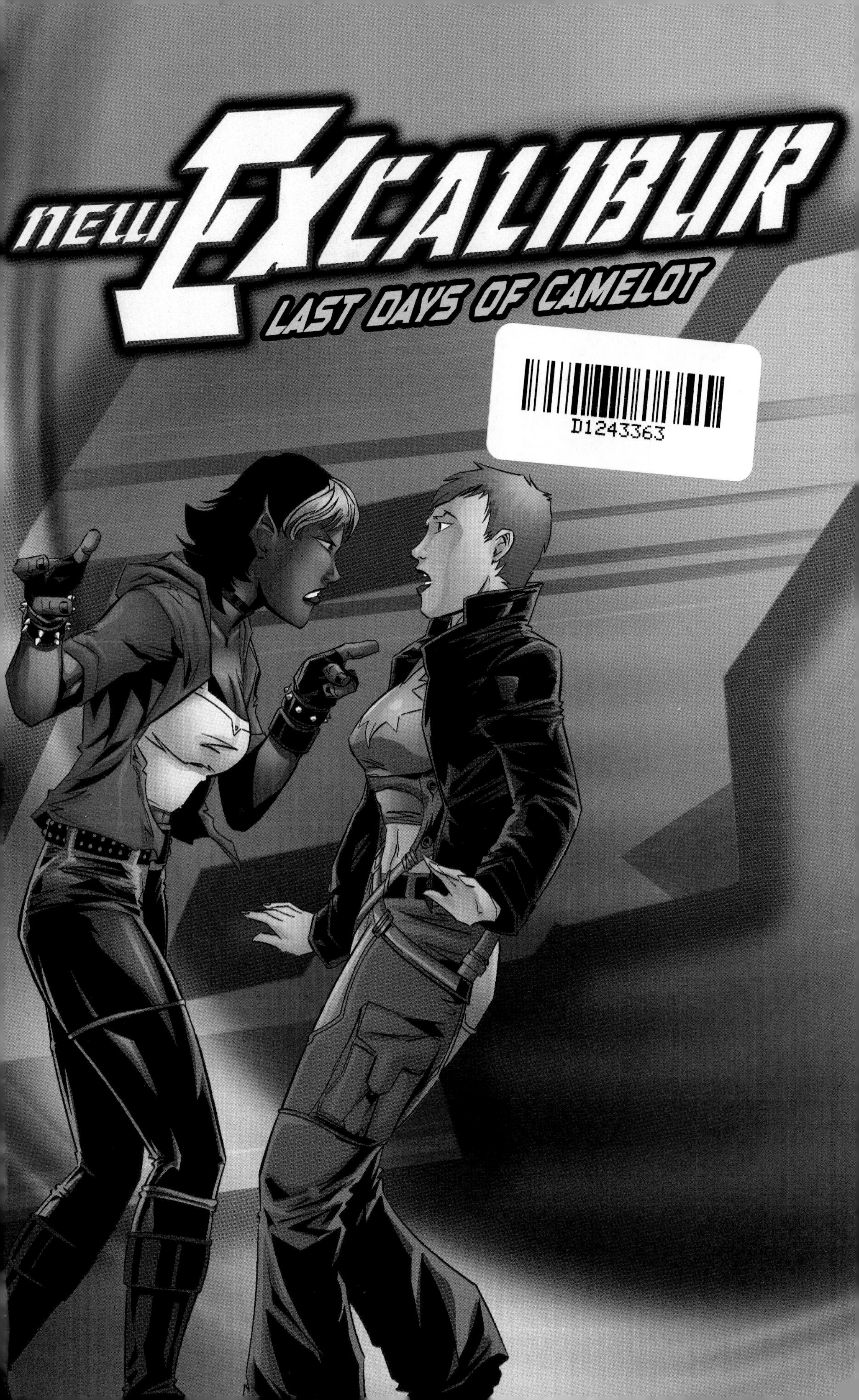
new EXCALIBUR
LAST DAYS OF CAMELOT

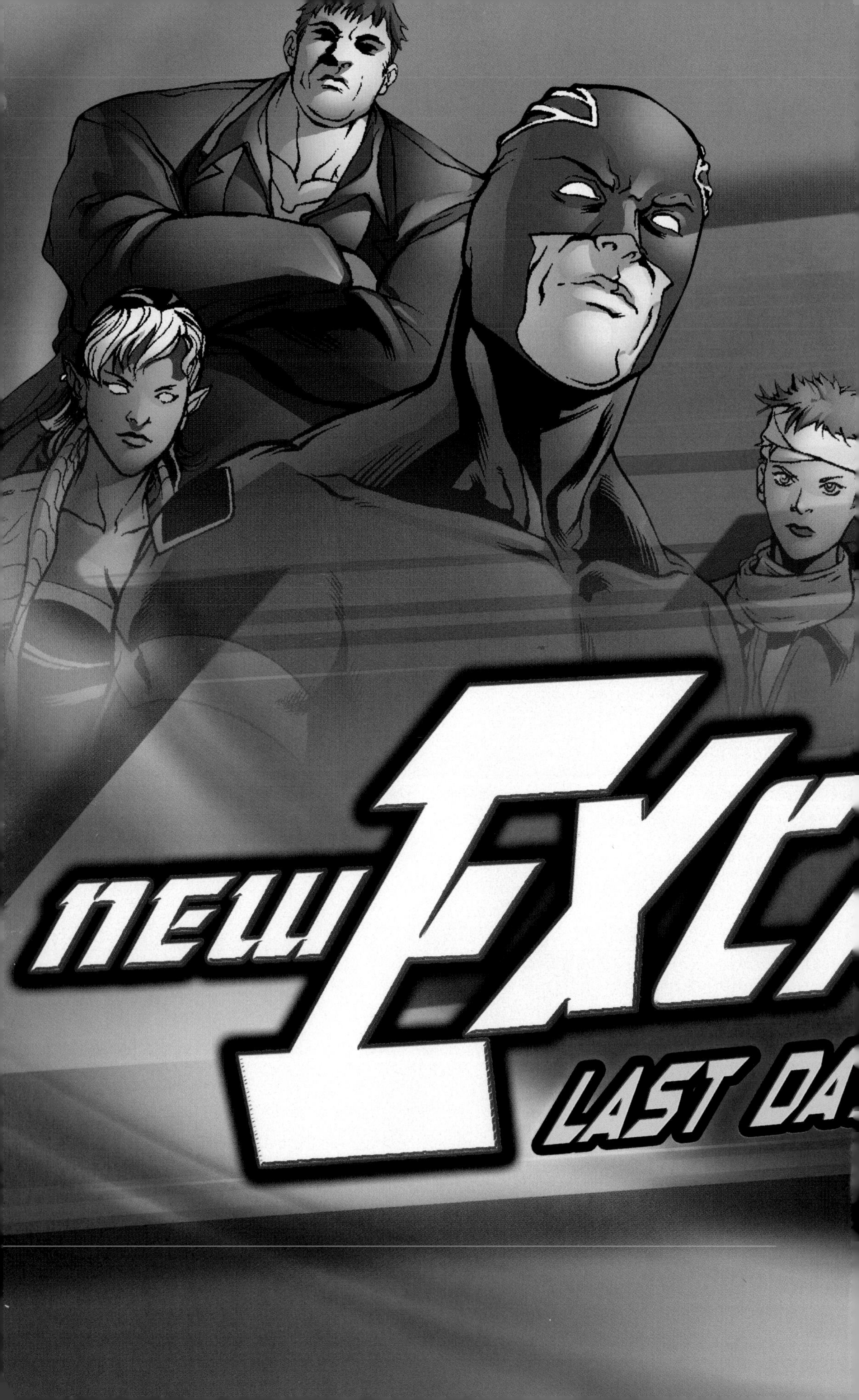
new
LAST

Writer: Frank Tieri
Issue #8, Story: Chris Claremont & Christopher Yost
Dialogue: Christopher Yost
**Pencils: Michael Ryan (Issues #8, 10-12) & Jim Calafiore
(Issues #13-15)**
Inks: Rick Ketcham (Issues #8, 10-12) & Mark McKenna (Issues #13-15)
Art (Issue #8): Scott Kolins
Colors: Pete Pantazis (Issues #8, 10-12), Wil Quintana (Issue #9) & Tom Chu
(Issues #13-15)
Letters: Tom Orzechowski

Assistant Editor: Sean Ryar
Editors: Nick Lowe & Mike Mart:

Collection Editor: Jennifer Grünwalc
Assistant Editor: Michael Shor
Associate Editor: Mark D. Beazle
Senior Editor, Special Projects: Jeff Youngquis
Senior Vice President of Sales: David Gabrie
Production: Jerron Quality Colo
Vice President of Creative: Tom Marvell

Editor in Chief: Joe Quesada
Publisher: Dan Buckle

ALIBUR

S OF CAMELOT

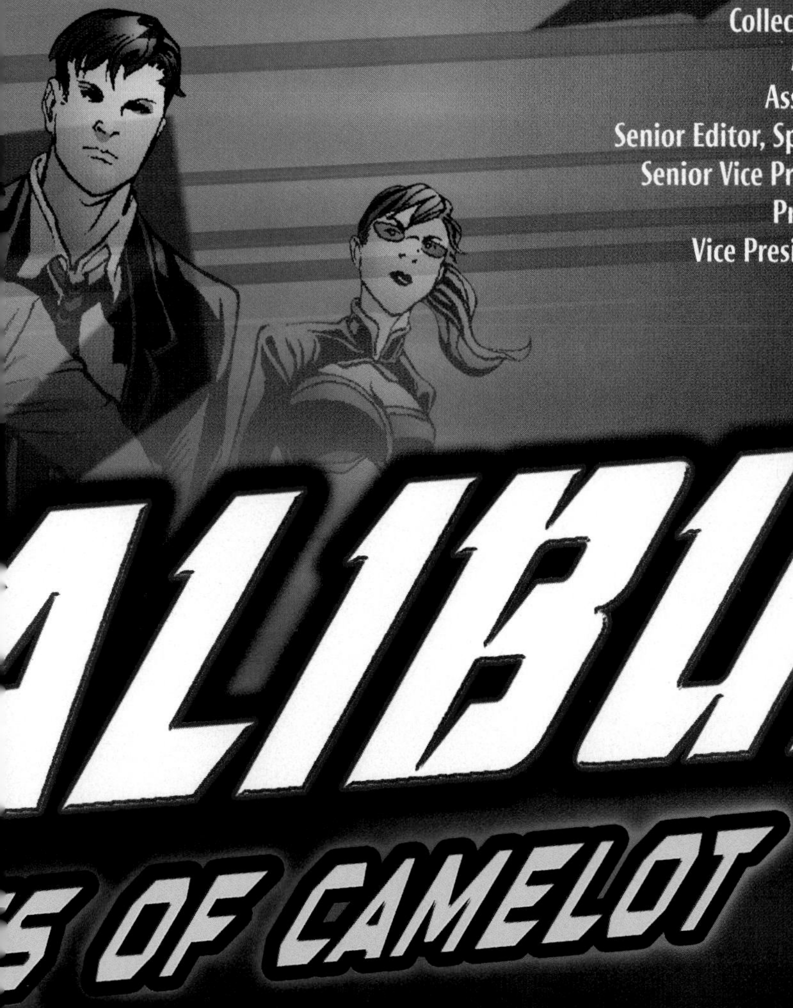

PREVIOUSLY

In the aftermath of M-DAY, five disparate heroes are brought together in London: CAPTAIN BRITAIN, JUGGERNAU NOCTURNE, DAZZLER and SAGE. Together with government agent PETE WISDOM (an agent of MI-13, the division of H Majesty's Intelligence Service devoted to the supernatural) they stand as a symbol of might in the service of right.

Recently, the team has fought what appeared to be an evil team of X-MEN. Where this team came from, or what the want, has yet to be discovered. Excalibur was able to take down this team of dark X-Men, but during a prison transfe their leader, an evil Professor Xavier, was able to break free. He immediately gained control of Sage's mind. SI succeeded in defeating Dark Charles, but it appears he's not gone for good. The team must now make a final decisic on the fate of this most dangerous threat...

#8

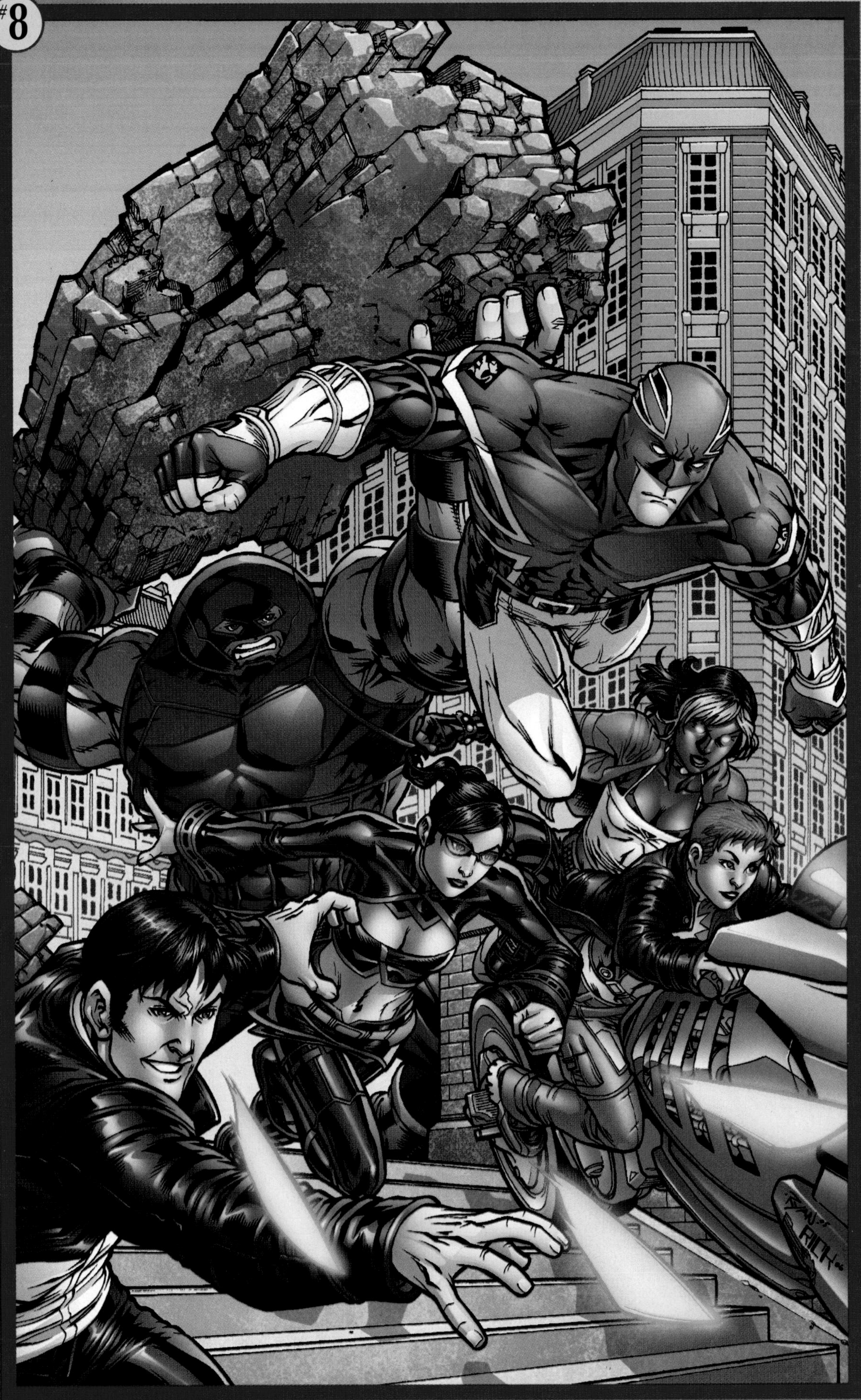

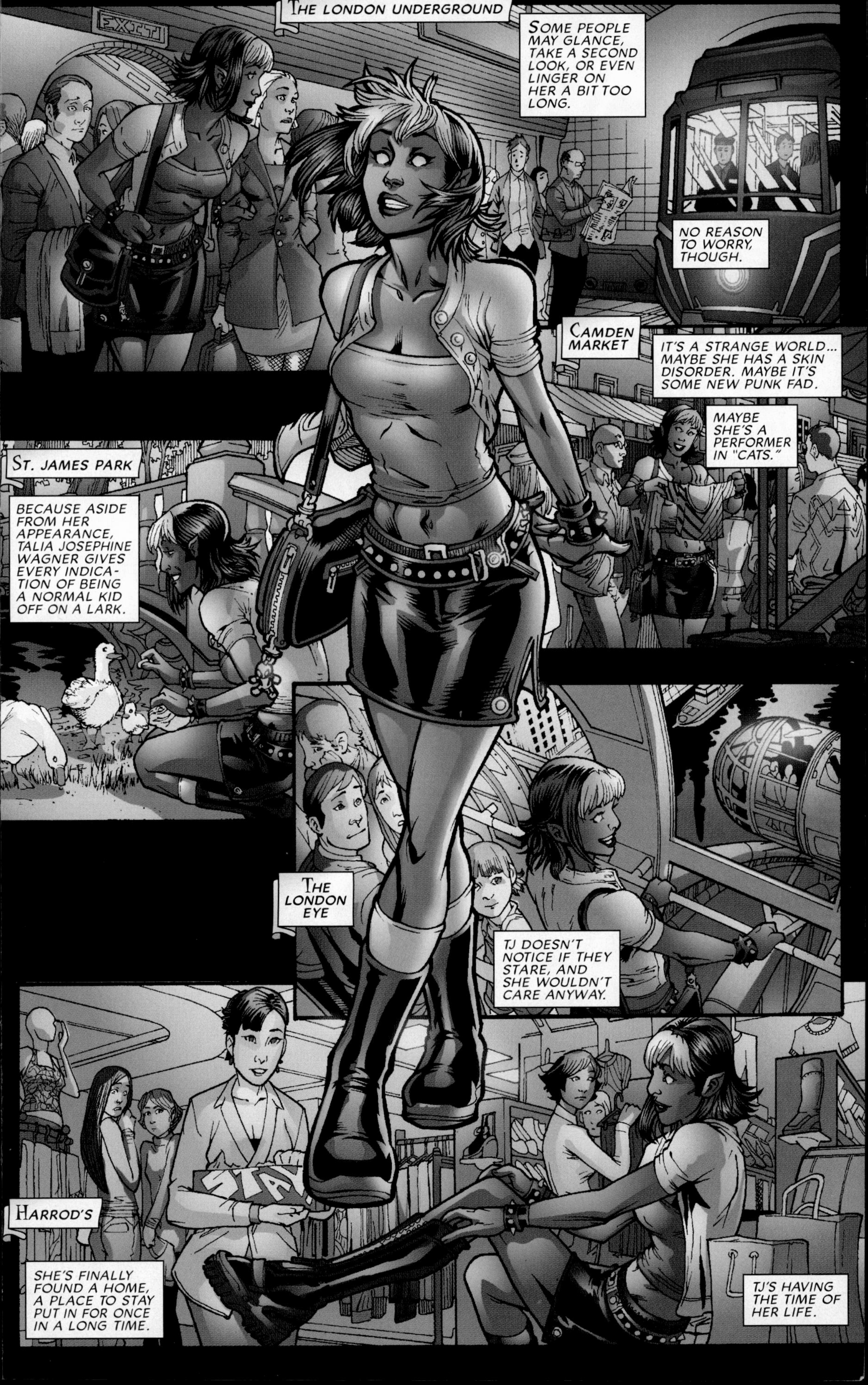
THE LONDON UNDERGROUND
SOME PEOPLE MAY GLANCE, TAKE A SECOND LOOK, OR EVEN LINGER ON HER A BIT TOO LONG.
NO REASON TO WORRY, THOUGH.
CAMDEN MARKET
IT'S A STRANGE WORLD... MAYBE SHE HAS A SKIN DISORDER. MAYBE IT'S SOME NEW PUNK FAD.
MAYBE SHE'S A PERFORMER IN "CATS."
ST. JAMES PARK
BECAUSE ASIDE FROM HER APPEARANCE, TALIA JOSEPHINE WAGNER GIVES EVERY INDICATION OF BEING A NORMAL KID OFF ON A LARK.
THE LONDON EYE
TJ DOESN'T NOTICE IF THEY STARE, AND SHE WOULDN'T CARE ANYWAY.
HARROD'S
SHE'S FINALLY FOUND A HOME, A PLACE TO STAY PUT IN FOR ONCE IN A LONG TIME.
TJ'S HAVING THE TIME OF HER LIFE.

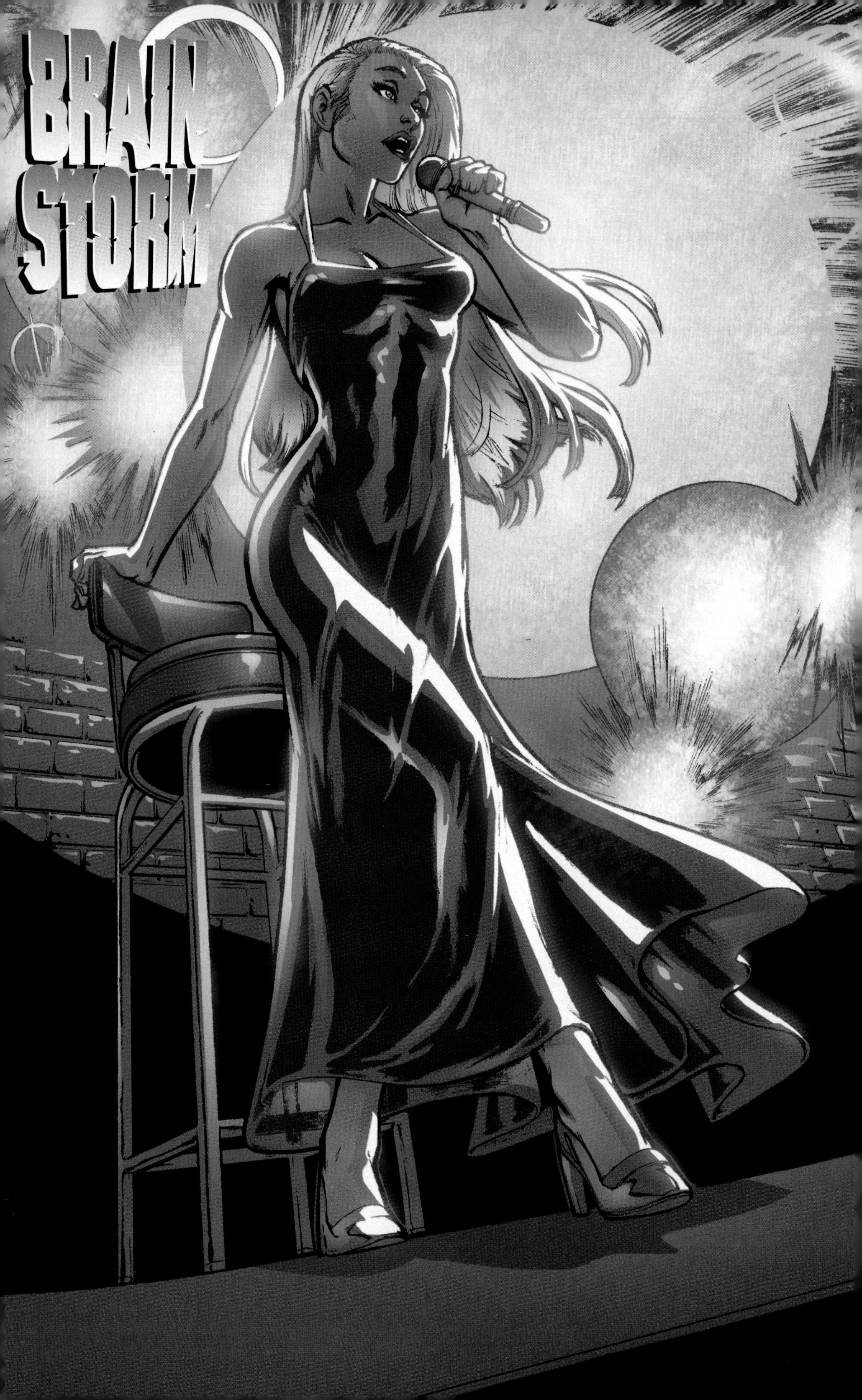
BRAIN STORM

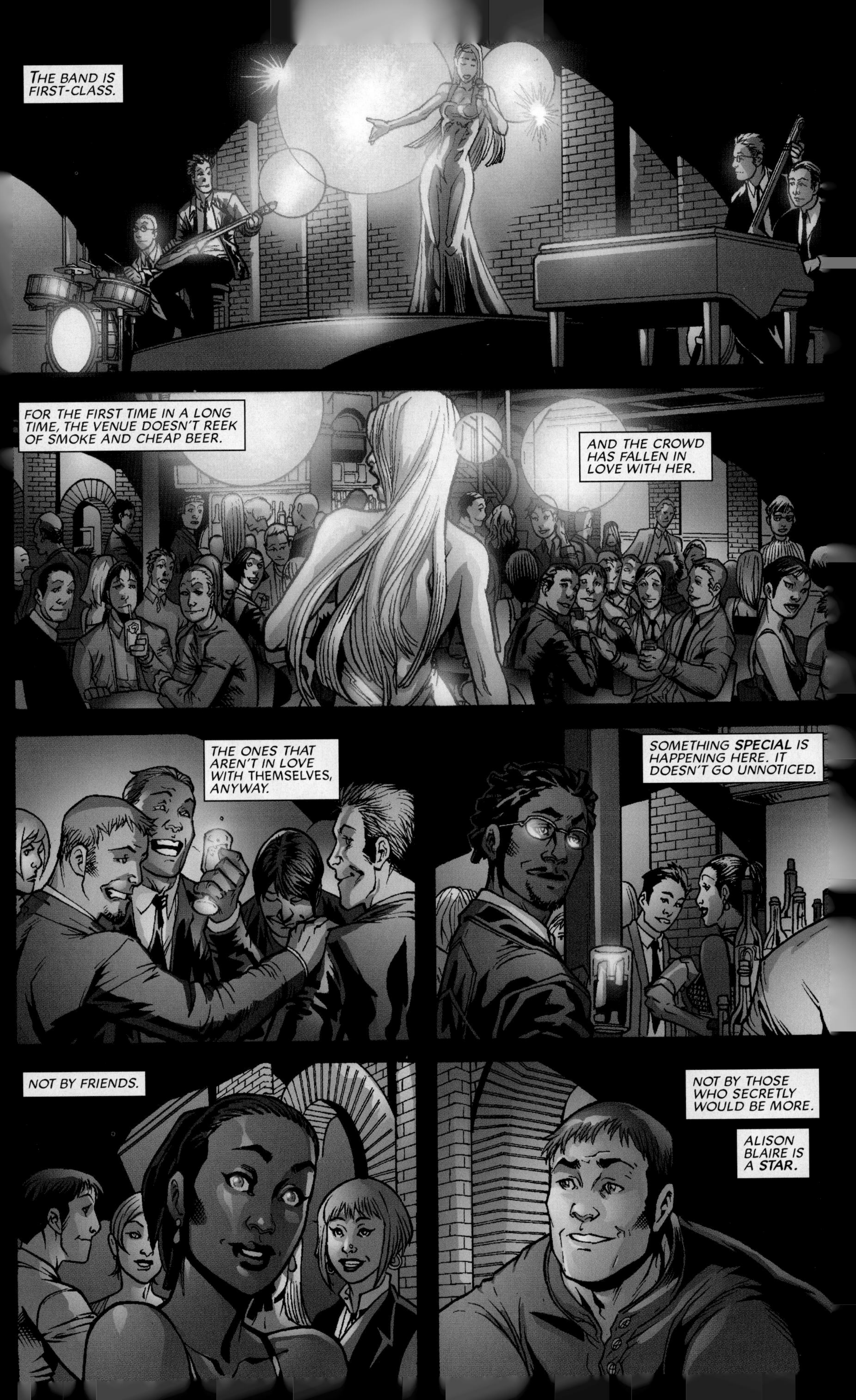
THE BAND IS FIRST-CLASS.
FOR THE FIRST TIME IN A LONG TIME, THE VENUE DOESN'T REEK OF SMOKE AND CHEAP BEER.
AND THE CROWD HAS FALLEN IN LOVE WITH HER.
THE ONES THAT AREN'T IN LOVE WITH THEMSELVES, ANYWAY.
SOMETHING SPECIAL IS HAPPENING HERE. IT DOESN'T GO UNNOTICED.
NOT BY FRIENDS.
NOT BY THOSE WHO SECRETLY WOULD BE MORE.
ALISON BLAIRE IS A STAR.

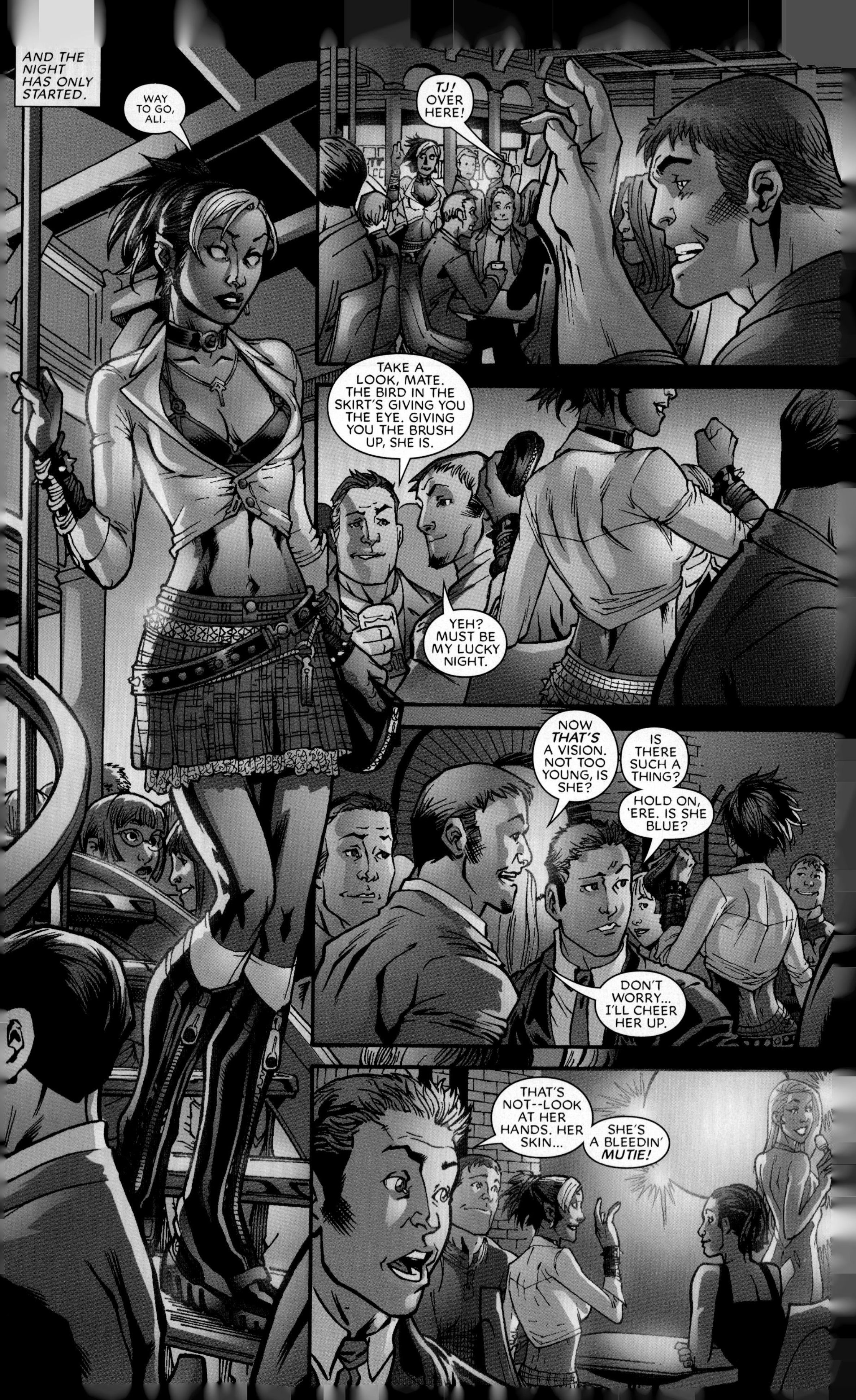
AND THE NIGHT HAS ONLY STARTED.
WAY TO GO, ALI.
TJ! OVER HERE!
TAKE A LOOK, MATE. THE BIRD IN THE SKIRT'S GIVING YOU THE EYE. GIVING YOU THE BRUSH UP, SHE IS.
YEH? MUST BE MY LUCKY NIGHT.
NOW THAT'S A VISION. NOT TOO YOUNG, IS SHE?
IS THERE SUCH A THING?
HOLD ON, 'ERE. IS SHE BLUE?
DON'T WORRY... I'LL CHEER HER UP.
THAT'S NOT--LOOK AT HER HANDS. HER SKIN...
SHE'S A BLEEDIN' MUTIE!

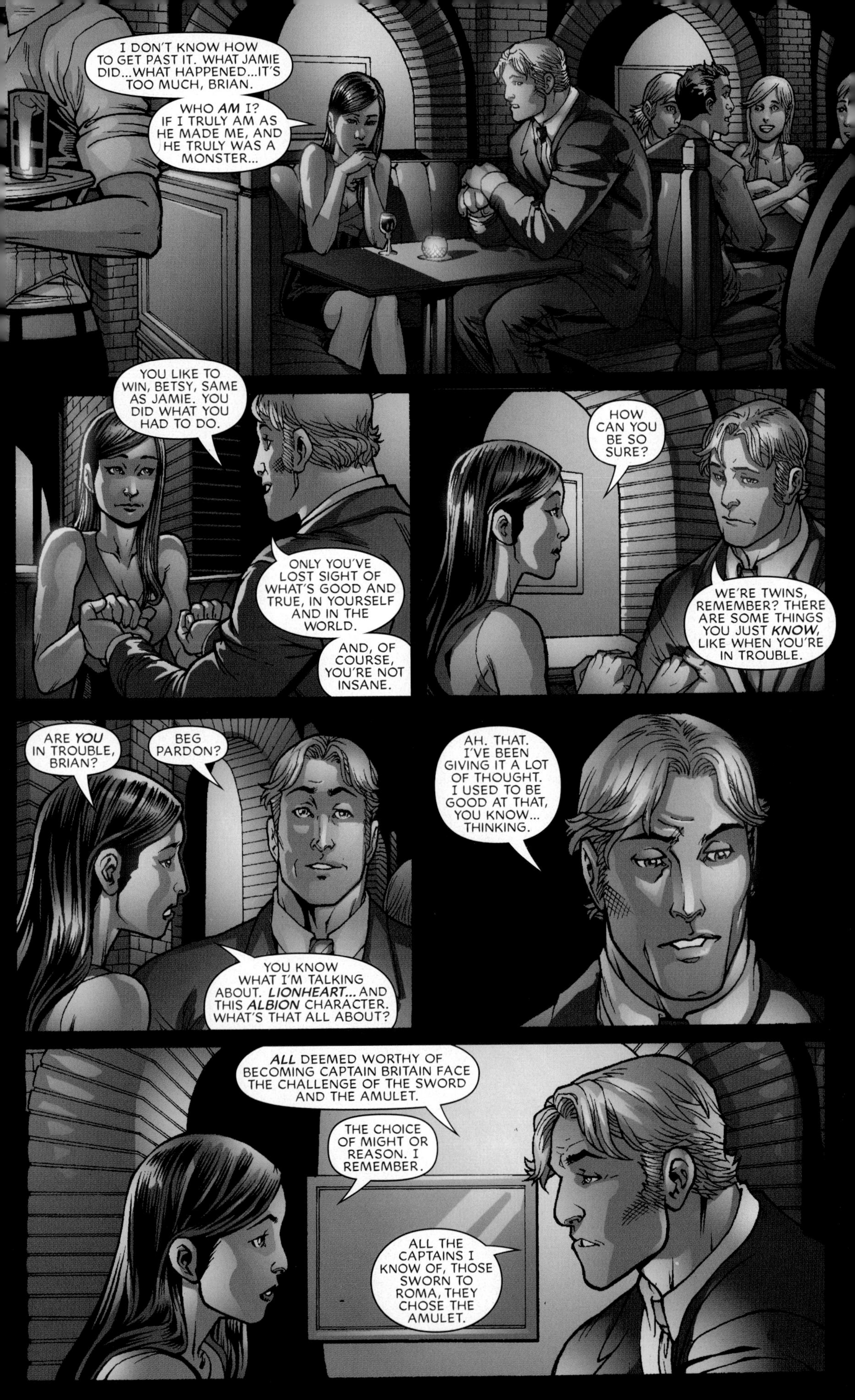
I DON'T KNOW HOW TO GET PAST IT. WHAT JAMIE DID...WHAT HAPPENED...IT'S TOO MUCH, BRIAN.
WHO *AM* I? IF I TRULY AM AS HE MADE ME, AND HE TRULY WAS A MONSTER...
YOU LIKE TO WIN, BETSY, SAME AS JAMIE. YOU DID WHAT YOU HAD TO DO.
ONLY YOU'VE LOST SIGHT OF WHAT'S GOOD AND TRUE, IN YOURSELF AND IN THE WORLD.
AND, OF COURSE, YOU'RE NOT INSANE.
HOW CAN YOU BE SO SURE?
WE'RE TWINS, REMEMBER? THERE ARE SOME THINGS YOU JUST *KNOW*, LIKE WHEN YOU'RE IN TROUBLE.
ARE *YOU* IN TROUBLE, BRIAN?
BEG PARDON?
YOU KNOW WHAT I'M TALKING ABOUT. *LIONHEART...* AND THIS *ALBION* CHARACTER. WHAT'S THAT ALL ABOUT?
AH. THAT. I'VE BEEN GIVING IT A LOT OF THOUGHT. I USED TO BE GOOD AT THAT, YOU KNOW... THINKING.
ALL DEEMED WORTHY OF BECOMING CAPTAIN BRITAIN FACE THE CHALLENGE OF THE SWORD AND THE AMULET.
THE CHOICE OF MIGHT OR REASON. I REMEMBER.
ALL THE CAPTAINS I KNOW OF, THOSE SWORN TO ROMA, THEY CHOSE THE AMULET.

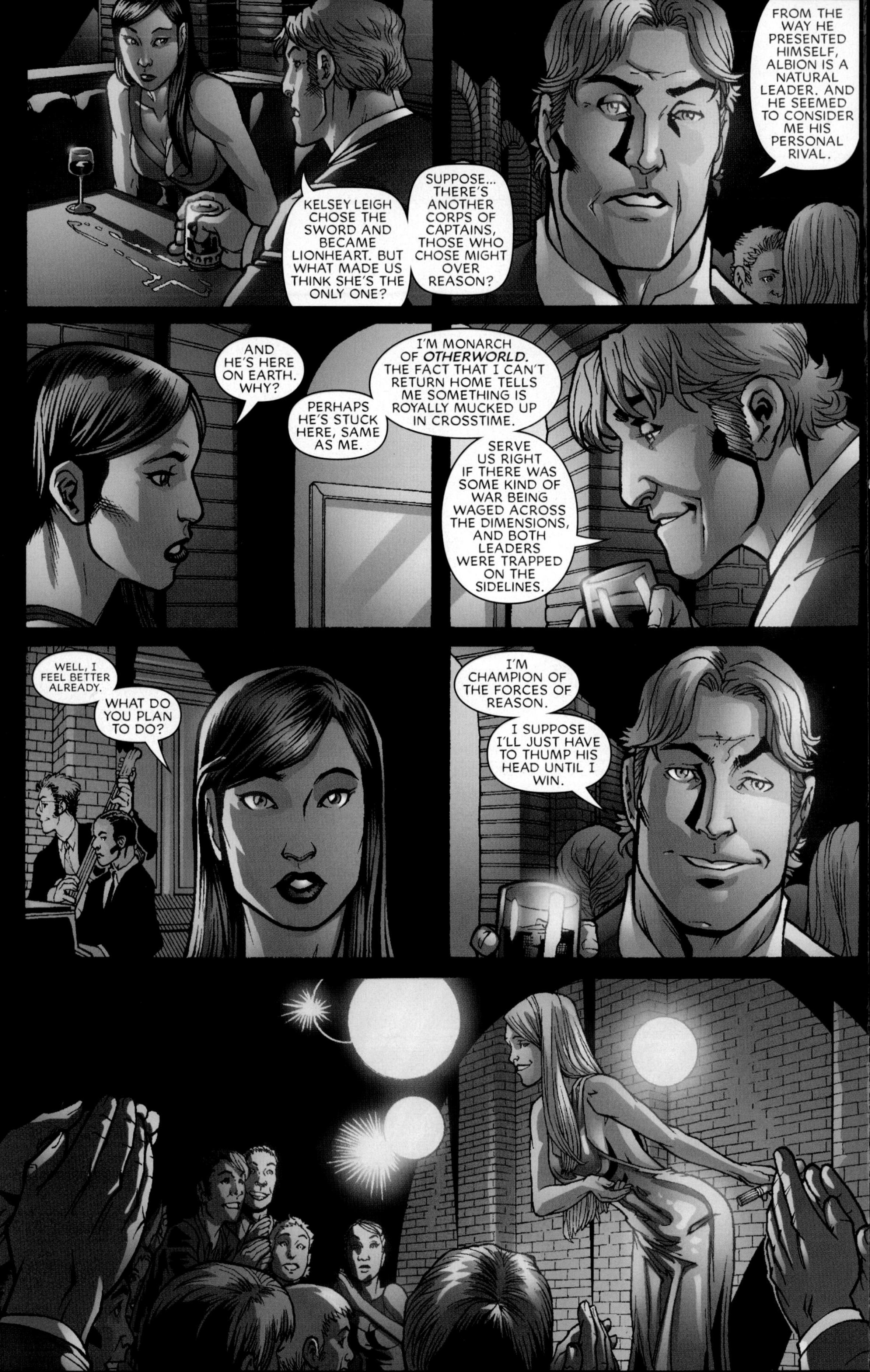
KELSEY LEIGH CHOSE THE SWORD AND BECAME LIONHEART. BUT WHAT MADE US THINK SHE'S THE ONLY ONE?
SUPPOSE... THERE'S ANOTHER CORPS OF CAPTAINS, THOSE WHO CHOSE MIGHT OVER REASON?
FROM THE WAY HE PRESENTED HIMSELF, ALBION IS A NATURAL LEADER. AND HE SEEMED TO CONSIDER ME HIS PERSONAL RIVAL.
AND HE'S HERE ON EARTH. WHY?
PERHAPS HE'S STUCK HERE, SAME AS ME.
I'M MONARCH OF *OTHERWORLD*. THE FACT THAT I CAN'T RETURN HOME TELLS ME SOMETHING IS ROYALLY MUCKED UP IN CROSSTIME.
SERVE US RIGHT IF THERE WAS SOME KIND OF WAR BEING WAGED ACROSS THE DIMENSIONS, AND BOTH LEADERS WERE TRAPPED ON THE SIDELINES.
WELL, I FEEL BETTER ALREADY.
WHAT DO YOU PLAN TO DO?
I'M CHAMPION OF THE FORCES OF REASON.
I SUPPOSE I'LL JUST HAVE TO THUMP HIS HEAD UNTIL I WIN.

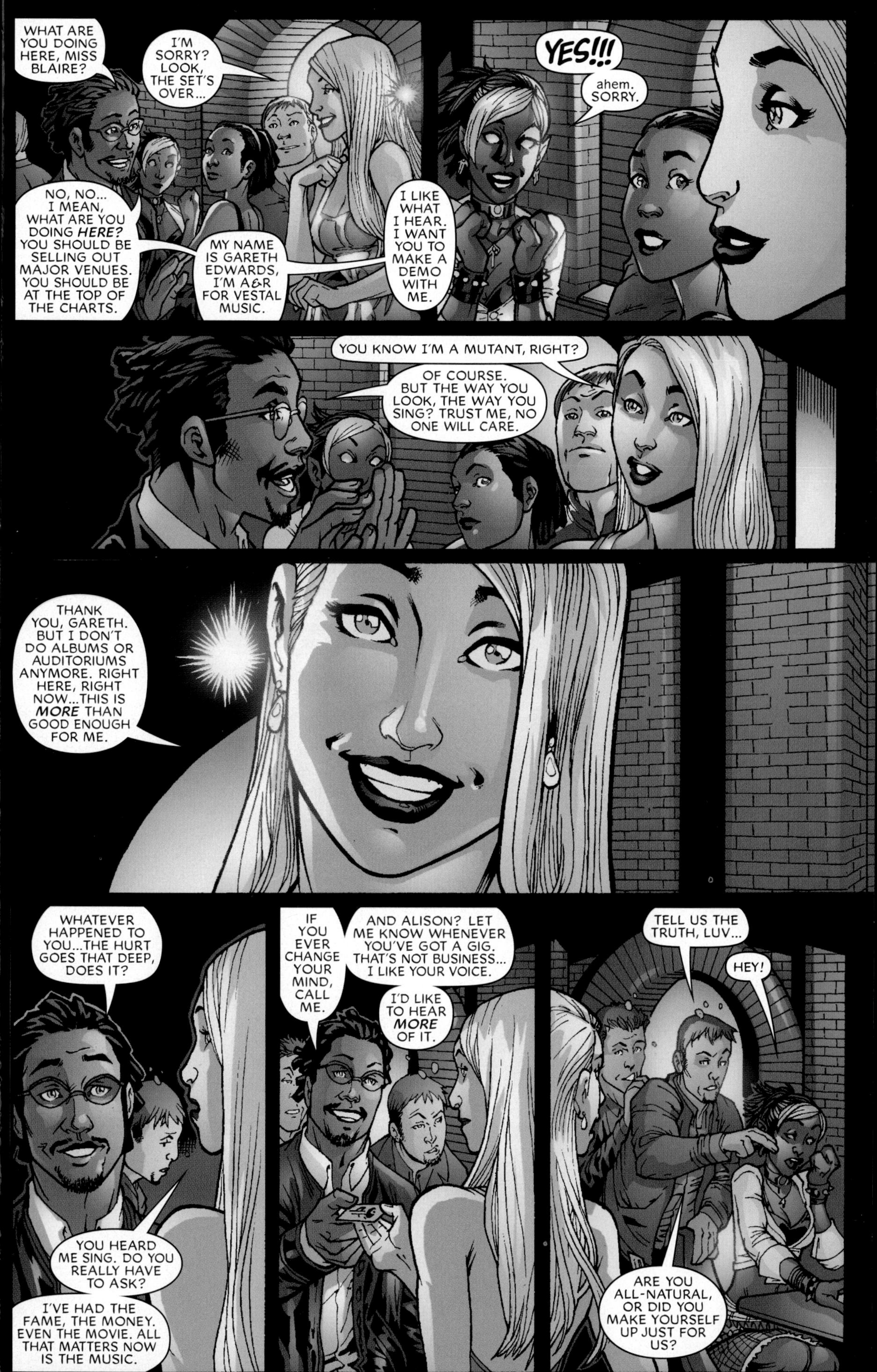
WHAT ARE YOU DOING HERE, MISS BLAIRE?
I'M SORRY? LOOK, THE SET'S OVER...
NO, NO... I MEAN, WHAT ARE YOU DOING *HERE?* YOU SHOULD BE SELLING OUT MAJOR VENUES. YOU SHOULD BE AT THE TOP OF THE CHARTS.
MY NAME IS GARETH EDWARDS, I'M A&R FOR VESTAL MUSIC.
I LIKE WHAT I HEAR. I WANT YOU TO MAKE A DEMO WITH ME.
YES!!!
ahem. SORRY.
YOU KNOW I'M A MUTANT, RIGHT?
OF COURSE. BUT THE WAY YOU LOOK, THE WAY YOU SING? TRUST ME, NO ONE WILL CARE.
THANK YOU, GARETH. BUT I DON'T DO ALBUMS OR AUDITORIUMS ANYMORE. RIGHT HERE, RIGHT NOW...THIS IS *MORE* THAN GOOD ENOUGH FOR ME.
WHATEVER HAPPENED TO YOU...THE HURT GOES THAT DEEP, DOES IT?
YOU HEARD ME SING. DO YOU REALLY HAVE TO ASK?
I'VE HAD THE FAME, THE MONEY. EVEN THE MOVIE. ALL THAT MATTERS NOW IS THE MUSIC.
IF YOU EVER CHANGE YOUR MIND, CALL ME.
AND ALISON? LET ME KNOW WHENEVER YOU'VE GOT A GIG. THAT'S NOT BUSINESS... I LIKE YOUR VOICE.
I'D LIKE TO HEAR *MORE* OF IT.
TELL US THE TRUTH, LUV...
HEY!
ARE YOU ALL-NATURAL, OR DID YOU MAKE YOURSELF UP JUST FOR US?

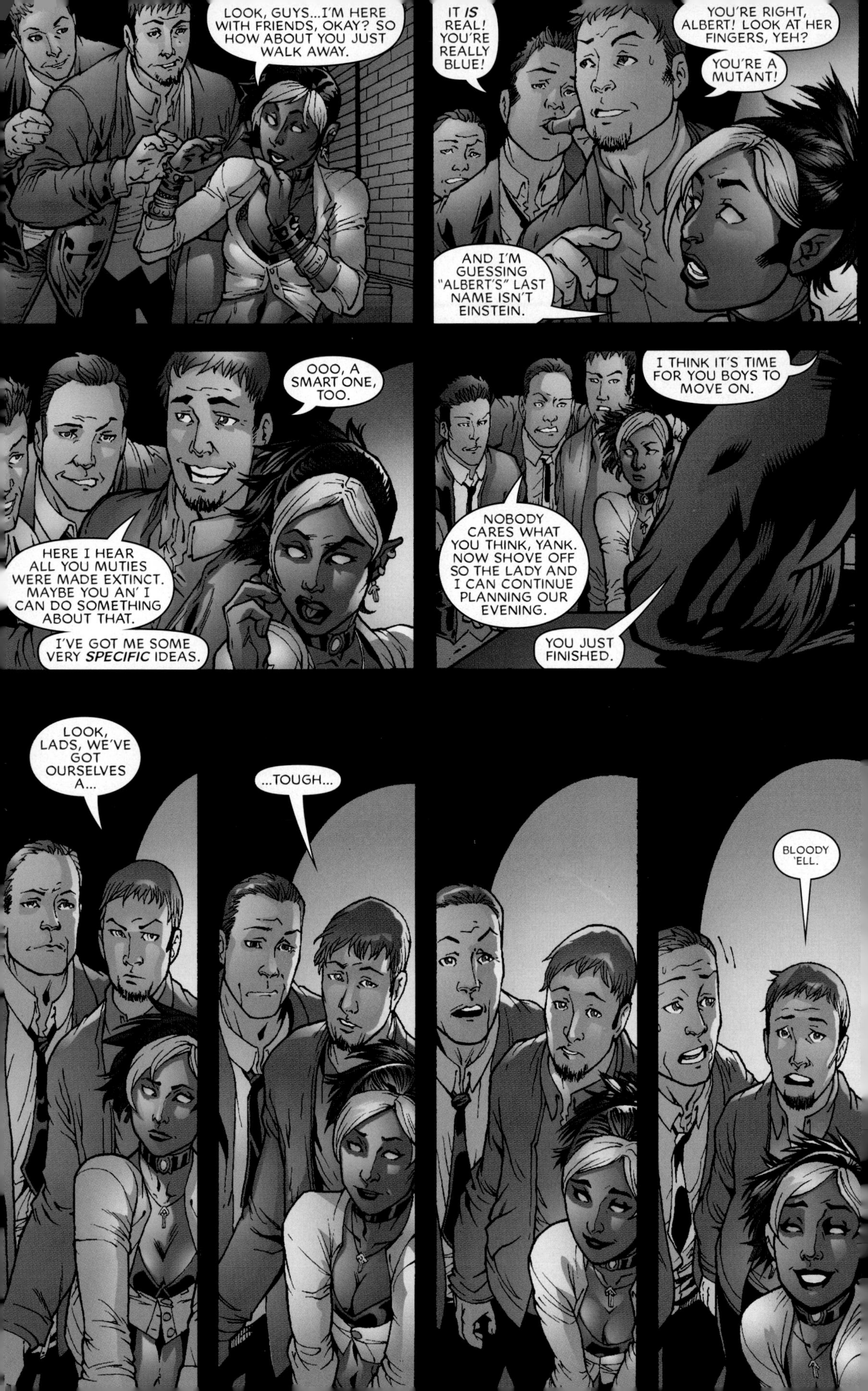
LOOK, GUYS...I'M HERE WITH FRIENDS, OKAY? SO HOW ABOUT YOU JUST WALK AWAY.
IT IS REAL! YOU'RE REALLY BLUE!
YOU'RE RIGHT, ALBERT! LOOK AT HER FINGERS, YEH?
YOU'RE A MUTANT!
AND I'M GUESSING "ALBERT'S" LAST NAME ISN'T EINSTEIN.
OOO, A SMART ONE, TOO.
HERE I HEAR ALL YOU MUTIES WERE MADE EXTINCT. MAYBE YOU AN' I CAN DO SOMETHING ABOUT THAT.
I'VE GOT ME SOME VERY SPECIFIC IDEAS.
I THINK IT'S TIME FOR YOU BOYS TO MOVE ON.
NOBODY CARES WHAT YOU THINK, YANK. NOW SHOVE OFF SO THE LADY AND I CAN CONTINUE PLANNING OUR EVENING.
YOU JUST FINISHED.
LOOK, LADS, WE'VE GOT OURSELVES A...
...TOUGH...
BLOODY 'ELL.

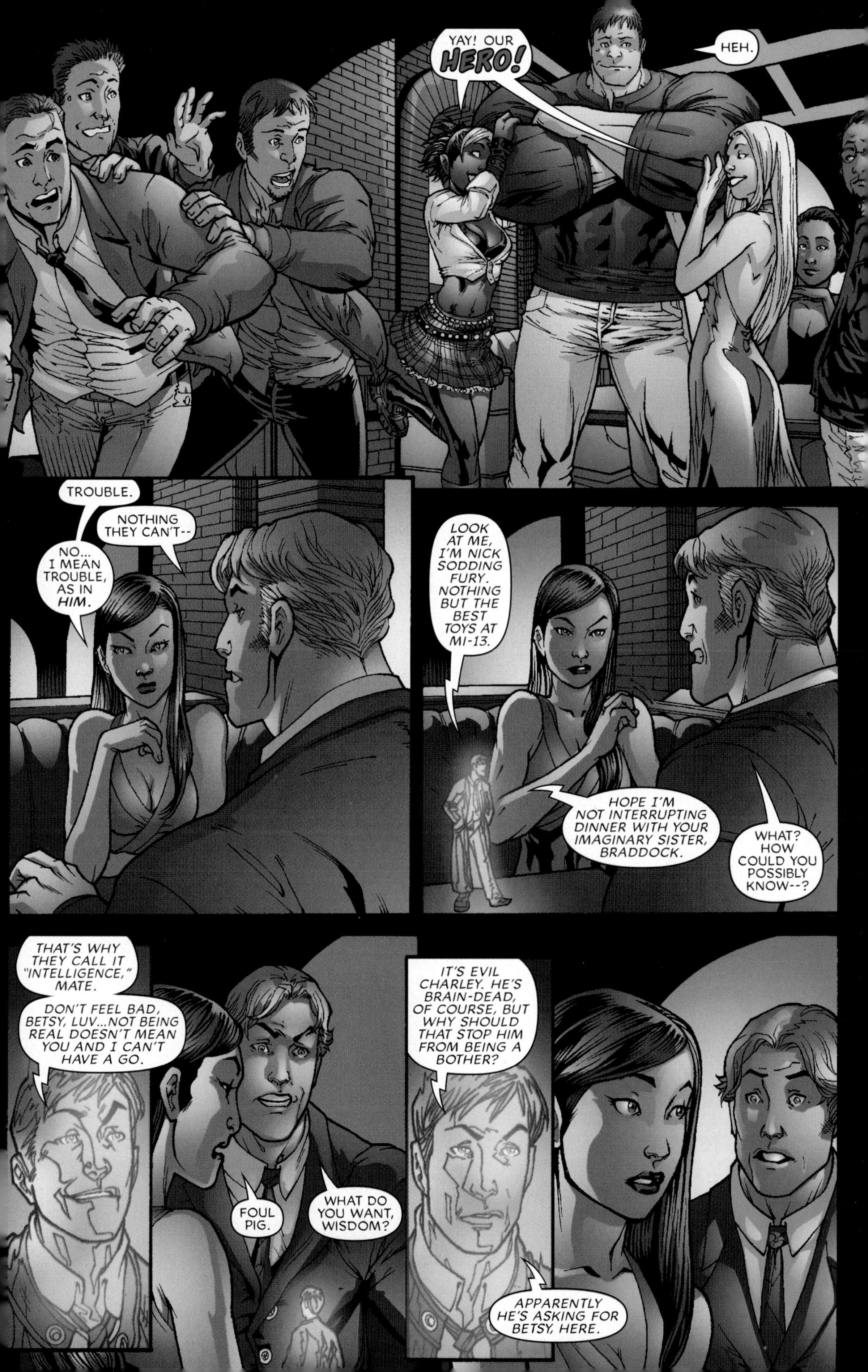
YAY! OUR HERO!
HEH.
TROUBLE.
NOTHING THEY CAN'T--
NO... I MEAN TROUBLE, AS IN HIM.
LOOK AT ME, I'M NICK SODDING FURY. NOTHING BUT THE BEST TOYS AT MI-13.
HOPE I'M NOT INTERRUPTING DINNER WITH YOUR IMAGINARY SISTER, BRADDOCK.
WHAT? HOW COULD YOU POSSIBLY KNOW--?
THAT'S WHY THEY CALL IT "INTELLIGENCE," MATE.
DON'T FEEL BAD, BETSY, LUV...NOT BEING REAL DOESN'T MEAN YOU AND I CAN'T HAVE A GO.
FOUL PIG.
WHAT DO YOU WANT, WISDOM?
IT'S EVIL CHARLEY. HE'S BRAIN-DEAD, OF COURSE, BUT WHY SHOULD THAT STOP HIM FROM BEING A BOTHER?
APPARENTLY HE'S ASKING FOR BETSY, HERE.

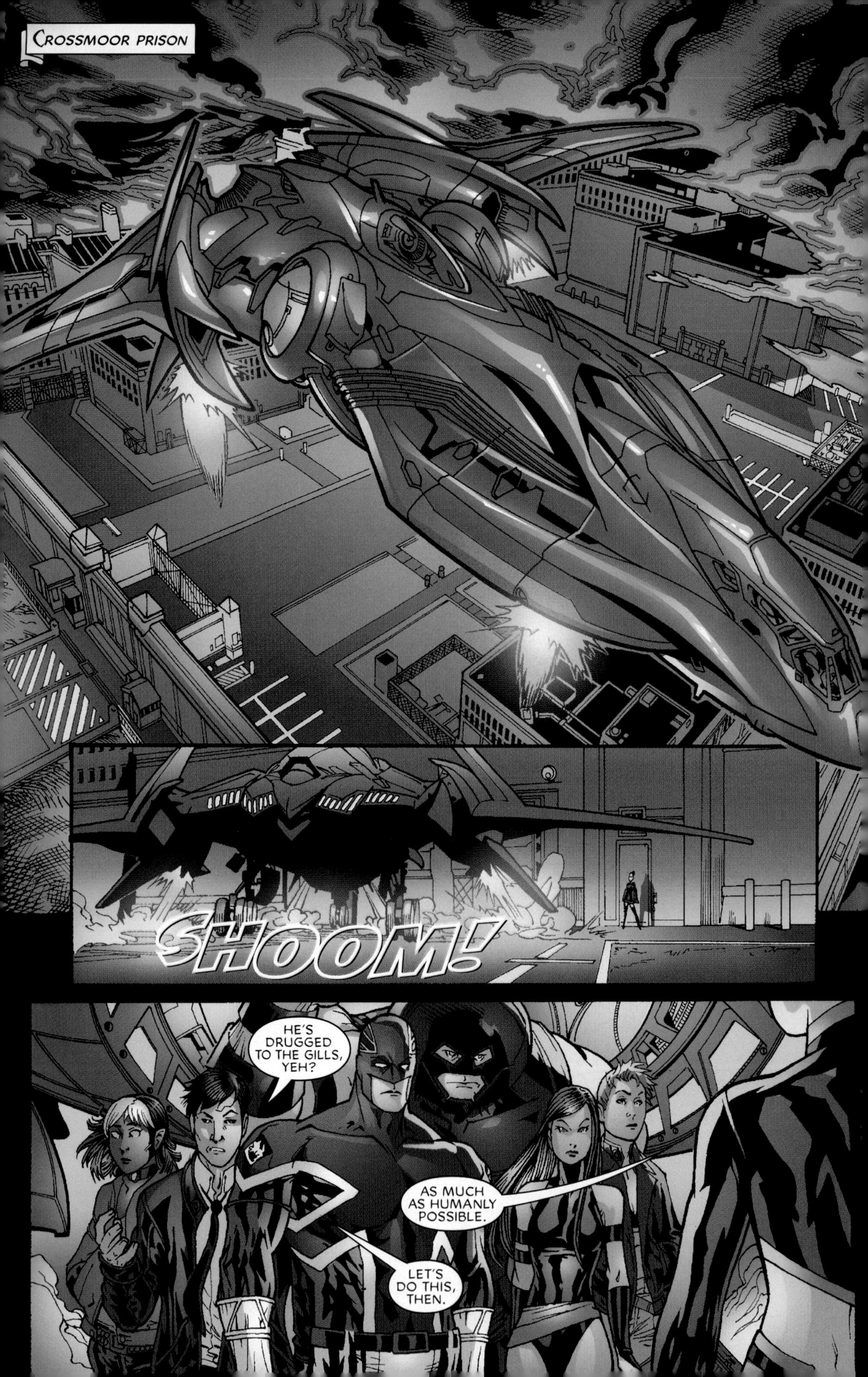
CROSSMOOR PRISON
SHOOM!
HE'S DRUGGED TO THE GILLS, YEH?
AS MUCH AS HUMANLY POSSIBLE.
LET'S DO THIS, THEN.

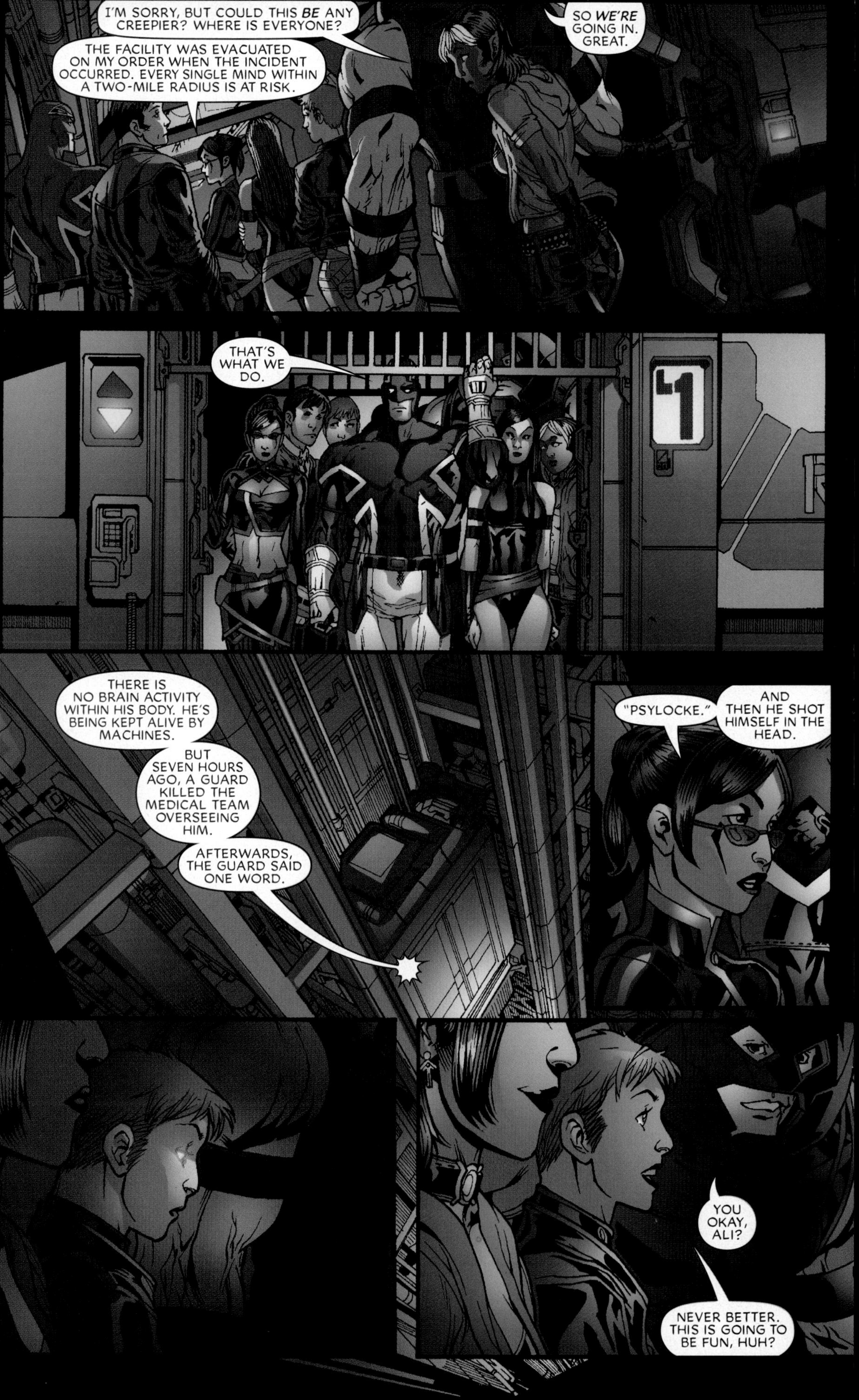
I'M SORRY, BUT COULD THIS *BE* ANY CREEPIER? WHERE IS EVERYONE?
THE FACILITY WAS EVACUATED ON MY ORDER WHEN THE INCIDENT OCCURRED. EVERY SINGLE MIND WITHIN A TWO-MILE RADIUS IS AT RISK.
SO *WE'RE* GOING IN. GREAT.
THAT'S WHAT WE DO.
THERE IS NO BRAIN ACTIVITY WITHIN HIS BODY. HE'S BEING KEPT ALIVE BY MACHINES.
BUT SEVEN HOURS AGO, A GUARD KILLED THE MEDICAL TEAM OVERSEEING HIM.
AFTERWARDS, THE GUARD SAID ONE WORD.
"PSYLOCKE."
AND THEN HE SHOT HIMSELF IN THE HEAD.
YOU OKAY, ALI?
NEVER BETTER. THIS IS GOING TO BE FUN, HUH?

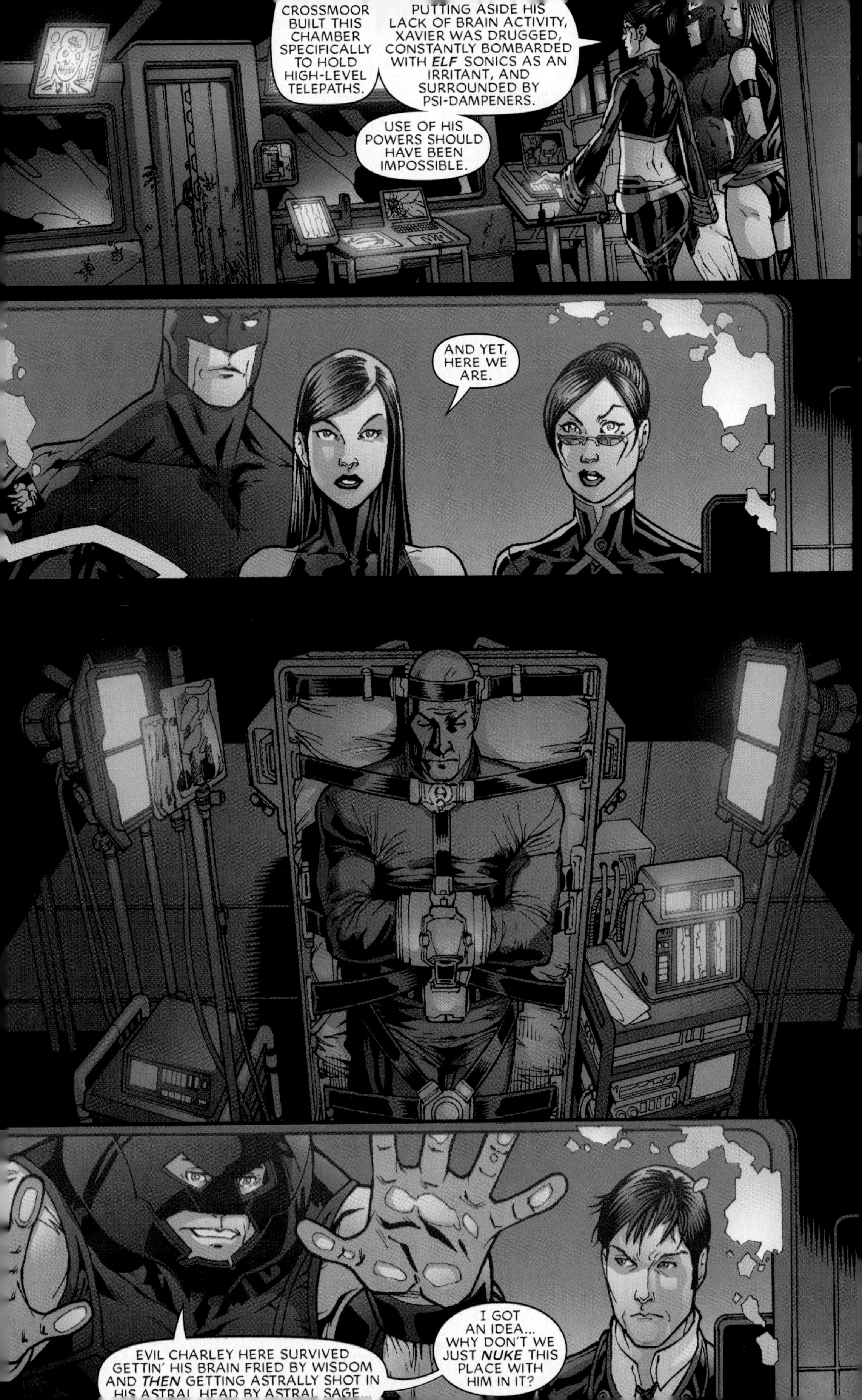
CROSSMOOR BUILT THIS CHAMBER SPECIFICALLY TO HOLD HIGH-LEVEL TELEPATHS.
PUTTING ASIDE HIS LACK OF BRAIN ACTIVITY, XAVIER WAS DRUGGED, CONSTANTLY BOMBARDED WITH ELF SONICS AS AN IRRITANT, AND SURROUNDED BY PSI-DAMPENERS.
USE OF HIS POWERS SHOULD HAVE BEEN IMPOSSIBLE.
AND YET, HERE WE ARE.
EVIL CHARLEY HERE SURVIVED GETTIN' HIS BRAIN FRIED BY WISDOM AND THEN GETTING ASTRALLY SHOT IN HIS ASTRAL HEAD BY ASTRAL SAGE...
I GOT AN IDEA... WHY DON'T WE JUST NUKE THIS PLACE WITH HIM IN IT?

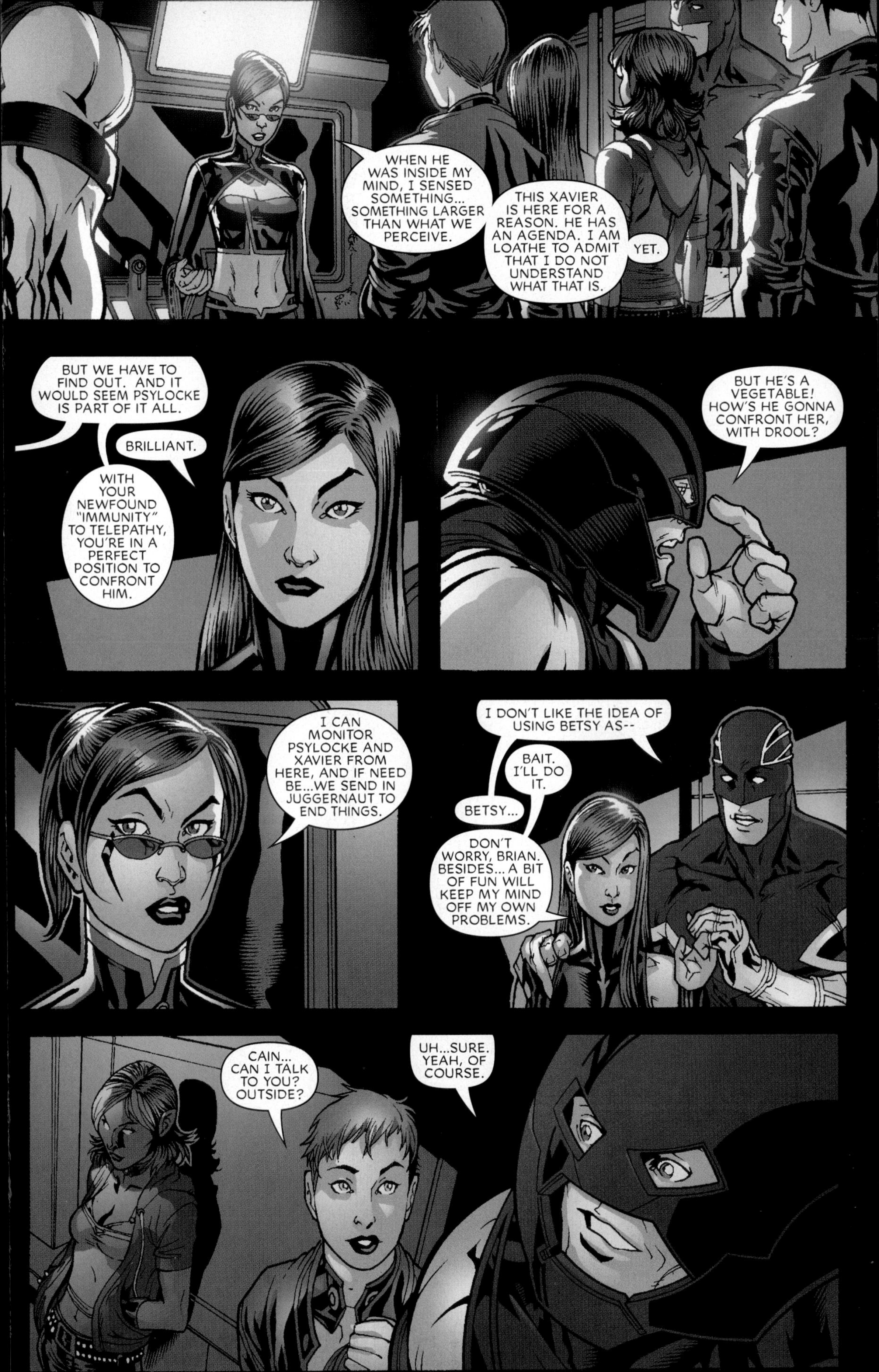
WHEN HE WAS INSIDE MY MIND, I SENSED SOMETHING... SOMETHING LARGER THAN WHAT WE PERCEIVE.
THIS XAVIER IS HERE FOR A REASON. HE HAS AN AGENDA. I AM LOATHE TO ADMIT THAT I DO NOT UNDERSTAND WHAT THAT IS.
YET.
BUT WE HAVE TO FIND OUT. AND IT WOULD SEEM PSYLOCKE IS PART OF IT ALL.
WITH YOUR NEWFOUND "IMMUNITY" TO TELEPATHY, YOU'RE IN A PERFECT POSITION TO CONFRONT HIM.
BRILLIANT.
BUT HE'S A VEGETABLE! HOW'S HE GONNA CONFRONT HER, WITH DROOL?
I CAN MONITOR PSYLOCKE AND XAVIER FROM HERE, AND IF NEED BE...WE SEND IN JUGGERNAUT TO END THINGS.
I DON'T LIKE THE IDEA OF USING BETSY AS--
BAIT. I'LL DO IT.
BETSY...
DON'T WORRY, BRIAN. BESIDES... A BIT OF FUN WILL KEEP MY MIND OFF MY OWN PROBLEMS.
CAIN... CAN I TALK TO YOU? OUTSIDE?
UH...SURE. YEAH, OF COURSE.

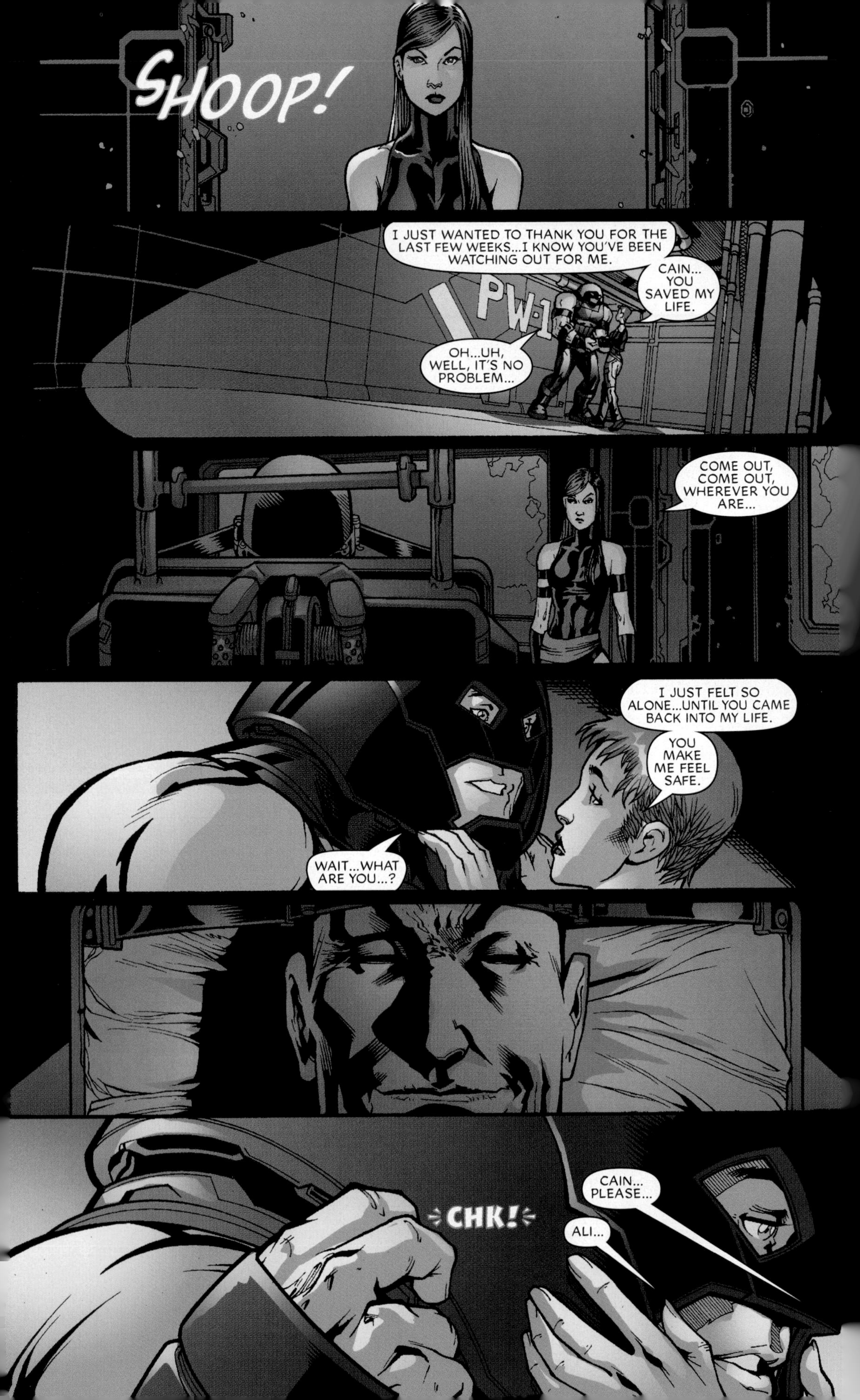
SHOOP!
I JUST WANTED TO THANK YOU FOR THE LAST FEW WEEKS...I KNOW YOU'VE BEEN WATCHING OUT FOR ME.
CAIN... YOU SAVED MY LIFE.
PW-1
OH...UH, WELL, IT'S NO PROBLEM...
COME OUT, COME OUT, WHEREVER YOU ARE...
I JUST FELT SO ALONE...UNTIL YOU CAME BACK INTO MY LIFE.
YOU MAKE ME FEEL SAFE.
WAIT...WHAT ARE YOU...?
CAIN... PLEASE...
CHK!
ALI...

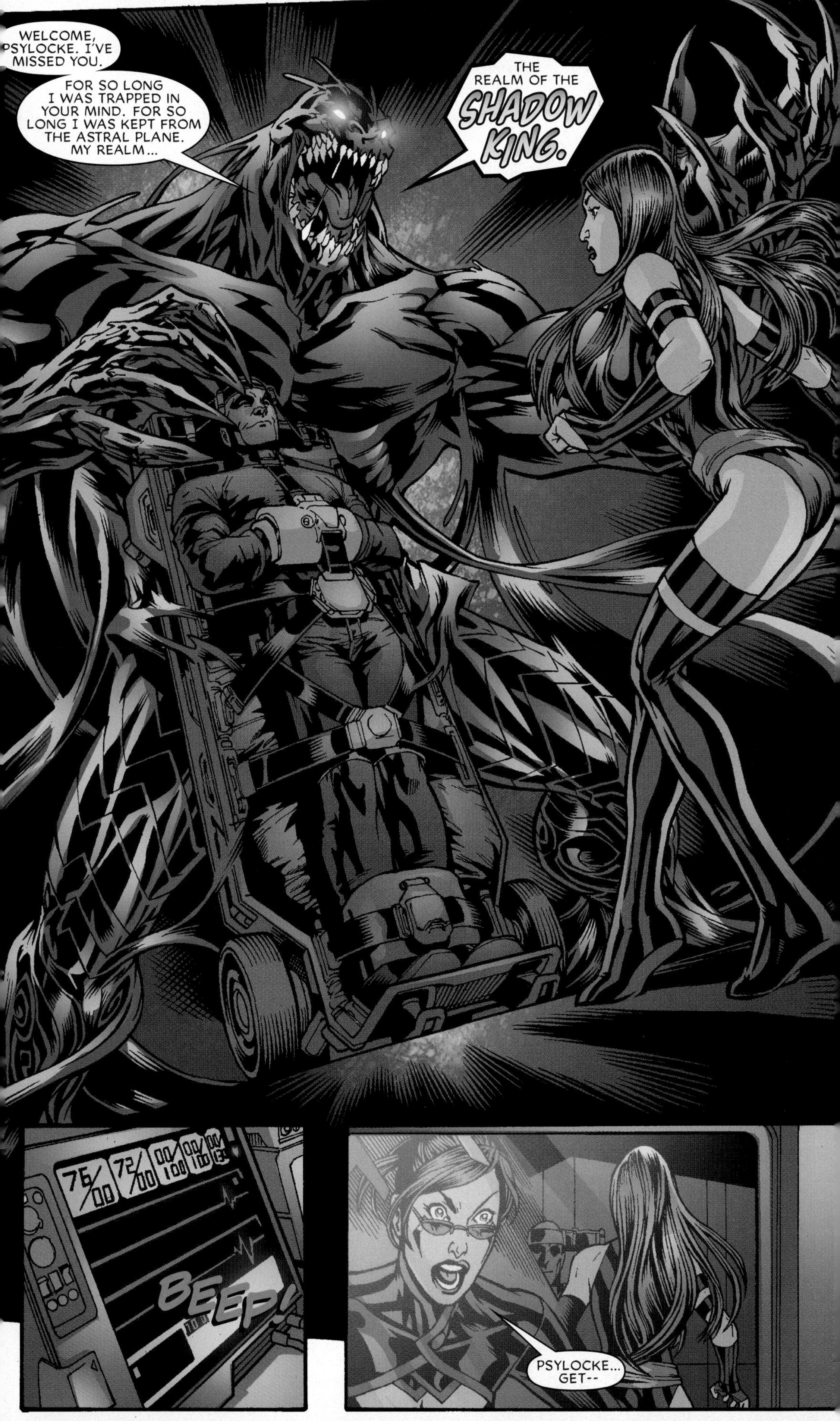
WELCOME, PSYLOCKE. I'VE MISSED YOU.
FOR SO LONG I WAS TRAPPED IN YOUR MIND. FOR SO LONG I WAS KEPT FROM THE ASTRAL PLANE. MY REALM...
THE REALM OF THE SHADOW KING.
BEEP!
PSYLOCKE... GET--

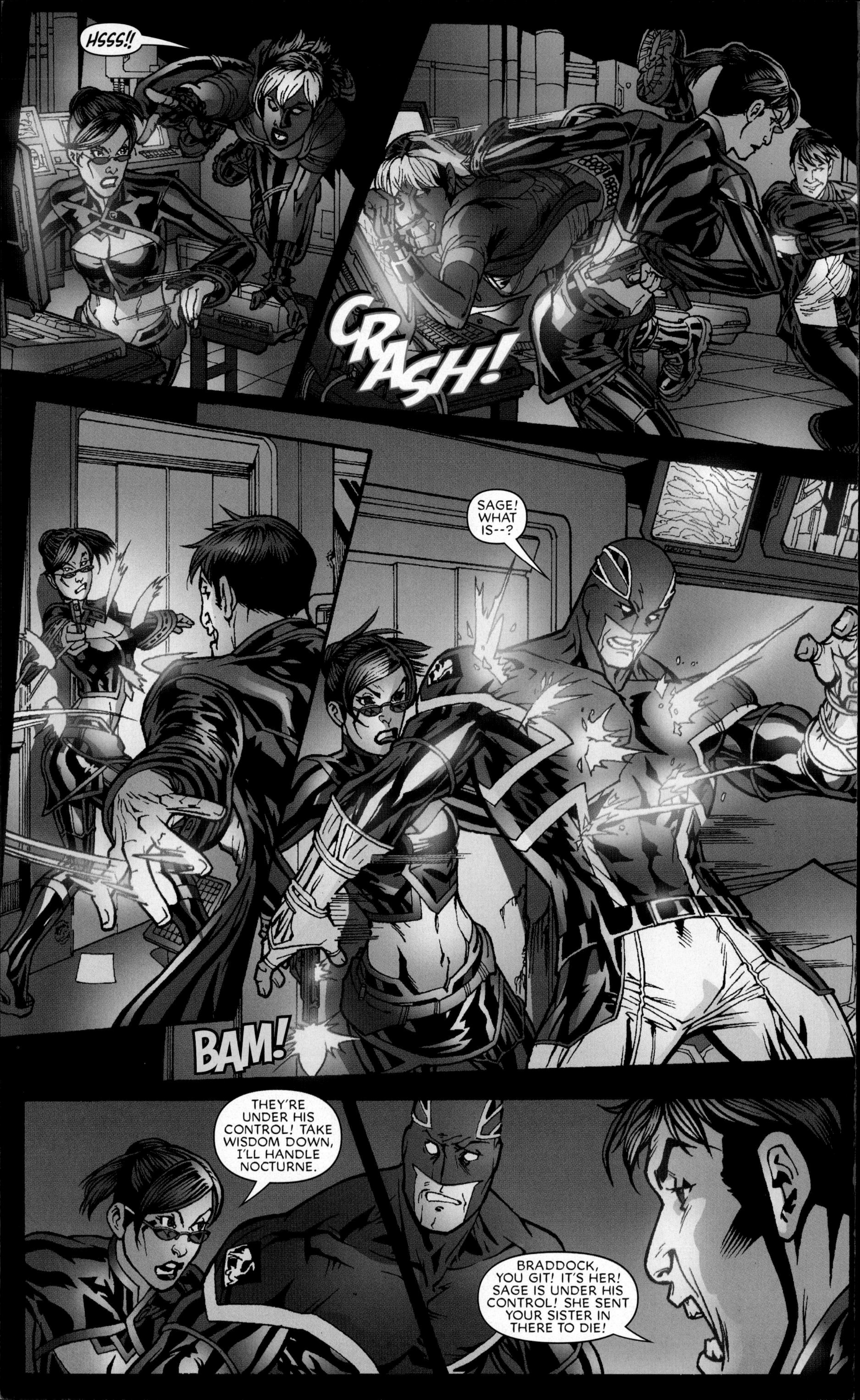
HSSS!!
CRASH!
SAGE! WHAT IS--?
BAM!
THEY'RE UNDER HIS CONTROL! TAKE WISDOM DOWN, I'LL HANDLE NOCTURNE.
BRADDOCK, YOU GIT! IT'S HER! SAGE IS UNDER HIS CONTROL! SHE SENT YOUR SISTER IN THERE TO DIE!

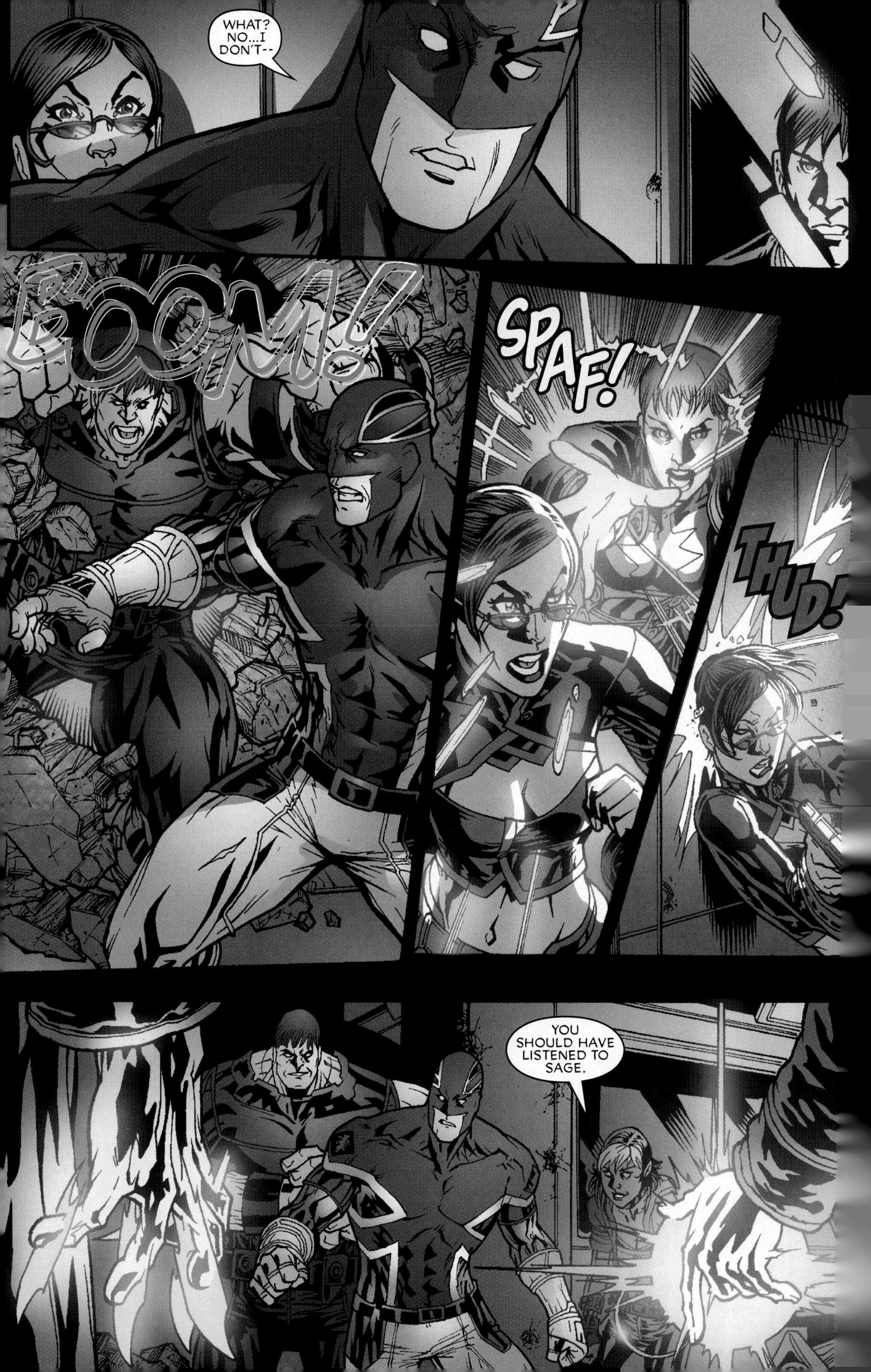
WHAT? NO...I DON'T--
BOOM!
SPAF!
THUD!
YOU SHOULD HAVE LISTENED TO SAGE.

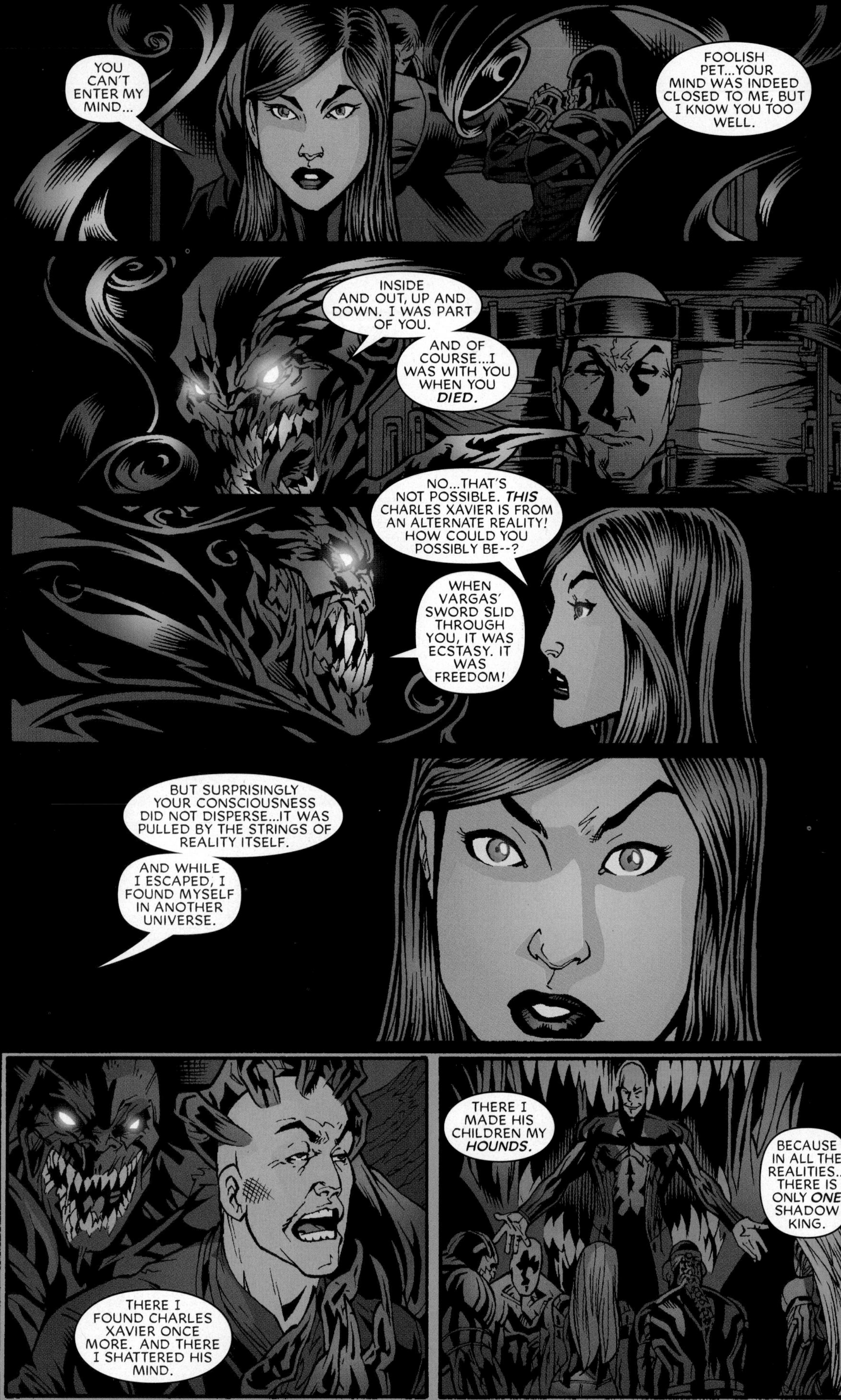
YOU CAN'T ENTER MY MIND...
FOOLISH PET...YOUR MIND WAS INDEED CLOSED TO ME, BUT I KNOW YOU TOO WELL.
INSIDE AND OUT, UP AND DOWN. I WAS PART OF YOU.
AND OF COURSE...I WAS WITH YOU WHEN YOU *DIED.*
NO...THAT'S NOT POSSIBLE. *THIS* CHARLES XAVIER IS FROM AN ALTERNATE REALITY! HOW COULD YOU POSSIBLY BE--?
WHEN VARGAS' SWORD SLID THROUGH YOU, IT WAS ECSTASY. IT WAS FREEDOM!
BUT SURPRISINGLY YOUR CONSCIOUSNESS DID NOT DISPERSE...IT WAS PULLED BY THE STRINGS OF REALITY ITSELF.
AND WHILE I ESCAPED, I FOUND MYSELF IN ANOTHER UNIVERSE.
THERE I FOUND CHARLES XAVIER ONCE MORE. AND THERE I SHATTERED HIS MIND.
THERE I MADE HIS CHILDREN MY *HOUNDS.*
BECAUSE IN ALL THE REALITIES... THERE IS ONLY *ONE* SHADOW KING.

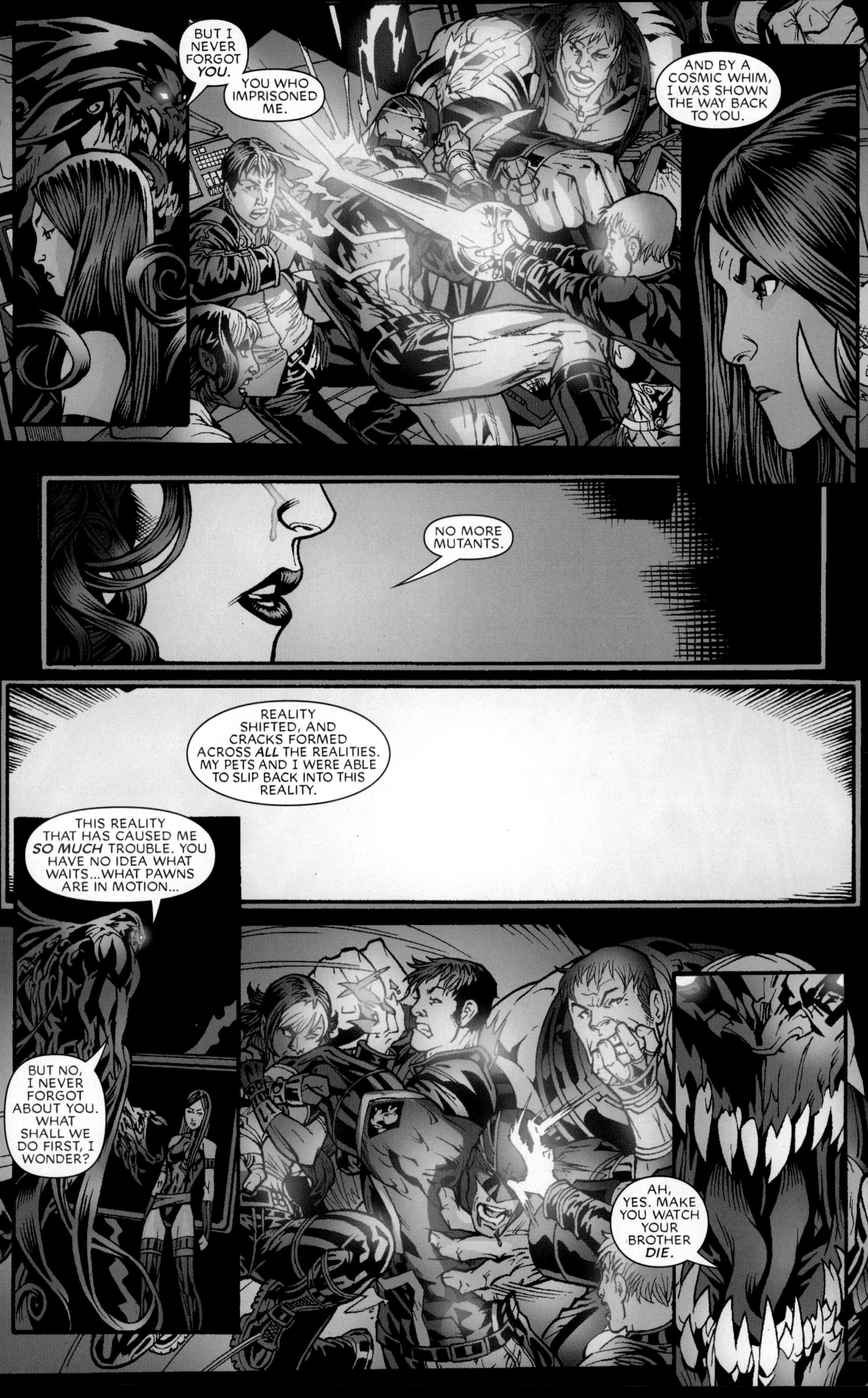
BUT I NEVER FORGOT *YOU.*
YOU WHO IMPRISONED ME.
AND BY A COSMIC WHIM, I WAS SHOWN THE WAY BACK TO YOU.
NO MORE MUTANTS.
REALITY SHIFTED, AND CRACKS FORMED ACROSS *ALL* THE REALITIES. MY PETS AND I WERE ABLE TO SLIP BACK INTO THIS REALITY.
THIS REALITY THAT HAS CAUSED ME *SO MUCH* TROUBLE. YOU HAVE NO IDEA WHAT WAITS...WHAT PAWNS ARE IN MOTION...
BUT NO, I NEVER FORGOT ABOUT YOU. WHAT SHALL WE DO FIRST, I WONDER?
AH, YES. MAKE YOU WATCH YOUR BROTHER *DIE.*

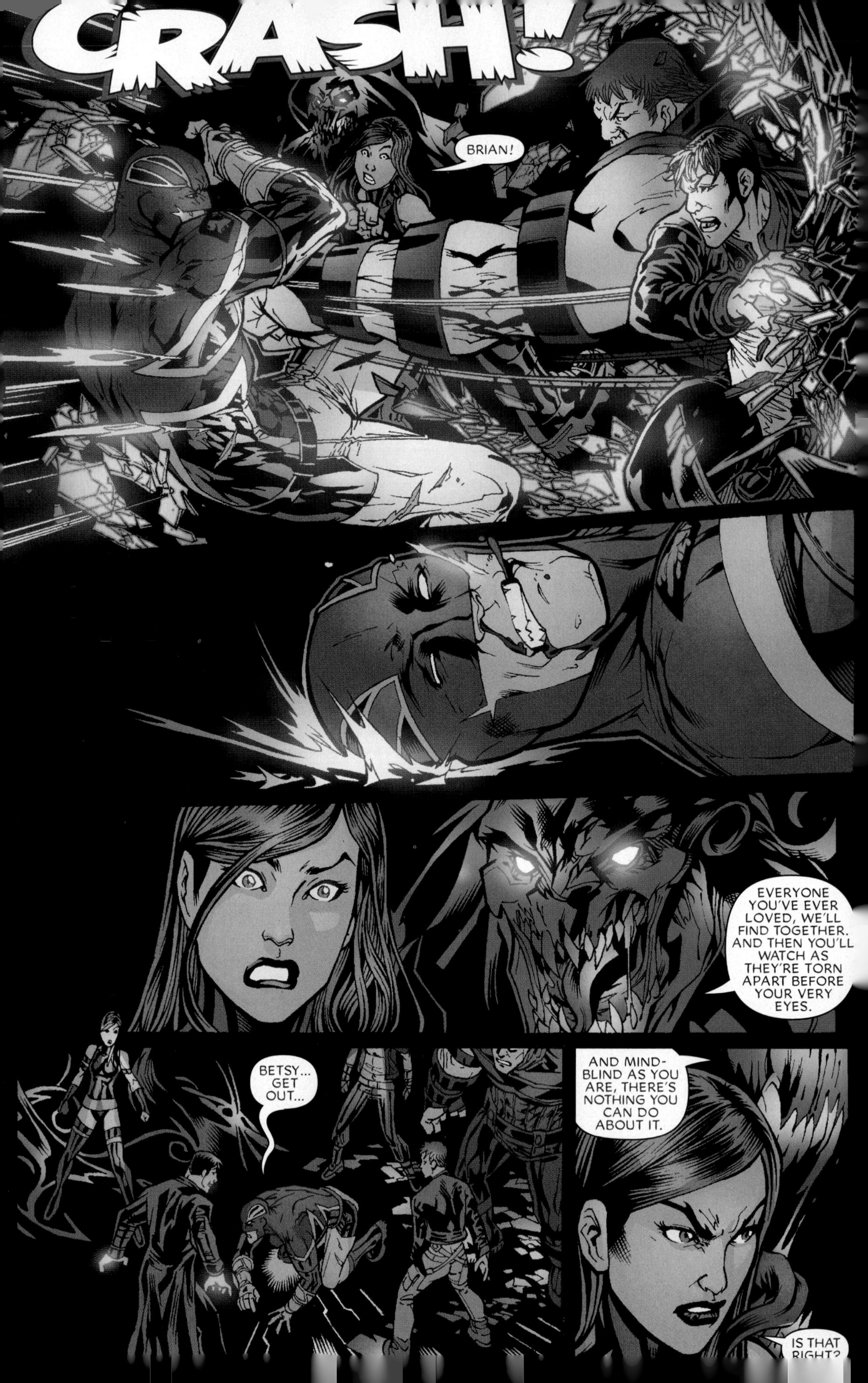
CRASH!
BRIAN!
EVERYONE YOU'VE EVER LOVED, WE'LL FIND TOGETHER. AND THEN YOU'LL WATCH AS THEY'RE TORN APART BEFORE YOUR VERY EYES.
BETSY... GET OUT...
AND MIND-BLIND AS YOU ARE, THERE'S NOTHING YOU CAN DO ABOUT IT.
IS THAT RIGHT?

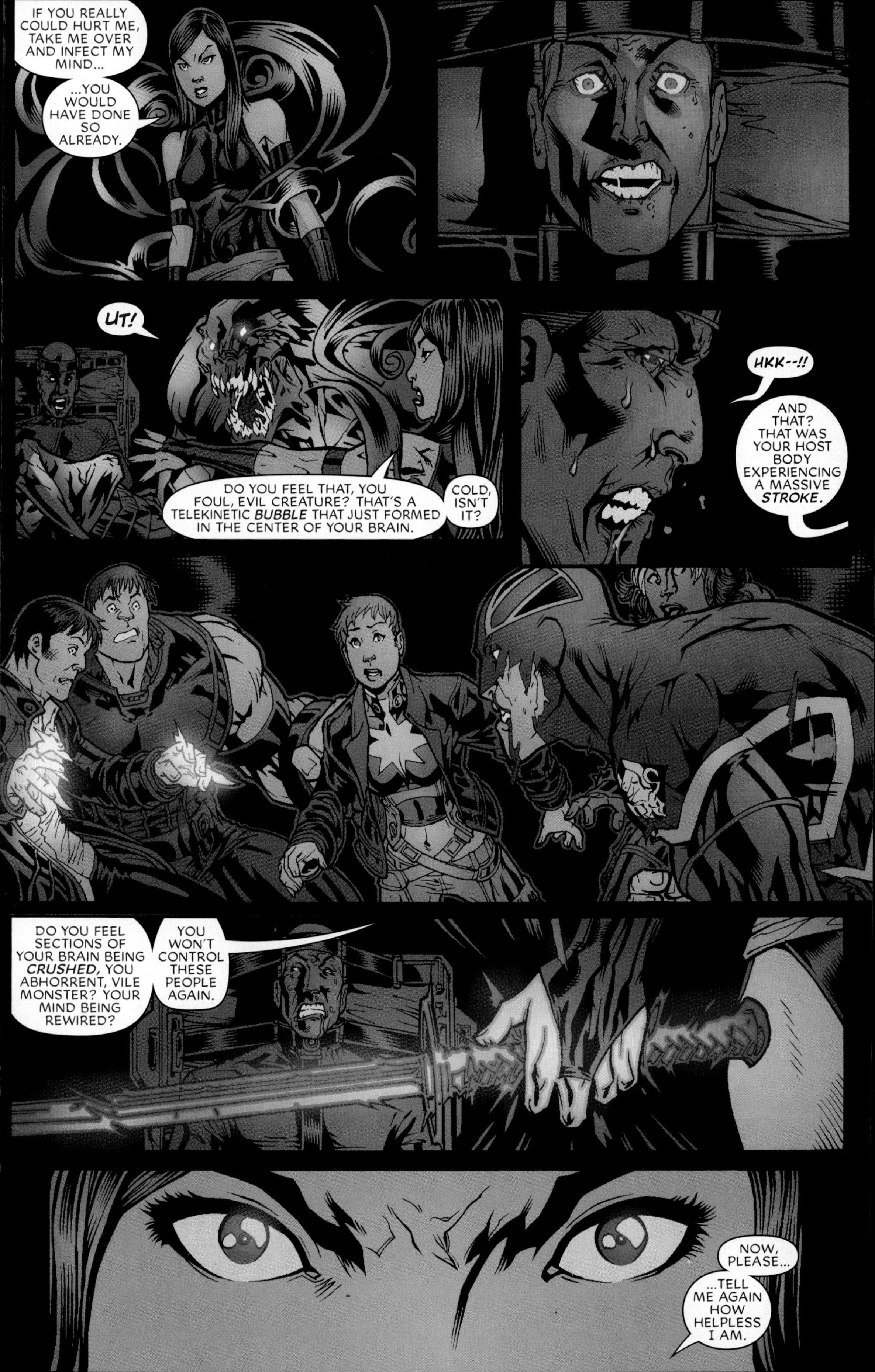
IF YOU REALLY COULD HURT ME, TAKE ME OVER AND INFECT MY MIND...
...YOU WOULD HAVE DONE SO ALREADY.
UT!
DO YOU FEEL THAT, YOU FOUL, EVIL CREATURE? THAT'S A TELEKINETIC BUBBLE THAT JUST FORMED IN THE CENTER OF YOUR BRAIN.
COLD, ISN'T IT?
HKK--!!
AND THAT? THAT WAS YOUR HOST BODY EXPERIENCING A MASSIVE STROKE.
DO YOU FEEL SECTIONS OF YOUR BRAIN BEING CRUSHED, YOU ABHORRENT, VILE MONSTER? YOUR MIND BEING REWIRED?
YOU WON'T CONTROL THESE PEOPLE AGAIN.
NOW, PLEASE...
...TELL ME AGAIN HOW HELPLESS I AM.

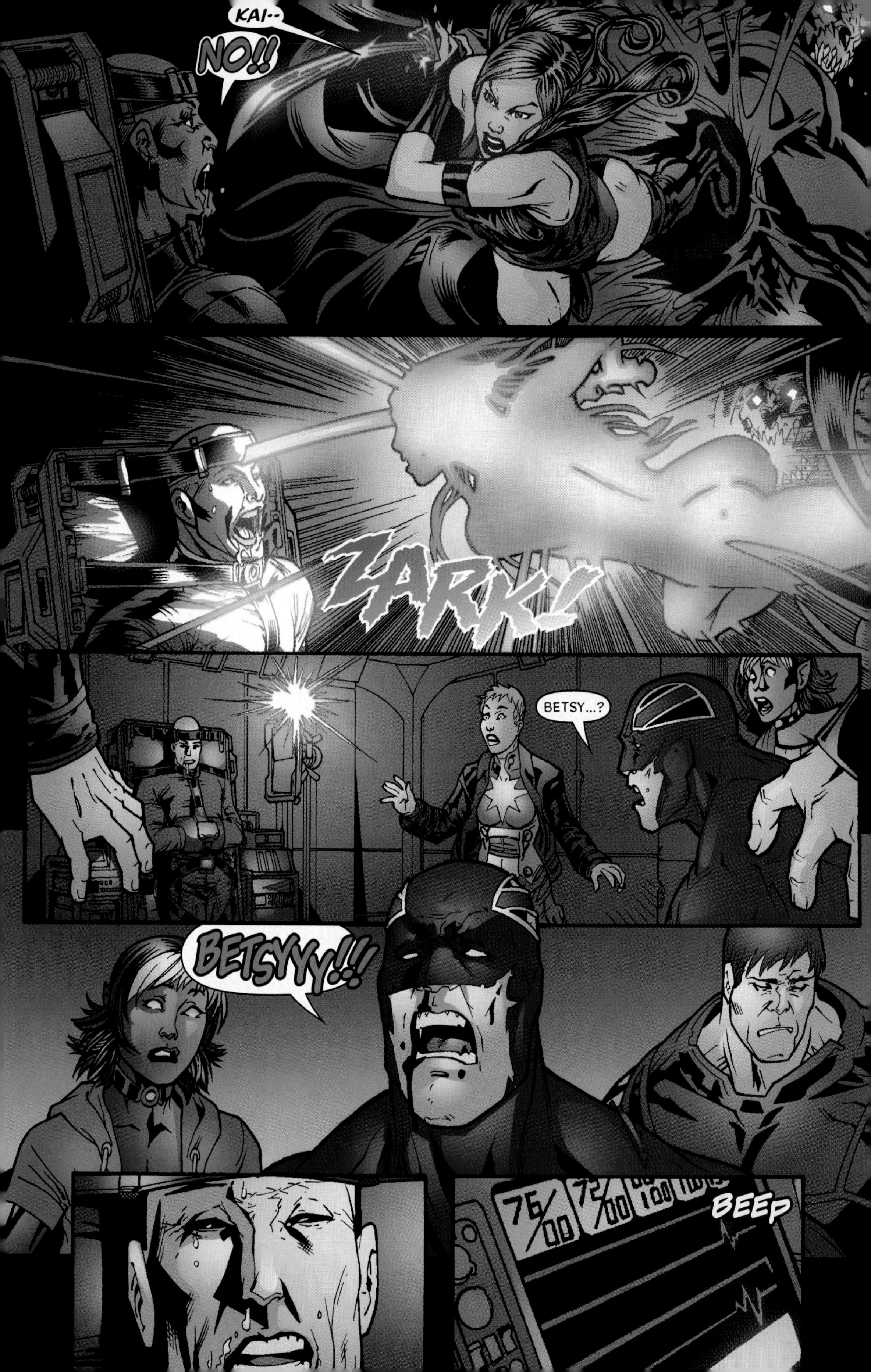
KAI--
NO!!
ZARK!
BETSY...?
BETSYYY!!!
76/00
72/00
BEEP

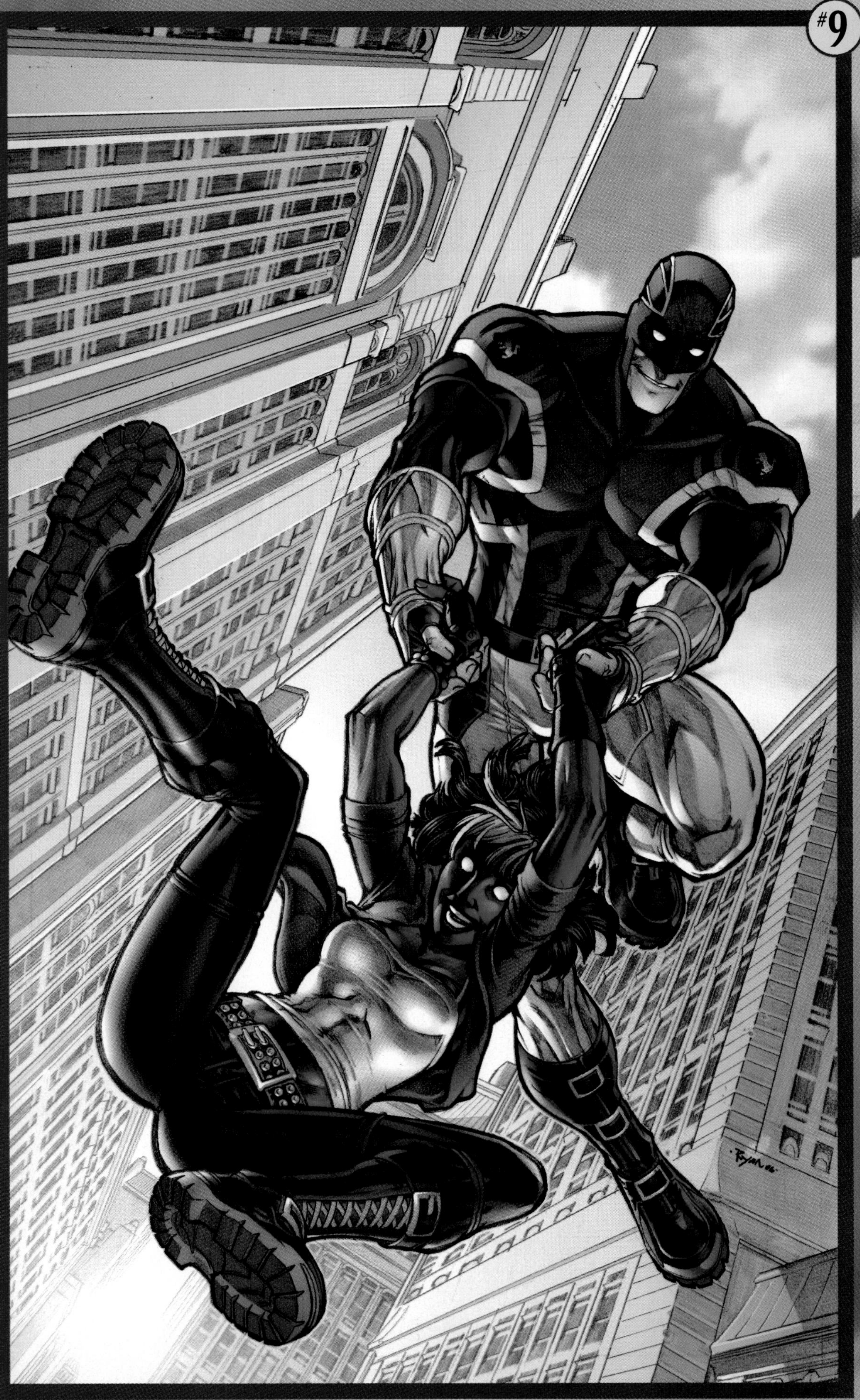
#9

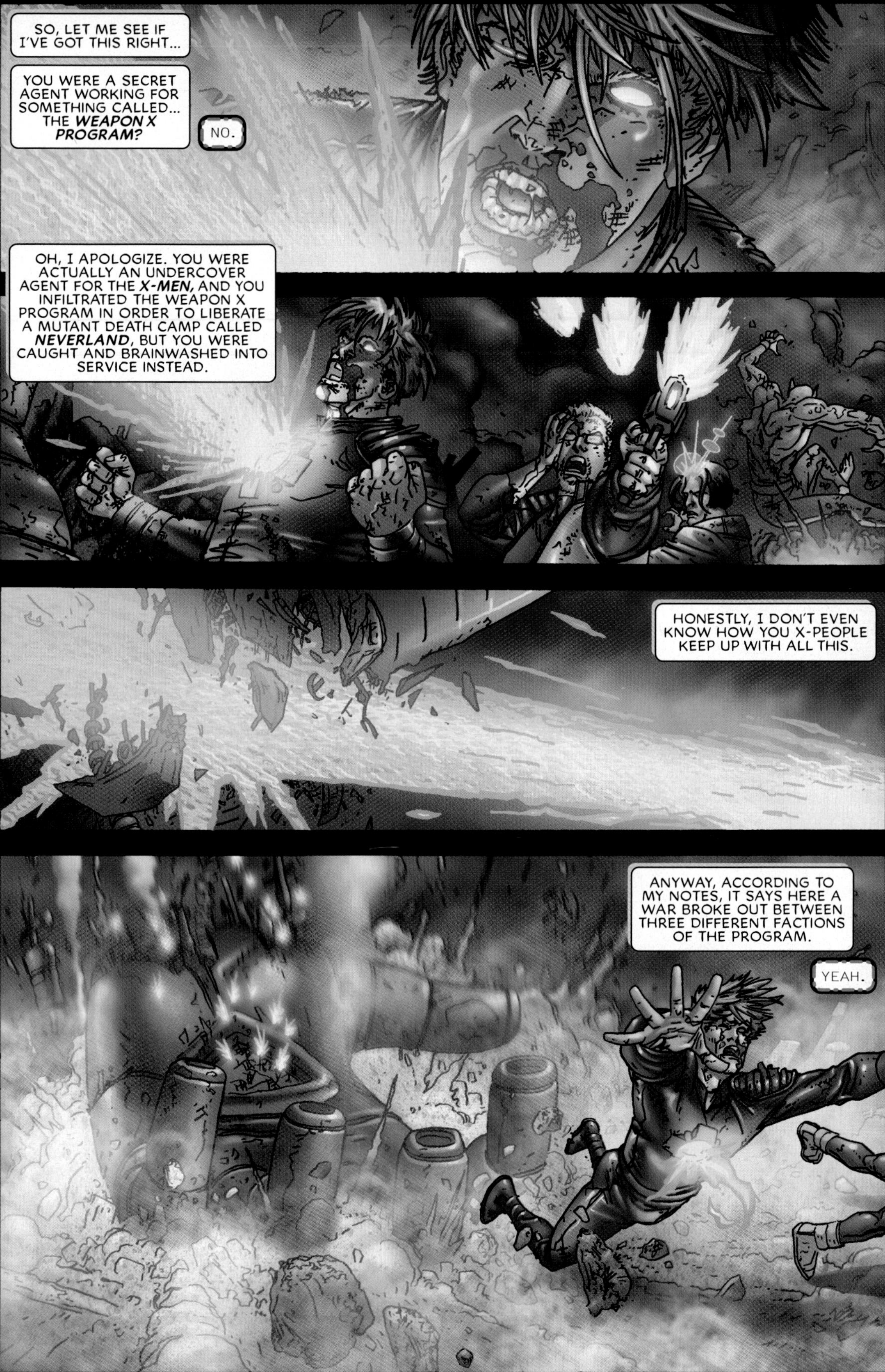
SO, LET ME SEE IF I'VE GOT THIS RIGHT...
YOU WERE A SECRET AGENT WORKING FOR SOMETHING CALLED... THE *WEAPON X PROGRAM?*
NO.
OH, I APOLOGIZE. YOU WERE ACTUALLY AN UNDERCOVER AGENT FOR THE *X-MEN,* AND YOU INFILTRATED THE WEAPON X PROGRAM IN ORDER TO LIBERATE A MUTANT DEATH CAMP CALLED *NEVERLAND*, BUT YOU WERE CAUGHT AND BRAINWASHED INTO SERVICE INSTEAD.
HONESTLY, I DON'T EVEN KNOW HOW YOU X-PEOPLE KEEP UP WITH ALL THIS.
ANYWAY, ACCORDING TO MY NOTES, IT SAYS HERE A WAR BROKE OUT BETWEEN THREE DIFFERENT FACTIONS OF THE PROGRAM.
YEAH.

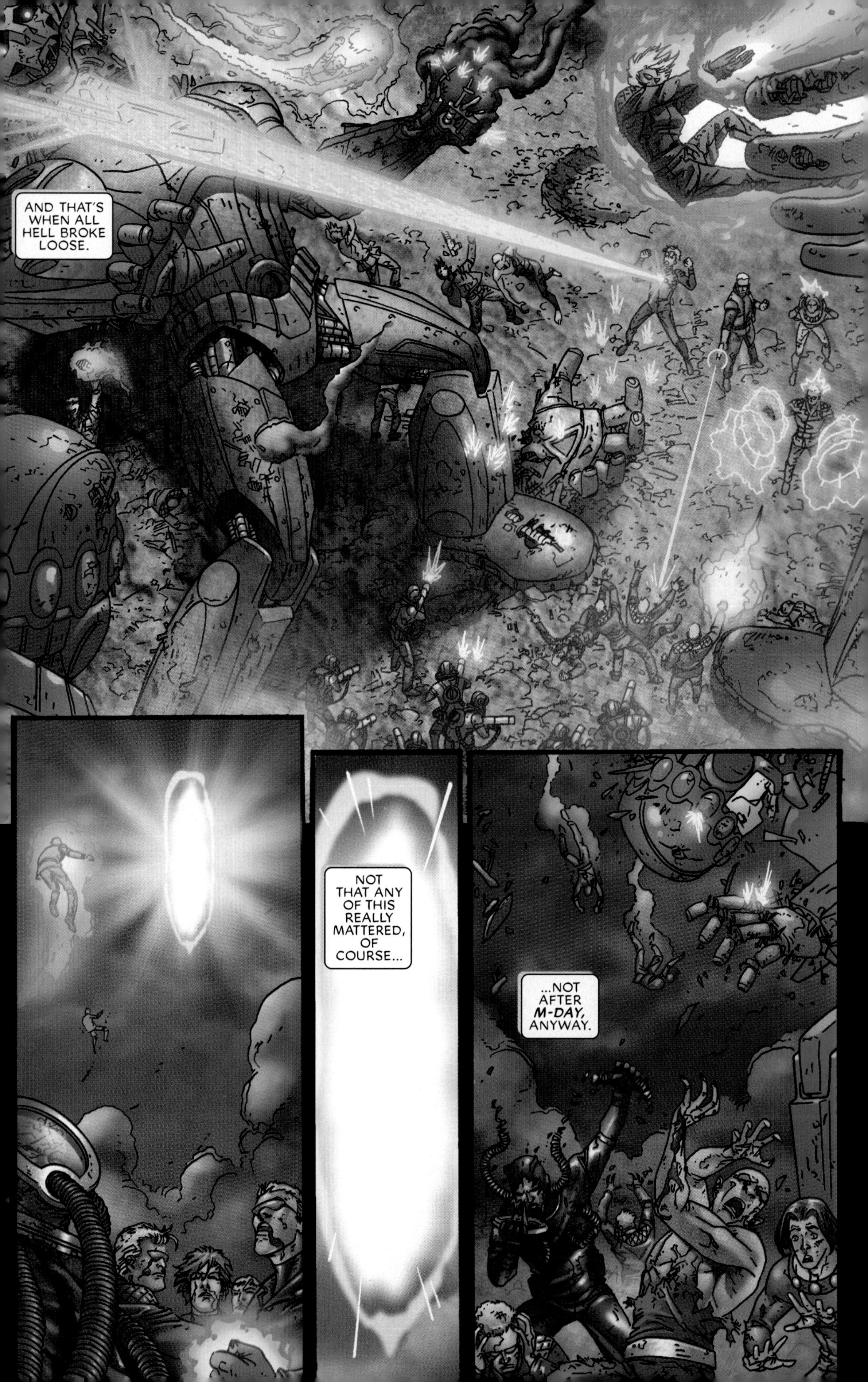
AND THAT'S WHEN ALL HELL BROKE LOOSE.
NOT THAT ANY OF THIS REALLY MATTERED, OF COURSE...
...NOT AFTER **M-DAY,** ANYWAY.

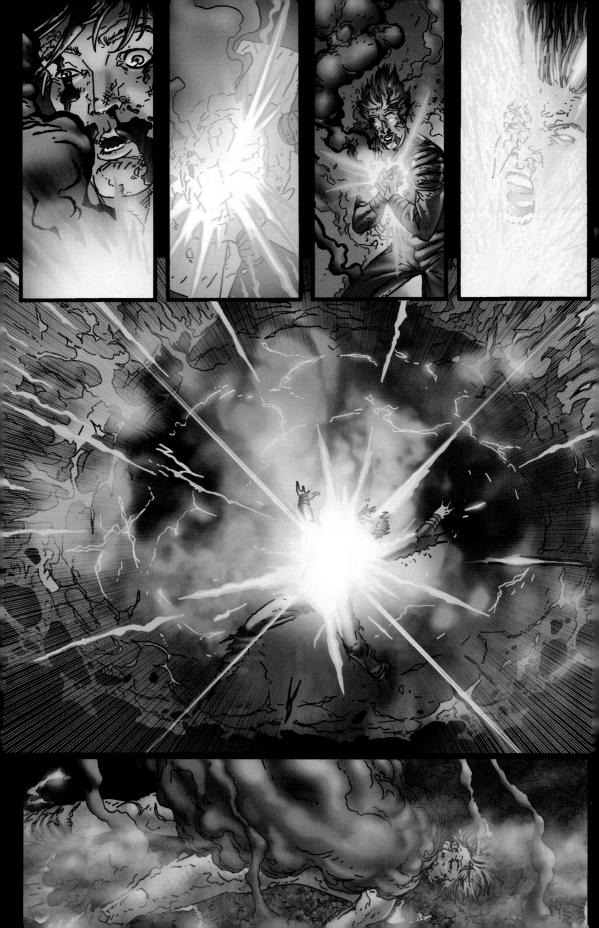

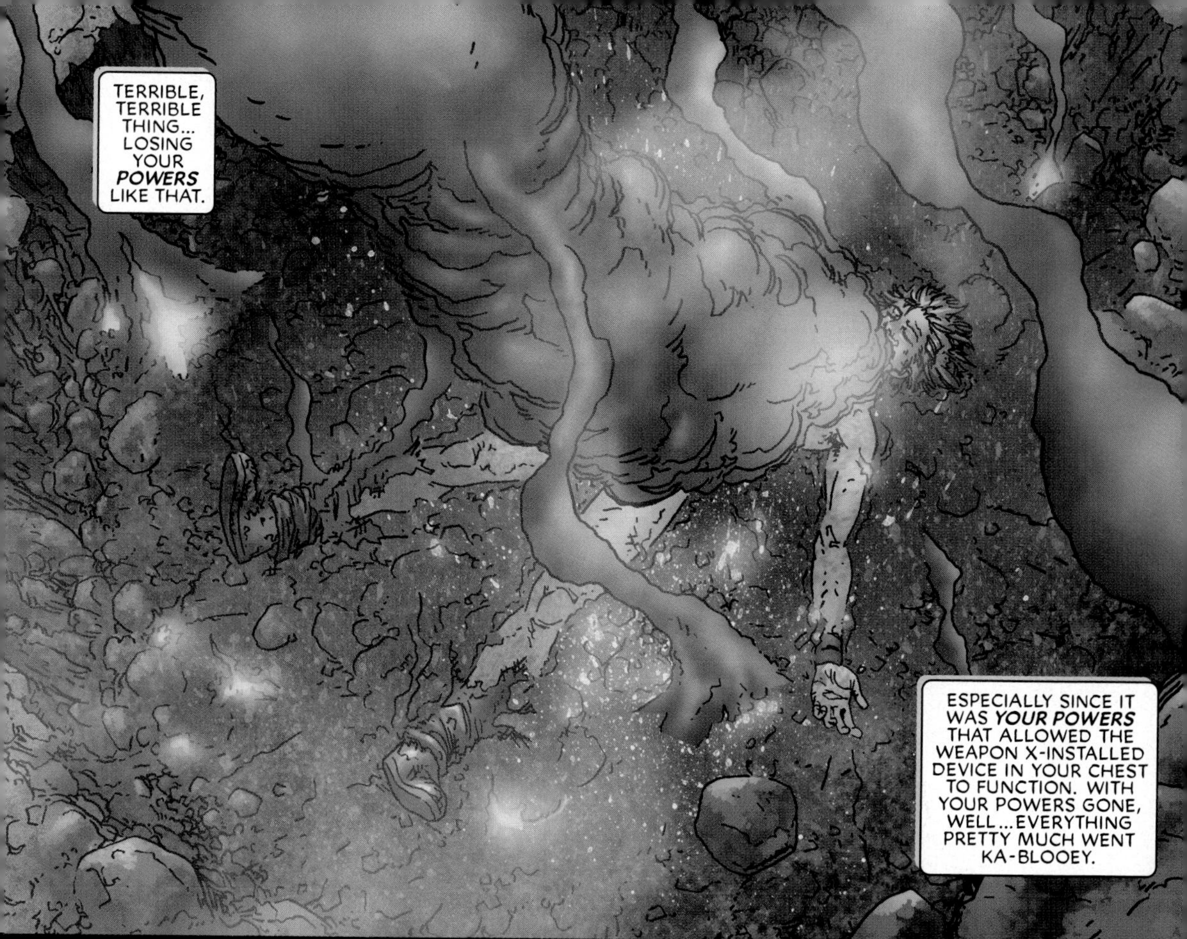
TERRIBLE, TERRIBLE THING... LOSING YOUR **POWERS** LIKE THAT.
ESPECIALLY SINCE IT WAS **YOUR POWERS** THAT ALLOWED THE WEAPON X-INSTALLED DEVICE IN YOUR CHEST TO FUNCTION. WITH YOUR POWERS GONE, WELL... EVERYTHING PRETTY MUCH WENT KA-BLOOEY.

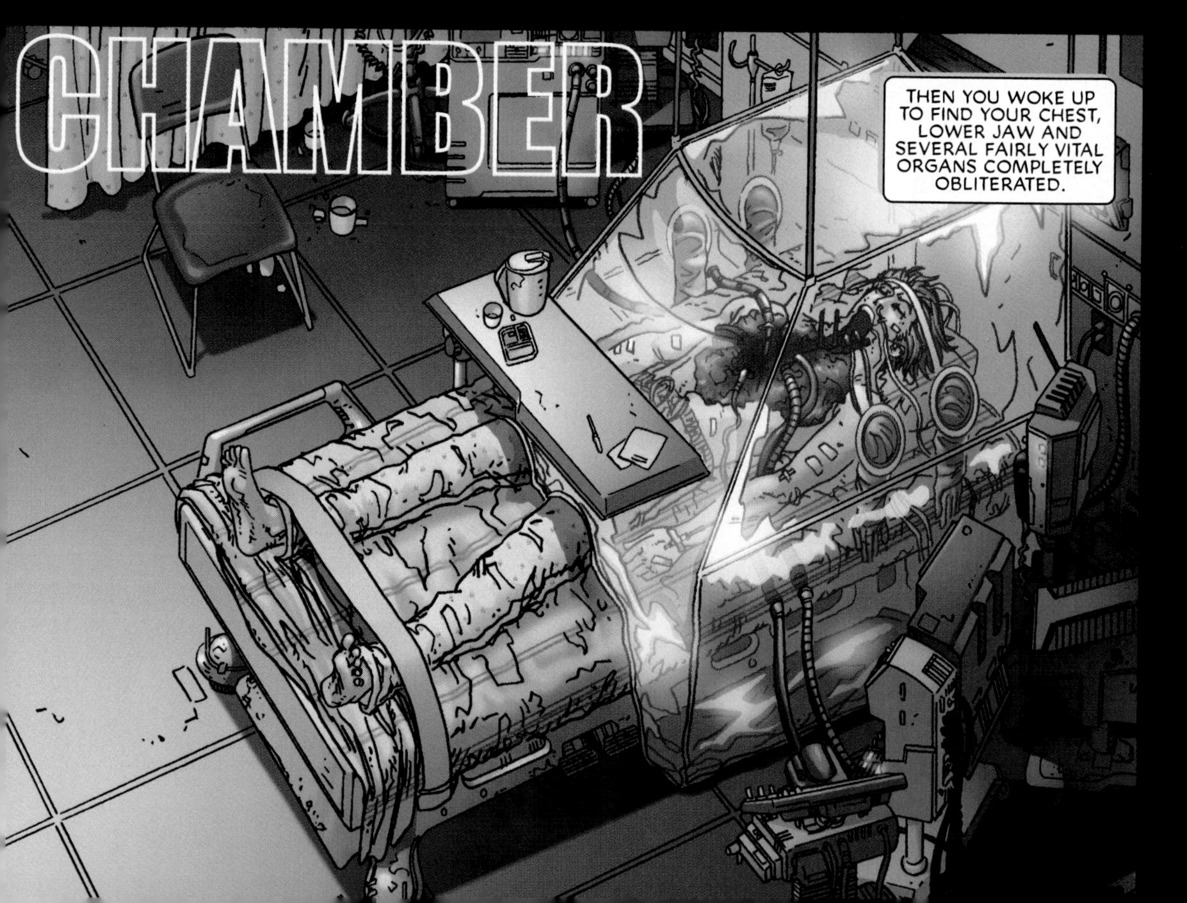
CHAMBER
THEN YOU WOKE UP TO FIND YOUR CHEST, LOWER JAW AND SEVERAL FAIRLY VITAL ORGANS COMPLETELY OBLITERATED.

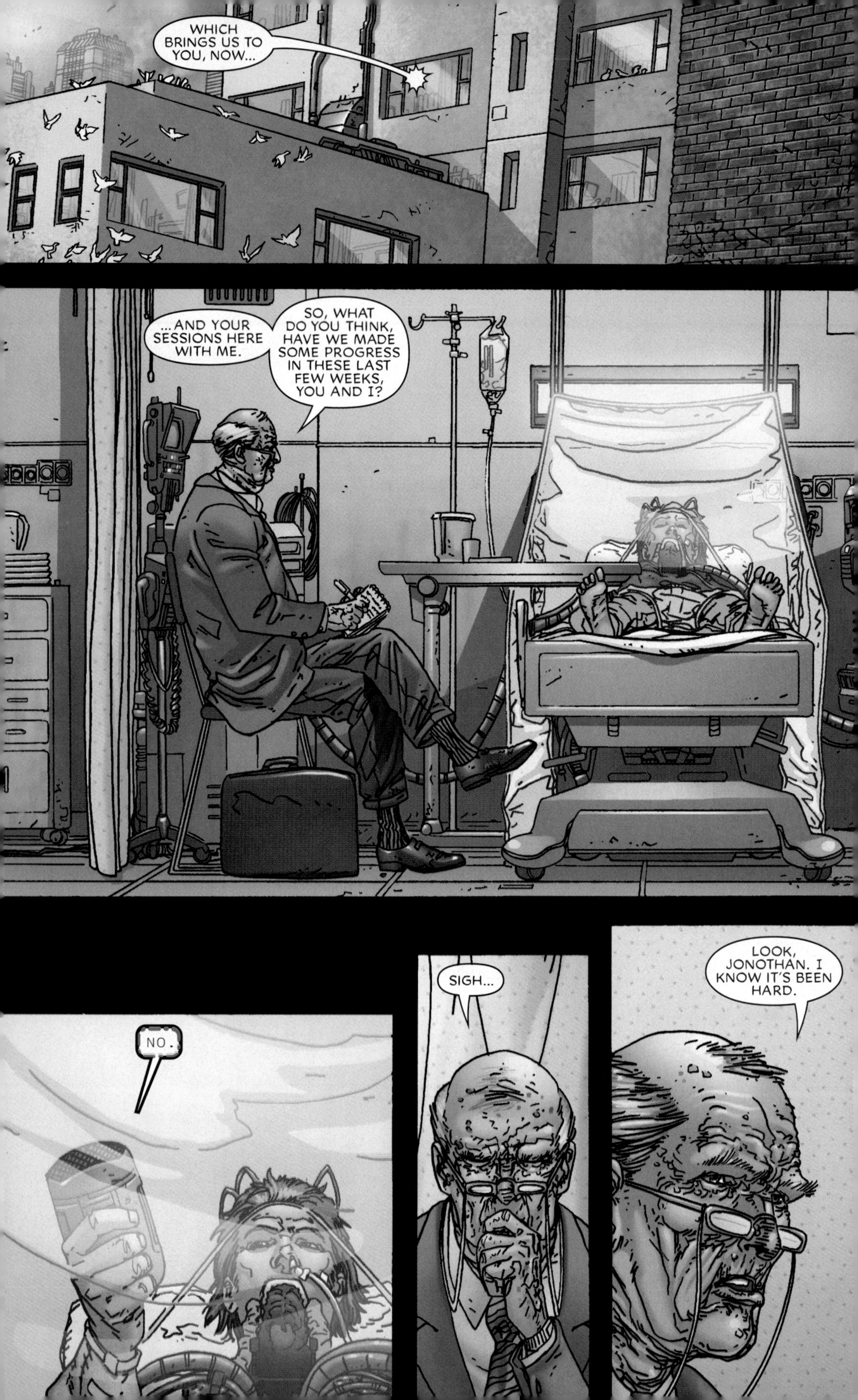
WHICH BRINGS US TO YOU, NOW...
...AND YOUR SESSIONS HERE WITH ME.
SO, WHAT DO YOU THINK, HAVE WE MADE SOME PROGRESS IN THESE LAST FEW WEEKS, YOU AND I?
NO.
SIGH...
LOOK, JONOTHAN. I KNOW IT'S BEEN HARD.

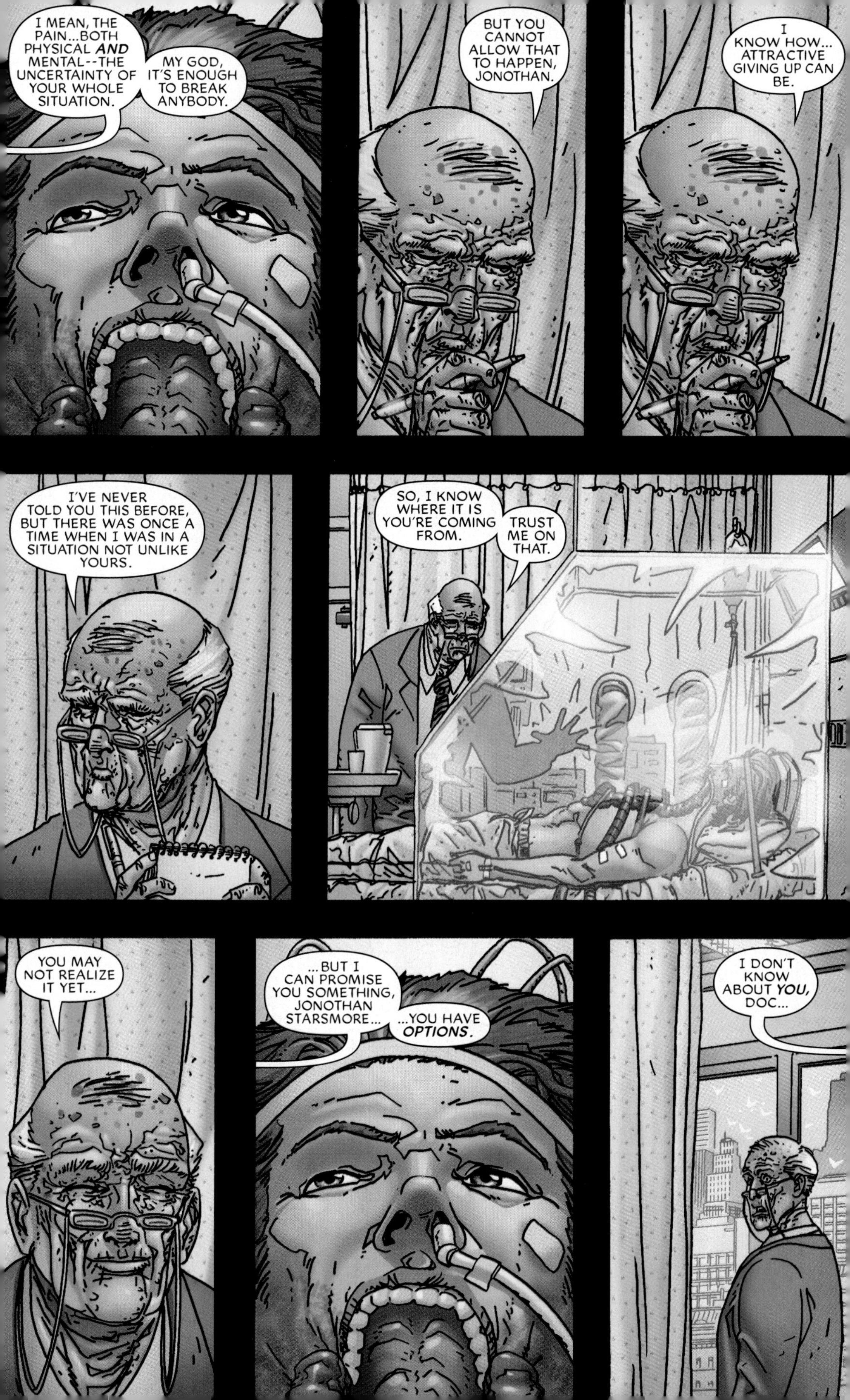
I MEAN, THE PAIN...BOTH PHYSICAL *AND* MENTAL--THE UNCERTAINTY OF YOUR WHOLE SITUATION.
MY GOD, IT'S ENOUGH TO BREAK ANYBODY.
BUT YOU CANNOT ALLOW THAT TO HAPPEN, JONOTHAN.
I KNOW HOW... ATTRACTIVE GIVING UP CAN BE.
I'VE NEVER TOLD YOU THIS BEFORE, BUT THERE WAS ONCE A TIME WHEN I WAS IN A SITUATION NOT UNLIKE YOURS.
SO, I KNOW WHERE IT IS YOU'RE COMING FROM.
TRUST ME ON THAT.
YOU MAY NOT REALIZE IT YET...
...BUT I CAN PROMISE YOU SOMETHING, JONOTHAN STARSMORE...
...YOU HAVE *OPTIONS*.
I DON'T KNOW ABOUT *YOU,* DOC...

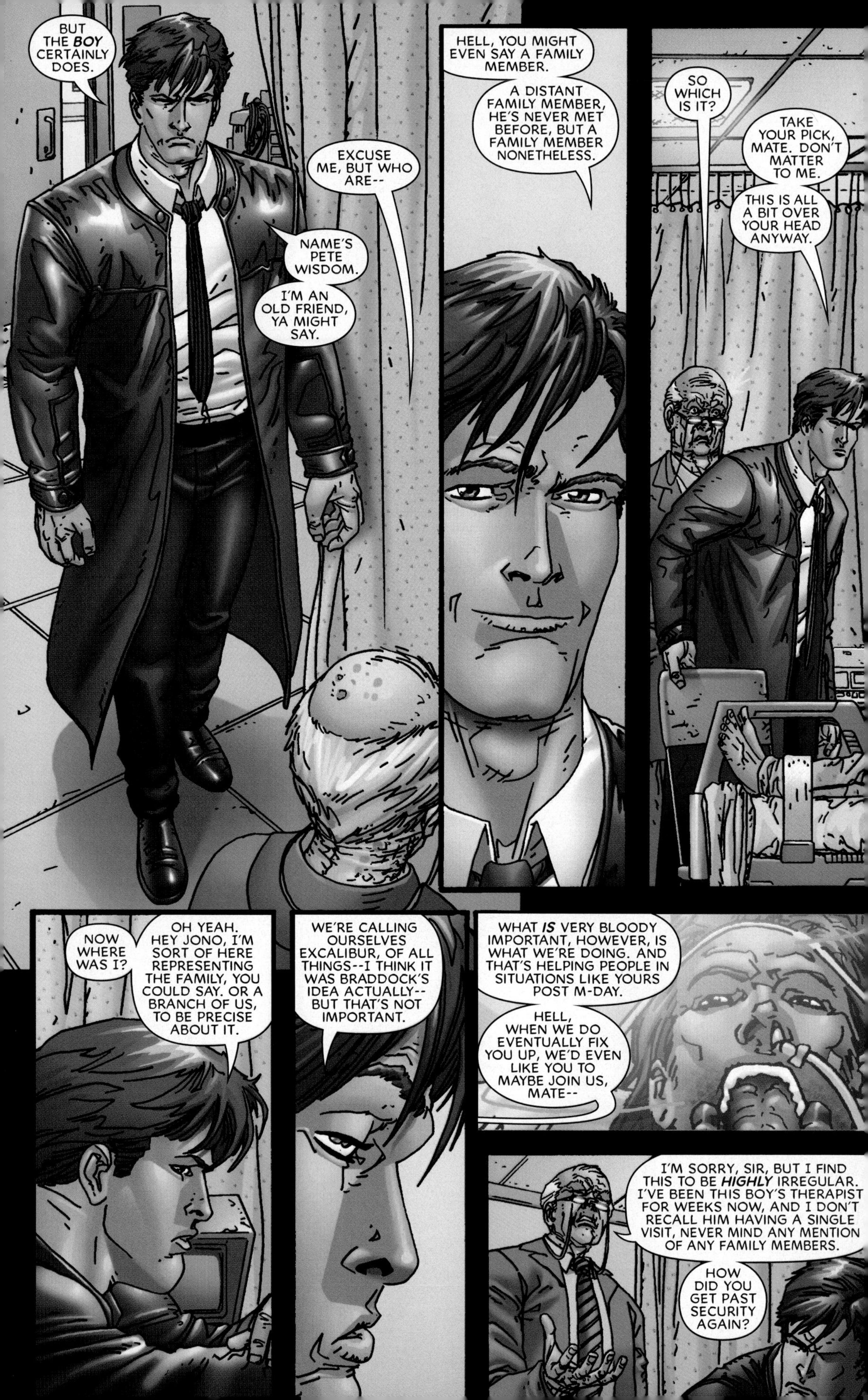

BUT THE *BOY* CERTAINLY DOES.
EXCUSE ME, BUT WHO ARE--
NAME'S PETE WISDOM.
I'M AN OLD FRIEND, YA MIGHT SAY.
HELL, YOU MIGHT EVEN SAY A FAMILY MEMBER.
A DISTANT FAMILY MEMBER, HE'S NEVER MET BEFORE, BUT A FAMILY MEMBER NONETHELESS.
SO WHICH IS IT?
TAKE YOUR PICK, MATE. DON'T MATTER TO ME.
THIS IS ALL A BIT OVER YOUR HEAD ANYWAY.
NOW WHERE WAS I?
OH YEAH. HEY JONO, I'M SORT OF HERE REPRESENTING THE FAMILY, YOU COULD SAY. OR A BRANCH OF US, TO BE PRECISE ABOUT IT.
WE'RE CALLING OURSELVES EXCALIBUR, OF ALL THINGS--I THINK IT WAS BRADDOCK'S IDEA ACTUALLY--BUT THAT'S NOT IMPORTANT.
WHAT *IS* VERY BLOODY IMPORTANT, HOWEVER, IS WHAT WE'RE DOING. AND THAT'S HELPING PEOPLE IN SITUATIONS LIKE YOURS POST M-DAY.
HELL, WHEN WE DO EVENTUALLY FIX YOU UP, WE'D EVEN LIKE YOU TO MAYBE JOIN US, MATE--
I'M SORRY, SIR, BUT I FIND THIS TO BE *HIGHLY* IRREGULAR. I'VE BEEN THIS BOY'S THERAPIST FOR WEEKS NOW, AND I DON'T RECALL HIM HAVING A SINGLE VISIT, NEVER MIND ANY MENTION OF ANY FAMILY MEMBERS.
HOW DID YOU GET PAST SECURITY AGAIN?

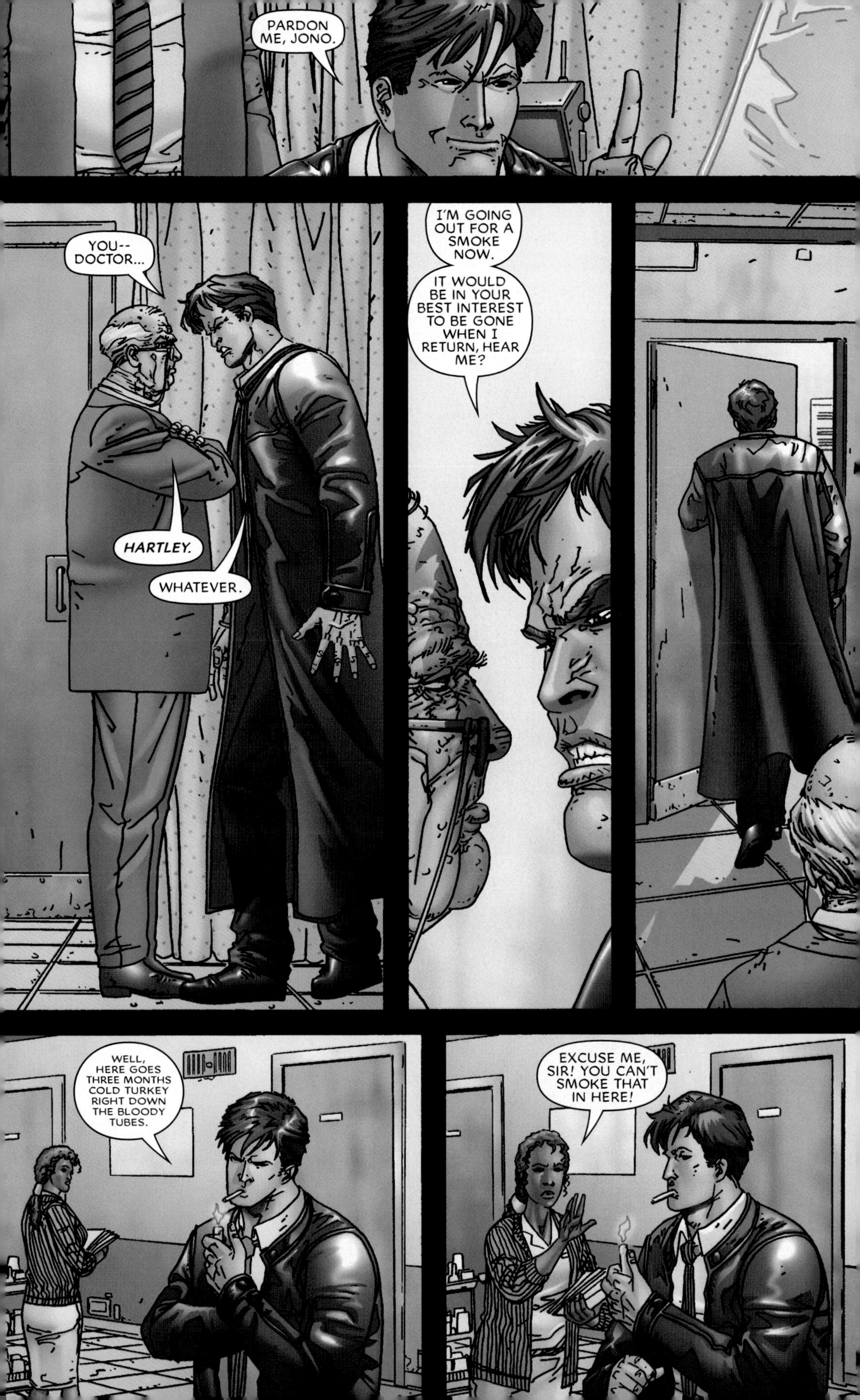
PARDON ME, JONO.
YOU-- DOCTOR...
HARTLEY.
WHATEVER.
I'M GOING OUT FOR A SMOKE NOW.
IT WOULD BE IN YOUR BEST INTEREST TO BE GONE WHEN I RETURN, HEAR ME?
WELL, HERE GOES THREE MONTHS COLD TURKEY RIGHT DOWN THE BLOODY TUBES.
EXCUSE ME, SIR! YOU CAN'T SMOKE THAT IN HERE!

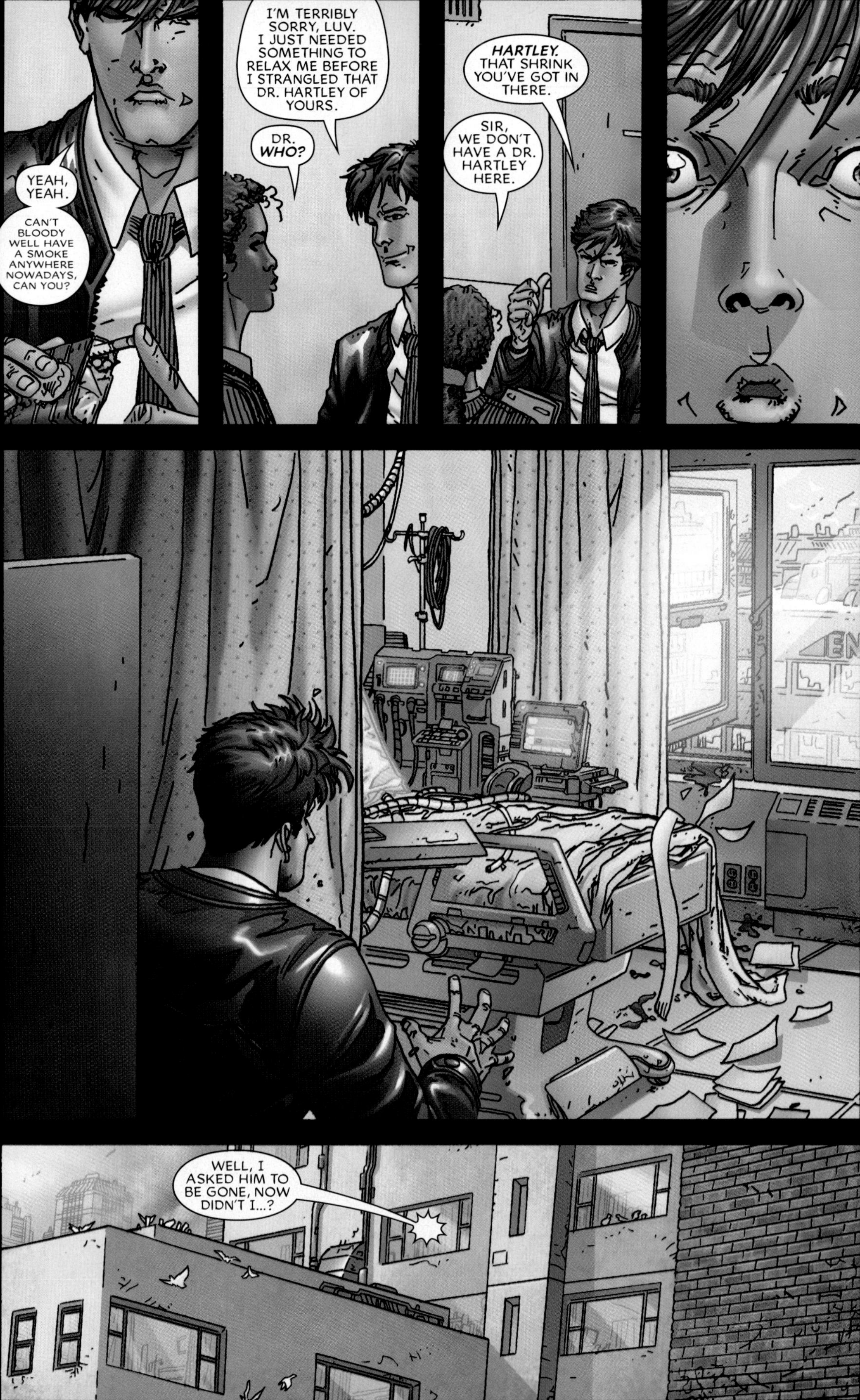
YEAH, YEAH.
CAN'T BLOODY WELL HAVE A SMOKE ANYWHERE NOWADAYS, CAN YOU?
I'M TERRIBLY SORRY, LUV. I JUST NEEDED SOMETHING TO RELAX ME BEFORE I STRANGLED THAT DR. HARTLEY OF YOURS.
DR. *WHO?*
HARTLEY. THAT SHRINK YOU'VE GOT IN THERE.
SIR, WE DON'T HAVE A DR. HARTLEY HERE.
WELL, I ASKED HIM TO BE GONE, NOW DIDN'T I...?

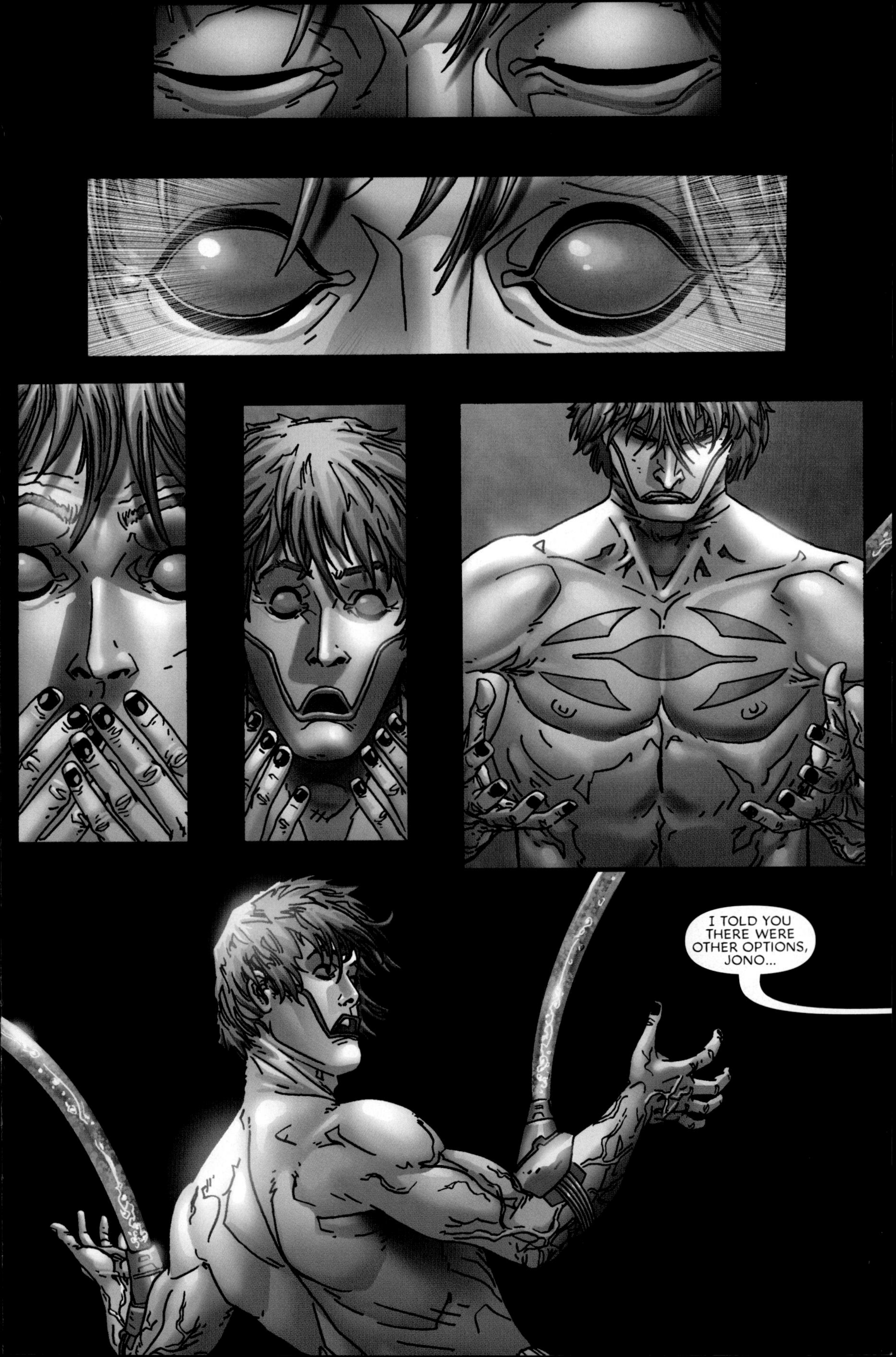
I TOLD YOU THERE WERE OTHER OPTIONS, JONO...

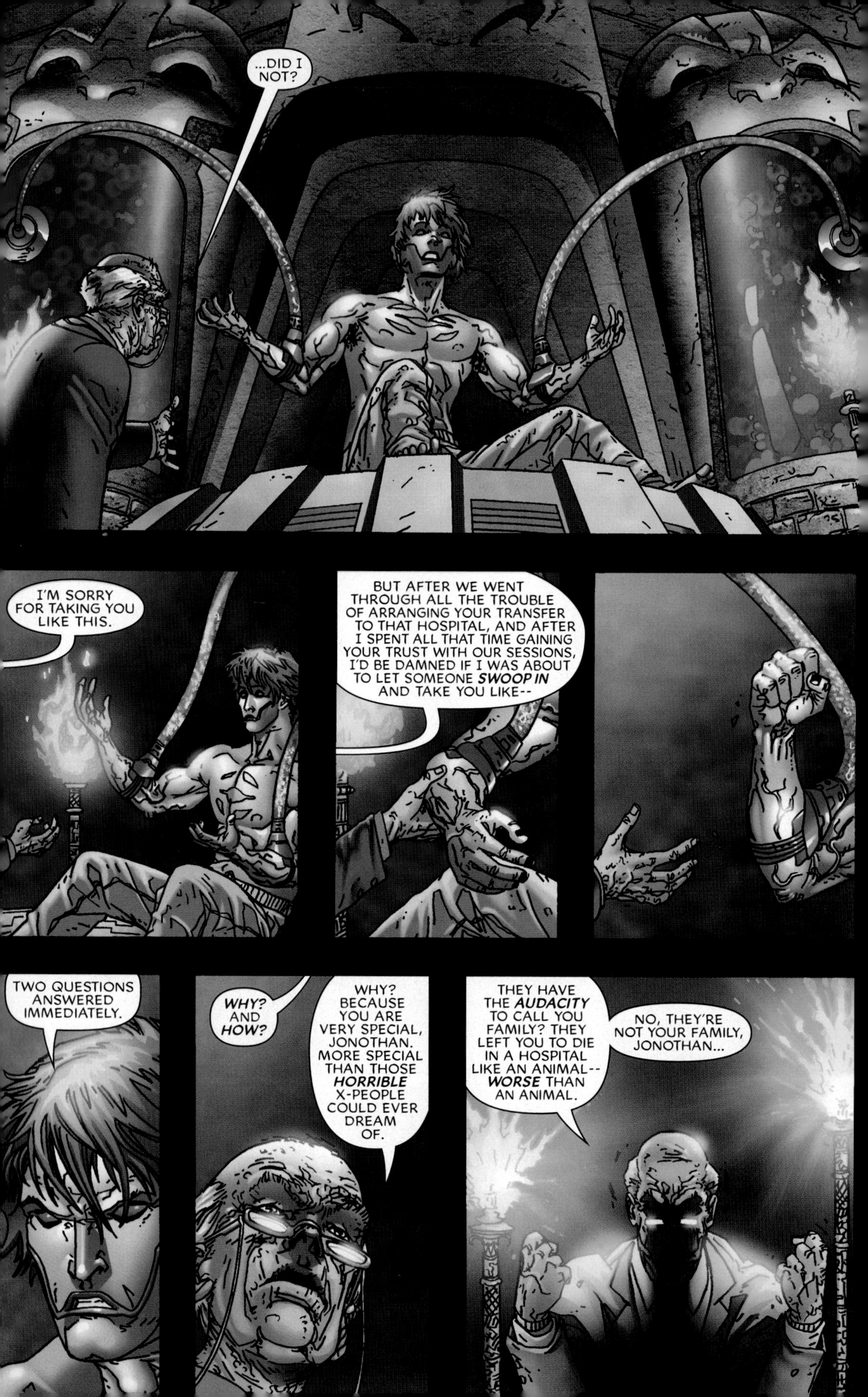
...DID I NOT?
I'M SORRY FOR TAKING YOU LIKE THIS.
BUT AFTER WE WENT THROUGH ALL THE TROUBLE OF ARRANGING YOUR TRANSFER TO THAT HOSPITAL, AND AFTER I SPENT ALL THAT TIME GAINING YOUR TRUST WITH OUR SESSIONS, I'D BE DAMNED IF I WAS ABOUT TO LET SOMEONE **SWOOP IN** AND TAKE YOU LIKE--
TWO QUESTIONS ANSWERED IMMEDIATELY.
WHY? AND **HOW?**
WHY? BECAUSE YOU ARE VERY SPECIAL, JONOTHAN. MORE SPECIAL THAN THOSE **HORRIBLE** X-PEOPLE COULD EVER DREAM OF.
THEY HAVE THE **AUDACITY** TO CALL YOU FAMILY? THEY LEFT YOU TO DIE IN A HOSPITAL LIKE AN ANIMAL-- **WORSE** THAN AN ANIMAL.
NO, THEY'RE NOT YOUR FAMILY, JONOTHAN...

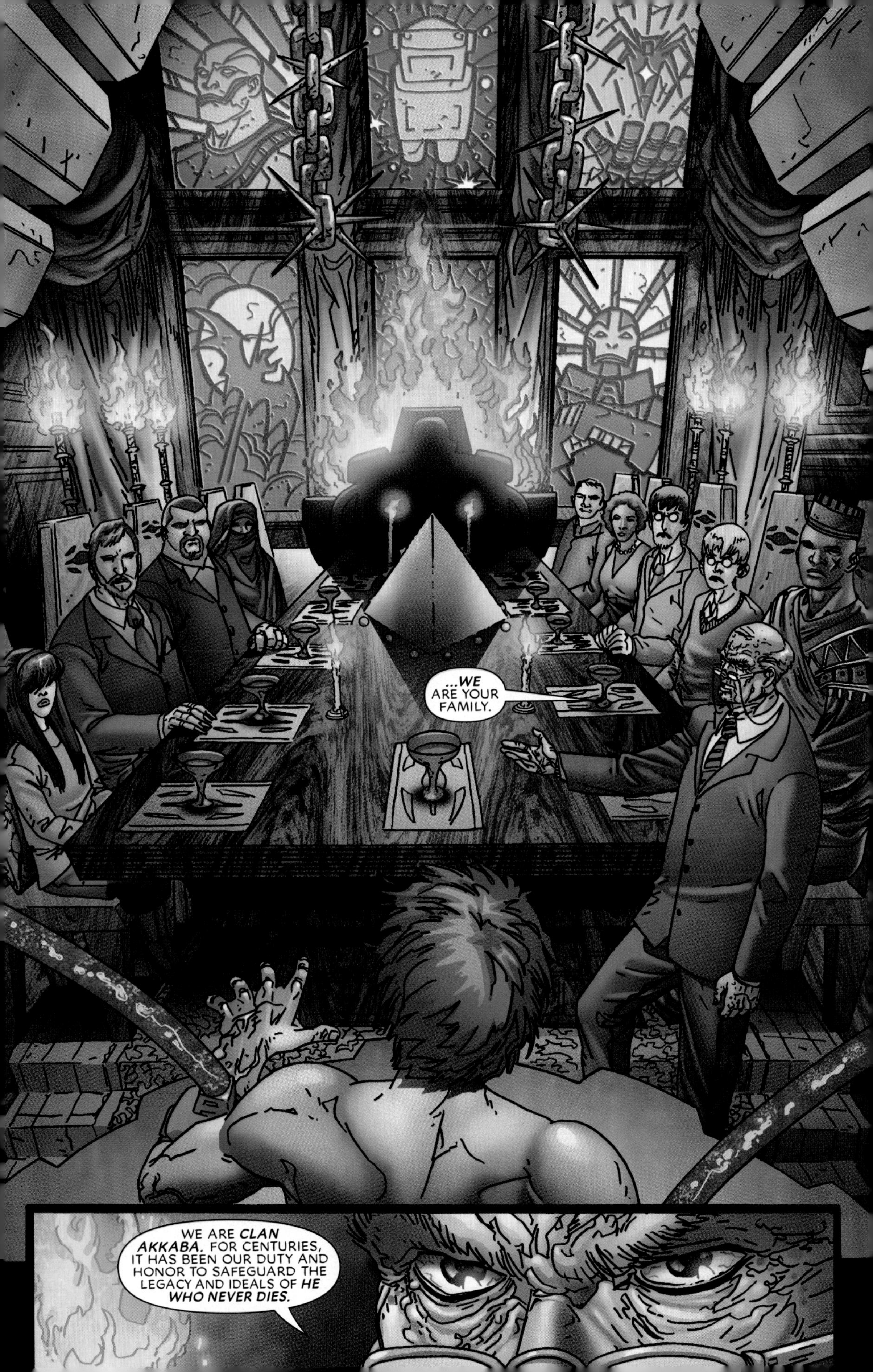
...WE ARE YOUR FAMILY.
WE ARE CLAN AKKABA. FOR CENTURIES, IT HAS BEEN OUR DUTY AND HONOR TO SAFEGUARD THE LEGACY AND IDEALS OF HE WHO NEVER DIES.

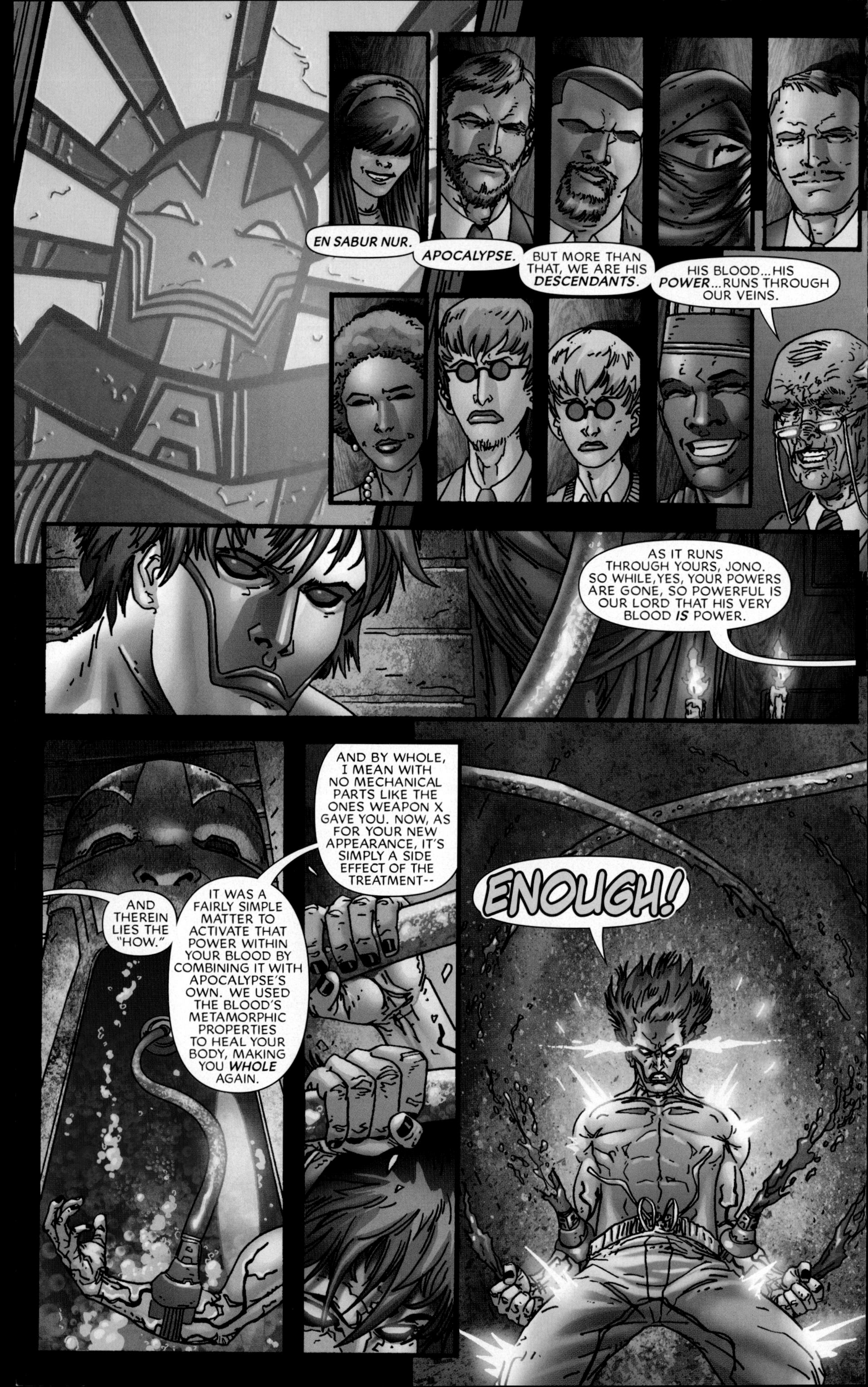
EN SABUR NUR.
APOCALYPSE.
BUT MORE THAN THAT, WE ARE HIS DESCENDANTS.
HIS BLOOD...HIS POWER...RUNS THROUGH OUR VEINS.
AS IT RUNS THROUGH YOURS, JONO. SO WHILE, YES, YOUR POWERS ARE GONE, SO POWERFUL IS OUR LORD THAT HIS VERY BLOOD IS POWER.
AND THEREIN LIES THE "HOW."
IT WAS A FAIRLY SIMPLE MATTER TO ACTIVATE THAT POWER WITHIN YOUR BLOOD BY COMBINING IT WITH APOCALYPSE'S OWN. WE USED THE BLOOD'S METAMORPHIC PROPERTIES TO HEAL YOUR BODY, MAKING YOU WHOLE AGAIN.
AND BY WHOLE, I MEAN WITH NO MECHANICAL PARTS LIKE THE ONES WEAPON X GAVE YOU. NOW, AS FOR YOUR NEW APPEARANCE, IT'S SIMPLY A SIDE EFFECT OF THE TREATMENT--
ENOUGH!

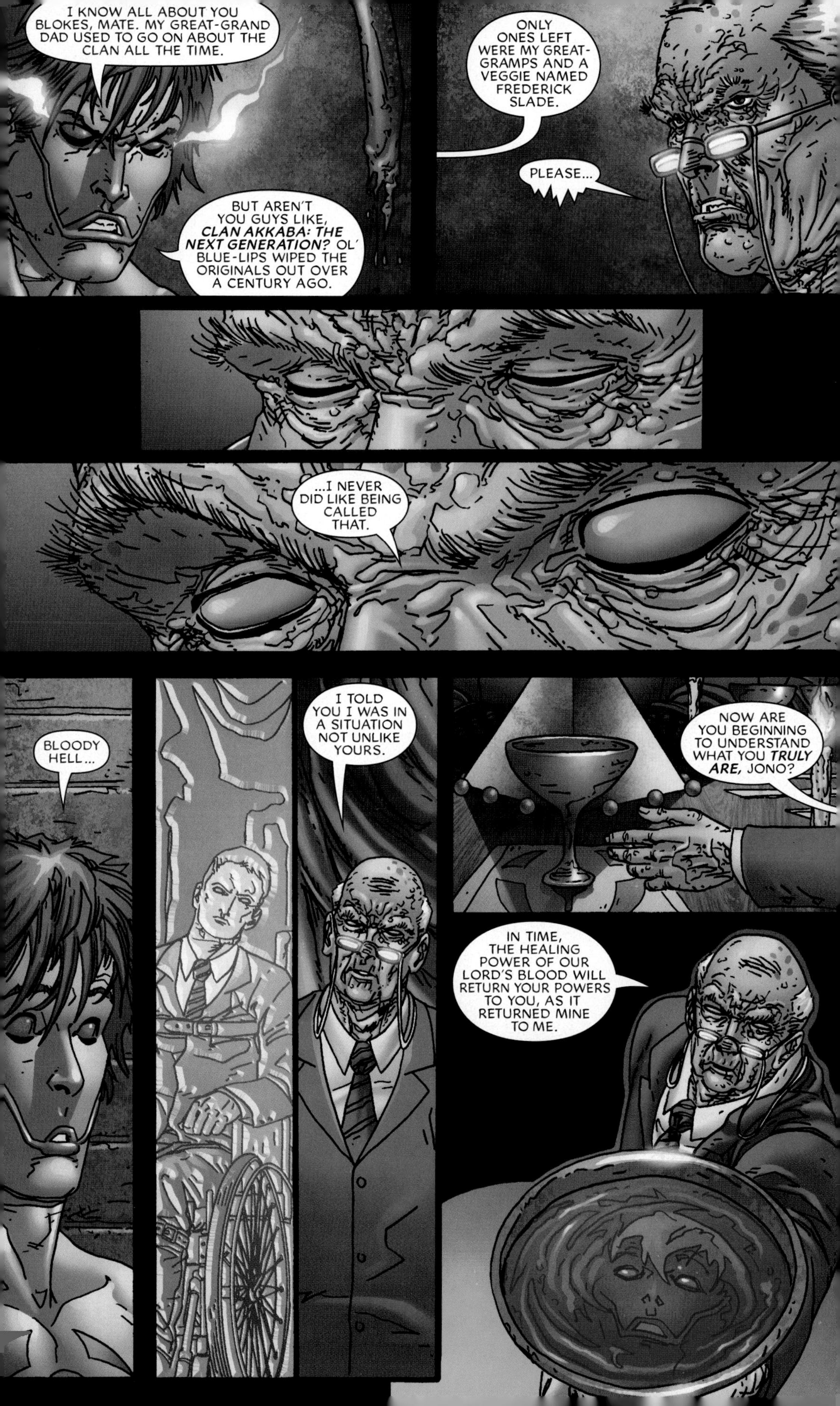
I KNOW ALL ABOUT YOU BLOKES, MATE. MY GREAT-GRAND DAD USED TO GO ON ABOUT THE CLAN ALL THE TIME.
BUT AREN'T YOU GUYS LIKE, ***CLAN AKKABA: THE NEXT GENERATION?*** OL' BLUE-LIPS WIPED THE ORIGINALS OUT OVER A CENTURY AGO.
ONLY ONES LEFT WERE MY GREAT-GRAMPS AND A VEGGIE NAMED FREDERICK SLADE.
PLEASE...
...I NEVER DID LIKE BEING CALLED THAT.
BLOODY HELL...
I TOLD YOU I WAS IN A SITUATION NOT UNLIKE YOURS.
NOW ARE YOU BEGINNING TO UNDERSTAND WHAT YOU ***TRULY ARE,*** JONO?
IN TIME, THE HEALING POWER OF OUR LORD'S BLOOD WILL RETURN YOUR POWERS TO YOU, AS IT RETURNED MINE TO ME.

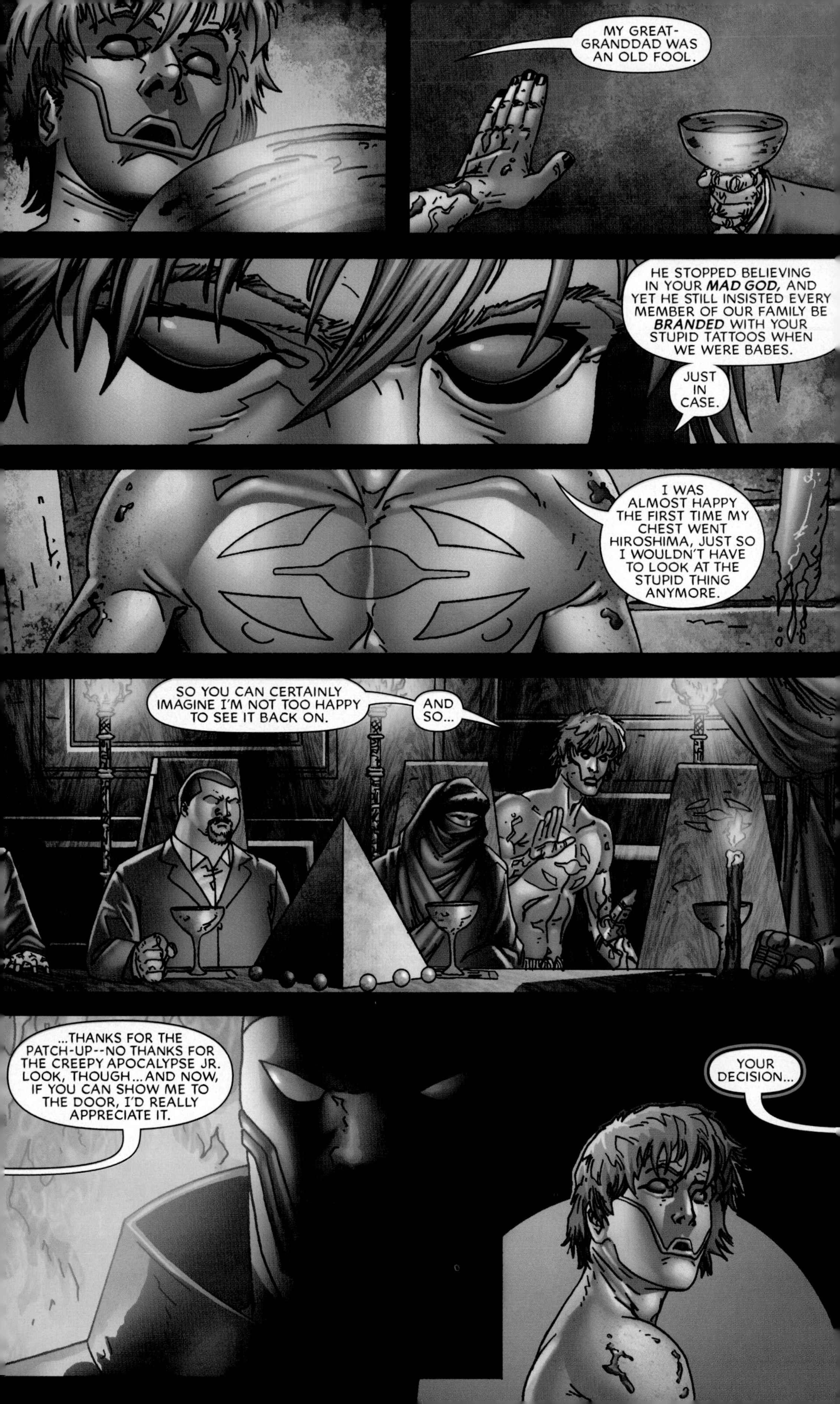

MY GREAT-GRANDDAD WAS AN OLD FOOL.
HE STOPPED BELIEVING IN YOUR ***MAD GOD,*** AND YET HE STILL INSISTED EVERY MEMBER OF OUR FAMILY BE ***BRANDED*** WITH YOUR STUPID TATTOOS WHEN WE WERE BABES.
JUST IN CASE.
I WAS ALMOST HAPPY THE FIRST TIME MY CHEST WENT HIROSHIMA, JUST SO I WOULDN'T HAVE TO LOOK AT THE STUPID THING ANYMORE.
SO YOU CAN CERTAINLY IMAGINE I'M NOT TOO HAPPY TO SEE IT BACK ON.
AND SO...
...THANKS FOR THE PATCH-UP--NO THANKS FOR THE CREEPY APOCALYPSE JR. LOOK, THOUGH...AND NOW, IF YOU CAN SHOW ME TO THE DOOR, I'D REALLY APPRECIATE IT.
YOUR DECISION...

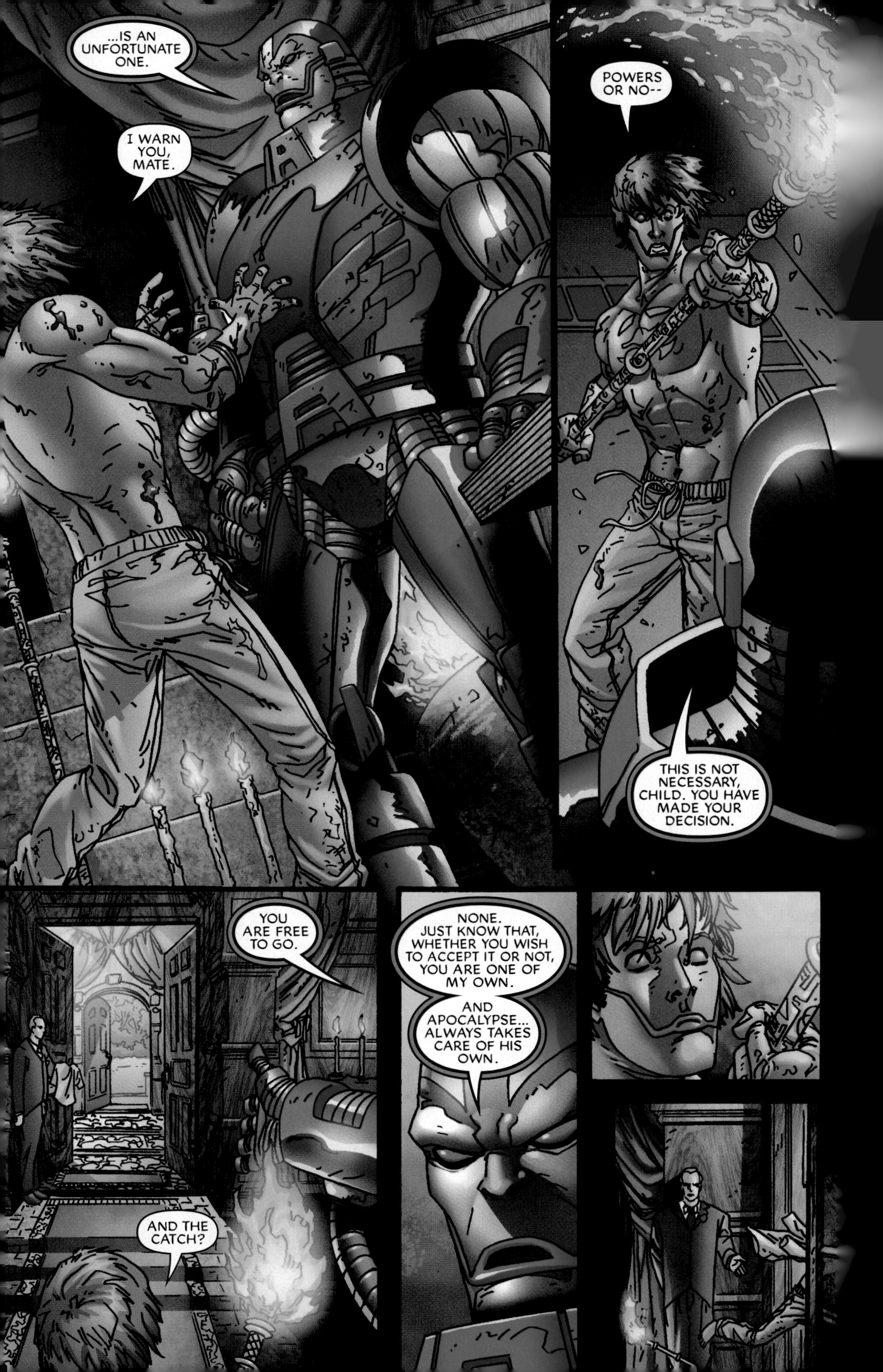
...IS AN UNFORTUNATE ONE.
I WARN YOU, MATE.
POWERS OR NO--
THIS IS NOT NECESSARY, CHILD. YOU HAVE MADE YOUR DECISION.
YOU ARE FREE TO GO.
AND THE CATCH?
NONE. JUST KNOW THAT, WHETHER YOU WISH TO ACCEPT IT OR NOT, YOU ARE ONE OF MY OWN.
AND APOCALYPSE... ALWAYS TAKES CARE OF HIS OWN.

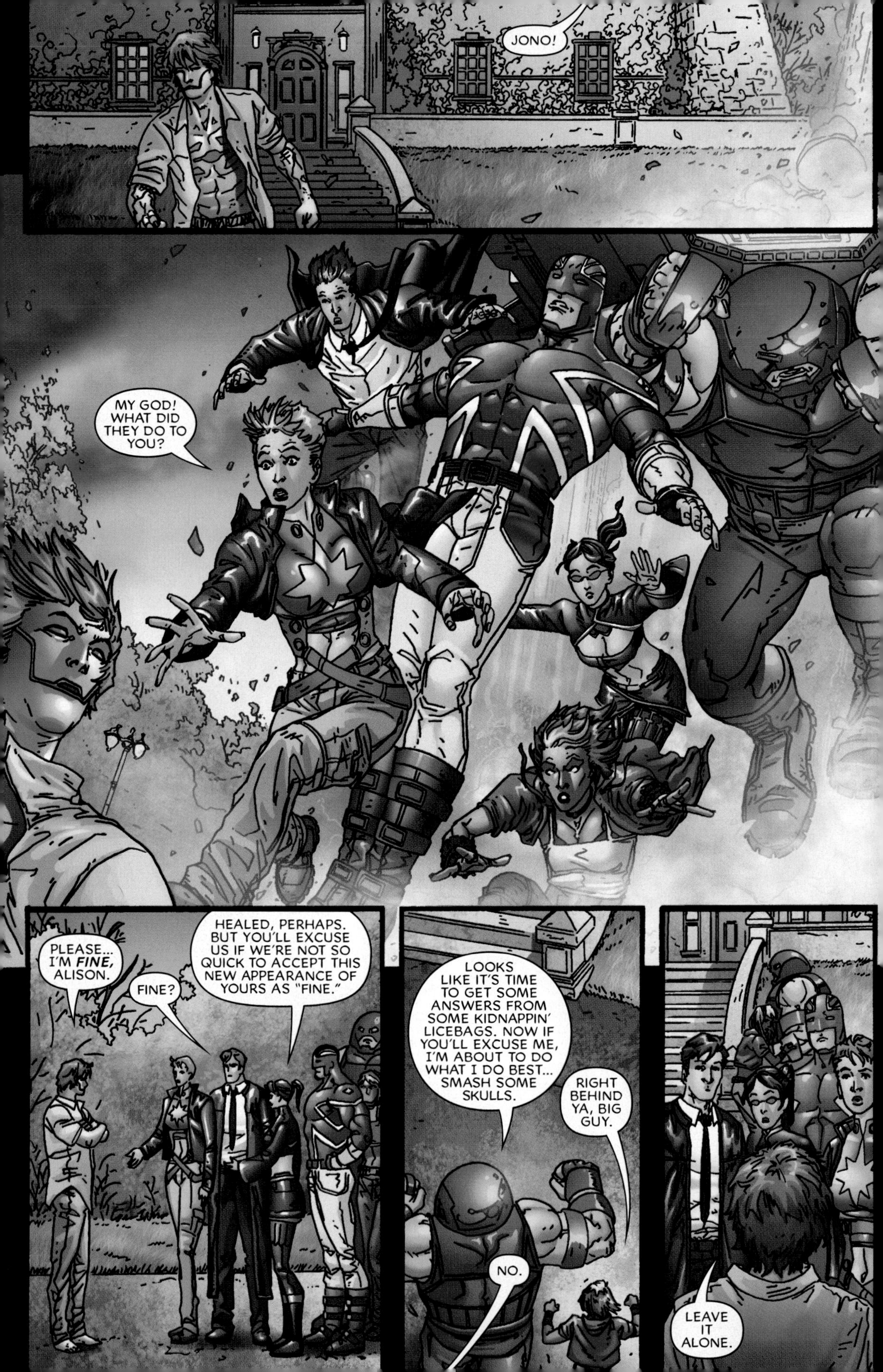
JONO!
MY GOD! WHAT DID THEY DO TO YOU?
PLEASE... I'M *FINE,* ALISON.
FINE?
HEALED, PERHAPS. BUT YOU'LL EXCUSE US IF WE'RE NOT SO QUICK TO ACCEPT THIS NEW APPEARANCE OF YOURS AS "FINE."
LOOKS LIKE IT'S TIME TO GET SOME ANSWERS FROM SOME KIDNAPPIN' LICEBAGS. NOW IF YOU'LL EXCUSE ME, I'M ABOUT TO DO WHAT I DO BEST... SMASH SOME SKULLS.
RIGHT BEHIND YA, BIG GUY.
NO.
LEAVE IT ALONE.

LEAVE IT ALONE? AM I HEARING THIS KID RIGHT?

OBVIOUSLY YOU'VE BEEN THROUGH SOME KIND OF *TRAUMA*, JONO...YOU'RE NOT THINKING CLEARLY. IF NOTHING ELSE, I'D LIKE TO GET YOU BACK TO OUR HEADQUARTERS AND SEE WHAT EXACTLY THEY'VE DONE TO YOU. IT COULD BE DANGEROUS--

I SAID I WAS FINE, DIDN'T I? WHATEVER HAPPENED IN THERE IS MY BUSINESS AND NONE OF YOURS.

LOOK, SON. I KNOW WE DON'T KNOW EACH OTHER THAT WELL, BUT--

YOU'RE WRONG, CAPTAIN.

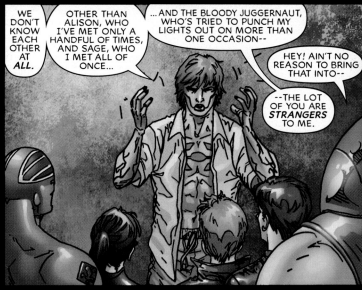

WE DON'T KNOW EACH OTHER AT *ALL*.

OTHER THAN ALISON, WHO I'VE MET ONLY A HANDFUL OF TIMES, AND SAGE, WHO I MET ALL OF ONCE...

...AND THE BLOODY JUGGERNAUT, WHO'S TRIED TO PUNCH MY LIGHTS OUT ON MORE THAN ONE OCCASION--

HEY! AIN'T NO REASON TO BRING THAT INTO--

--THE LOT OF YOU ARE *STRANGERS* TO ME.

AND NOW YOU ALL SWOOP IN AND SAVE ME? *YOU* PEOPLE?

DON'T YOU *GET* IT?

NOT EVERYONE WANTS TO BE SAVED.

NOT EVERYONE WANTS TO PLAY DRESS-UP AS PART OF THE BRAND-SPANKIN'-NEW X-MEN-TEAM-OF-THE-MONTH.

NOT EVERYONE EVEN WANTS POWERS.

SOME OF US JUST WANT TO BE LEFT THE HELL ALONE.

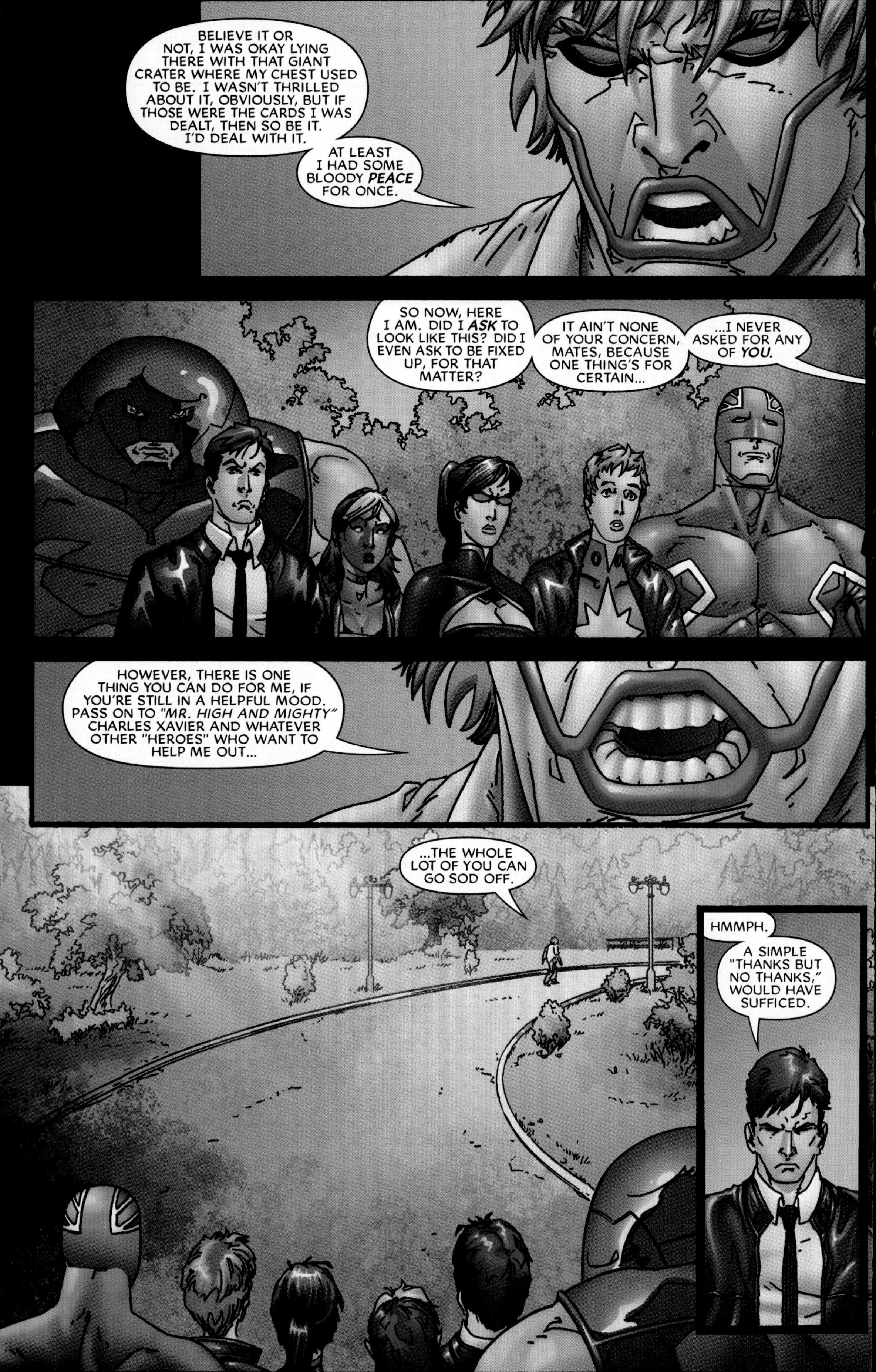
BELIEVE IT OR NOT, I WAS OKAY LYING THERE WITH THAT GIANT CRATER WHERE MY CHEST USED TO BE. I WASN'T THRILLED ABOUT IT, OBVIOUSLY, BUT IF THOSE WERE THE CARDS I WAS DEALT, THEN SO BE IT. I'D DEAL WITH IT.
AT LEAST I HAD SOME BLOODY *PEACE* FOR ONCE.
SO NOW, HERE I AM. DID I *ASK* TO LOOK LIKE THIS? DID I EVEN ASK TO BE FIXED UP, FOR THAT MATTER?
IT AIN'T NONE OF YOUR CONCERN, MATES, BECAUSE ONE THING'S FOR CERTAIN...
...I NEVER ASKED FOR ANY OF *YOU.*
HOWEVER, THERE IS ONE THING YOU CAN DO FOR ME, IF YOU'RE STILL IN A HELPFUL MOOD. PASS ON TO *"MR. HIGH AND MIGHTY"* CHARLES XAVIER AND WHATEVER OTHER "HEROES" WHO WANT TO HELP ME OUT...
...THE WHOLE LOT OF YOU CAN GO SOD OFF.
HMMPH.
A SIMPLE "THANKS BUT NO THANKS," WOULD HAVE SUFFICED.

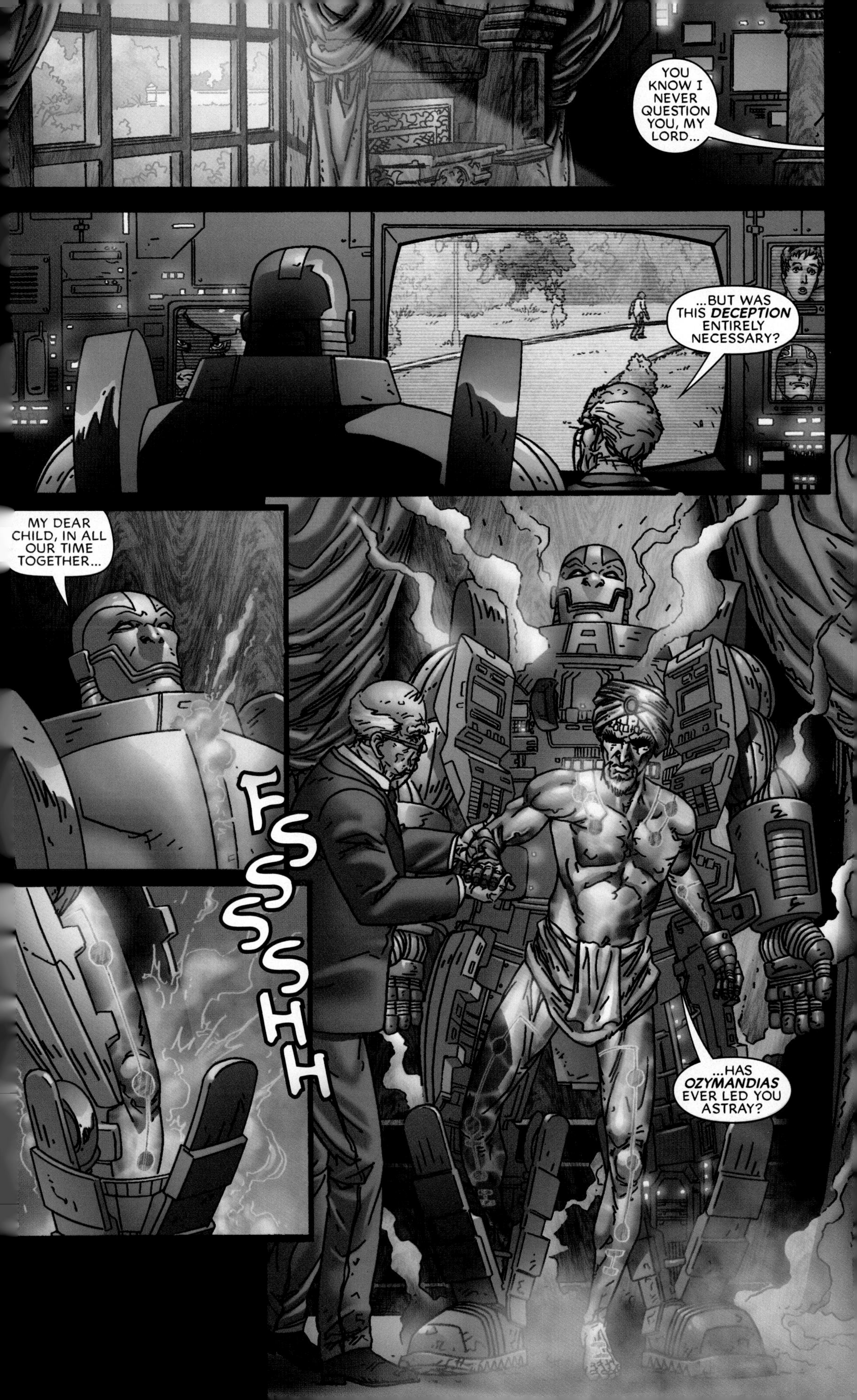
YOU KNOW I NEVER QUESTION YOU, MY LORD...
...BUT WAS THIS DECEPTION ENTIRELY NECESSARY?
MY DEAR CHILD, IN ALL OUR TIME TOGETHER...
FSSSSHH
...HAS OZYMANDIAS EVER LED YOU ASTRAY?

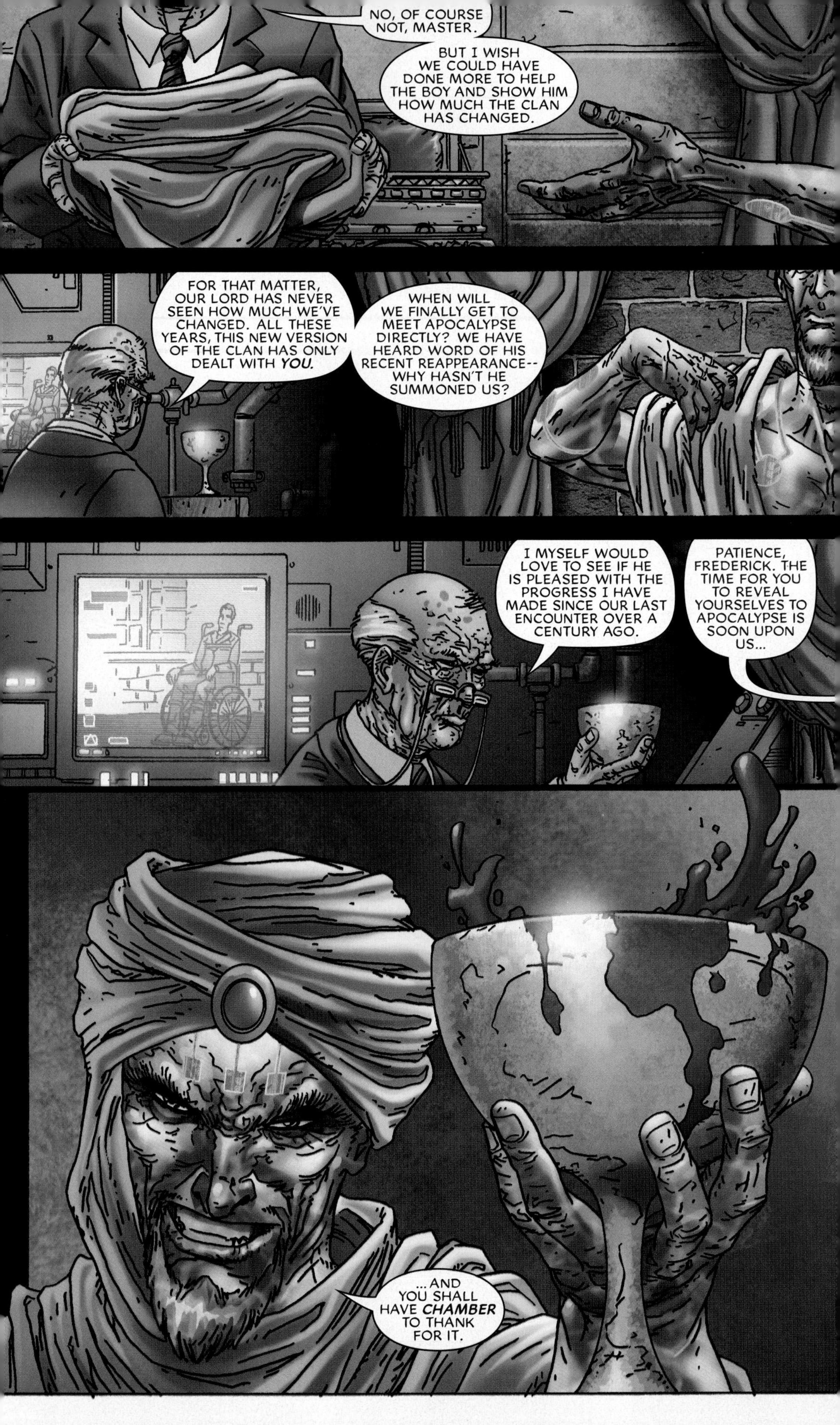
NO, OF COURSE NOT, MASTER.
BUT I WISH WE COULD HAVE DONE MORE TO HELP THE BOY AND SHOW HIM HOW MUCH THE CLAN HAS CHANGED.
FOR THAT MATTER, OUR LORD HAS NEVER SEEN HOW MUCH WE'VE CHANGED. ALL THESE YEARS, THIS NEW VERSION OF THE CLAN HAS ONLY DEALT WITH *YOU.*
WHEN WILL WE FINALLY GET TO MEET APOCALYPSE DIRECTLY? WE HAVE HEARD WORD OF HIS RECENT REAPPEARANCE-- WHY HASN'T HE SUMMONED US?
I MYSELF WOULD LOVE TO SEE IF HE IS PLEASED WITH THE PROGRESS I HAVE MADE SINCE OUR LAST ENCOUNTER OVER A CENTURY AGO.
PATIENCE, FREDERICK. THE TIME FOR YOU TO REVEAL YOURSELVES TO APOCALYPSE IS SOON UPON US...
...AND YOU SHALL HAVE *CHAMBER* TO THANK FOR IT.

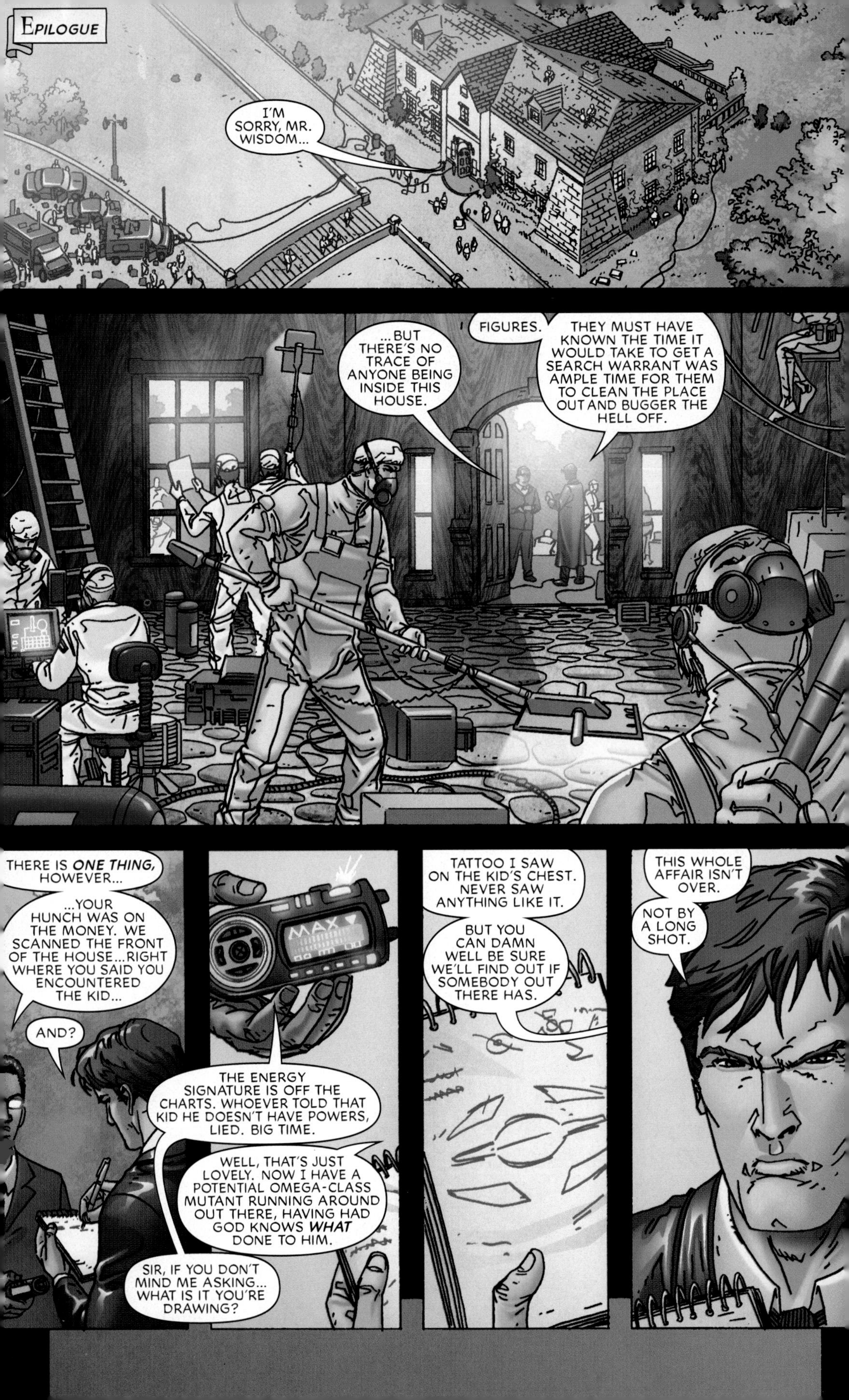
EPILOGUE
I'M SORRY, MR. WISDOM...
...BUT THERE'S NO TRACE OF ANYONE BEING INSIDE THIS HOUSE.
FIGURES.
THEY MUST HAVE KNOWN THE TIME IT WOULD TAKE TO GET A SEARCH WARRANT WAS AMPLE TIME FOR THEM TO CLEAN THE PLACE OUT AND BUGGER THE HELL OFF.
THERE IS ONE THING, HOWEVER...
...YOUR HUNCH WAS ON THE MONEY. WE SCANNED THE FRONT OF THE HOUSE...RIGHT WHERE YOU SAID YOU ENCOUNTERED THE KID...
AND?
MAX
THE ENERGY SIGNATURE IS OFF THE CHARTS. WHOEVER TOLD THAT KID HE DOESN'T HAVE POWERS, LIED. BIG TIME.
WELL, THAT'S JUST LOVELY. NOW I HAVE A POTENTIAL OMEGA-CLASS MUTANT RUNNING AROUND OUT THERE, HAVING HAD GOD KNOWS WHAT DONE TO HIM.
SIR, IF YOU DON'T MIND ME ASKING... WHAT IS IT YOU'RE DRAWING?
TATTOO I SAW ON THE KID'S CHEST. NEVER SAW ANYTHING LIKE IT.
BUT YOU CAN DAMN WELL BE SURE WE'LL FIND OUT IF SOMEBODY OUT THERE HAS.
THIS WHOLE AFFAIR ISN'T OVER.
NOT BY A LONG SHOT.

#10

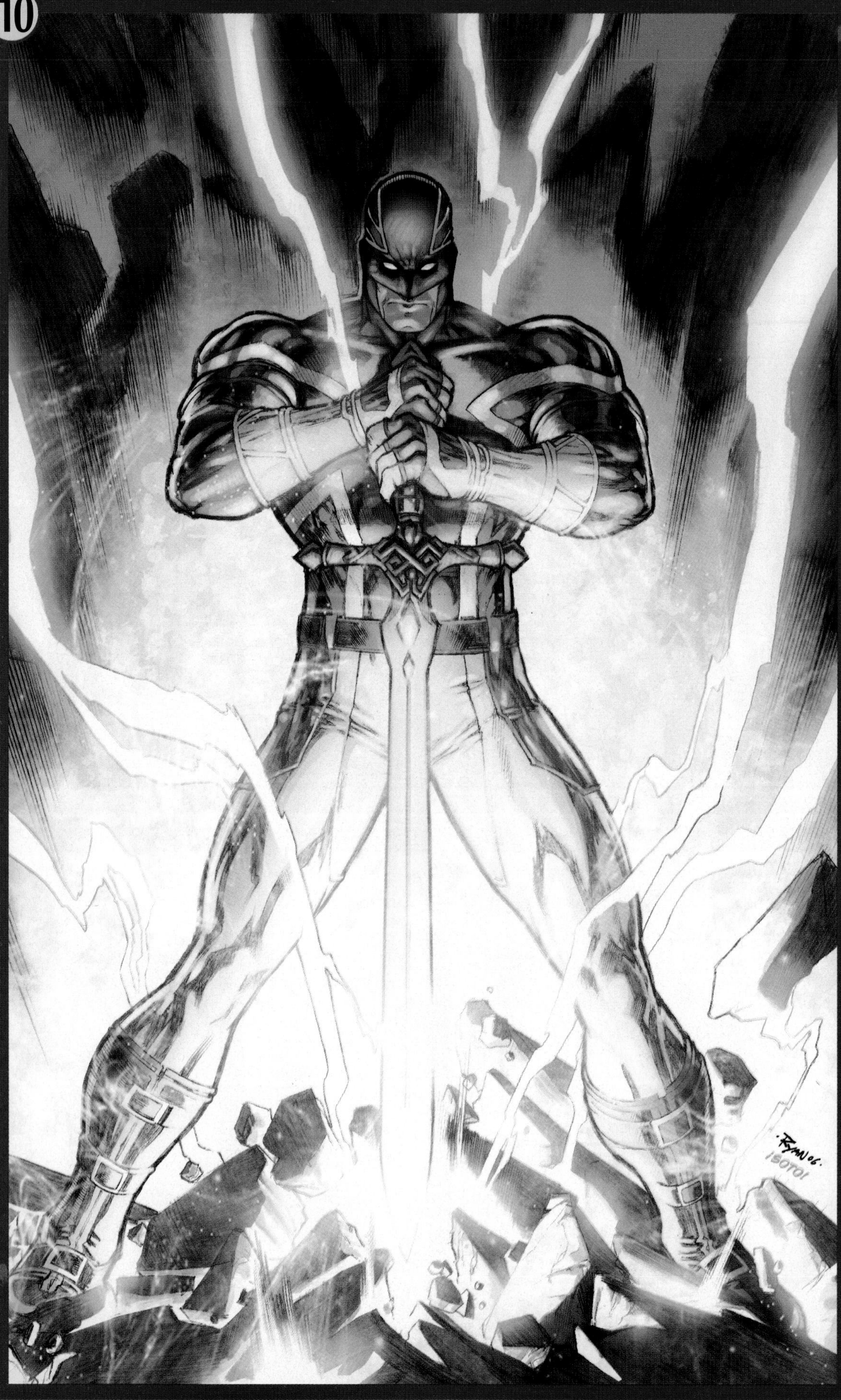

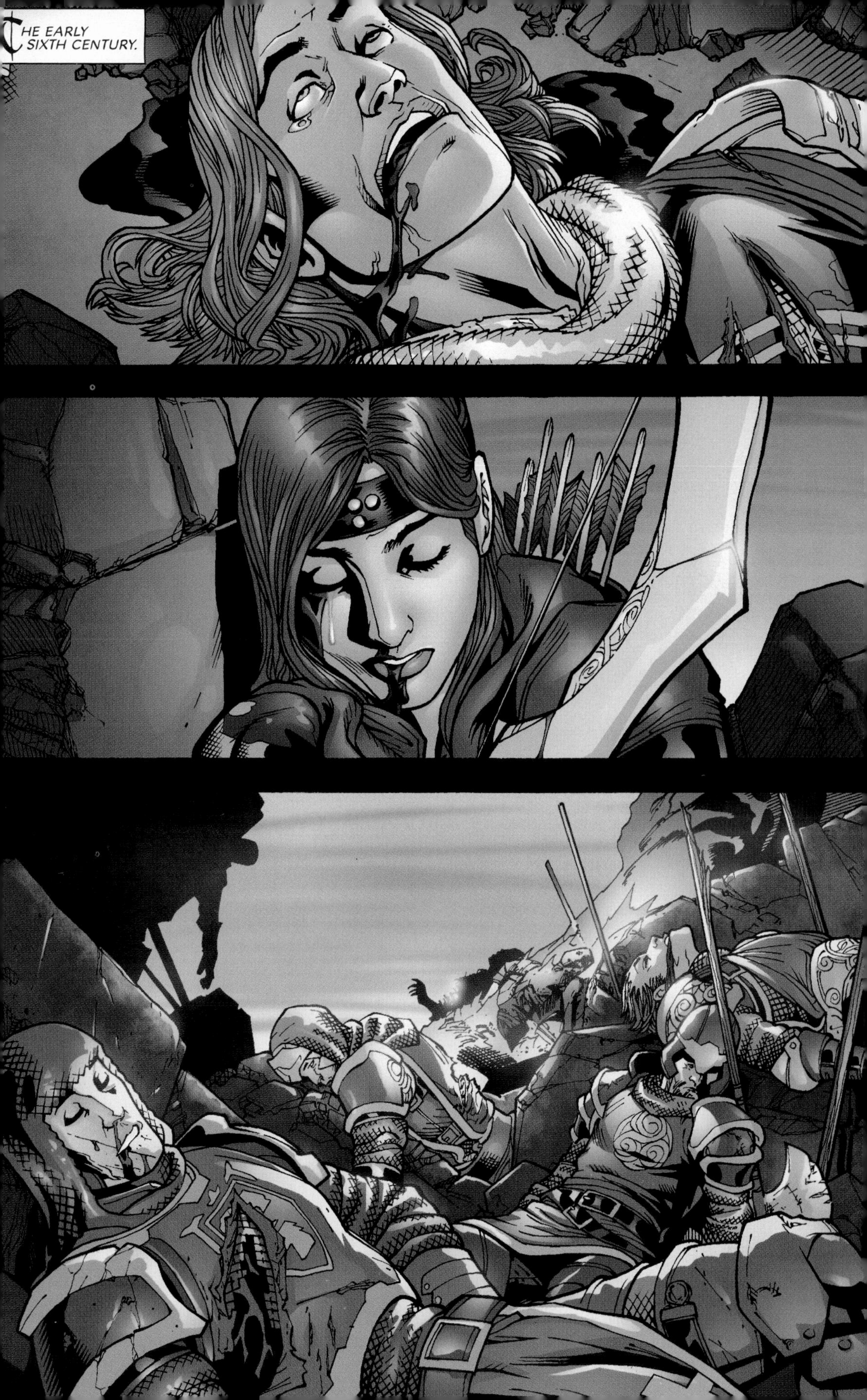
THE EARLY SIXTH CENTURY.

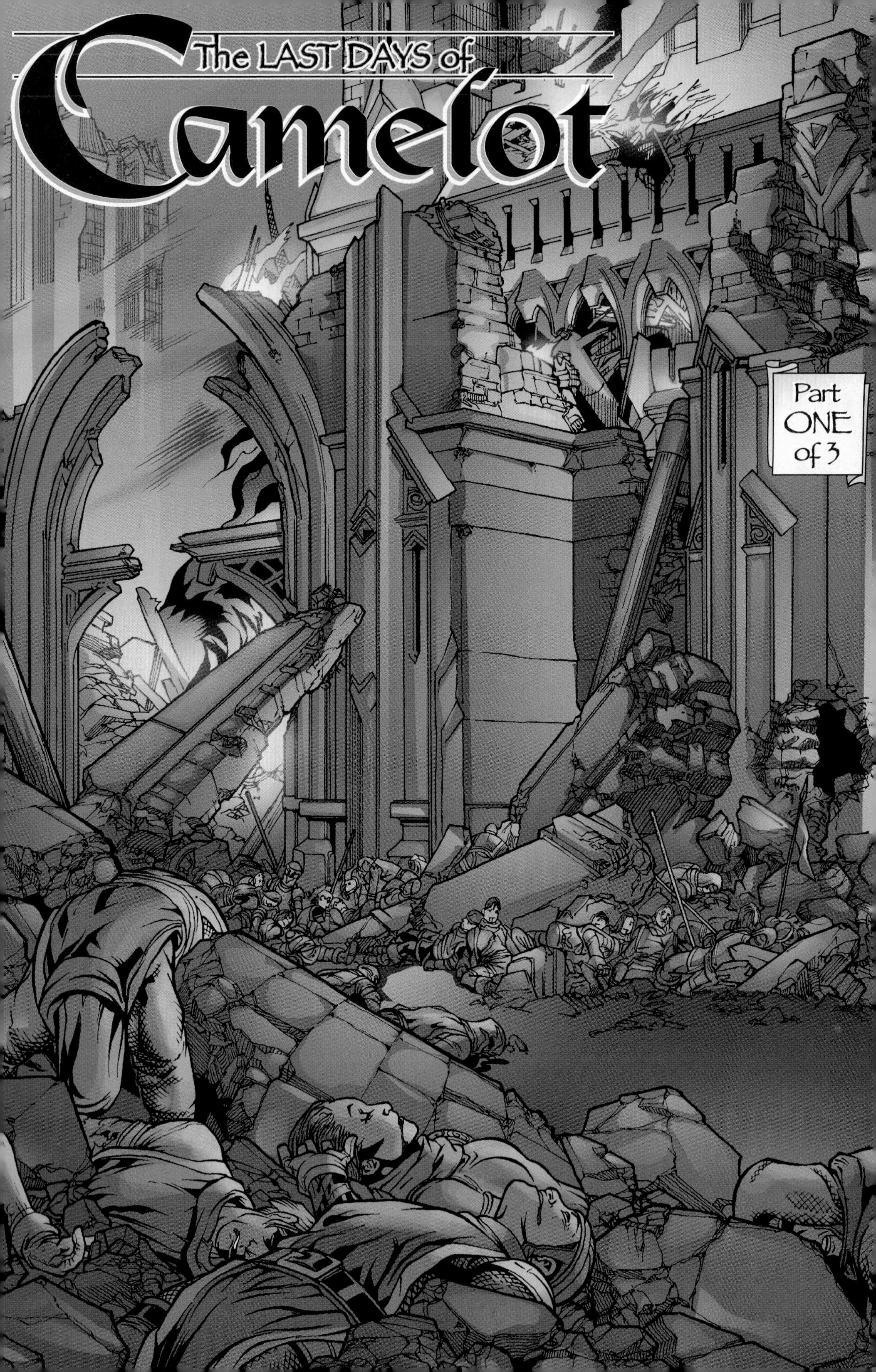

The LAST DAYS of
Camelot
Part ONE of 3

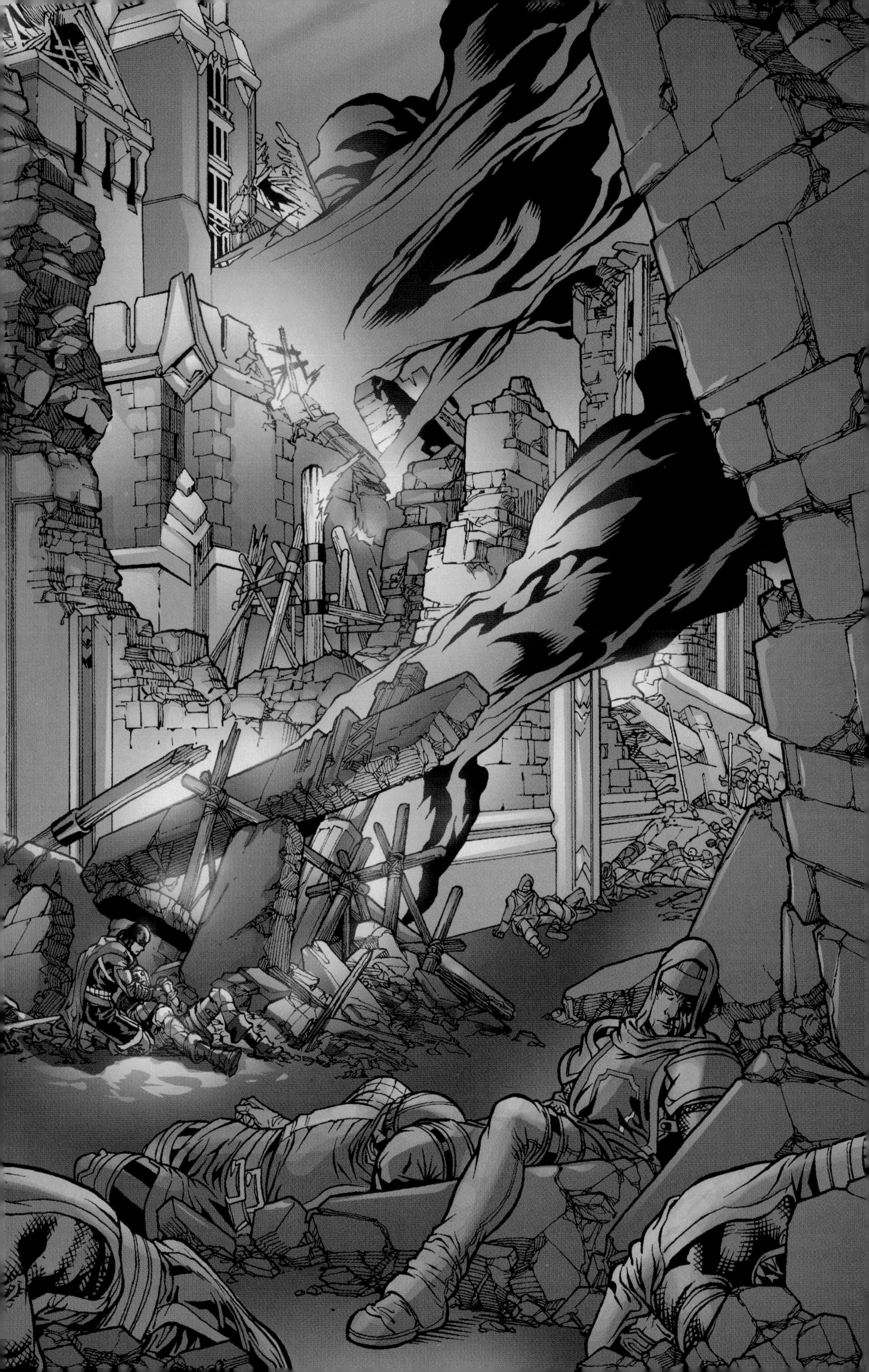

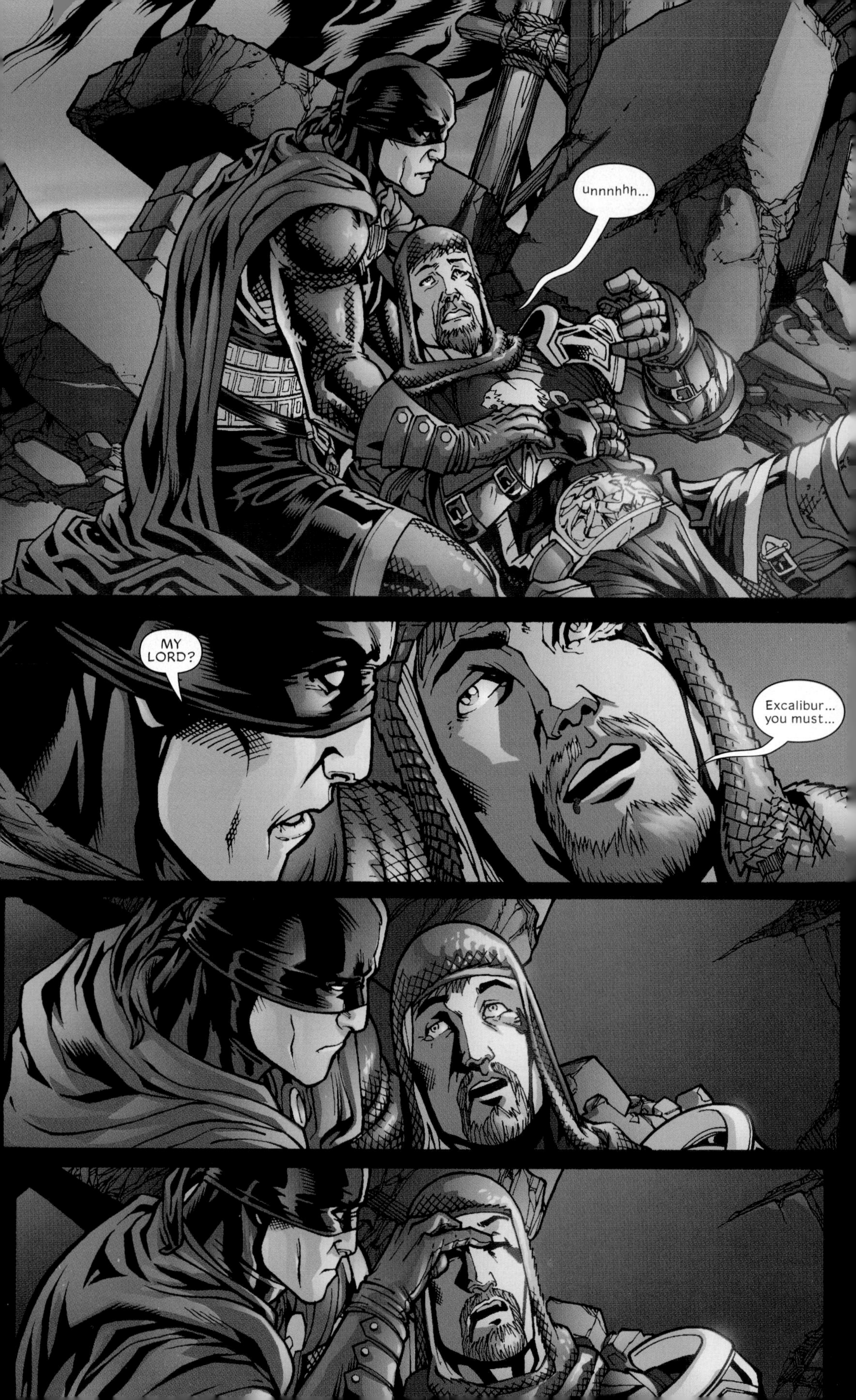
unnnhhh...
MY LORD?
Excalibur... you must...

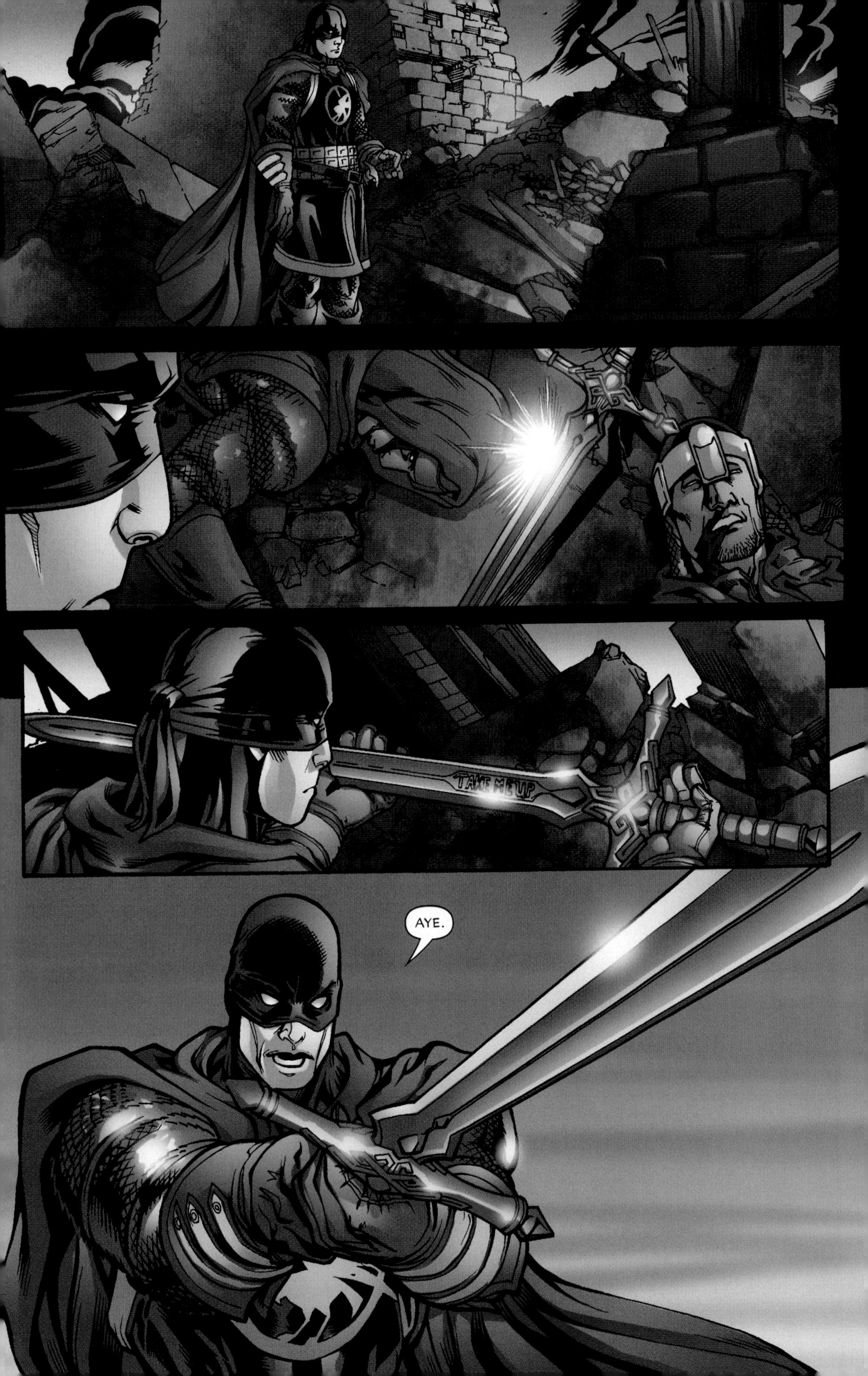
TAKE ME UP
AYE.

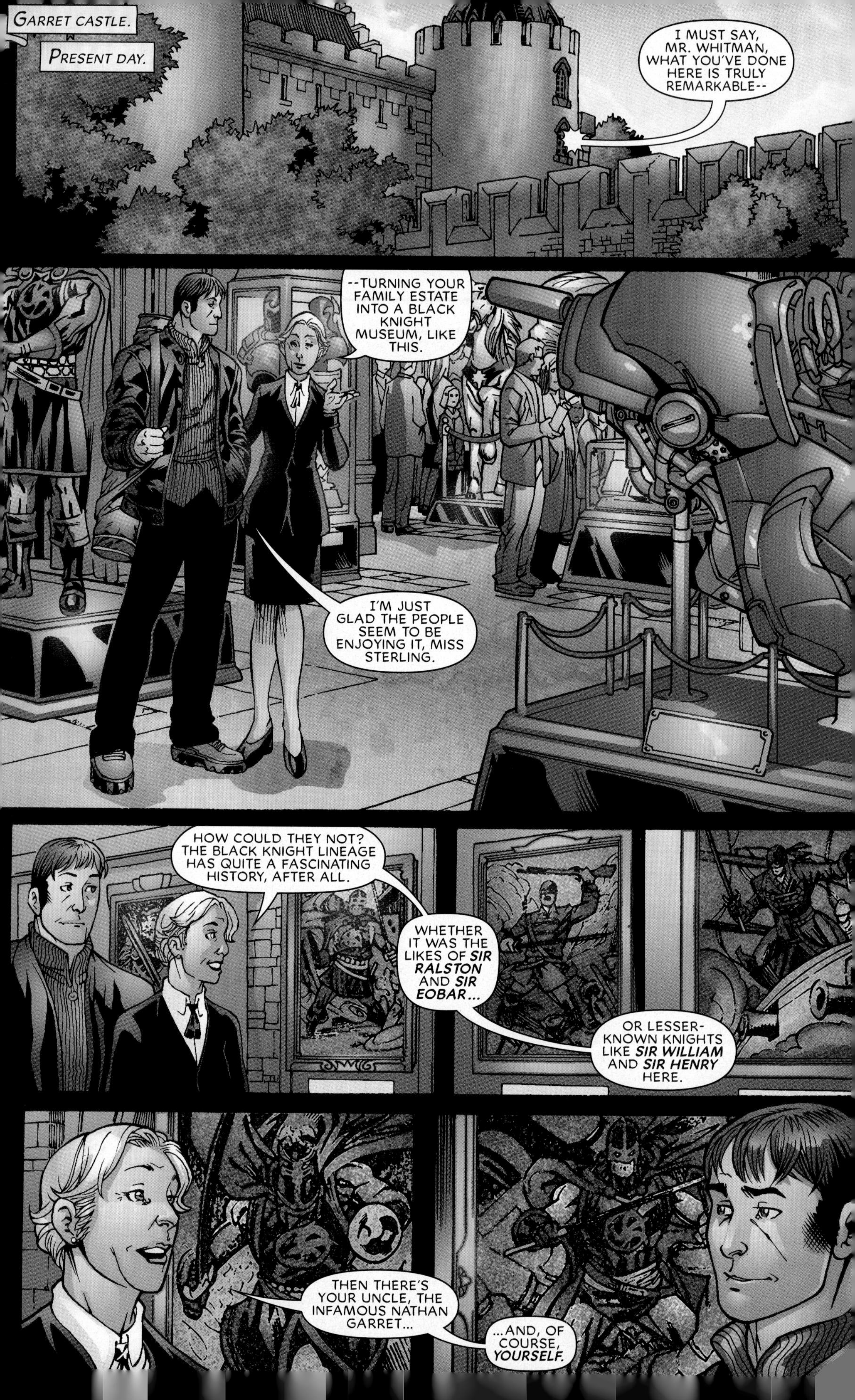

GARRET CASTLE.
PRESENT DAY.
I MUST SAY, MR. WHITMAN, WHAT YOU'VE DONE HERE IS TRULY REMARKABLE--
--TURNING YOUR FAMILY ESTATE INTO A BLACK KNIGHT MUSEUM, LIKE THIS.
I'M JUST GLAD THE PEOPLE SEEM TO BE ENJOYING IT, MISS STERLING.
HOW COULD THEY NOT? THE BLACK KNIGHT LINEAGE HAS QUITE A FASCINATING HISTORY, AFTER ALL.
WHETHER IT WAS THE LIKES OF SIR RALSTON AND SIR EOBAR...
OR LESSER-KNOWN KNIGHTS LIKE SIR WILLIAM AND SIR HENRY HERE.
THEN THERE'S YOUR UNCLE, THE INFAMOUS NATHAN GARRET...
...AND, OF COURSE, YOURSELF.

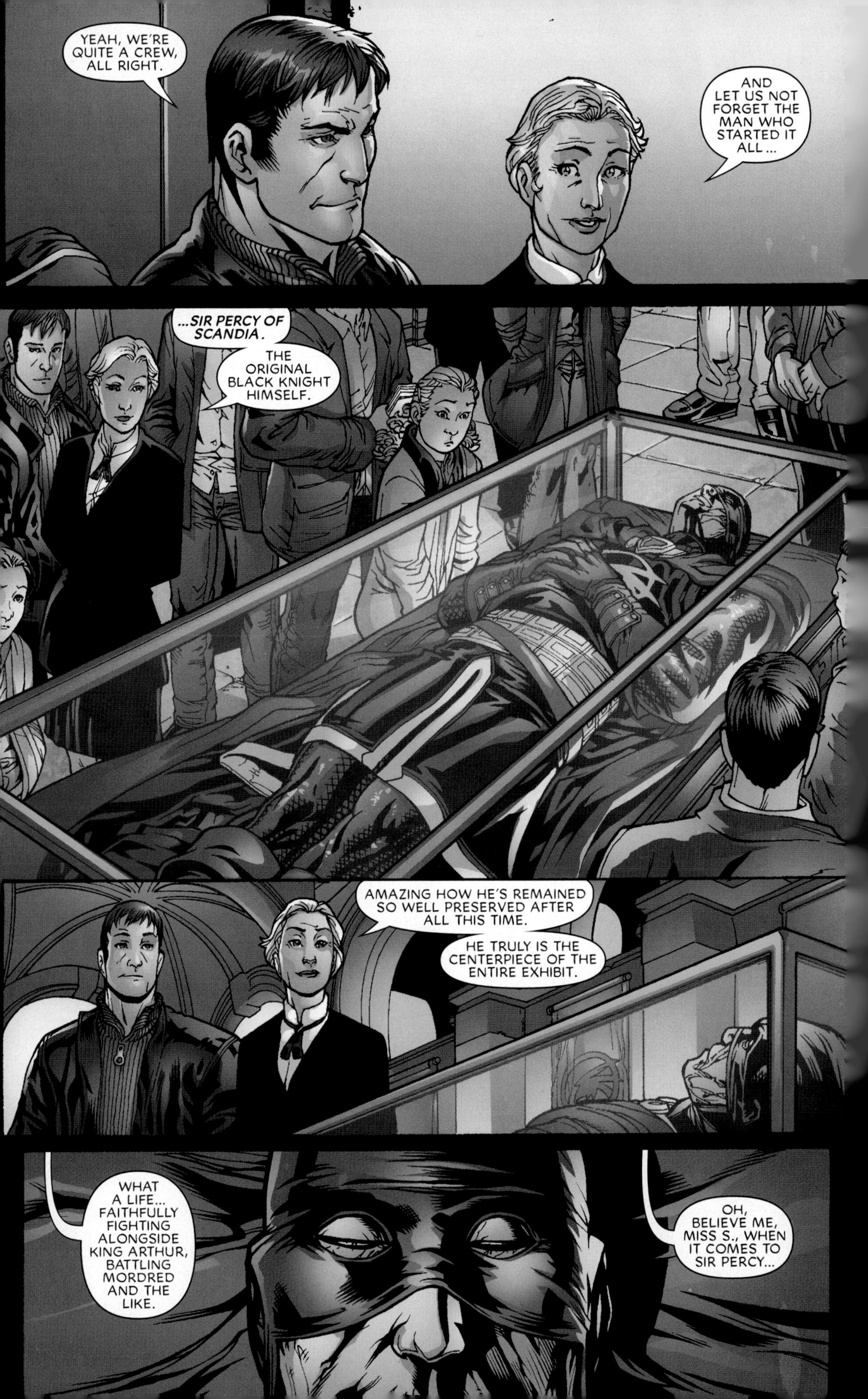
YEAH, WE'RE QUITE A CREW, ALL RIGHT.
AND LET US NOT FORGET THE MAN WHO STARTED IT ALL...
...SIR PERCY OF SCANDIA.
THE ORIGINAL BLACK KNIGHT HIMSELF.
AMAZING HOW HE'S REMAINED SO WELL PRESERVED AFTER ALL THIS TIME.
HE TRULY IS THE CENTERPIECE OF THE ENTIRE EXHIBIT.
WHAT A LIFE... FAITHFULLY FIGHTING ALONGSIDE KING ARTHUR, BATTLING MORDRED AND THE LIKE.
OH, BELIEVE ME, MISS S., WHEN IT COMES TO SIR PERCY...

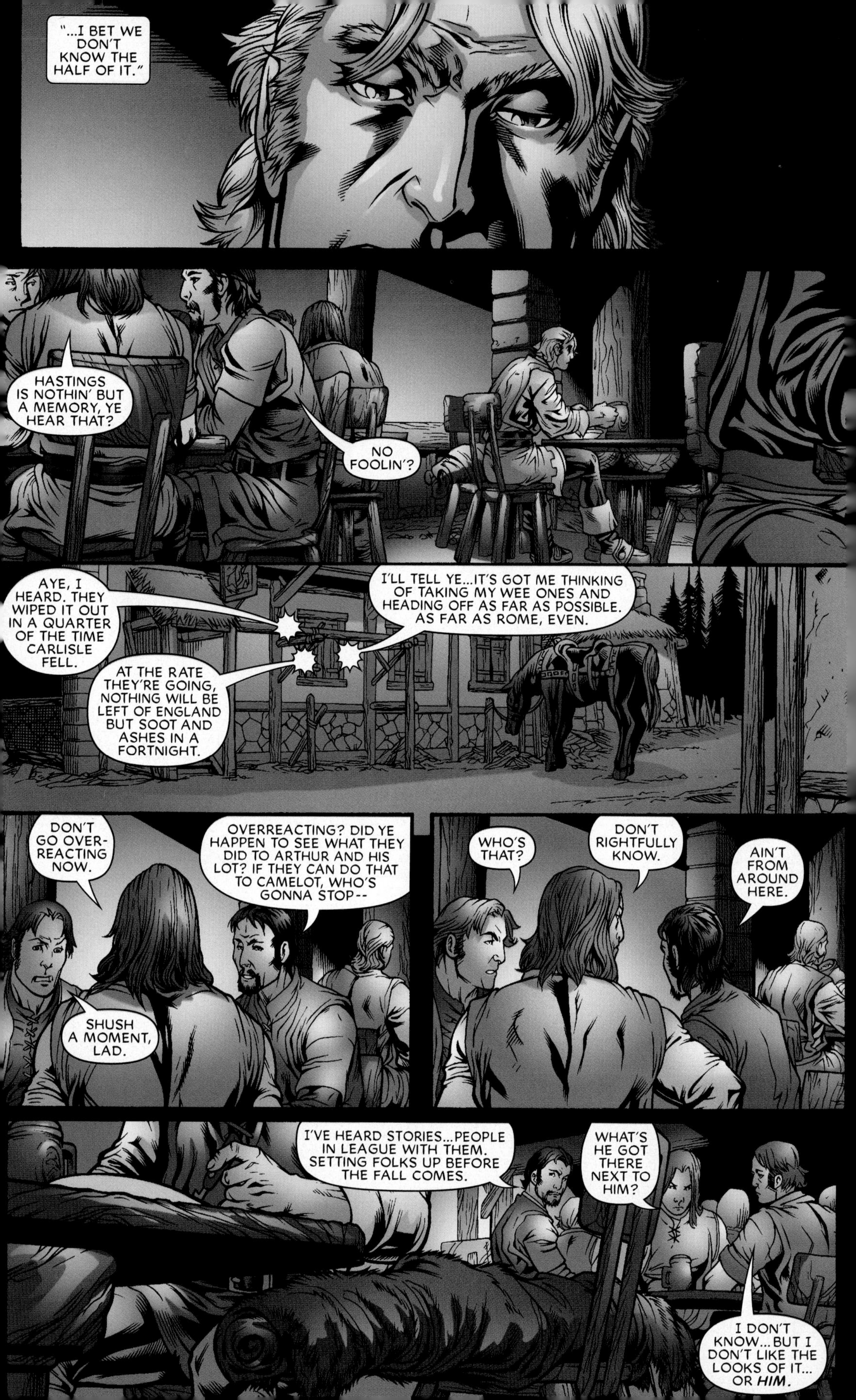
"...I BET WE DON'T KNOW THE HALF OF IT."
HASTINGS IS NOTHIN' BUT A MEMORY, YE HEAR THAT?
NO FOOLIN'?
AYE, I HEARD. THEY WIPED IT OUT IN A QUARTER OF THE TIME CARLISLE FELL.
I'LL TELL YE...IT'S GOT ME THINKING OF TAKING MY WEE ONES AND HEADING OFF AS FAR AS POSSIBLE. AS FAR AS ROME, EVEN.
AT THE RATE THEY'RE GOING, NOTHING WILL BE LEFT OF ENGLAND BUT SOOT AND ASHES IN A FORTNIGHT.
DON'T GO OVER-REACTING NOW.
OVERREACTING? DID YE HAPPEN TO SEE WHAT THEY DID TO ARTHUR AND HIS LOT? IF THEY CAN DO THAT TO CAMELOT, WHO'S GONNA STOP--
SHUSH A MOMENT, LAD.
WHO'S THAT?
DON'T RIGHTFULLY KNOW.
AIN'T FROM AROUND HERE.
I'VE HEARD STORIES...PEOPLE IN LEAGUE WITH THEM. SETTING FOLKS UP BEFORE THE FALL COMES.
WHAT'S HE GOT THERE NEXT TO HIM?
I DON'T KNOW...BUT I DON'T LIKE THE LOOKS OF IT... OR *HIM*.

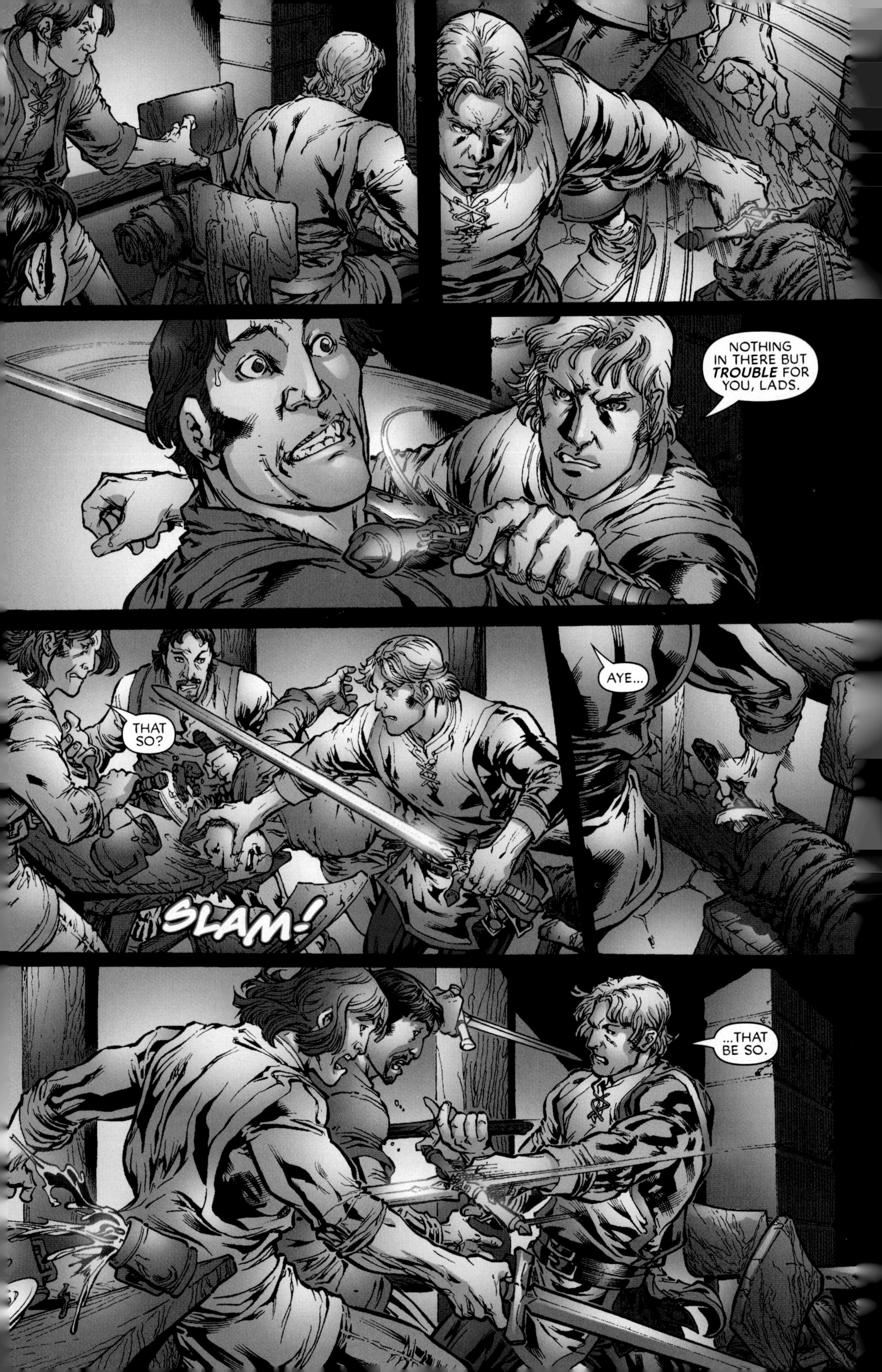
NOTHING IN THERE BUT TROUBLE FOR YOU, LADS.
THAT SO?
AYE...
SLAM!
...THAT BE SO.

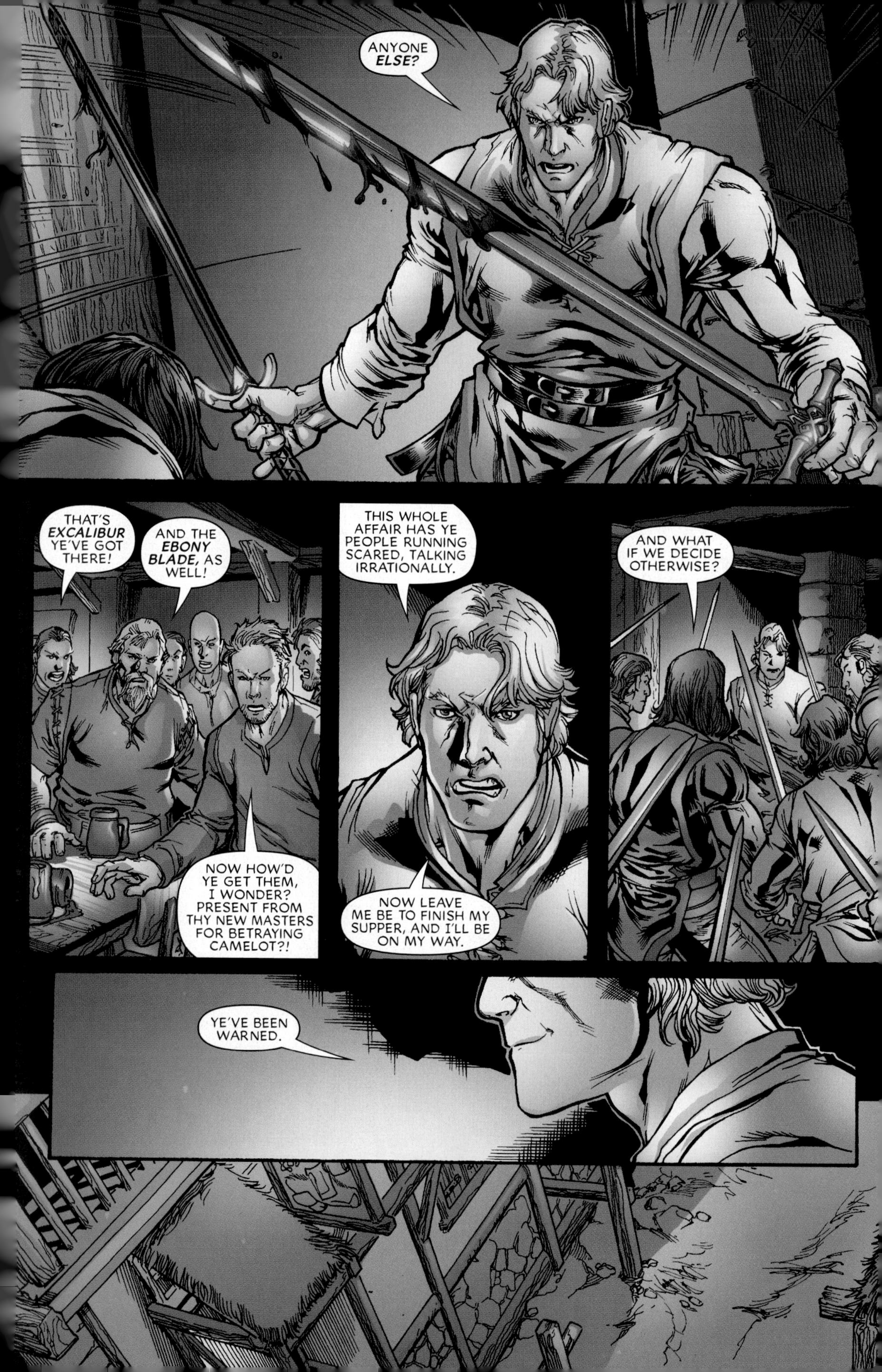

ANYONE *ELSE?*
THAT'S *EXCALIBUR* YE'VE GOT THERE!
AND THE *EBONY BLADE,* AS WELL!
NOW HOW'D YE GET THEM, I WONDER? PRESENT FROM THY NEW MASTERS FOR BETRAYING CAMELOT?!
THIS WHOLE AFFAIR HAS YE PEOPLE RUNNING SCARED, TALKING IRRATIONALLY.
NOW LEAVE ME BE TO FINISH MY SUPPER, AND I'LL BE ON MY WAY.
AND WHAT IF WE DECIDE OTHERWISE?
YE'VE BEEN WARNED.

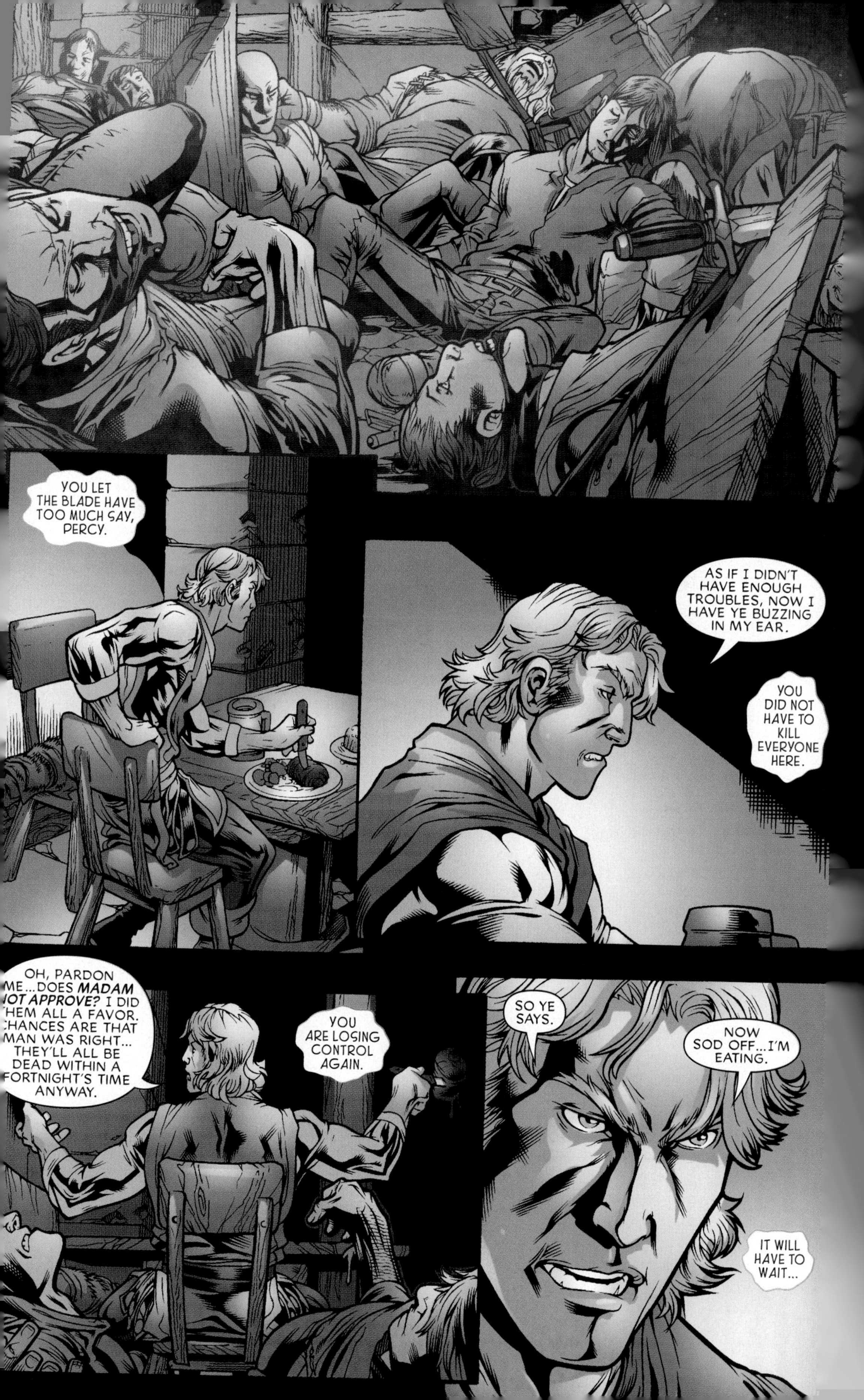
YOU LET THE BLADE HAVE TOO MUCH SAY, PERCY.
AS IF I DIDN'T HAVE ENOUGH TROUBLES, NOW I HAVE YE BUZZING IN MY EAR.
YOU DID NOT HAVE TO KILL EVERYONE HERE.
OH, PARDON ME...DOES MADAM NOT APPROVE? I DID THEM ALL A FAVOR. CHANCES ARE THAT MAN WAS RIGHT... THEY'LL ALL BE DEAD WITHIN A FORTNIGHT'S TIME ANYWAY.
YOU ARE LOSING CONTROL AGAIN.
SO YE SAYS.
NOW SOD OFF...I'M EATING.
IT WILL HAVE TO WAIT...

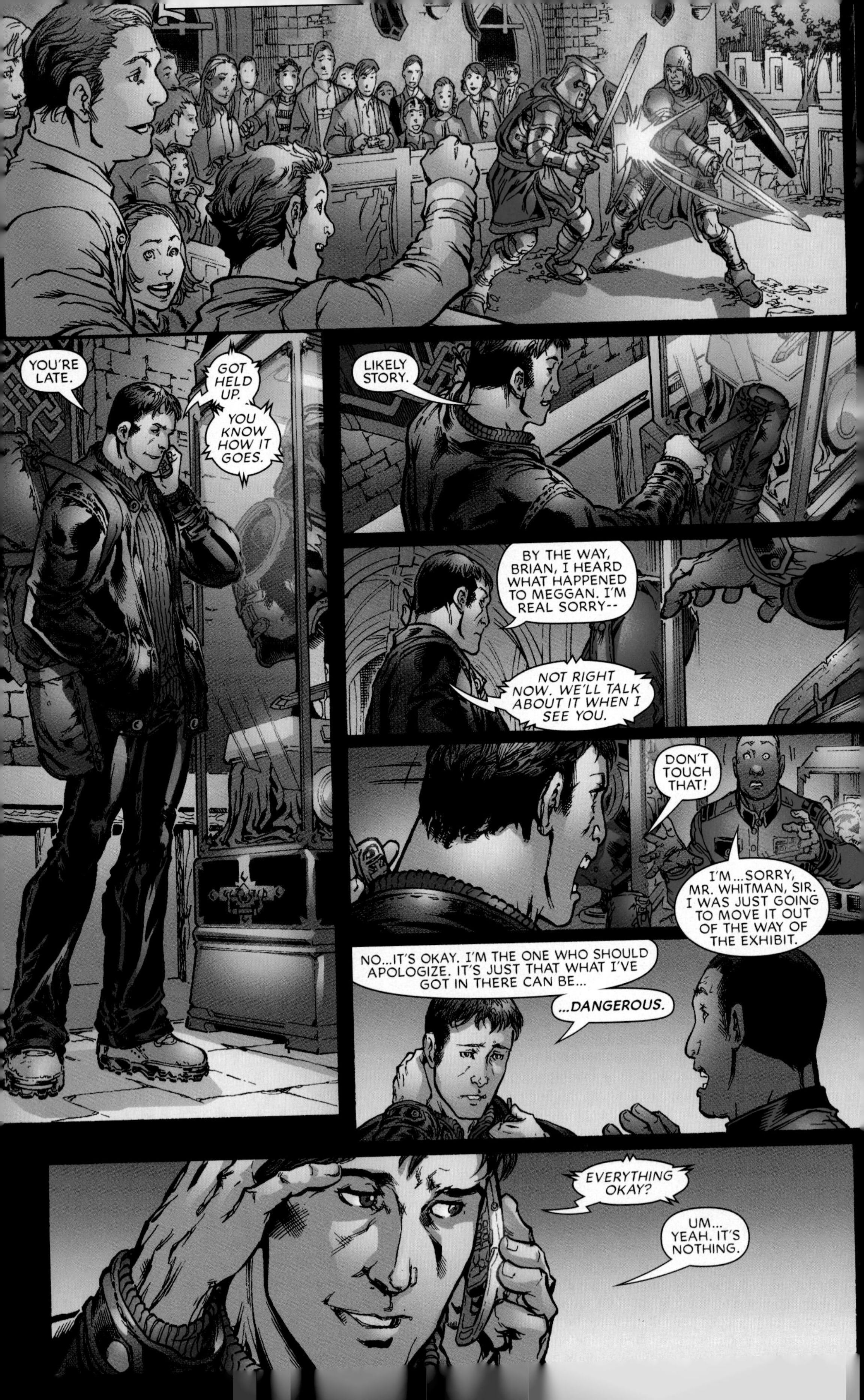
YOU'RE LATE.
GOT HELD UP.
YOU KNOW HOW IT GOES.
LIKELY STORY.
BY THE WAY, BRIAN, I HEARD WHAT HAPPENED TO MEGGAN. I'M REAL SORRY--
NOT RIGHT NOW. WE'LL TALK ABOUT IT WHEN I SEE YOU.
DON'T TOUCH THAT!
I'M...SORRY, MR. WHITMAN, SIR. I WAS JUST GOING TO MOVE IT OUT OF THE WAY OF THE EXHIBIT.
NO...IT'S OKAY. I'M THE ONE WHO SHOULD APOLOGIZE. IT'S JUST THAT WHAT I'VE GOT IN THERE CAN BE...
...DANGEROUS.
EVERYTHING OKAY?
UM... YEAH. IT'S NOTHING.

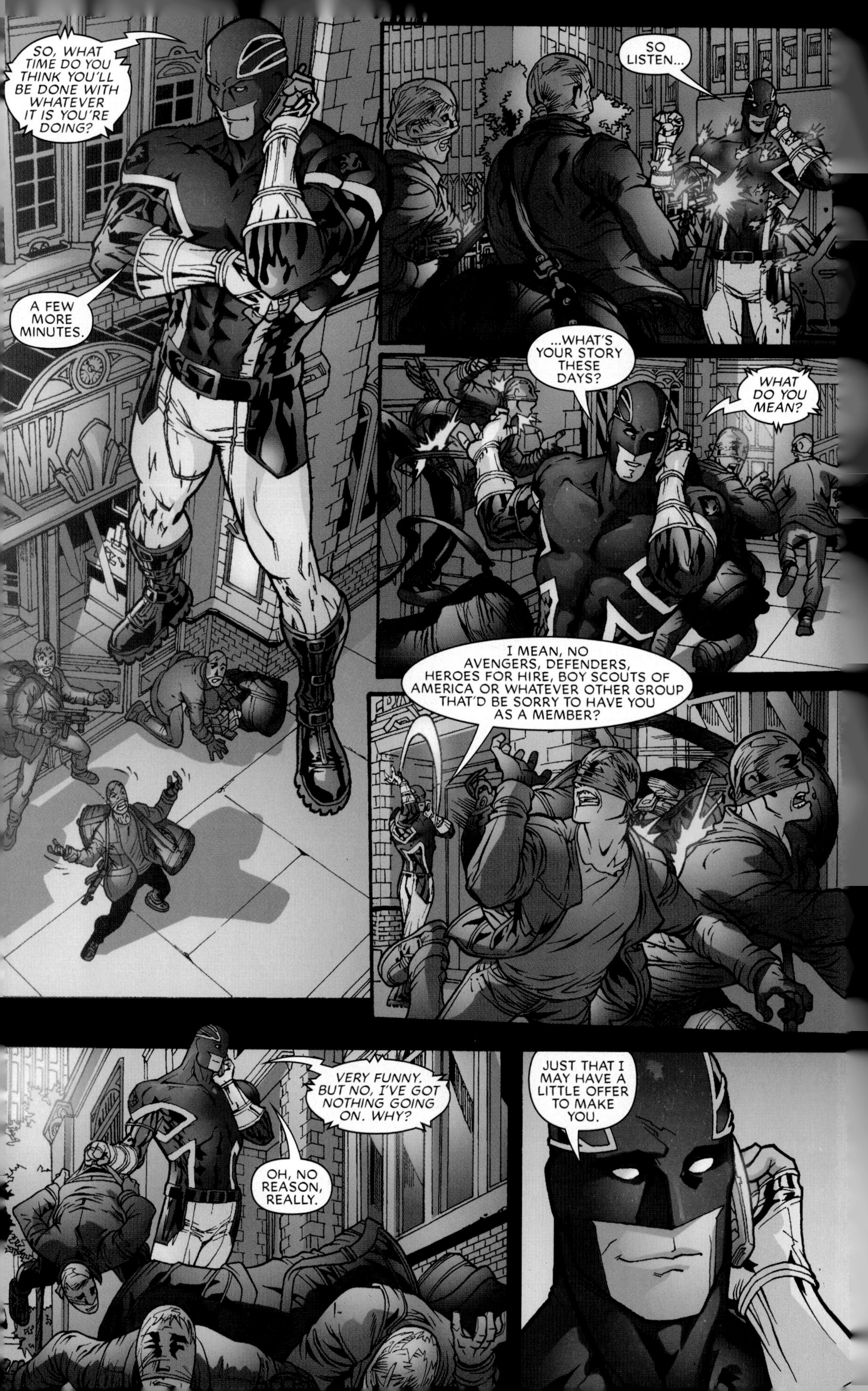
SO, WHAT TIME DO YOU THINK YOU'LL BE DONE WITH WHATEVER IT IS YOU'RE DOING?
A FEW MORE MINUTES.
SO LISTEN...
...WHAT'S YOUR STORY THESE DAYS?
WHAT DO YOU MEAN?
I MEAN, NO AVENGERS, DEFENDERS, HEROES FOR HIRE, BOY SCOUTS OF AMERICA OR WHATEVER OTHER GROUP THAT'D BE SORRY TO HAVE YOU AS A MEMBER?
VERY FUNNY. BUT NO, I'VE GOT NOTHING GOING ON. WHY?
OH, NO REASON, REALLY.
JUST THAT I MAY HAVE A LITTLE OFFER TO MAKE YOU.

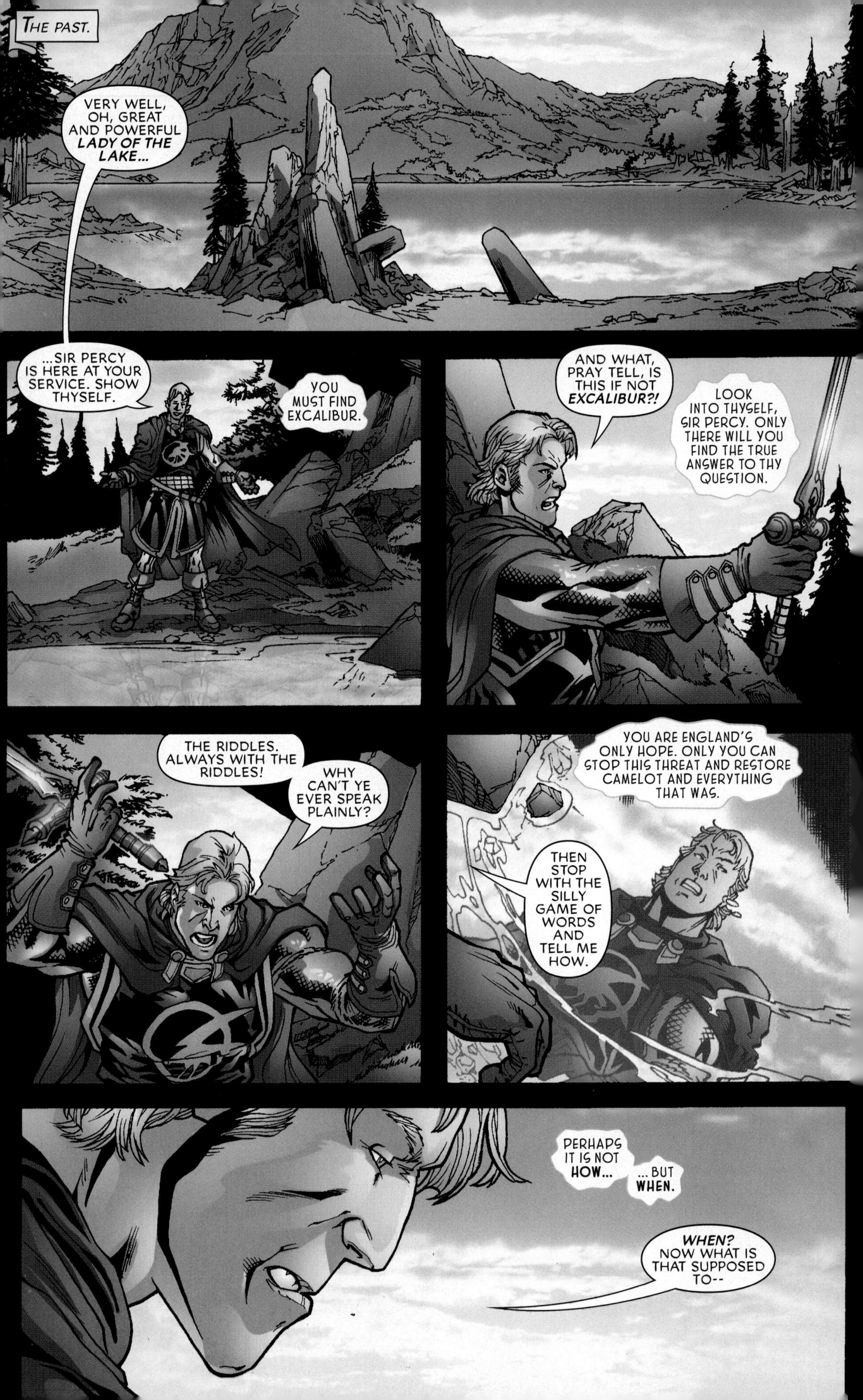

THE PAST.
VERY WELL, OH, GREAT AND POWERFUL LADY OF THE LAKE...
...SIR PERCY IS HERE AT YOUR SERVICE. SHOW THYSELF.
YOU MUST FIND EXCALIBUR.
AND WHAT, PRAY TELL, IS THIS IF NOT EXCALIBUR?!
LOOK INTO THYSELF, SIR PERCY. ONLY THERE WILL YOU FIND THE TRUE ANSWER TO THY QUESTION.
THE RIDDLES. ALWAYS WITH THE RIDDLES!
WHY CAN'T YE EVER SPEAK PLAINLY?
YOU ARE ENGLAND'S ONLY HOPE. ONLY YOU CAN STOP THIS THREAT AND RESTORE CAMELOT AND EVERYTHING THAT WAS.
THEN STOP WITH THE SILLY GAME OF WORDS AND TELL ME HOW.
PERHAPS IT IS NOT HOW...
...BUT WHEN.
WHEN? NOW WHAT IS THAT SUPPOSED TO--

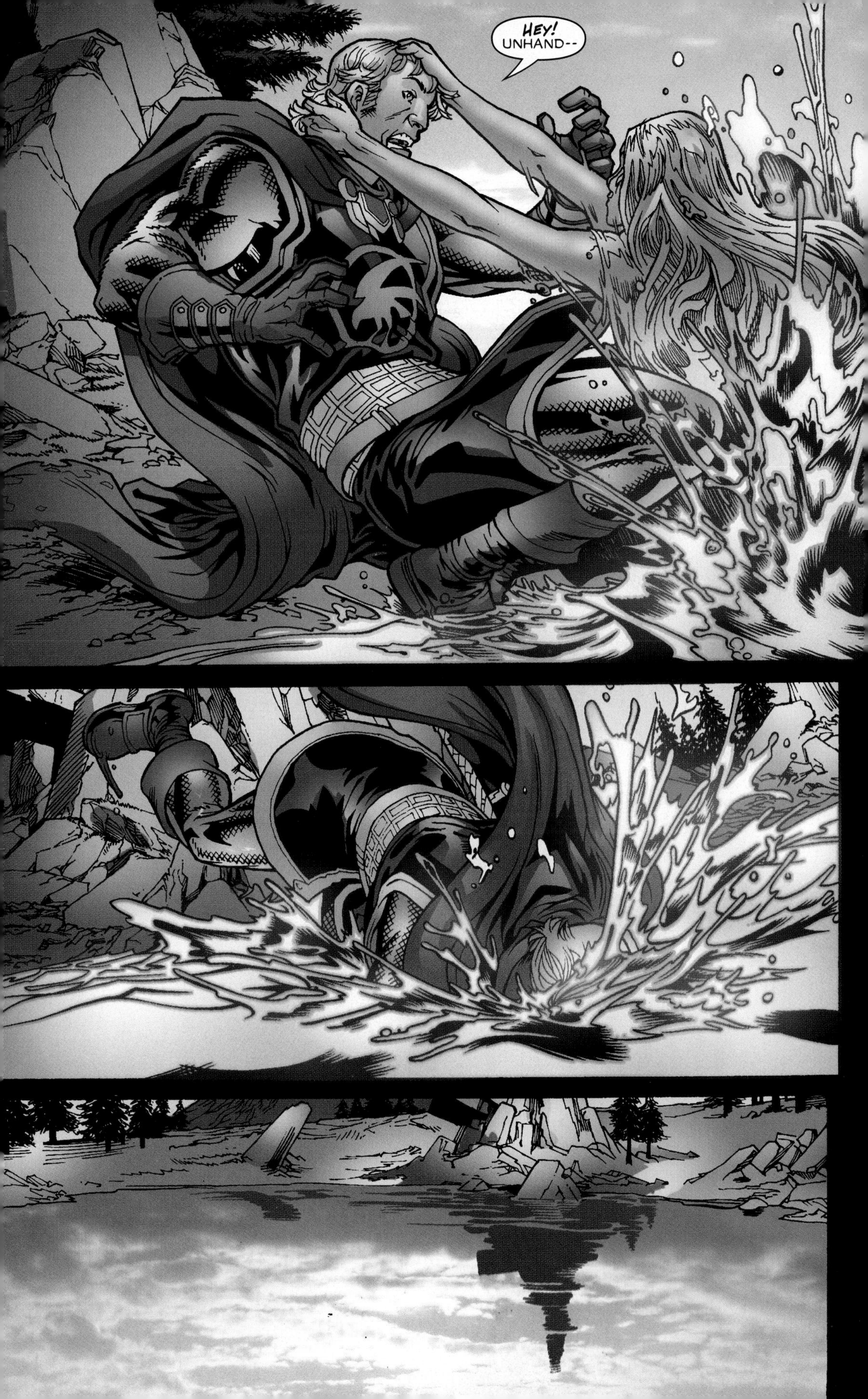
HEY! UNHAND--

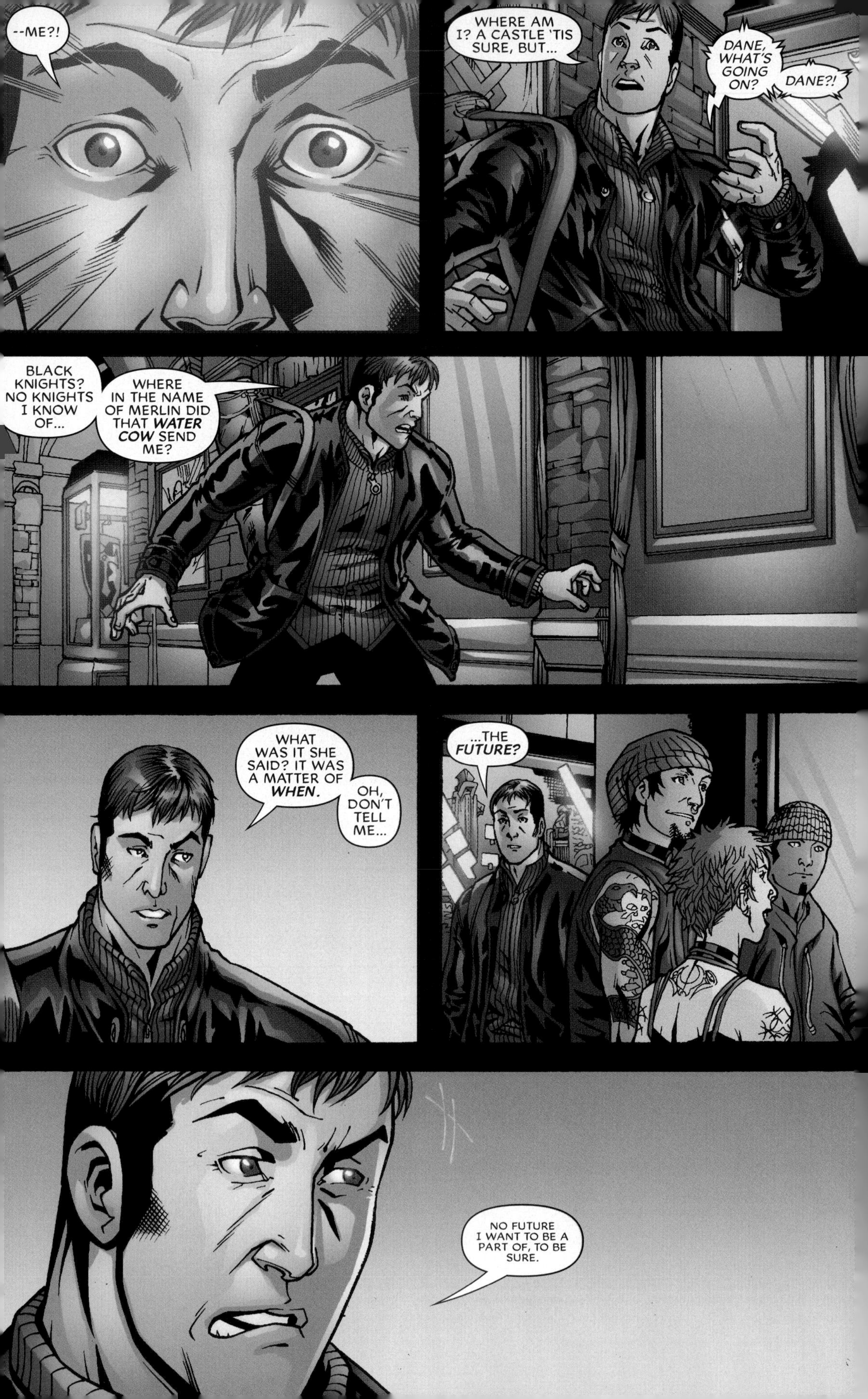
--ME?!
WHERE AM I? A CASTLE 'TIS SURE, BUT...
DANE, WHAT'S GOING ON?
DANE?!
BLACK KNIGHTS? NO KNIGHTS I KNOW OF...
WHERE IN THE NAME OF MERLIN DID THAT WATER COW SEND ME?
WHAT WAS IT SHE SAID? IT WAS A MATTER OF WHEN.
OH, DON'T TELL ME...
...THE FUTURE?
NO FUTURE I WANT TO BE A PART OF, TO BE SURE.

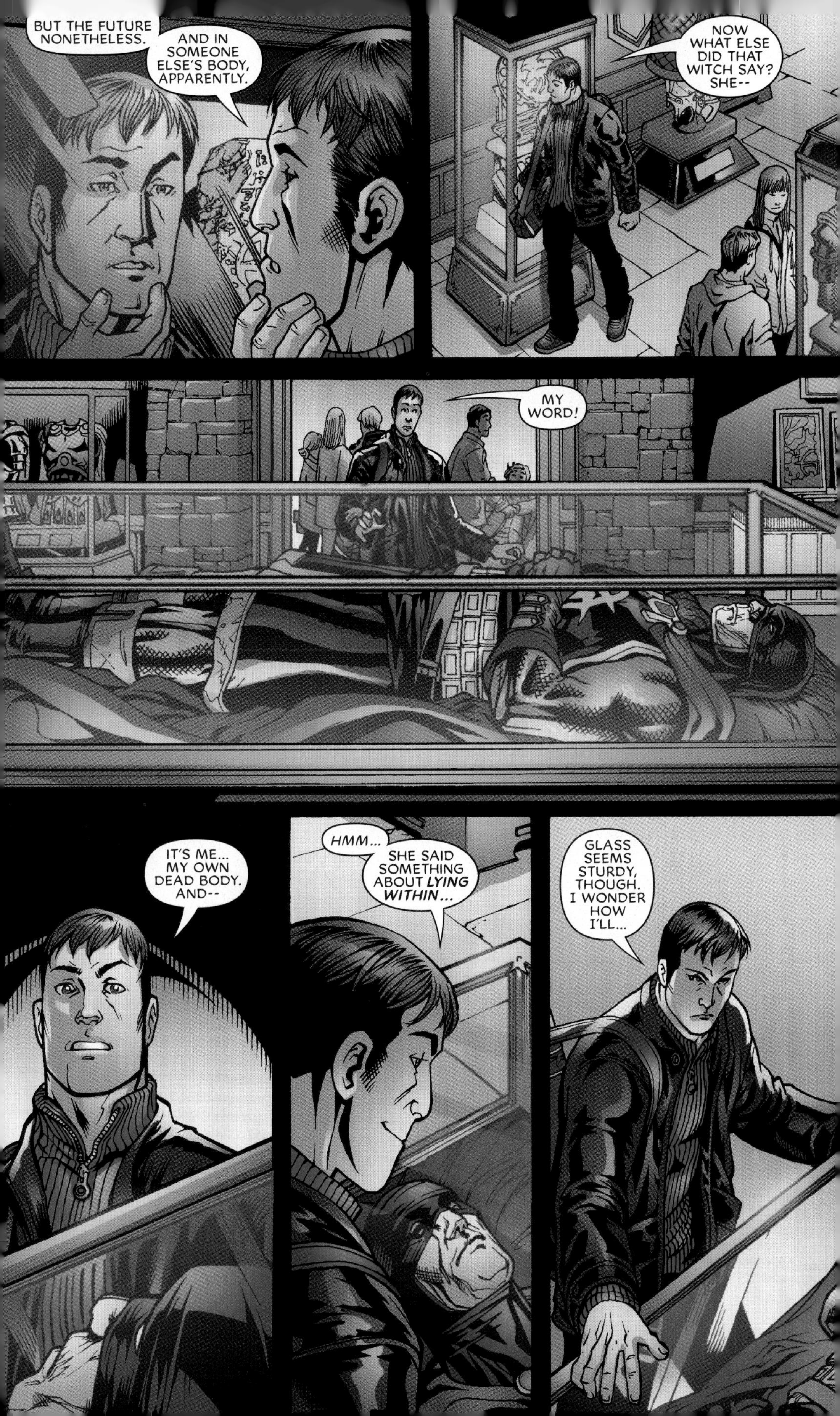
BUT THE FUTURE NONETHELESS.
AND IN SOMEONE ELSE'S BODY, APPARENTLY.
NOW WHAT ELSE DID THAT WITCH SAY? SHE--
MY WORD!
IT'S ME... MY OWN DEAD BODY. AND--
HMM...
SHE SAID SOMETHING ABOUT *LYING WITHIN*...
GLASS SEEMS STURDY, THOUGH. I WONDER HOW I'LL...

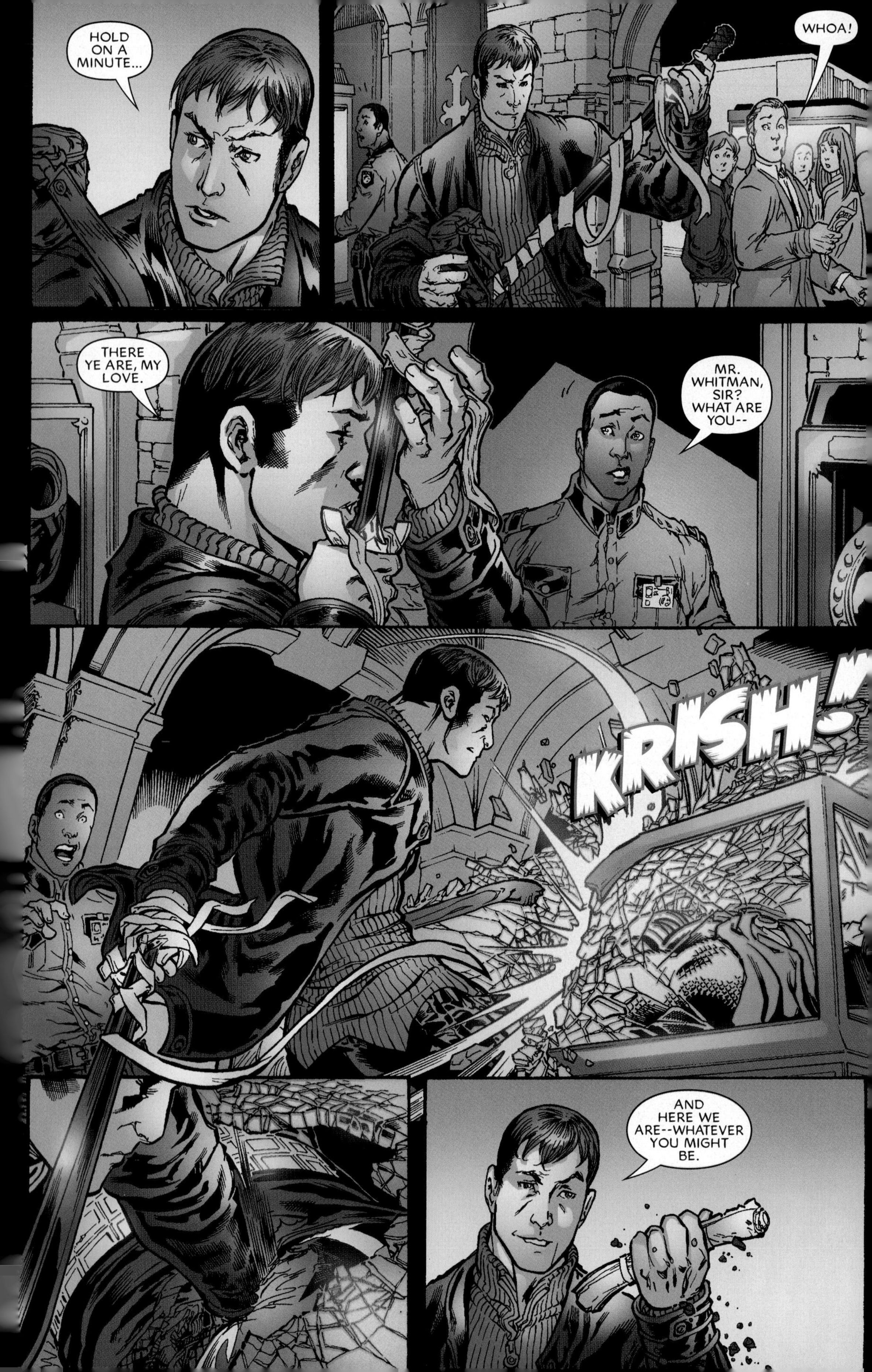
HOLD ON A MINUTE...
WHOA!
THERE YE ARE, MY LOVE.
MR. WHITMAN, SIR? WHAT ARE YOU--
KRISH!
AND HERE WE ARE--WHATEVER YOU MIGHT BE.

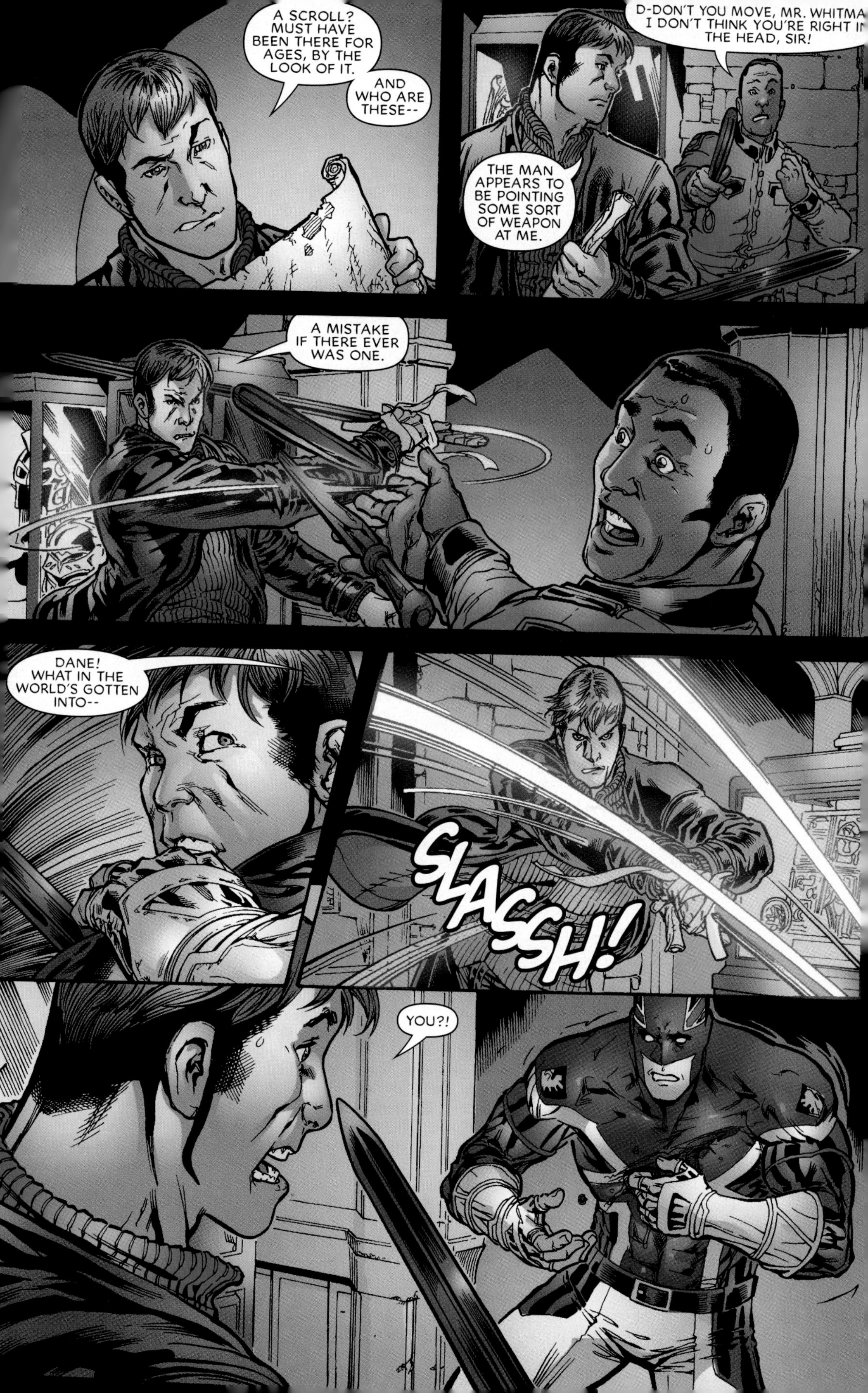
A SCROLL? MUST HAVE BEEN THERE FOR AGES, BY THE LOOK OF IT.
AND WHO ARE THESE--
D-DON'T YOU MOVE, MR. WHITMA
I DON'T THINK YOU'RE RIGHT I
THE HEAD, SIR!
THE MAN APPEARS TO BE POINTING SOME SORT OF WEAPON AT ME.
A MISTAKE IF THERE EVER WAS ONE.
DANE! WHAT IN THE WORLD'S GOTTEN INTO--
SLASSH!
YOU?!

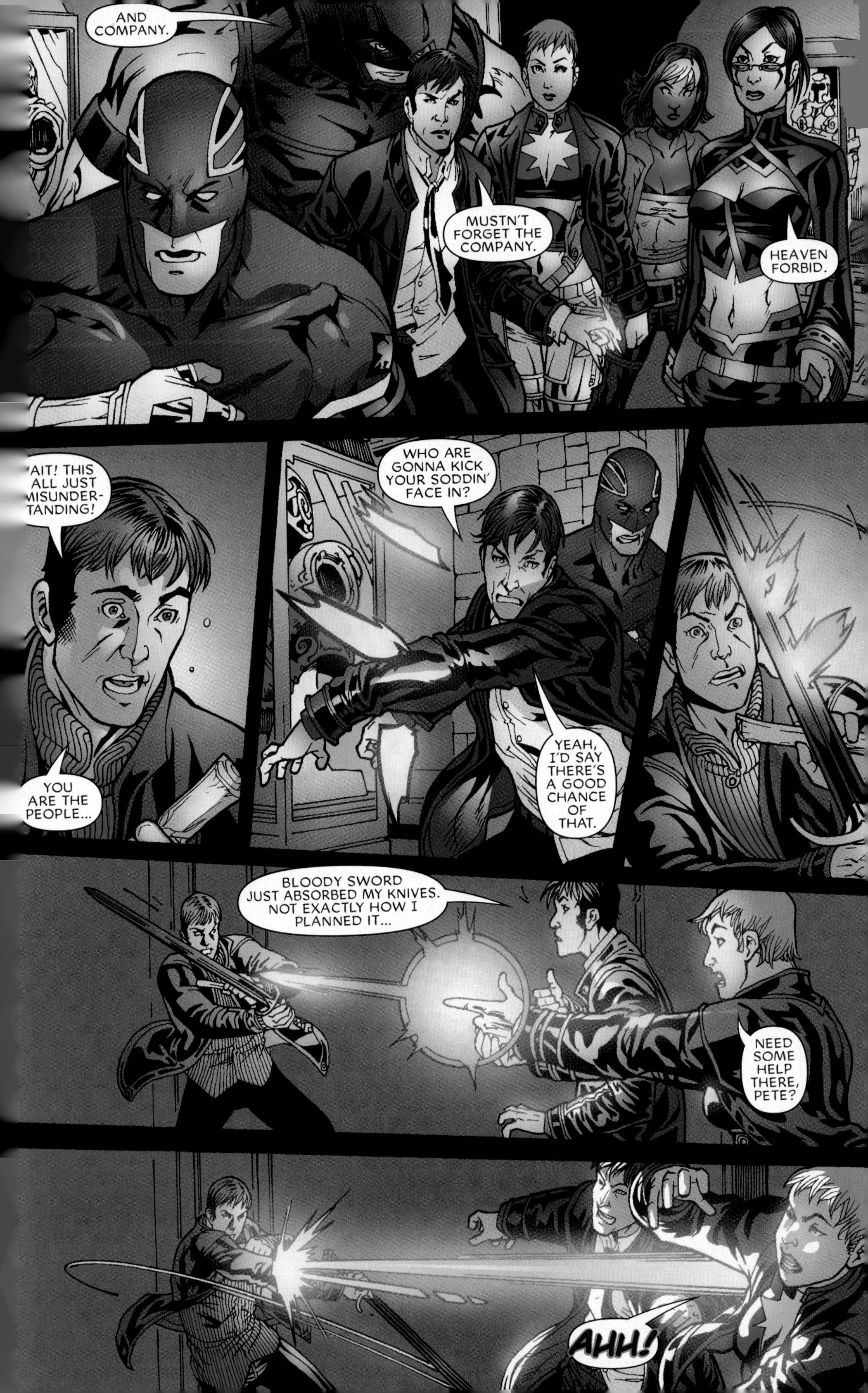

AND COMPANY.
MUSTN'T FORGET THE COMPANY.
HEAVEN FORBID.
AIT! THIS ALL JUST MISUNDER-TANDING!
YOU ARE THE PEOPLE...
WHO ARE GONNA KICK YOUR SODDIN' FACE IN?
YEAH, I'D SAY THERE'S A GOOD CHANCE OF THAT.
BLOODY SWORD JUST ABSORBED MY KNIVES. NOT EXACTLY HOW I PLANNED IT...
NEED SOME HELP THERE, PETE?
AHH!

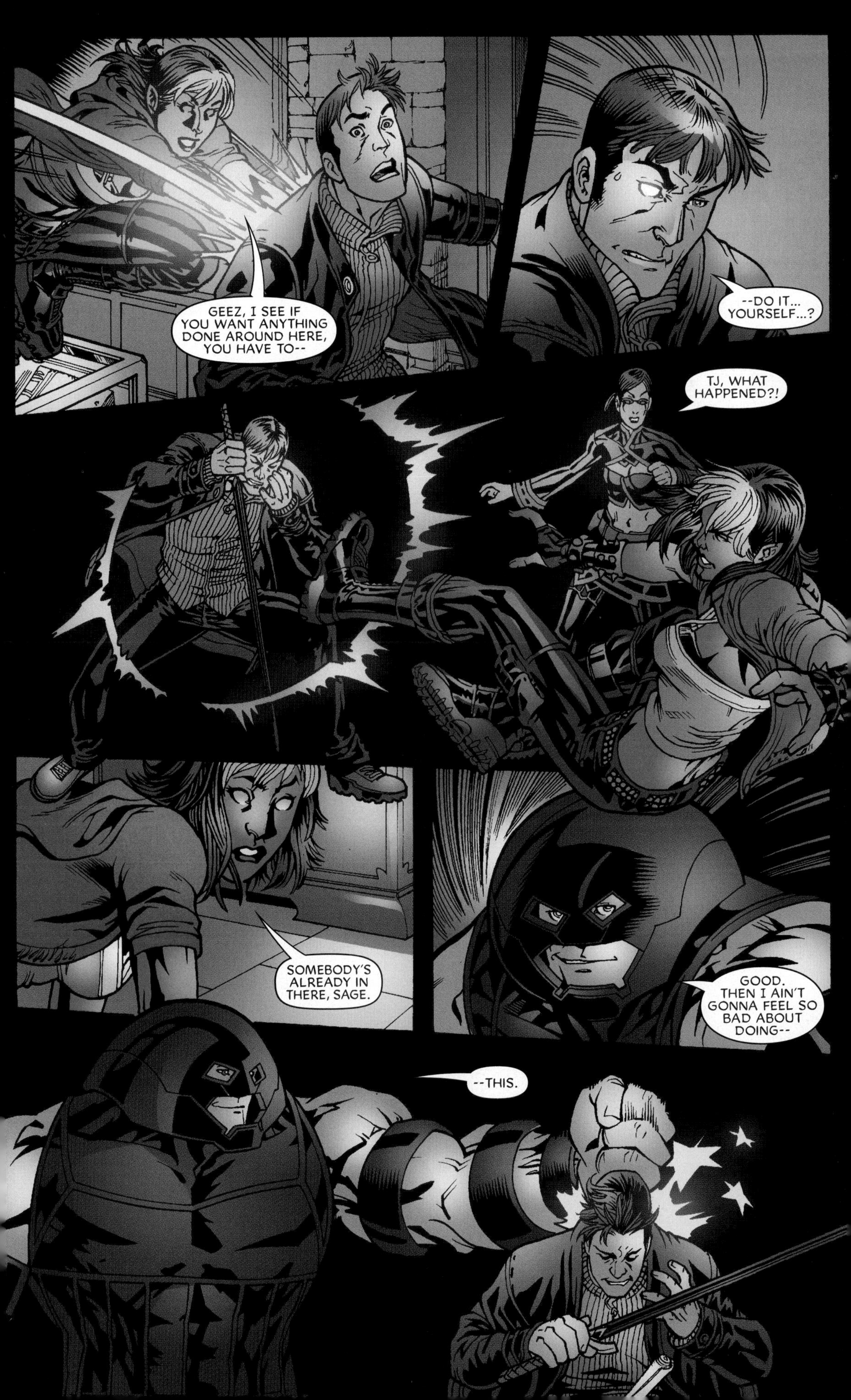
GEEZ, I SEE IF YOU WANT ANYTHING DONE AROUND HERE, YOU HAVE TO--
--DO IT... YOURSELF...?
TJ, WHAT HAPPENED?!
SOMEBODY'S ALREADY IN THERE, SAGE.
GOOD. THEN I AIN'T GONNA FEEL SO BAD ABOUT DOING--
--THIS.

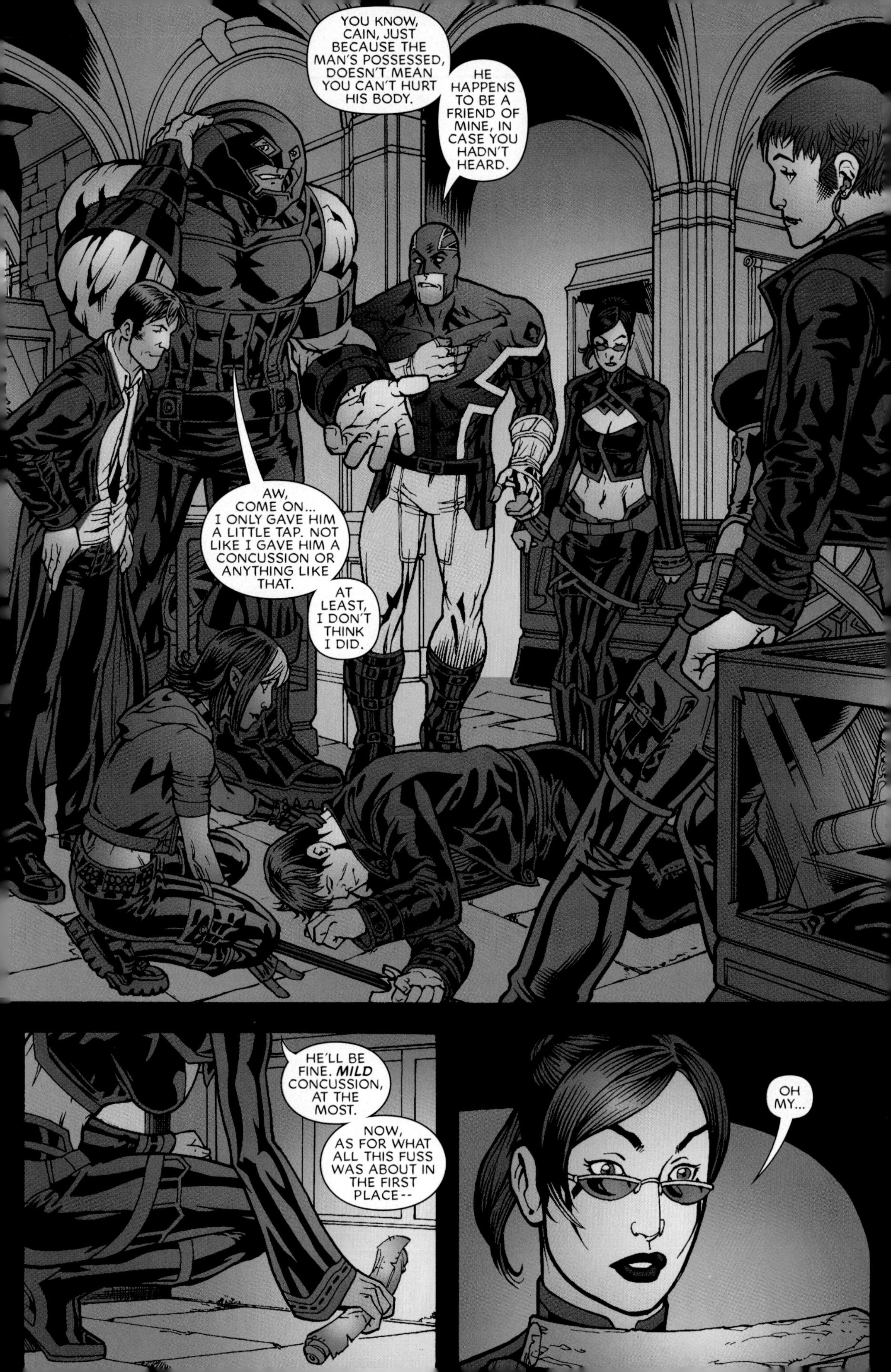
YOU KNOW, CAIN, JUST BECAUSE THE MAN'S POSSESSED, DOESN'T MEAN YOU CAN'T HURT HIS BODY.
HE HAPPENS TO BE A FRIEND OF MINE, IN CASE YOU HADN'T HEARD.
AW, COME ON... I ONLY GAVE HIM A LITTLE TAP. NOT LIKE I GAVE HIM A CONCUSSION OR ANYTHING LIKE THAT.
AT LEAST, I DON'T THINK I DID.
HE'LL BE FINE. ***MILD*** CONCUSSION, AT THE MOST.
NOW, AS FOR WHAT ALL THIS FUSS WAS ABOUT IN THE FIRST PLACE--
OH MY...

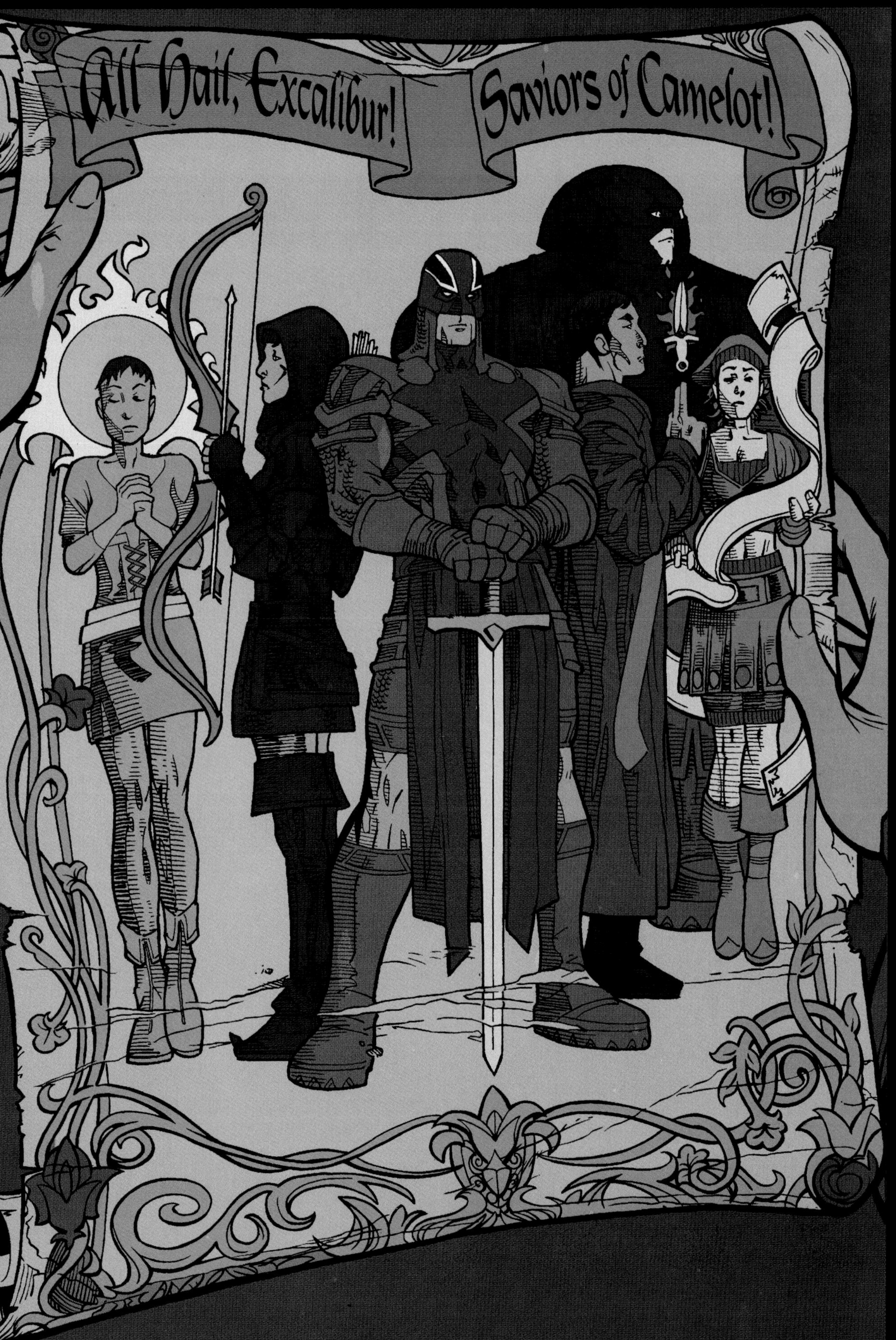
All Hail, Excalibur!
Saviors of Camelot!

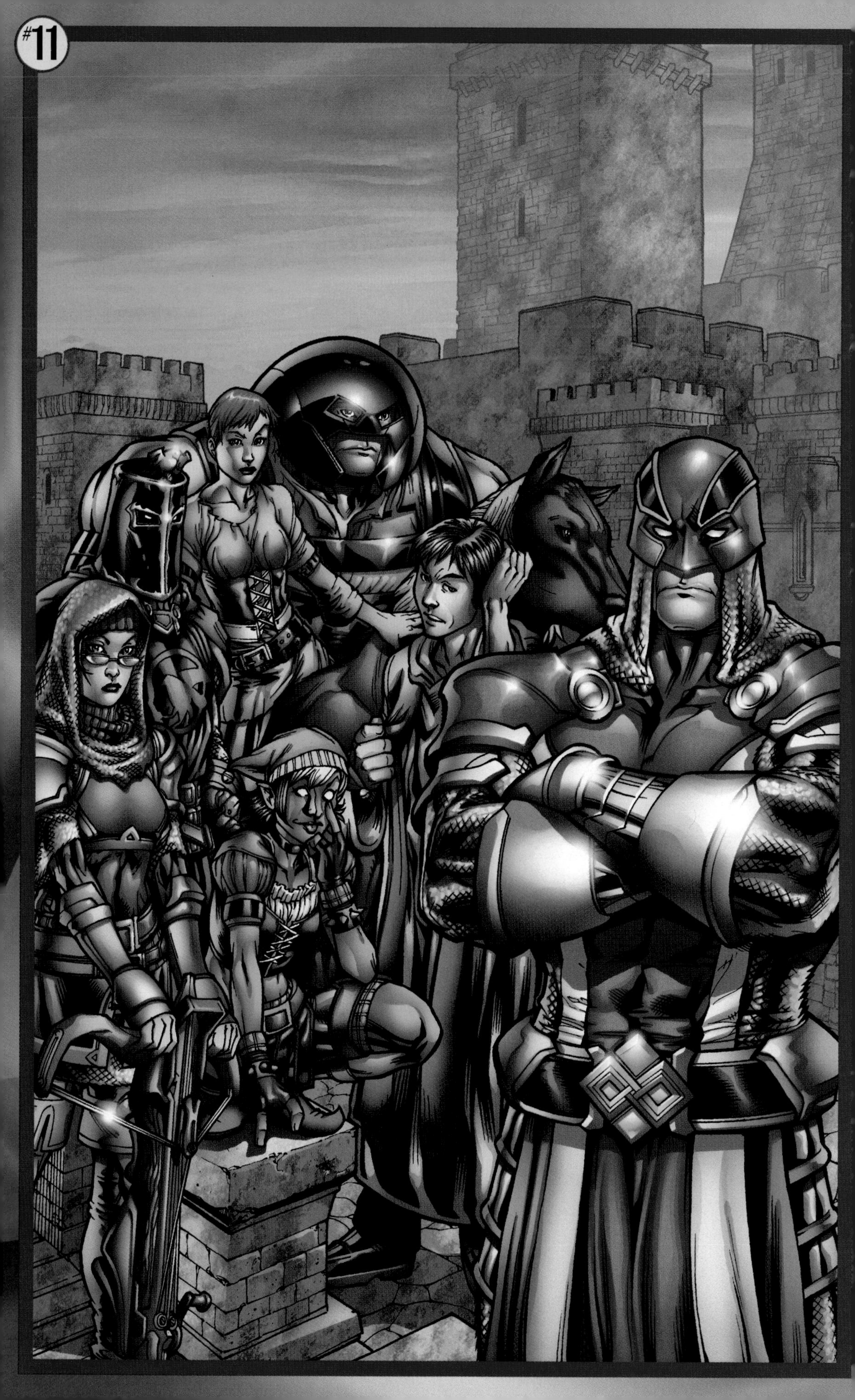
#11

SO LET ME SEE IF I'VE GOT THIS STRAIGHT...

...THIS FRIEND OF YOURS, WHAT'S-HIS-FACE...

DANE WHITMAN. OR THE *BLACK KNIGHT*, IF YOU PREFER.

RIGHT.

HE'S BEEN *POSSESSED*.

YEP.

BY THIS ORIGINAL BLACK KNIGHT FELLOW, SIR...

PERCY.

PERCY. BLOODY HELL, WHAT A NAME.

ANYWAY, THIS SIR PERCY BLOKE CLAIMS HE'S SOMEHOW COME INTO THE FUTURE BECAUSE CAMELOT--

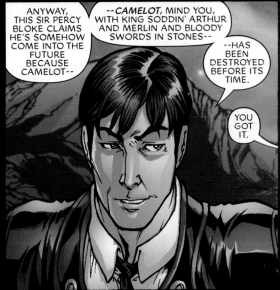

--*CAMELOT*, MIND YOU, WITH KING SODDIN' ARTHUR AND MERLIN AND BLOODY SWORDS IN STONES--

--HAS BEEN DESTROYED BEFORE ITS TIME.

YOU GOT IT.

AND WE'RE THE ONLY ONES WHO CAN SAVE IT.

APPARENTLY.

BUT TO DO SO, WE'VE GOT TO GO BACK THROUGH TIME.

THAT WOULD STAND TO REASON, WOULDN'T IT?

OH, AND ONE LAST THING...

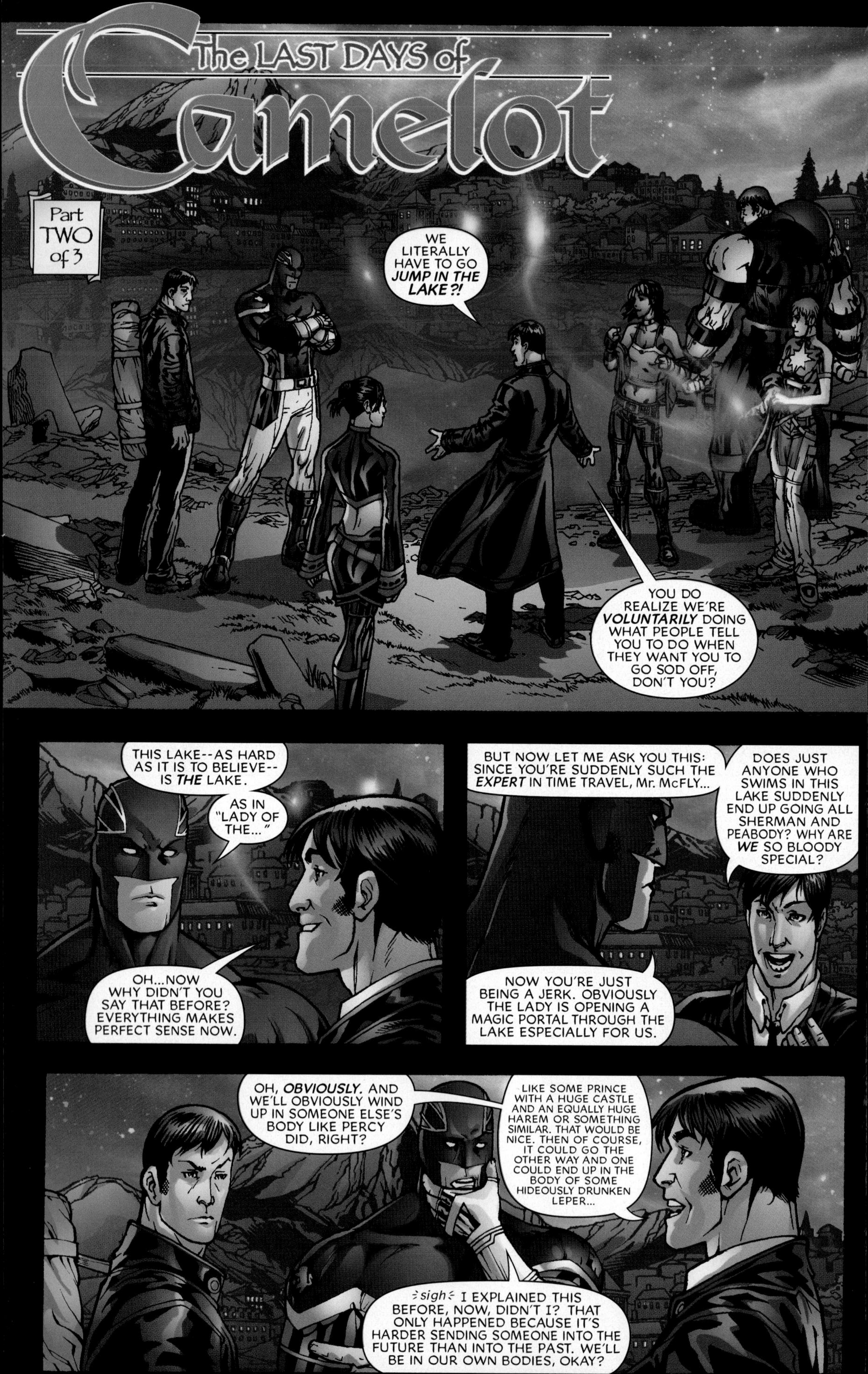
The LAST DAYS of Camelot
Part TWO of 3
WE LITERALLY HAVE TO GO JUMP IN THE LAKE?!
YOU DO REALIZE WE'RE VOLUNTARILY DOING WHAT PEOPLE TELL YOU TO DO WHEN THEY WANT YOU TO GO SOD OFF, DON'T YOU?
THIS LAKE--AS HARD AS IT IS TO BELIEVE--IS THE LAKE.
AS IN "LADY OF THE..."
OH...NOW WHY DIDN'T YOU SAY THAT BEFORE? EVERYTHING MAKES PERFECT SENSE NOW.
BUT NOW LET ME ASK YOU THIS: SINCE YOU'RE SUDDENLY SUCH THE EXPERT IN TIME TRAVEL, Mr. McFLY...
DOES JUST ANYONE WHO SWIMS IN THIS LAKE SUDDENLY END UP GOING ALL SHERMAN AND PEABODY? WHY ARE WE SO BLOODY SPECIAL?
NOW YOU'RE JUST BEING A JERK. OBVIOUSLY THE LADY IS OPENING A MAGIC PORTAL THROUGH THE LAKE ESPECIALLY FOR US.
OH, OBVIOUSLY. AND WE'LL OBVIOUSLY WIND UP IN SOMEONE ELSE'S BODY LIKE PERCY DID, RIGHT?
-LIKE SOME PRINCE WITH A HUGE CASTLE AND AN EQUALLY HUGE HAREM OR SOMETHING SIMILAR. THAT WOULD BE NICE. THEN OF COURSE, IT COULD GO THE OTHER WAY AND ONE COULD END UP IN THE BODY OF SOME HIDEOUSLY DRUNKEN LEPER...
sigh I EXPLAINED THIS BEFORE, NOW, DIDN'T I? THAT ONLY HAPPENED BECAUSE IT'S HARDER SENDING SOMEONE INTO THE FUTURE THAN INTO THE PAST. WE'LL BE IN OUR OWN BODIES, OKAY?

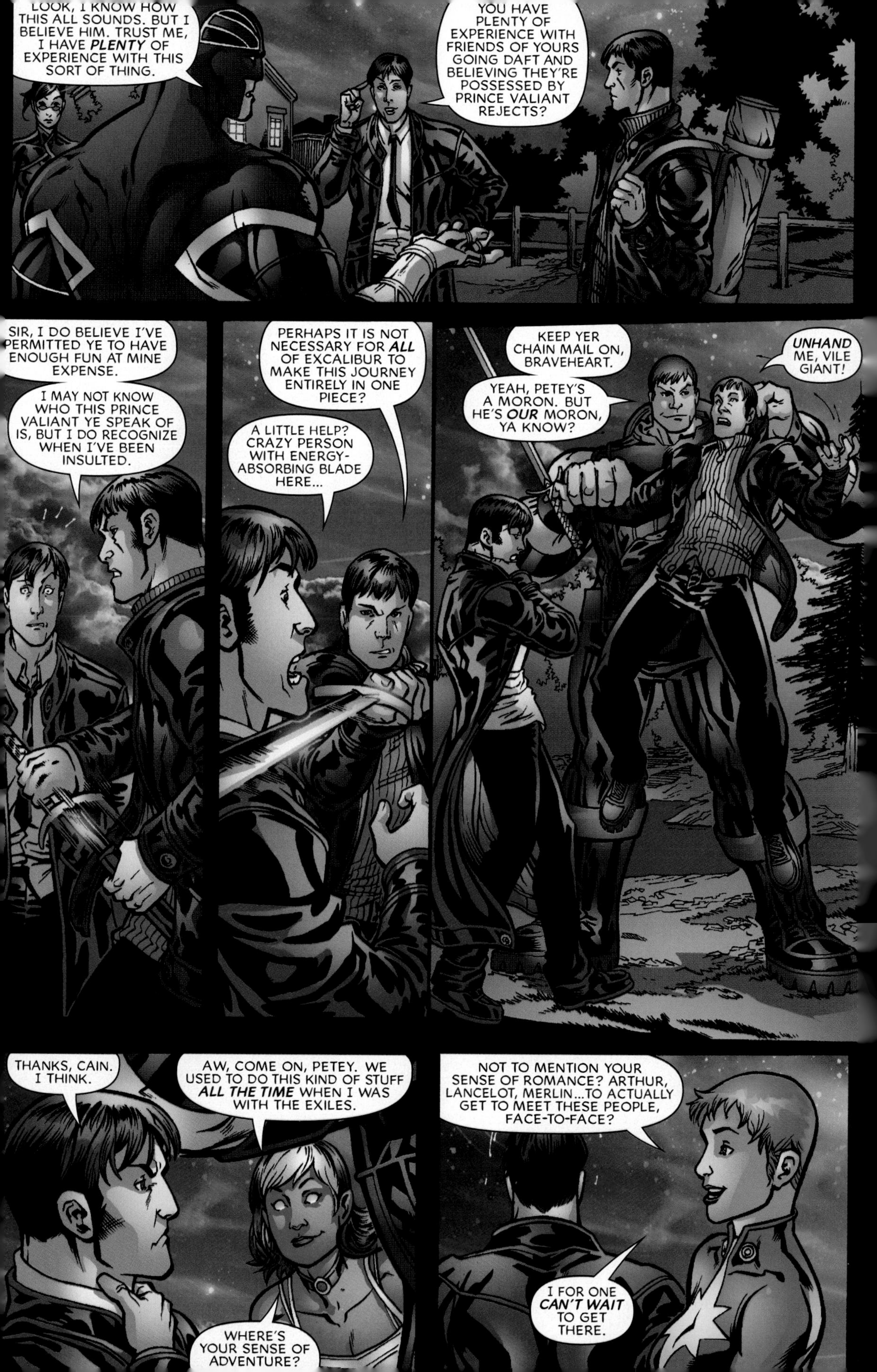
LOOK, I KNOW HOW THIS ALL SOUNDS. BUT I BELIEVE HIM. TRUST ME, I HAVE *PLENTY* OF EXPERIENCE WITH THIS SORT OF THING.
YOU HAVE PLENTY OF EXPERIENCE WITH FRIENDS OF YOURS GOING DAFT AND BELIEVING THEY'RE POSSESSED BY PRINCE VALIANT REJECTS?
SIR, I DO BELIEVE I'VE PERMITTED YE TO HAVE ENOUGH FUN AT MINE EXPENSE.
I MAY NOT KNOW WHO THIS PRINCE VALIANT YE SPEAK OF IS, BUT I DO RECOGNIZE WHEN I'VE BEEN INSULTED.
PERHAPS IT IS NOT NECESSARY FOR *ALL* OF EXCALIBUR TO MAKE THIS JOURNEY ENTIRELY IN ONE PIECE?
A LITTLE HELP? CRAZY PERSON WITH ENERGY-ABSORBING BLADE HERE...
KEEP YER CHAIN MAIL ON, BRAVEHEART.
YEAH, PETEY'S A MORON. BUT HE'S *OUR* MORON, YA KNOW?
UNHAND ME, VILE GIANT!
THANKS, CAIN. I THINK.
AW, COME ON, PETEY. WE USED TO DO THIS KIND OF STUFF *ALL THE TIME* WHEN I WAS WITH THE EXILES.
WHERE'S YOUR SENSE OF ADVENTURE?
NOT TO MENTION YOUR SENSE OF ROMANCE? ARTHUR, LANCELOT, MERLIN...TO ACTUALLY GET TO MEET THESE PEOPLE, FACE-TO-FACE?
I FOR ONE *CAN'T WAIT* TO GET THERE.

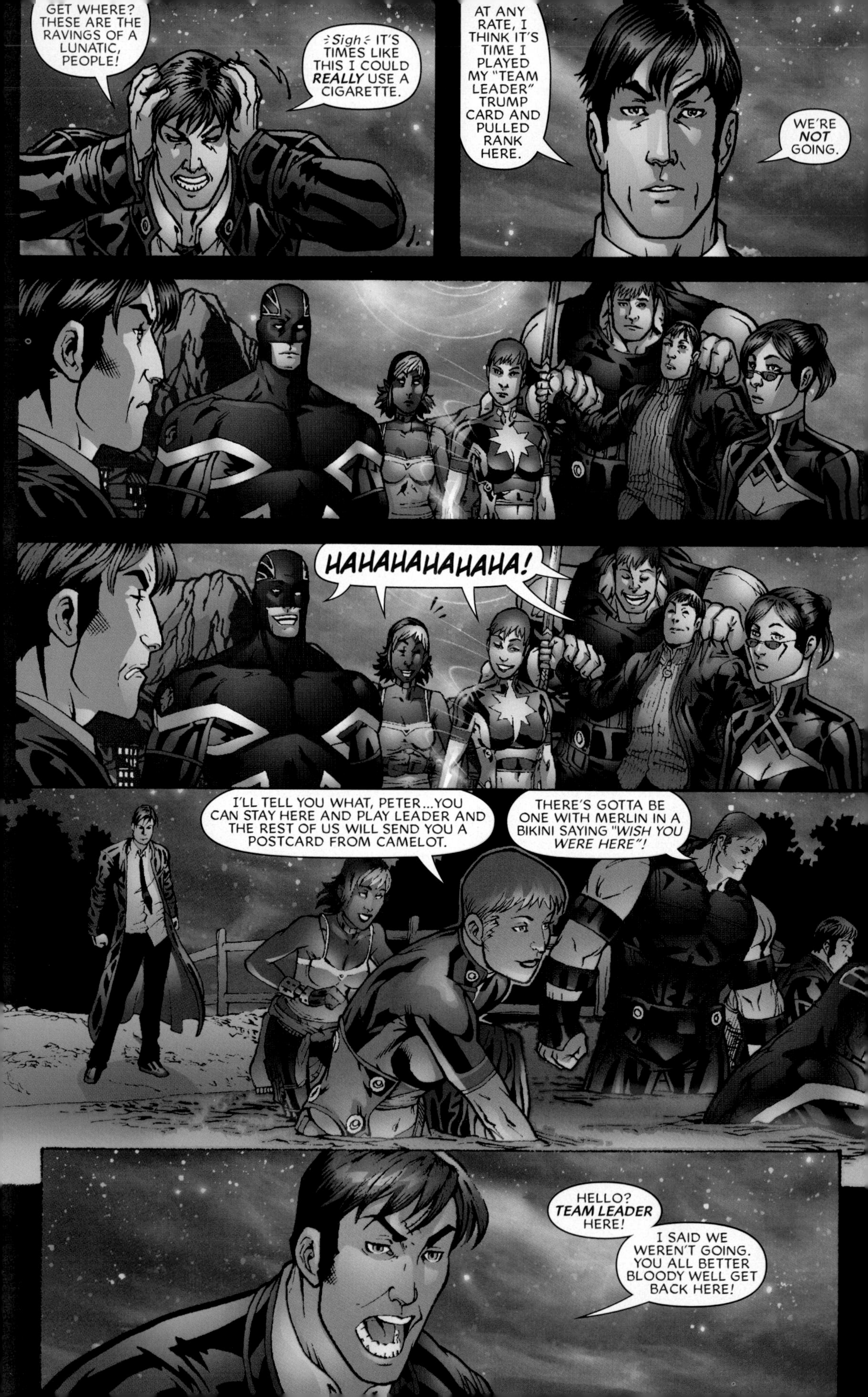
GET WHERE? THESE ARE THE RAVINGS OF A LUNATIC, PEOPLE!
Sigh IT'S TIMES LIKE THIS I COULD ***REALLY*** USE A CIGARETTE.
AT ANY RATE, I THINK IT'S TIME I PLAYED MY "TEAM LEADER" TRUMP CARD AND PULLED RANK HERE.
WE'RE ***NOT*** GOING.
HAHAHAHAHAHA!
I'LL TELL YOU WHAT, PETER...YOU CAN STAY HERE AND PLAY LEADER AND THE REST OF US WILL SEND YOU A POSTCARD FROM CAMELOT.
THERE'S GOTTA BE ONE WITH MERLIN IN A BIKINI SAYING "*WISH YOU WERE HERE*"!
HELLO? ***TEAM LEADER*** HERE!
I SAID WE WEREN'T GOING. YOU ALL BETTER BLOODY WELL GET BACK HERE!

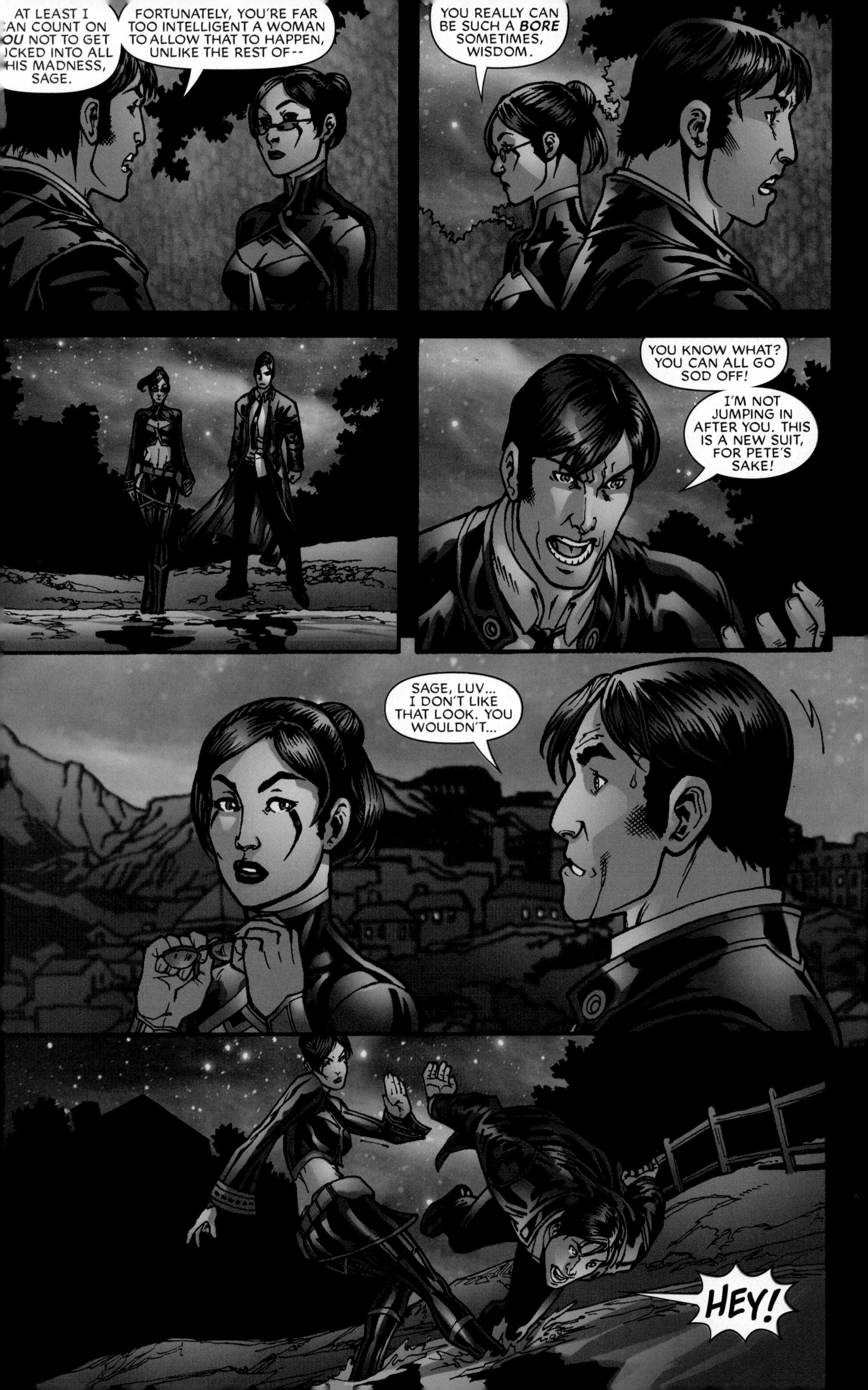
AT LEAST I CAN COUNT ON YOU NOT TO GET SUCKED INTO ALL THIS MADNESS, SAGE.
FORTUNATELY, YOU'RE FAR TOO INTELLIGENT A WOMAN TO ALLOW THAT TO HAPPEN, UNLIKE THE REST OF--
YOU REALLY CAN BE SUCH A *BORE* SOMETIMES, WISDOM.
YOU KNOW WHAT? YOU CAN ALL GO SOD OFF!
I'M NOT JUMPING IN AFTER YOU. THIS IS A NEW SUIT, FOR PETE'S SAKE!
SAGE, LUV... I DON'T LIKE THAT LOOK. YOU WOULDN'T...
HEY!

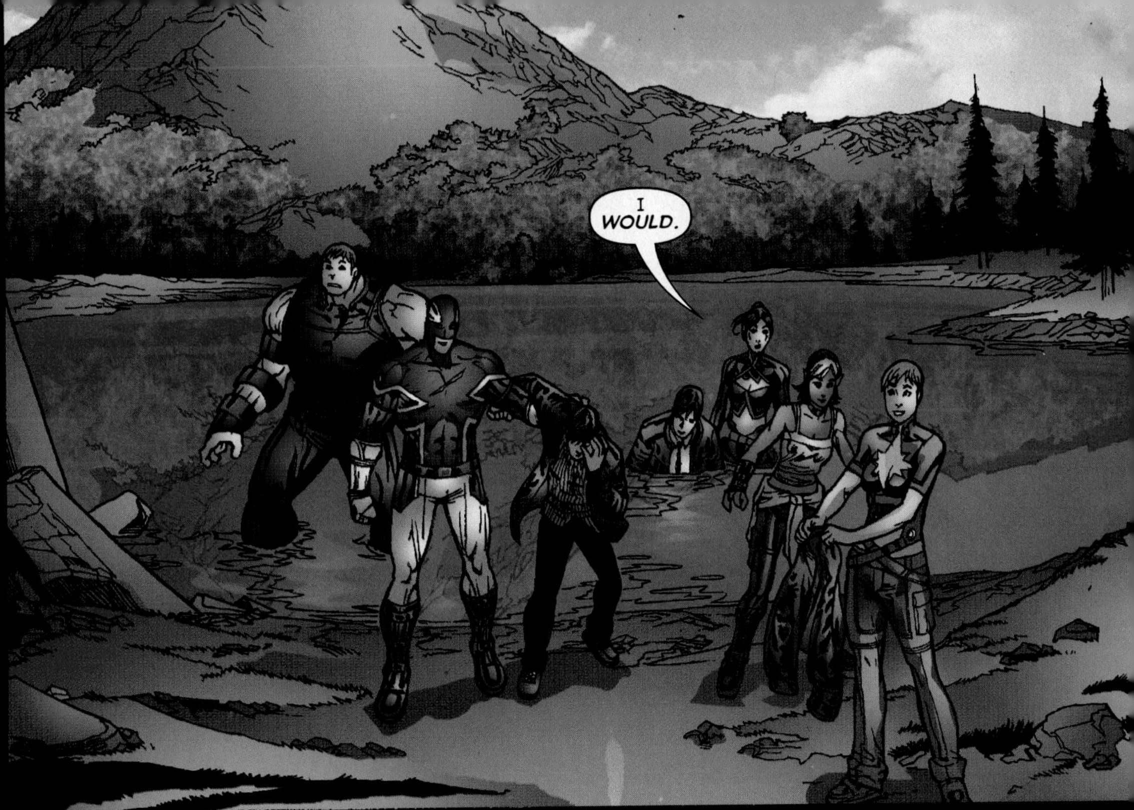
I WOULD.

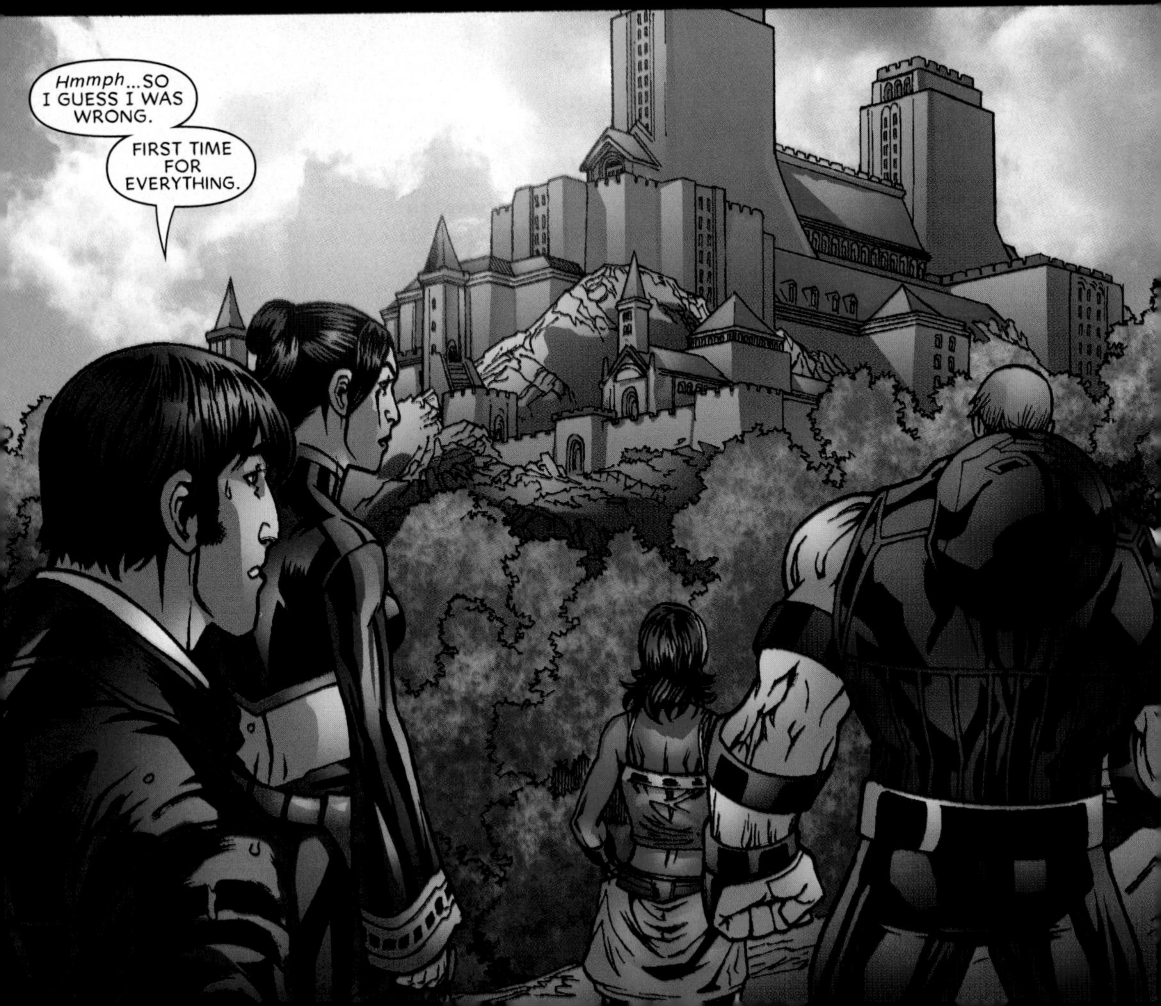
Hmmph...SO I GUESS I WAS WRONG.
FIRST TIME FOR EVERYTHING.

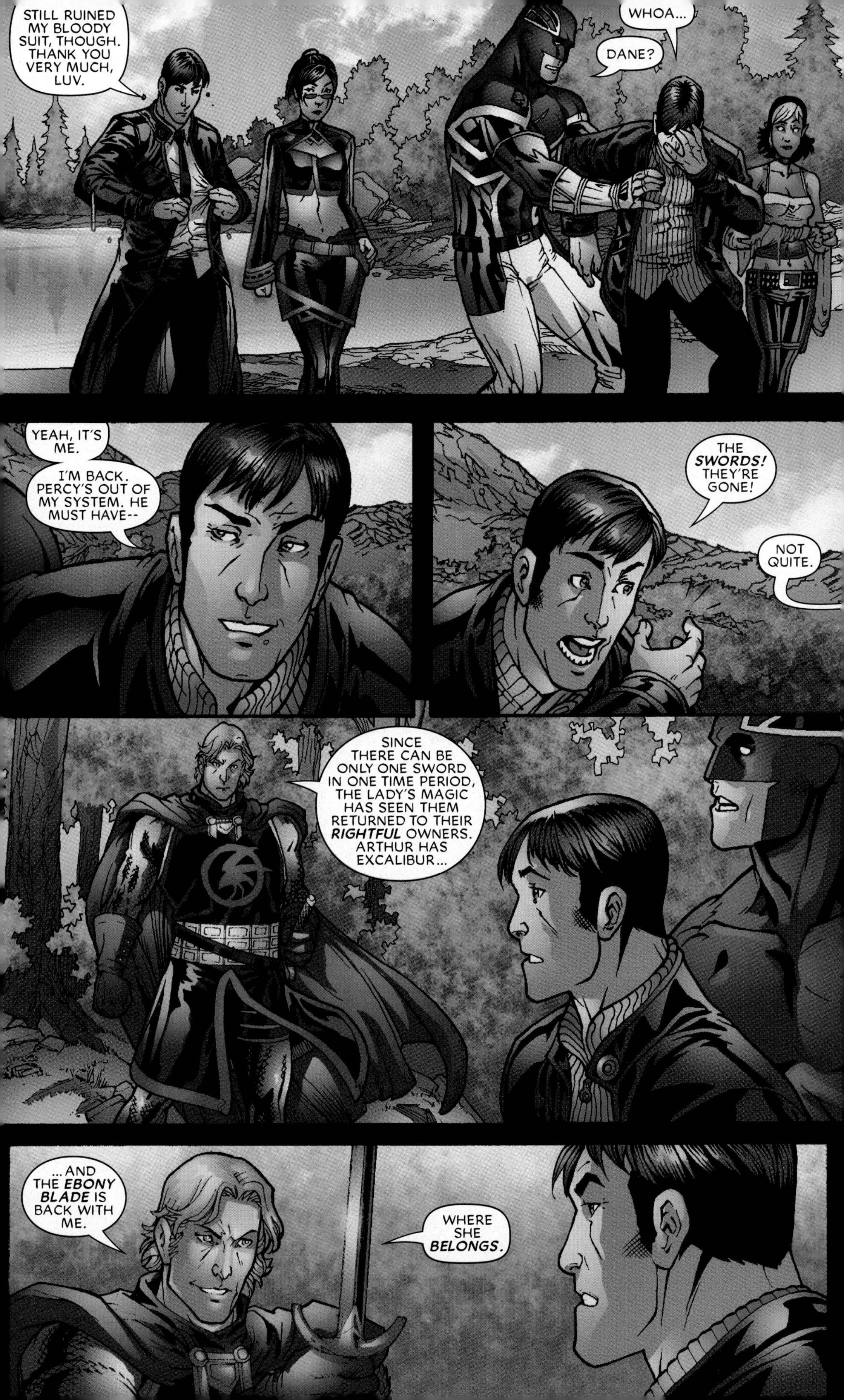
STILL RUINED MY BLOODY SUIT, THOUGH. THANK YOU VERY MUCH, LUV.
WHOA...
DANE?
YEAH, IT'S ME.
I'M BACK. PERCY'S OUT OF MY SYSTEM. HE MUST HAVE--
THE SWORDS! THEY'RE GONE!
NOT QUITE.
SINCE THERE CAN BE ONLY ONE SWORD IN ONE TIME PERIOD, THE LADY'S MAGIC HAS SEEN THEM RETURNED TO THEIR RIGHTFUL OWNERS. ARTHUR HAS EXCALIBUR...
...AND THE EBONY BLADE IS BACK WITH ME.
WHERE SHE BELONGS.

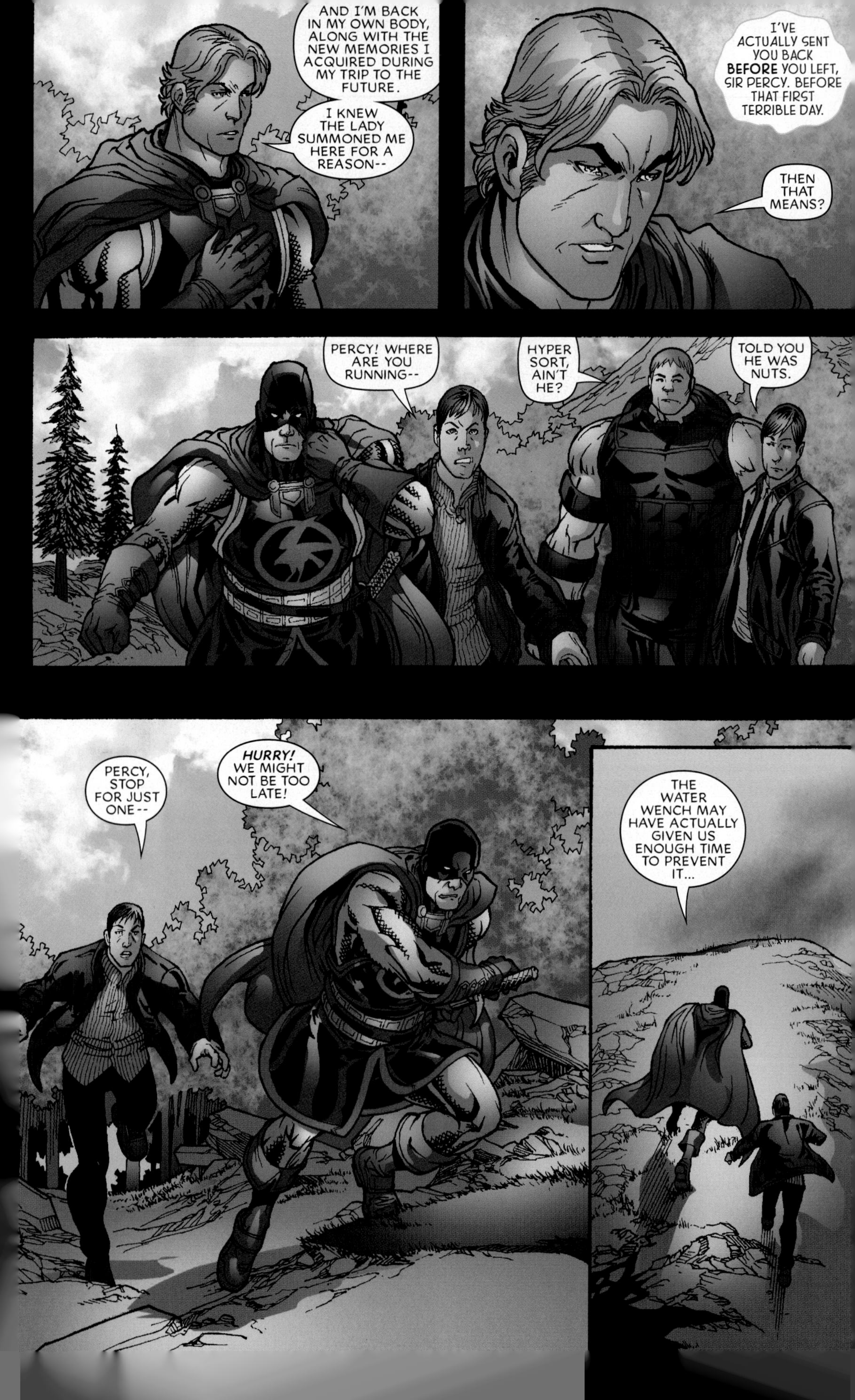
AND I'M BACK IN MY OWN BODY, ALONG WITH THE NEW MEMORIES I ACQUIRED DURING MY TRIP TO THE FUTURE.
I KNEW THE LADY SUMMONED ME HERE FOR A REASON--
I'VE ACTUALLY SENT YOU BACK **BEFORE** YOU LEFT, SIR PERCY. BEFORE THAT FIRST TERRIBLE DAY.
THEN THAT MEANS?
PERCY! WHERE ARE YOU RUNNING--
HYPER SORT, AIN'T HE?
TOLD YOU HE WAS NUTS.
PERCY, STOP FOR JUST ONE--
HURRY! WE MIGHT NOT BE TOO LATE!
THE WATER WENCH MAY HAVE ACTUALLY GIVEN US ENOUGH TIME TO PREVENT IT...

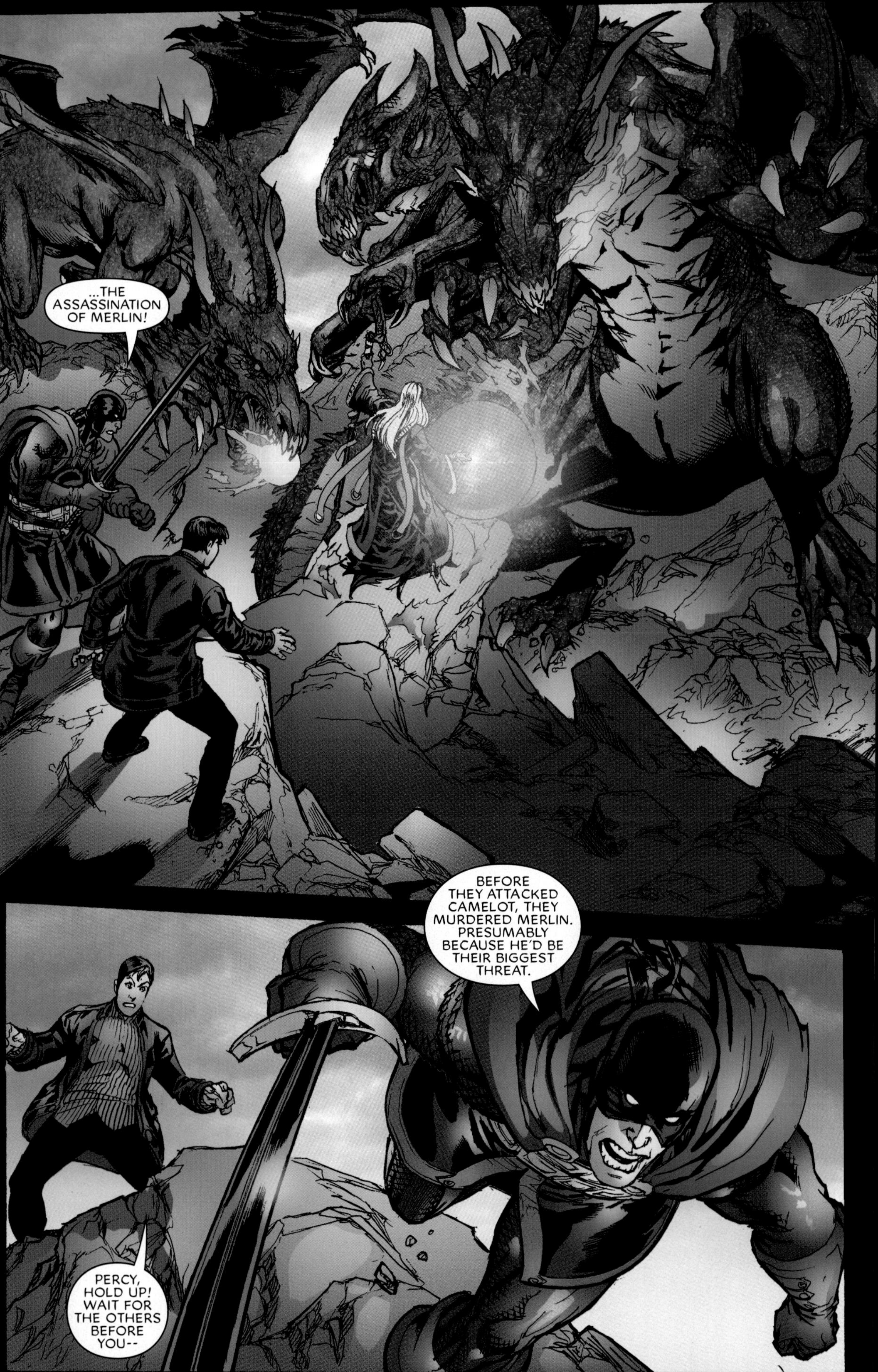
...THE ASSASSINATION OF MERLIN!
BEFORE THEY ATTACKED CAMELOT, THEY MURDERED MERLIN. PRESUMABLY BECAUSE HE'D BE THEIR BIGGEST THREAT.
PERCY, HOLD UP! WAIT FOR THE OTHERS BEFORE YOU--

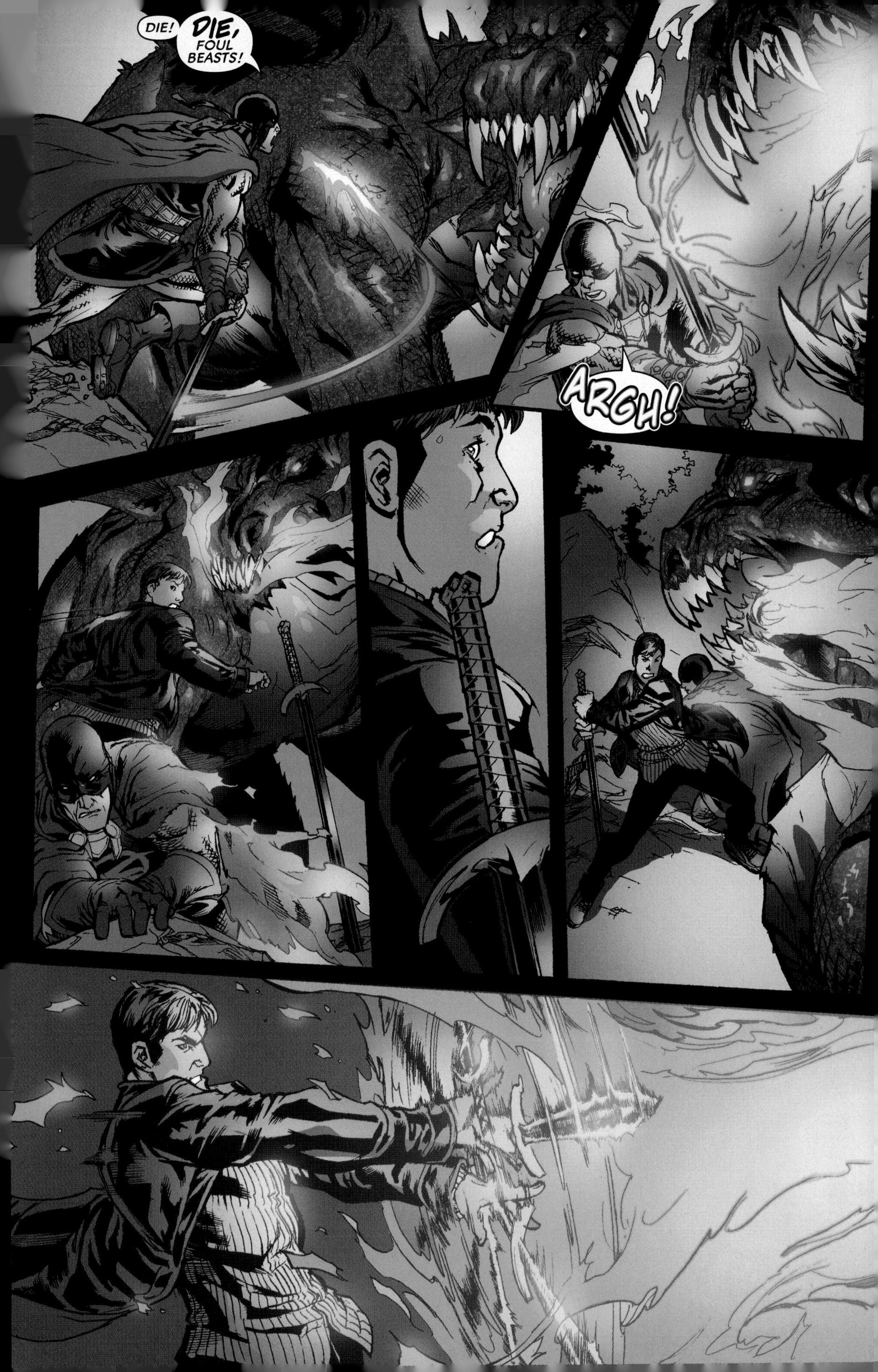
DIE!
DIE, FOUL BEASTS!
ARGH!

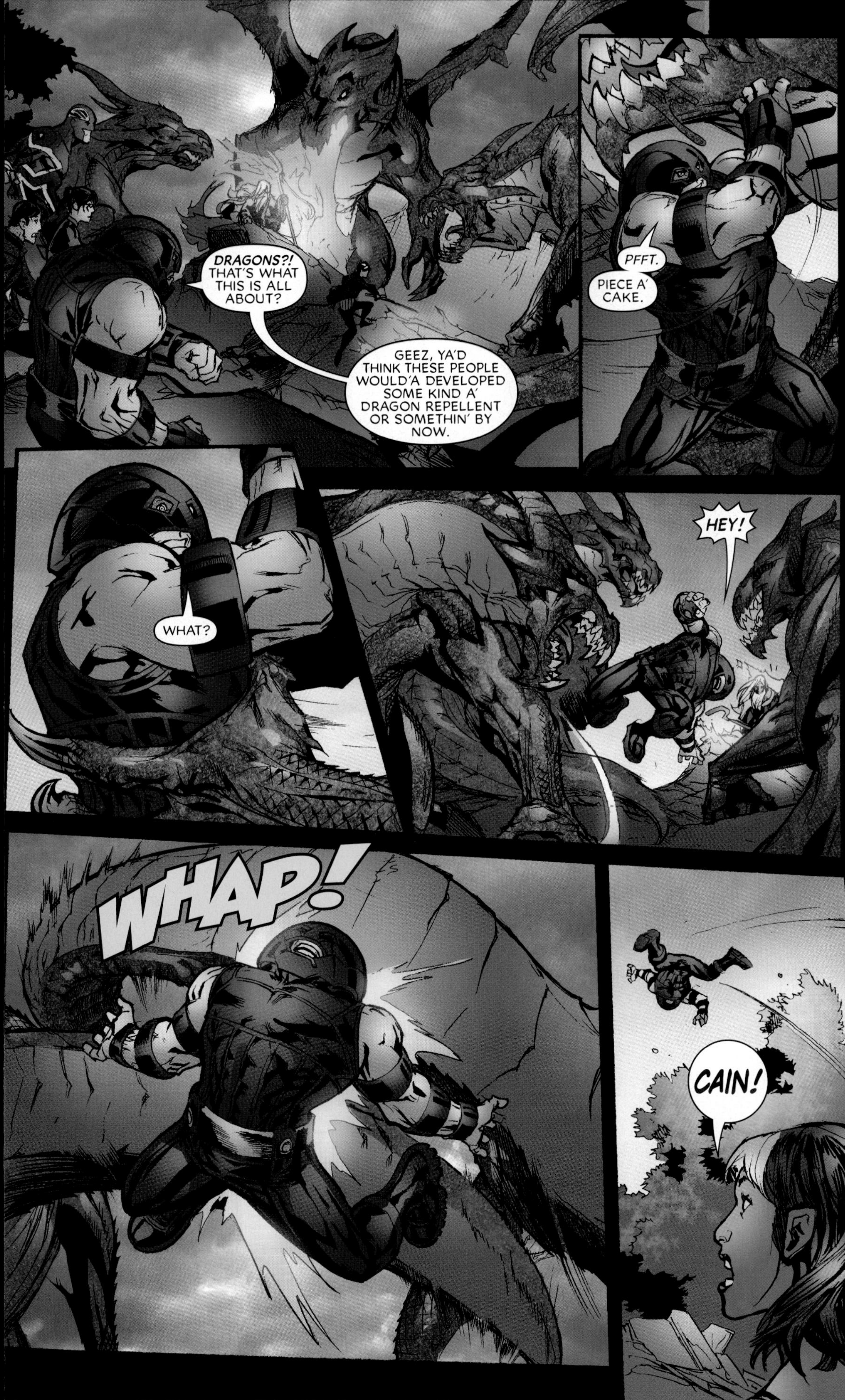
DRAGONS?! THAT'S WHAT THIS IS ALL ABOUT?
GEEZ, YA'D THINK THESE PEOPLE WOULD'A DEVELOPED SOME KIND A' DRAGON REPELLENT OR SOMETHIN' BY NOW.
PFFT.
PIECE A' CAKE.
WHAT?
HEY!
WHAP!
CAIN!

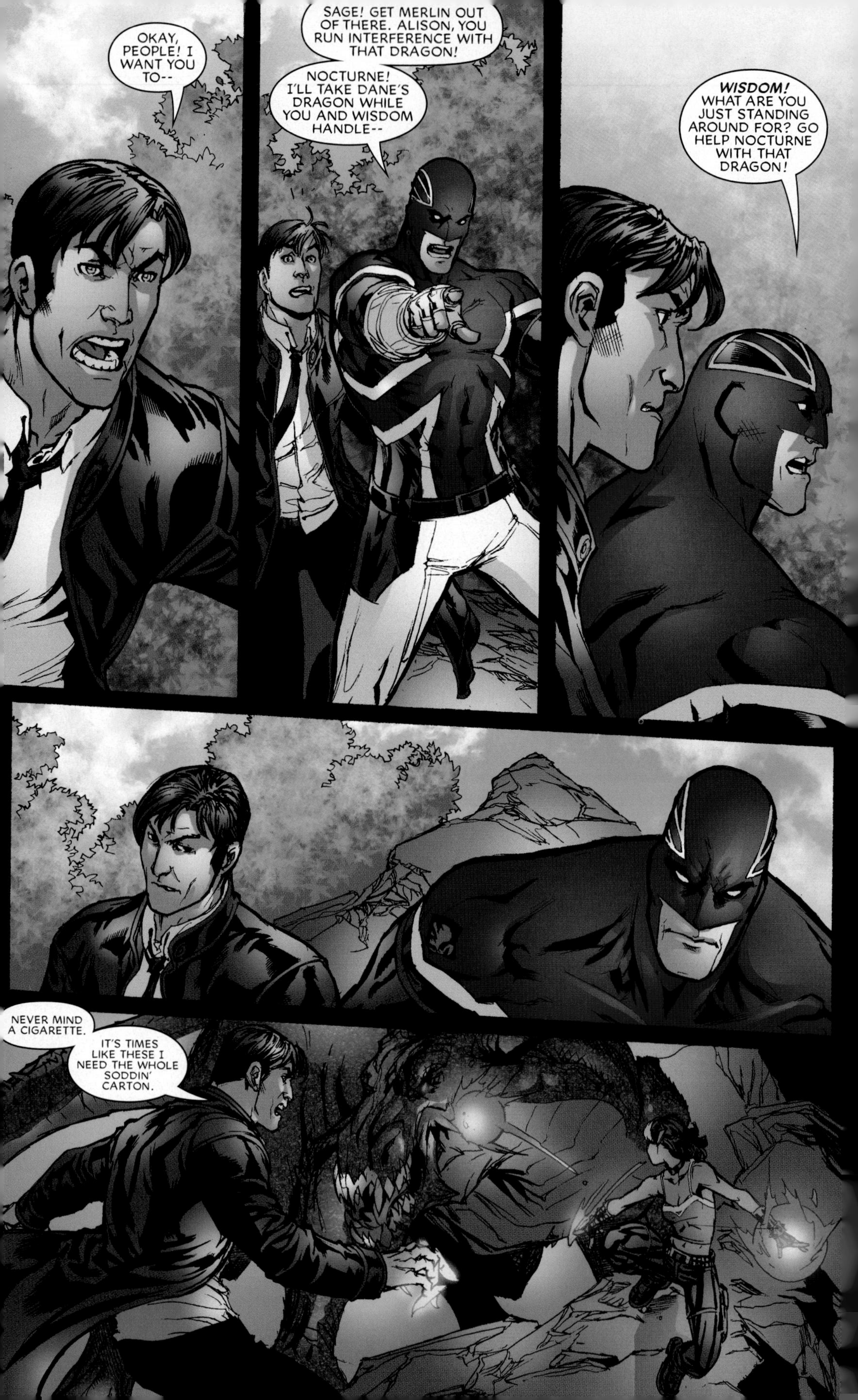
OKAY, PEOPLE! I WANT YOU TO--
SAGE! GET MERLIN OUT OF THERE. ALISON, YOU RUN INTERFERENCE WITH THAT DRAGON!
NOCTURNE! I'LL TAKE DANE'S DRAGON WHILE YOU AND WISDOM HANDLE--
WISDOM! WHAT ARE YOU JUST STANDING AROUND FOR? GO HELP NOCTURNE WITH THAT DRAGON!
NEVER MIND A CIGARETTE.
IT'S TIMES LIKE THESE I NEED THE WHOLE SODDIN' CARTON.

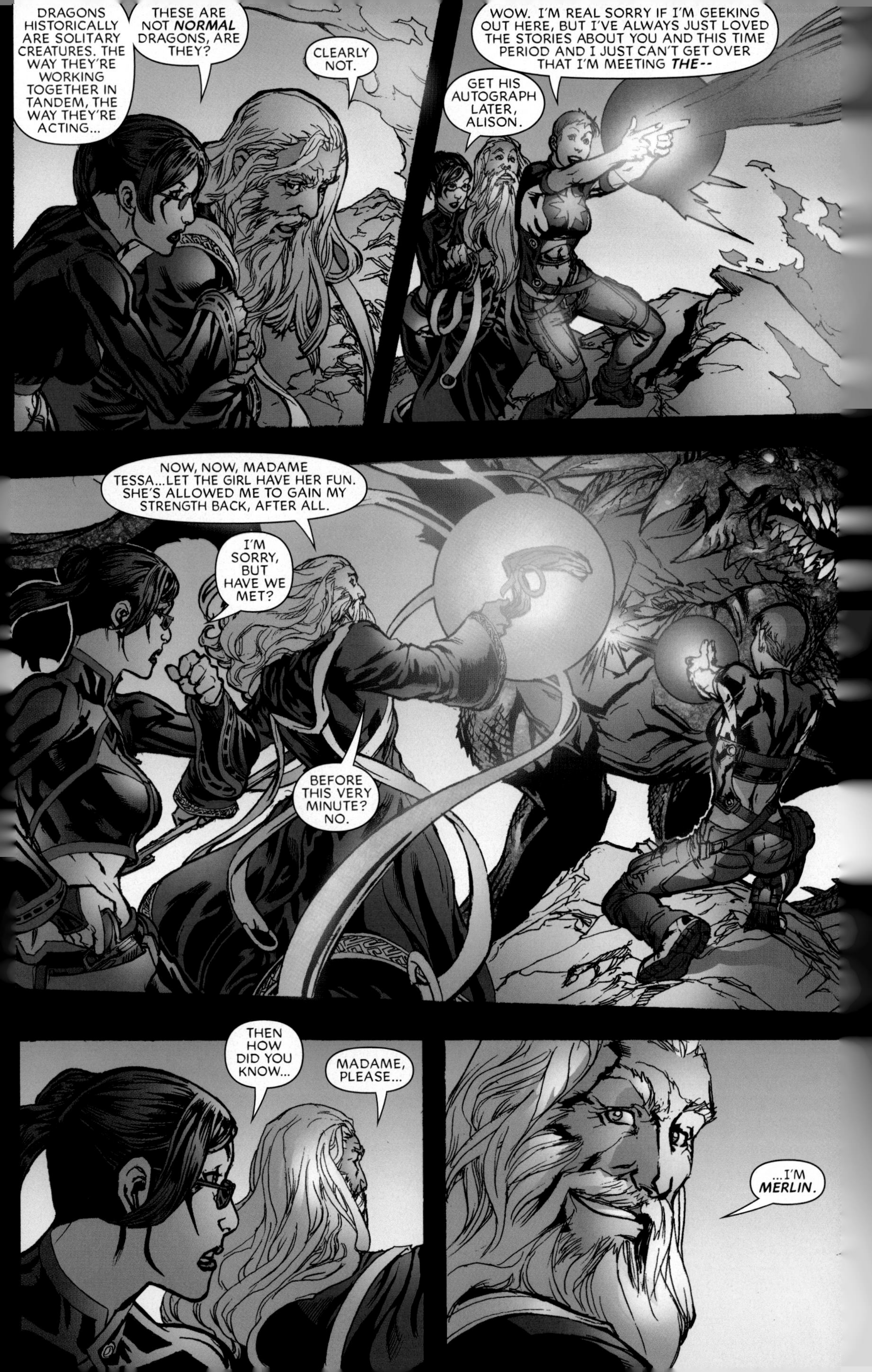
DRAGONS HISTORICALLY ARE SOLITARY CREATURES. THE WAY THEY'RE WORKING TOGETHER IN TANDEM, THE WAY THEY'RE ACTING...
THESE ARE NOT NORMAL DRAGONS, ARE THEY?
CLEARLY NOT.
WOW. I'M REAL SORRY IF I'M GEEKING OUT HERE, BUT I'VE ALWAYS JUST LOVED THE STORIES ABOUT YOU AND THIS TIME PERIOD AND I JUST CAN'T GET OVER THAT I'M MEETING THE--
GET HIS AUTOGRAPH LATER, ALISON.
NOW, NOW, MADAME TESSA...LET THE GIRL HAVE HER FUN. SHE'S ALLOWED ME TO GAIN MY STRENGTH BACK, AFTER ALL.
I'M SORRY, BUT HAVE WE MET?
BEFORE THIS VERY MINUTE? NO.
THEN HOW DID YOU KNOW...
MADAME, PLEASE...
...I'M MERLIN.

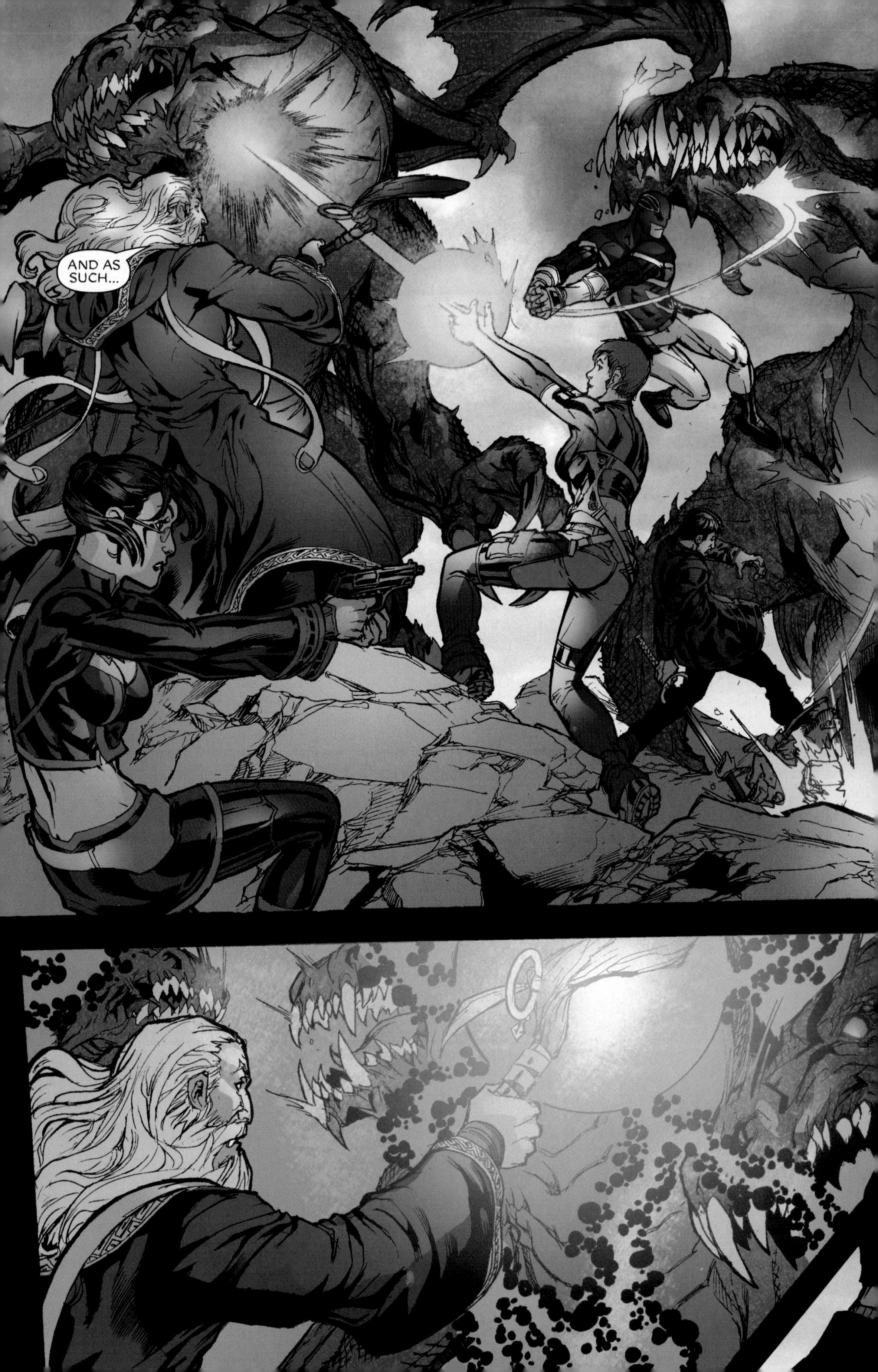
AND AS SUCH...

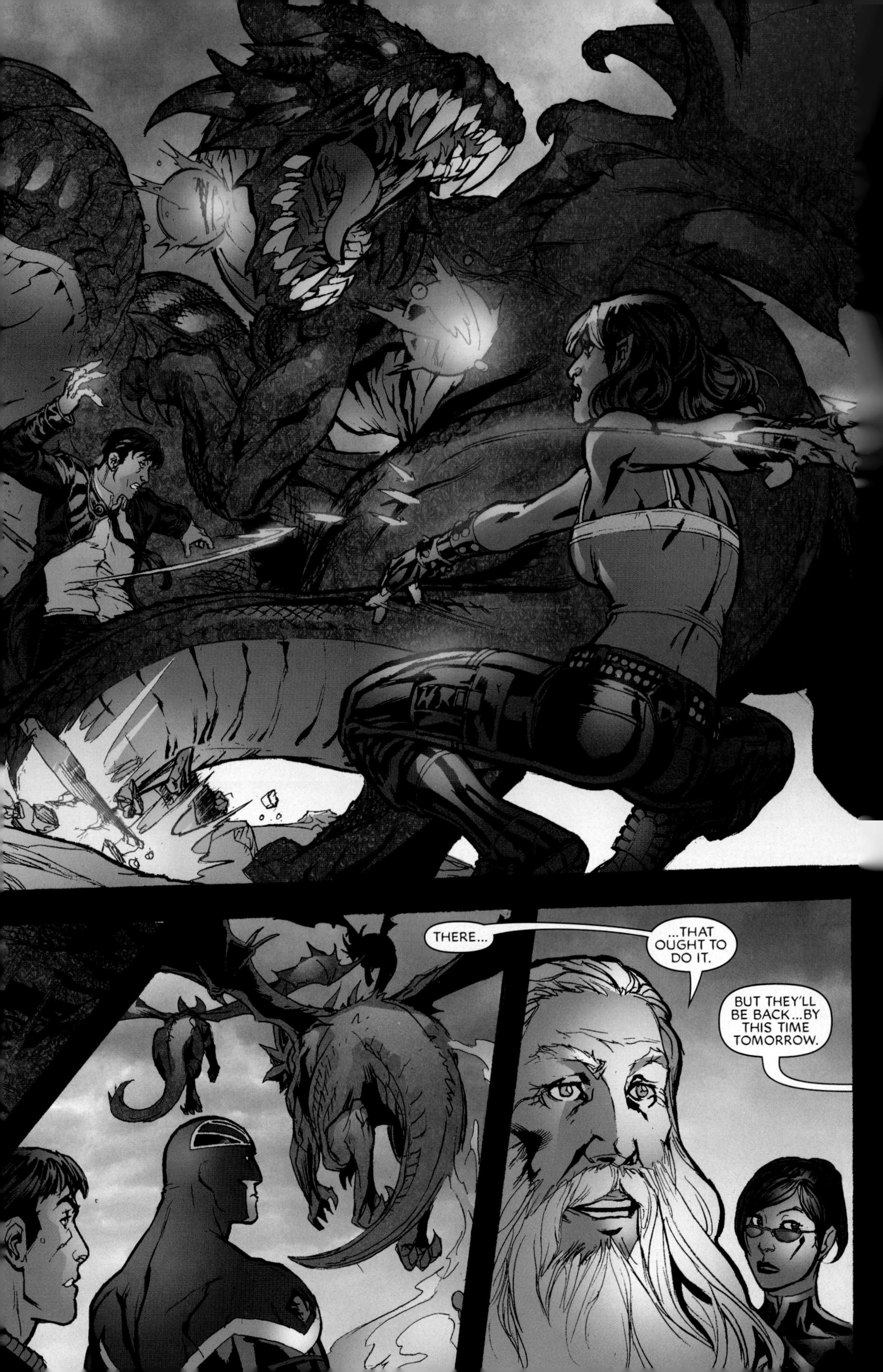
THERE...
...THAT OUGHT TO DO IT.
BUT THEY'LL BE BACK...BY THIS TIME TOMORROW.

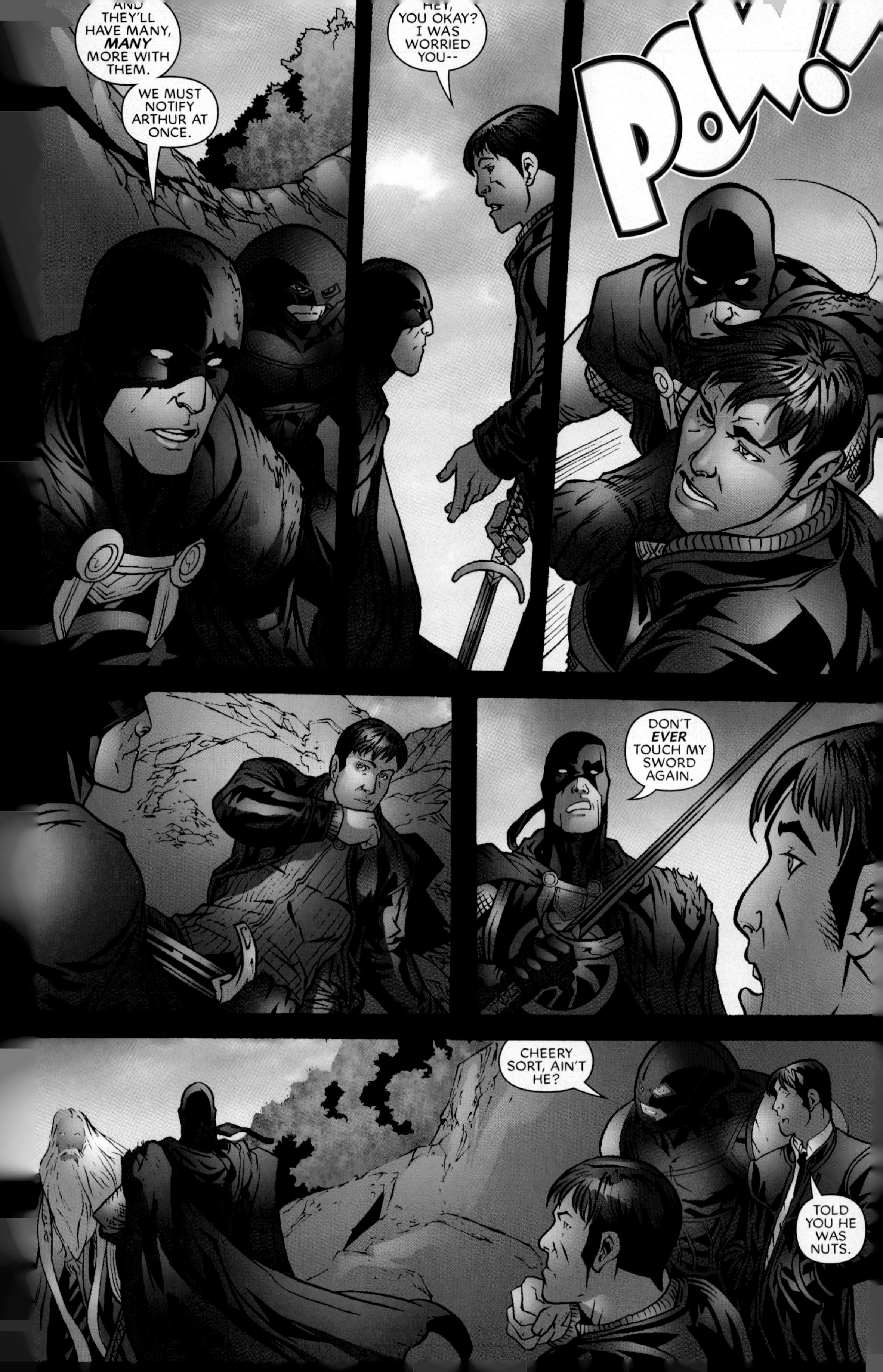
AND THEY'LL HAVE MANY, MANY MORE WITH THEM.
WE MUST NOTIFY ARTHUR AT ONCE.
HEY, YOU OKAY? I WAS WORRIED YOU--
POW!!
DON'T EVER TOUCH MY SWORD AGAIN.
CHEERY SORT, AIN'T HE?
TOLD YOU HE WAS NUTS.

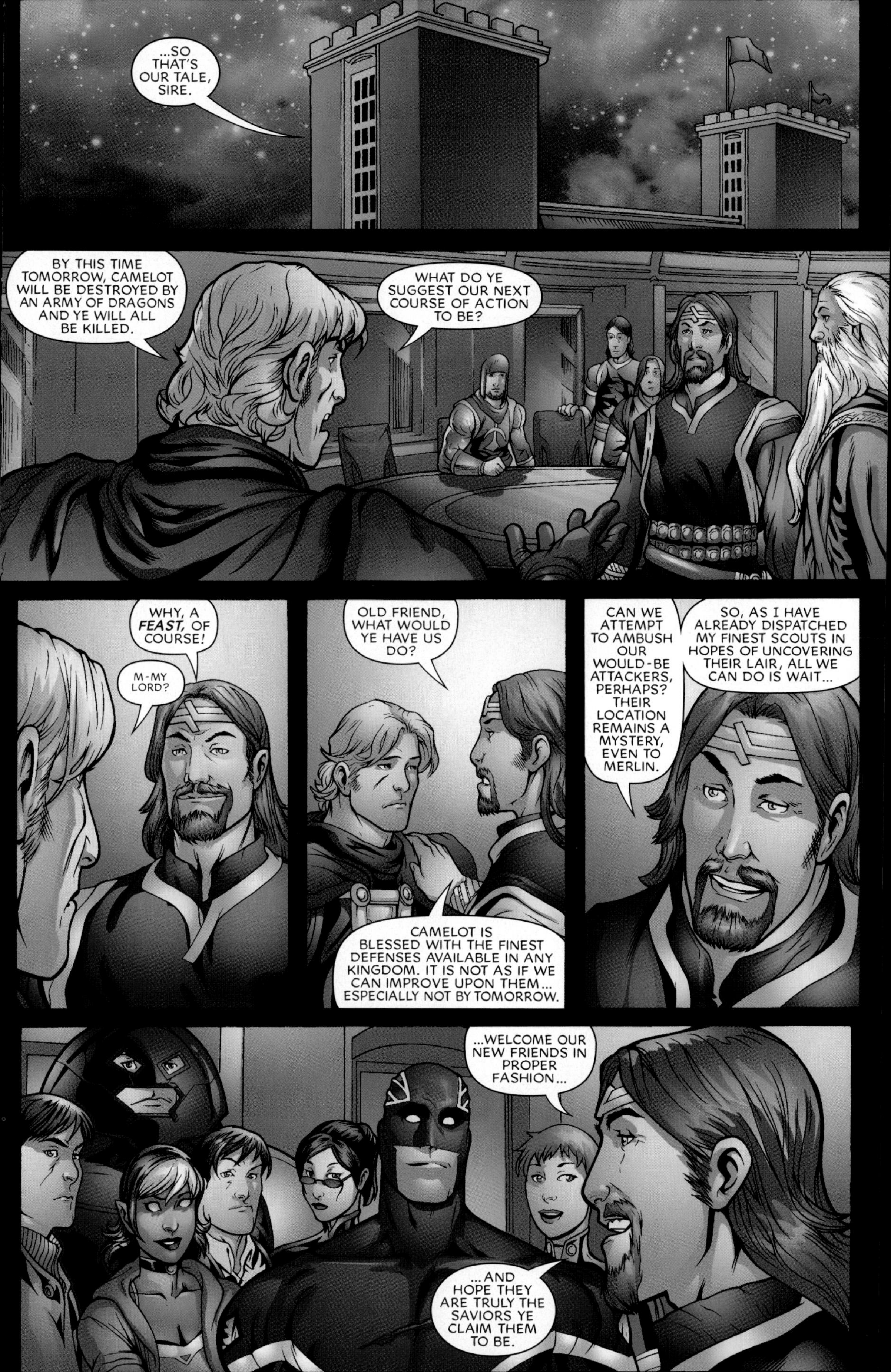
...SO THAT'S OUR TALE, SIRE.
BY THIS TIME TOMORROW, CAMELOT WILL BE DESTROYED BY AN ARMY OF DRAGONS AND YE WILL ALL BE KILLED.
WHAT DO YE SUGGEST OUR NEXT COURSE OF ACTION TO BE?
WHY, A FEAST, OF COURSE!
M-MY LORD?
OLD FRIEND, WHAT WOULD YE HAVE US DO?
CAMELOT IS BLESSED WITH THE FINEST DEFENSES AVAILABLE IN ANY KINGDOM. IT IS NOT AS IF WE CAN IMPROVE UPON THEM... ESPECIALLY NOT BY TOMORROW.
CAN WE ATTEMPT TO AMBUSH OUR WOULD-BE ATTACKERS, PERHAPS? THEIR LOCATION REMAINS A MYSTERY, EVEN TO MERLIN.
SO, AS I HAVE ALREADY DISPATCHED MY FINEST SCOUTS IN HOPES OF UNCOVERING THEIR LAIR, ALL WE CAN DO IS WAIT...
...WELCOME OUR NEW FRIENDS IN PROPER FASHION...
...AND HOPE THEY ARE TRULY THE SAVIORS YE CLAIM THEM TO BE.

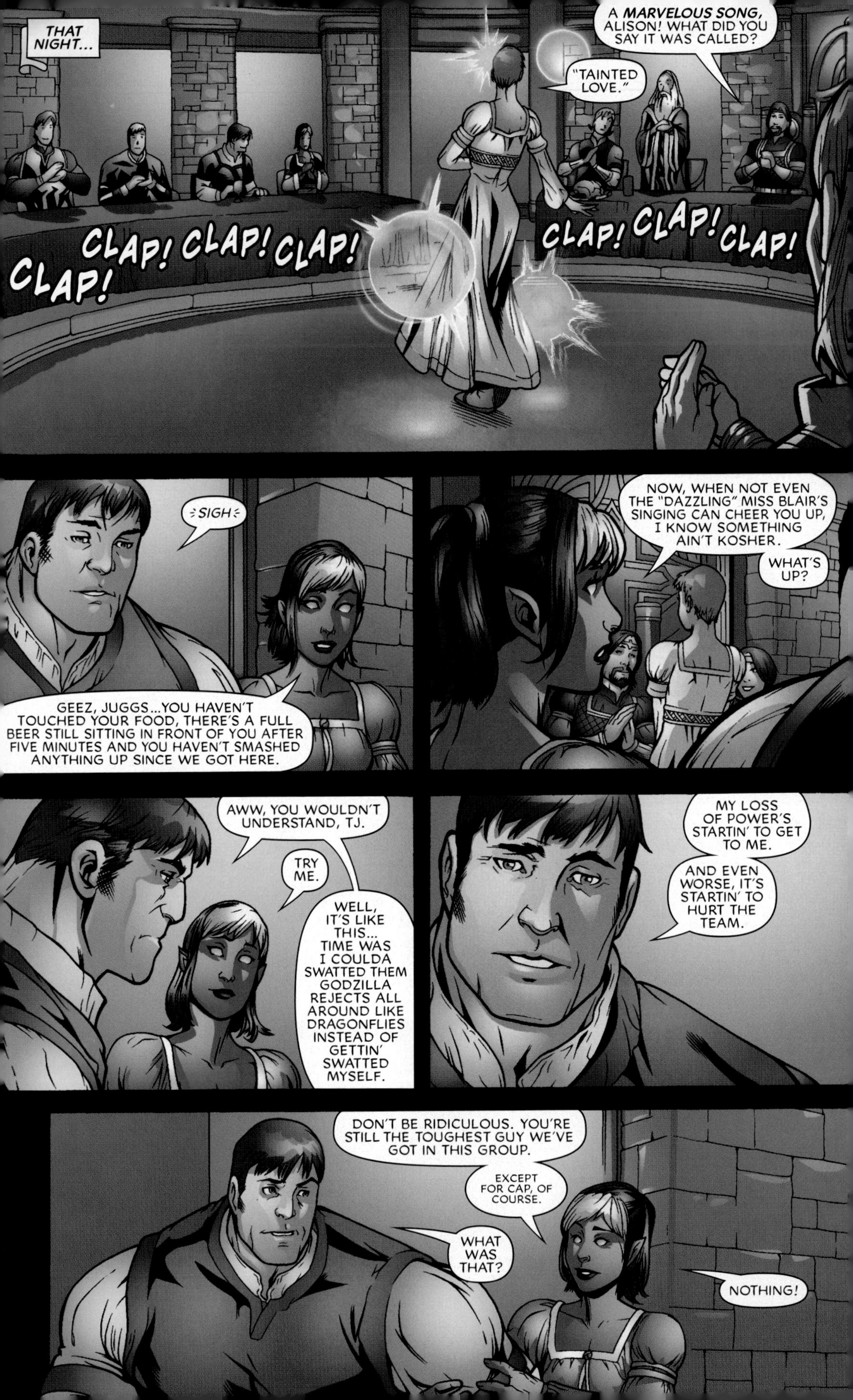
THAT NIGHT...
A MARVELOUS SONG, ALISON! WHAT DID YOU SAY IT WAS CALLED?
"TAINTED LOVE."
CLAP! CLAP! CLAP! CLAP!
CLAP! CLAP! CLAP!
SIGH
GEEZ, JUGGS...YOU HAVEN'T TOUCHED YOUR FOOD, THERE'S A FULL BEER STILL SITTING IN FRONT OF YOU AFTER FIVE MINUTES AND YOU HAVEN'T SMASHED ANYTHING UP SINCE WE GOT HERE.
NOW, WHEN NOT EVEN THE "DAZZLING" MISS BLAIR'S SINGING CAN CHEER YOU UP, I KNOW SOMETHING AIN'T KOSHER.
WHAT'S UP?
AWW, YOU WOULDN'T UNDERSTAND, TJ.
TRY ME.
WELL, IT'S LIKE THIS... TIME WAS I COULDA SWATTED THEM GODZILLA REJECTS ALL AROUND LIKE DRAGONFLIES INSTEAD OF GETTIN' SWATTED MYSELF.
MY LOSS OF POWER'S STARTIN' TO GET TO ME.
AND EVEN WORSE, IT'S STARTIN' TO HURT THE TEAM.
DON'T BE RIDICULOUS. YOU'RE STILL THE TOUGHEST GUY WE'VE GOT IN THIS GROUP.
EXCEPT FOR CAP, OF COURSE.
WHAT WAS THAT?
NOTHING!

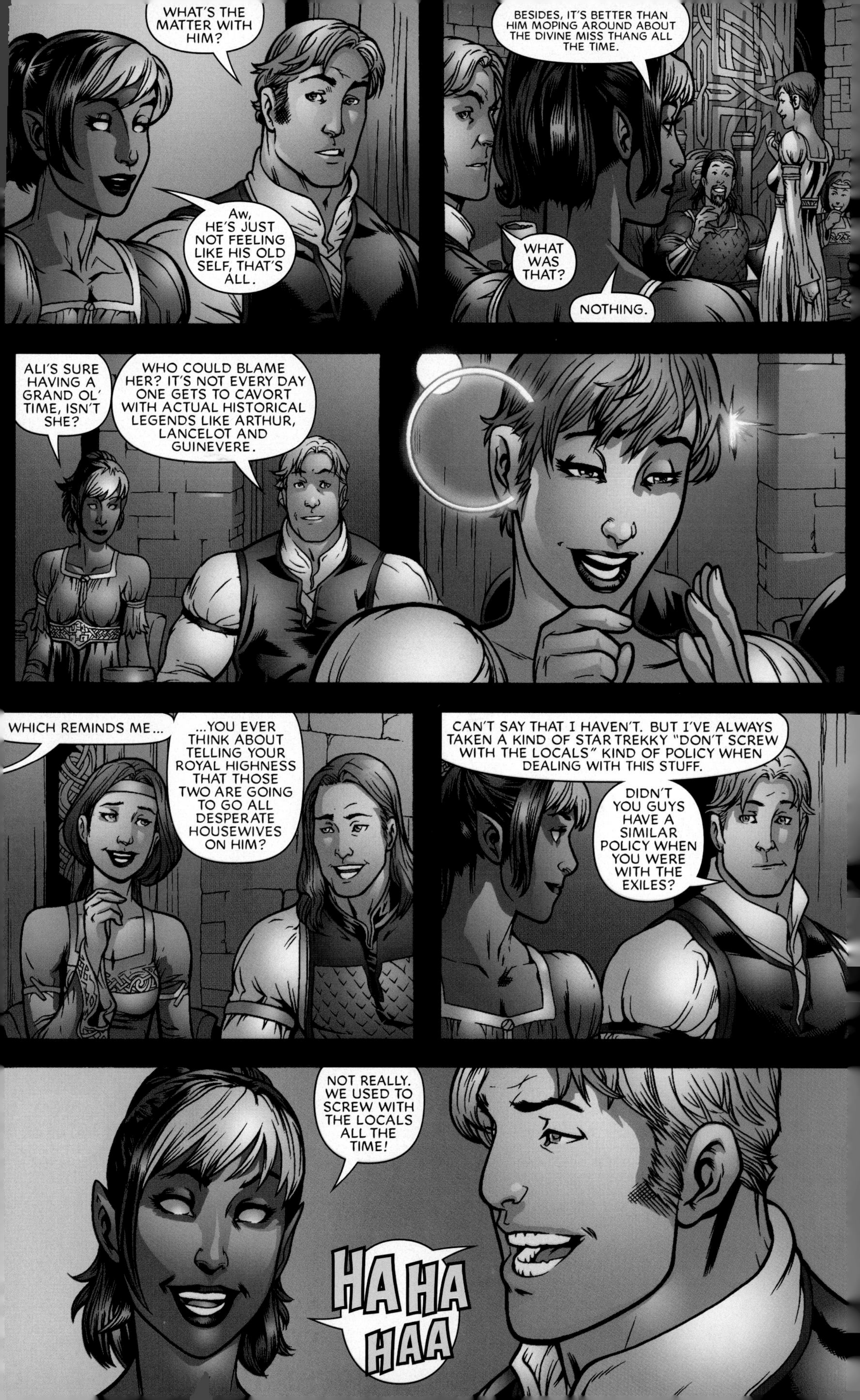

WHAT'S THE MATTER WITH HIM?
Aw, HE'S JUST NOT FEELING LIKE HIS OLD SELF, THAT'S ALL.
BESIDES, IT'S BETTER THAN HIM MOPING AROUND ABOUT THE DIVINE MISS THANG ALL THE TIME.
WHAT WAS THAT?
NOTHING.
ALI'S SURE HAVING A GRAND OL' TIME, ISN'T SHE?
WHO COULD BLAME HER? IT'S NOT EVERY DAY ONE GETS TO CAVORT WITH ACTUAL HISTORICAL LEGENDS LIKE ARTHUR, LANCELOT AND GUINEVERE.
WHICH REMINDS ME...
...YOU EVER THINK ABOUT TELLING YOUR ROYAL HIGHNESS THAT THOSE TWO ARE GOING TO GO ALL DESPERATE HOUSEWIVES ON HIM?
CAN'T SAY THAT I HAVEN'T. BUT I'VE ALWAYS TAKEN A KIND OF STAR TREKKY "DON'T SCREW WITH THE LOCALS" KIND OF POLICY WHEN DEALING WITH THIS STUFF.
DIDN'T YOU GUYS HAVE A SIMILAR POLICY WHEN YOU WERE WITH THE EXILES?
NOT REALLY. WE USED TO SCREW WITH THE LOCALS ALL THE TIME!
HA HA HA HAA

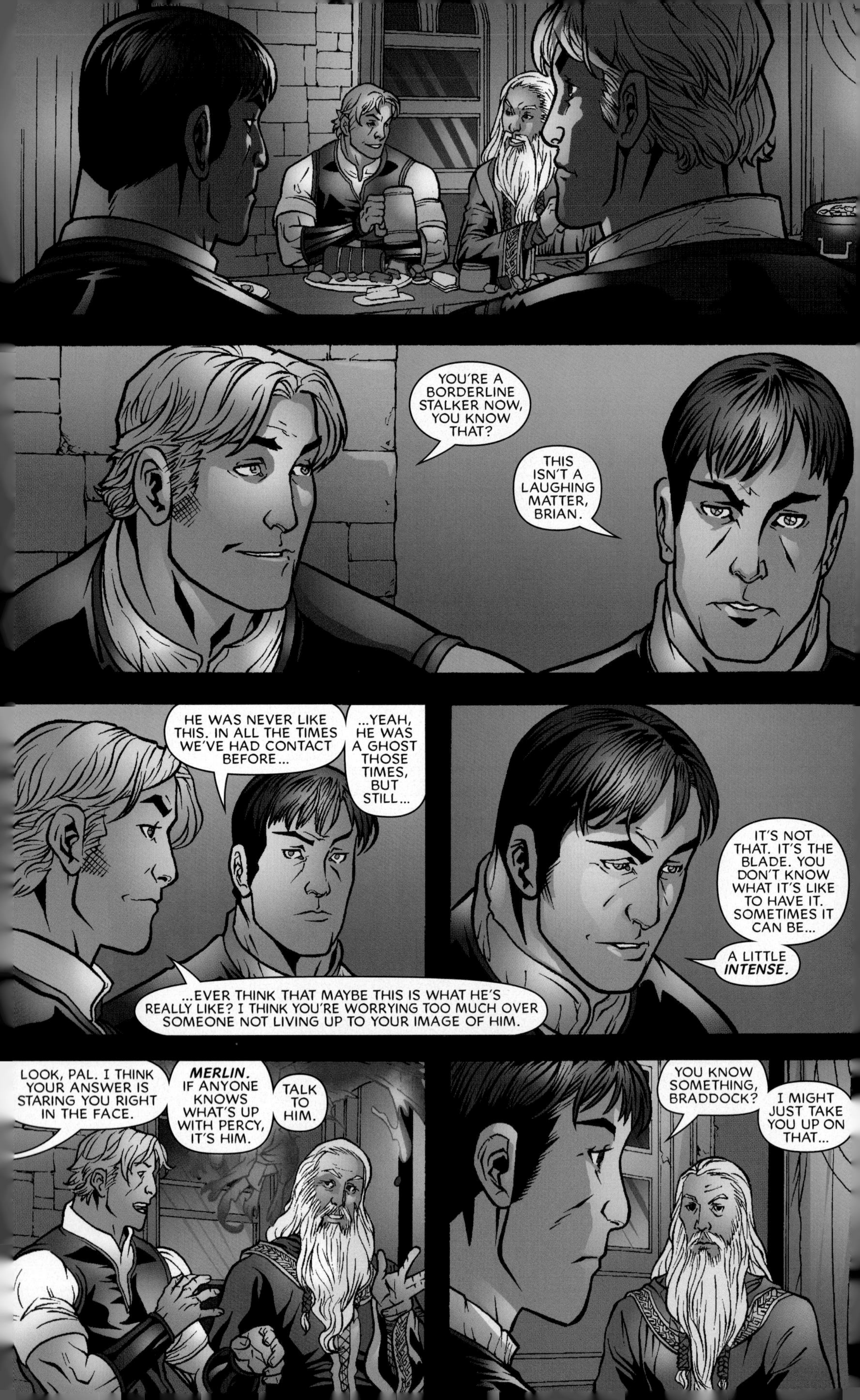
YOU'RE A BORDERLINE STALKER NOW, YOU KNOW THAT?
THIS ISN'T A LAUGHING MATTER, BRIAN.
HE WAS NEVER LIKE THIS. IN ALL THE TIMES WE'VE HAD CONTACT BEFORE...
...YEAH, HE WAS A GHOST THOSE TIMES, BUT STILL...
...EVER THINK THAT MAYBE THIS IS WHAT HE'S REALLY LIKE? I THINK YOU'RE WORRYING TOO MUCH OVER SOMEONE NOT LIVING UP TO YOUR IMAGE OF HIM.
IT'S NOT THAT. IT'S THE BLADE. YOU DON'T KNOW WHAT IT'S LIKE TO HAVE IT. SOMETIMES IT CAN BE...
A LITTLE ***INTENSE***.
LOOK, PAL. I THINK YOUR ANSWER IS STARING YOU RIGHT IN THE FACE.
MERLIN. IF ANYONE KNOWS WHAT'S UP WITH PERCY, IT'S HIM.
TALK TO HIM.
YOU KNOW SOMETHING, BRADDOCK?
I MIGHT JUST TAKE YOU UP ON THAT...

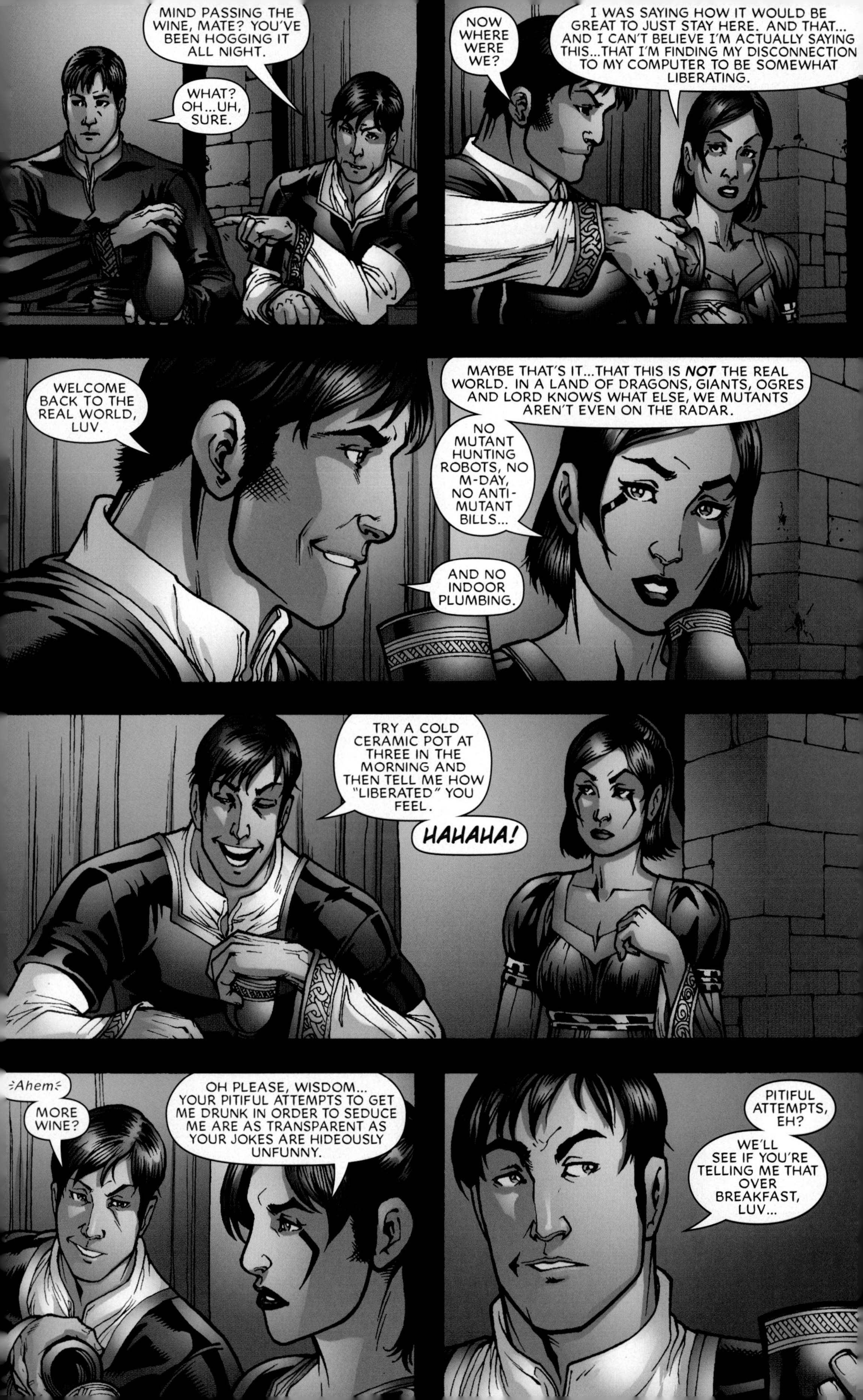
MIND PASSING THE WINE, MATE? YOU'VE BEEN HOGGING IT ALL NIGHT.
WHAT? OH...UH, SURE.
NOW WHERE WERE WE?
I WAS SAYING HOW IT WOULD BE GREAT TO JUST STAY HERE. AND THAT... AND I CAN'T BELIEVE I'M ACTUALLY SAYING THIS...THAT I'M FINDING MY DISCONNECTION TO MY COMPUTER TO BE SOMEWHAT LIBERATING.
WELCOME BACK TO THE REAL WORLD, LUV.
MAYBE THAT'S IT...THAT THIS IS *NOT* THE REAL WORLD. IN A LAND OF DRAGONS, GIANTS, OGRES AND LORD KNOWS WHAT ELSE, WE MUTANTS AREN'T EVEN ON THE RADAR.
NO MUTANT HUNTING ROBOTS, NO M-DAY, NO ANTI-MUTANT BILLS...
AND NO INDOOR PLUMBING.
TRY A COLD CERAMIC POT AT THREE IN THE MORNING AND THEN TELL ME HOW "LIBERATED" YOU FEEL.
HAHAHA!
Ahem
MORE WINE?
OH PLEASE, WISDOM... YOUR PITIFUL ATTEMPTS TO GET ME DRUNK IN ORDER TO SEDUCE ME ARE AS TRANSPARENT AS YOUR JOKES ARE HIDEOUSLY UNFUNNY.
PITIFUL ATTEMPTS, EH?
WE'LL SEE IF YOU'RE TELLING ME THAT OVER BREAKFAST, LUV...

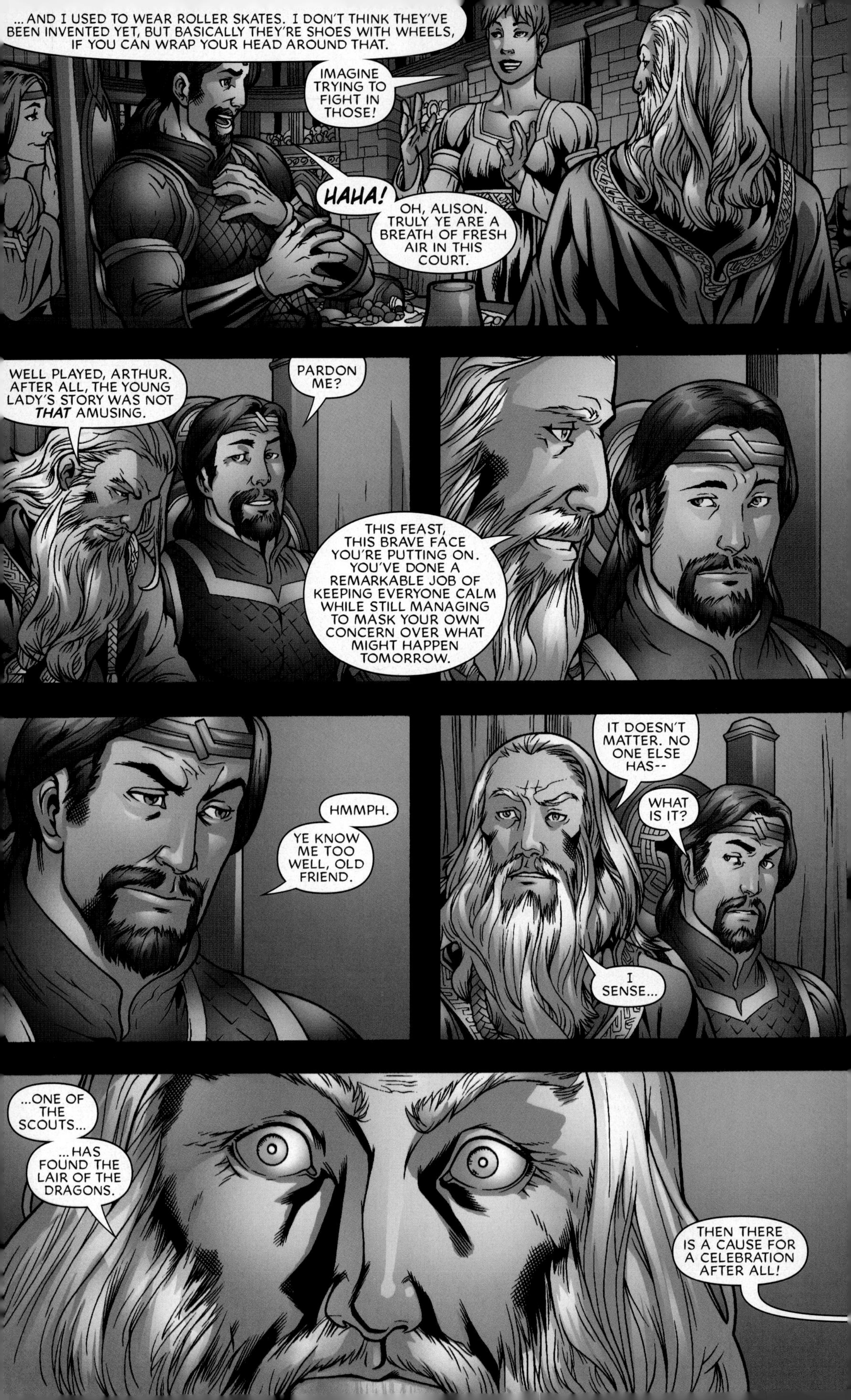
...AND I USED TO WEAR ROLLER SKATES. I DON'T THINK THEY'VE BEEN INVENTED YET, BUT BASICALLY THEY'RE SHOES WITH WHEELS, IF YOU CAN WRAP YOUR HEAD AROUND THAT.
IMAGINE TRYING TO FIGHT IN THOSE!
HAHA!
OH, ALISON. TRULY YE ARE A BREATH OF FRESH AIR IN THIS COURT.
WELL PLAYED, ARTHUR. AFTER ALL, THE YOUNG LADY'S STORY WAS NOT THAT AMUSING.
PARDON ME?
THIS FEAST, THIS BRAVE FACE YOU'RE PUTTING ON. YOU'VE DONE A REMARKABLE JOB OF KEEPING EVERYONE CALM WHILE STILL MANAGING TO MASK YOUR OWN CONCERN OVER WHAT MIGHT HAPPEN TOMORROW.
HMMPH.
YE KNOW ME TOO WELL, OLD FRIEND.
IT DOESN'T MATTER. NO ONE ELSE HAS--
WHAT IS IT?
I SENSE...
...ONE OF THE SCOUTS...
...HAS FOUND THE LAIR OF THE DRAGONS.
THEN THERE IS A CAUSE FOR A CELEBRATION AFTER ALL!

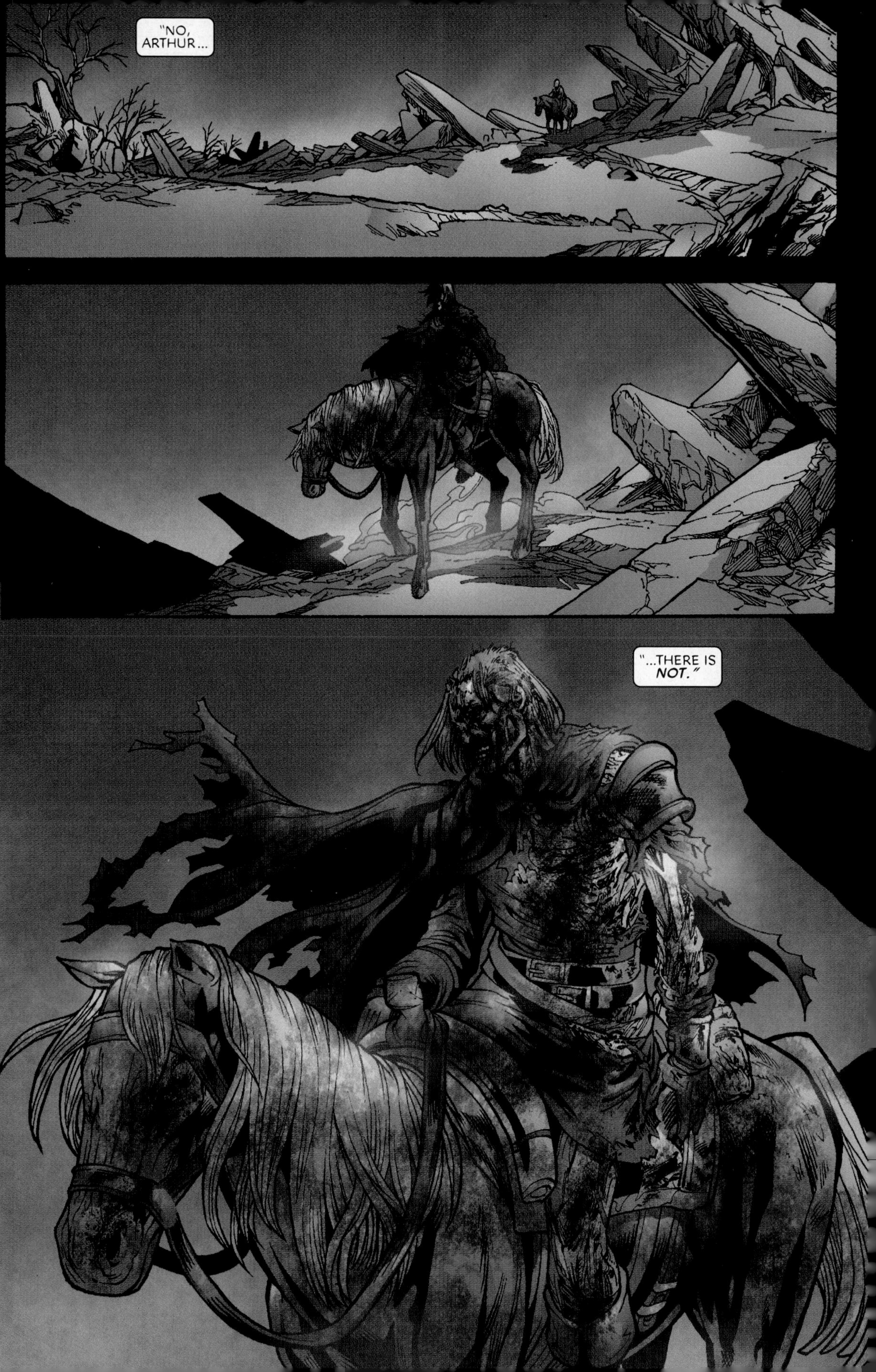
"NO, ARTHUR...
"...THERE IS *NOT.*"

#12

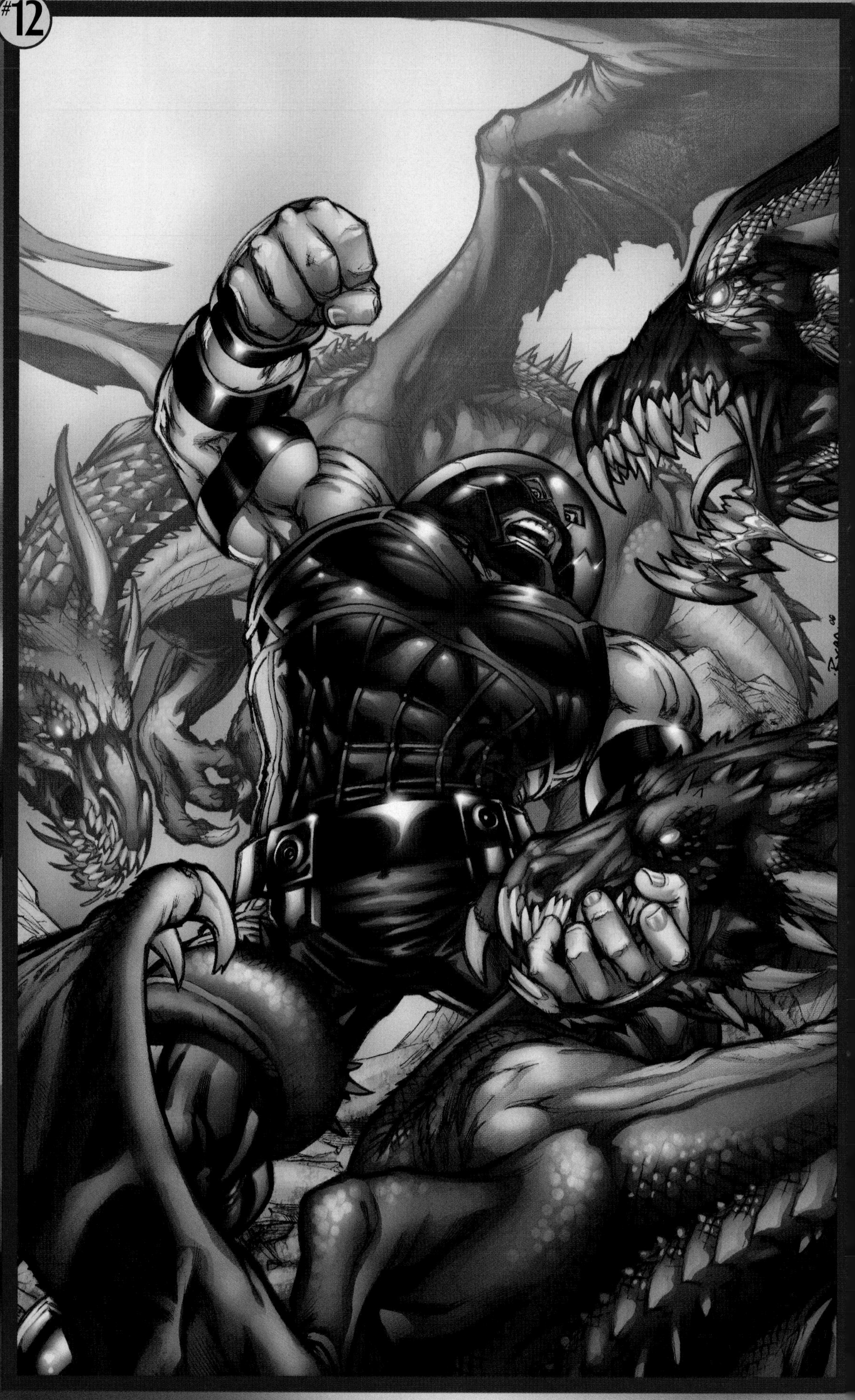

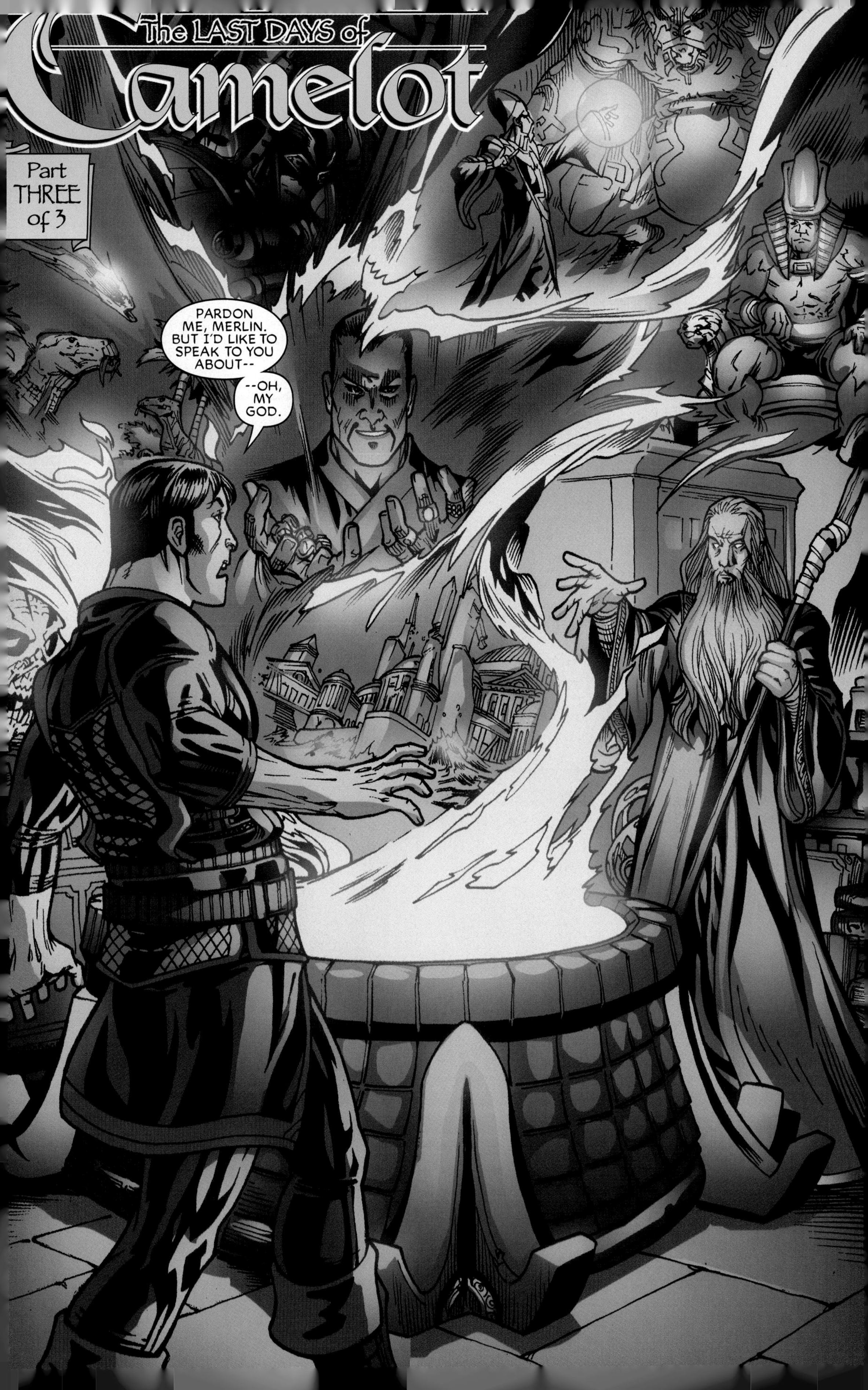

The LAST DAYS of Camelot
Part THREE of 3
PARDON ME, MERLIN. BUT I'D LIKE TO SPEAK TO YOU ABOUT--
--OH, MY GOD.

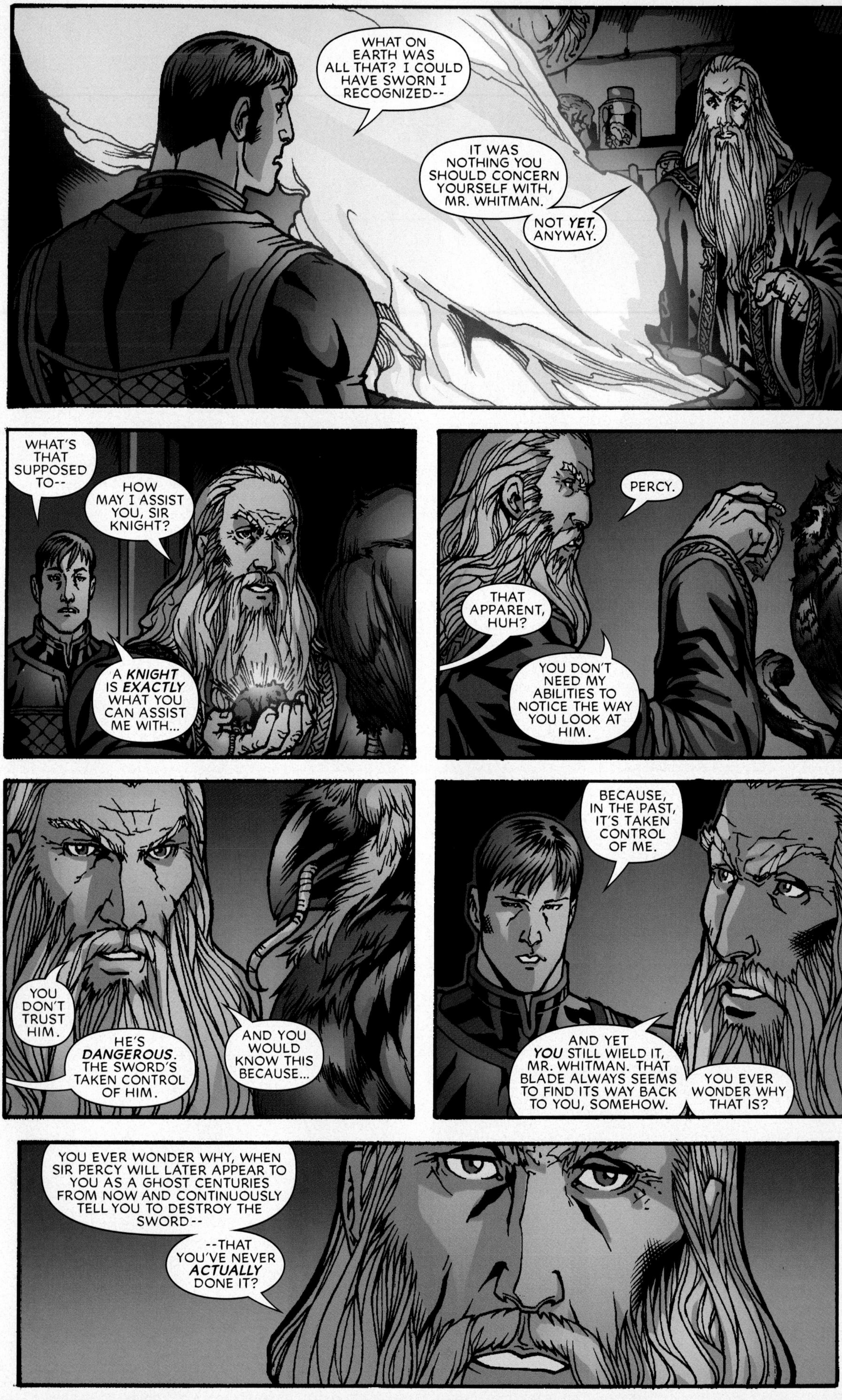
WHAT ON EARTH WAS ALL THAT? I COULD HAVE SWORN I RECOGNIZED--
IT WAS NOTHING YOU SHOULD CONCERN YOURSELF WITH, MR. WHITMAN.
NOT YET, ANYWAY.
WHAT'S THAT SUPPOSED TO--
HOW MAY I ASSIST YOU, SIR KNIGHT?
A KNIGHT IS EXACTLY WHAT YOU CAN ASSIST ME WITH...
PERCY.
THAT APPARENT, HUH?
YOU DON'T NEED MY ABILITIES TO NOTICE THE WAY YOU LOOK AT HIM.
YOU DON'T TRUST HIM.
HE'S DANGEROUS. THE SWORD'S TAKEN CONTROL OF HIM.
AND YOU WOULD KNOW THIS BECAUSE...
BECAUSE, IN THE PAST, IT'S TAKEN CONTROL OF ME.
AND YET YOU STILL WIELD IT, MR. WHITMAN. THAT BLADE ALWAYS SEEMS TO FIND ITS WAY BACK TO YOU, SOMEHOW.
YOU EVER WONDER WHY THAT IS?
YOU EVER WONDER WHY, WHEN SIR PERCY WILL LATER APPEAR TO YOU AS A GHOST CENTURIES FROM NOW AND CONTINUOUSLY TELL YOU TO DESTROY THE SWORD--
--THAT YOU'VE NEVER ACTUALLY DONE IT?

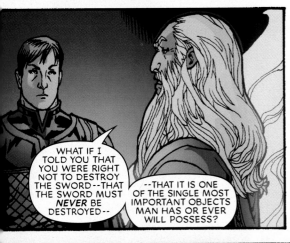

WHAT IF I TOLD YOU THAT YOU WERE RIGHT NOT TO DESTROY THE SWORD--THAT THE SWORD MUST *NEVER* BE DESTROYED--

--THAT IT IS ONE OF THE SINGLE MOST IMPORTANT OBJECTS MAN HAS OR EVER WILL POSSESS?

WHAT IF I TOLD YOU PERCY'S GHOST WAS LYING?

THAT HE WILL BECOME SO CORRUPTED BY THE SWORD THAT IT WILL AFFECT HIM BEYOND THE GRAVE...TO THE POINT WHERE HE'D RATHER SEE IT DESTROYED THAN HELD BY ANOTHER?

YOU WOULDN'T BE SURPRISED BY ANY OF THIS, MR. WHITMAN...

...WOULD YOU?

NO.

I GUESS DEEP DOWN, SOMEWAY... SOMEHOW, I'VE ALWAYS KNOWN IT.

BUT IF YOU KNOW PERCY WILL LIE ABOUT THE SWORD, THAT HE'LL TRY TO DESTROY IT... WHY DO YOU ALLOW HIM TO STILL POSSESS IT?

WHY DON'T YOU ASK HIM, YOUR-SELF?

WHAT?

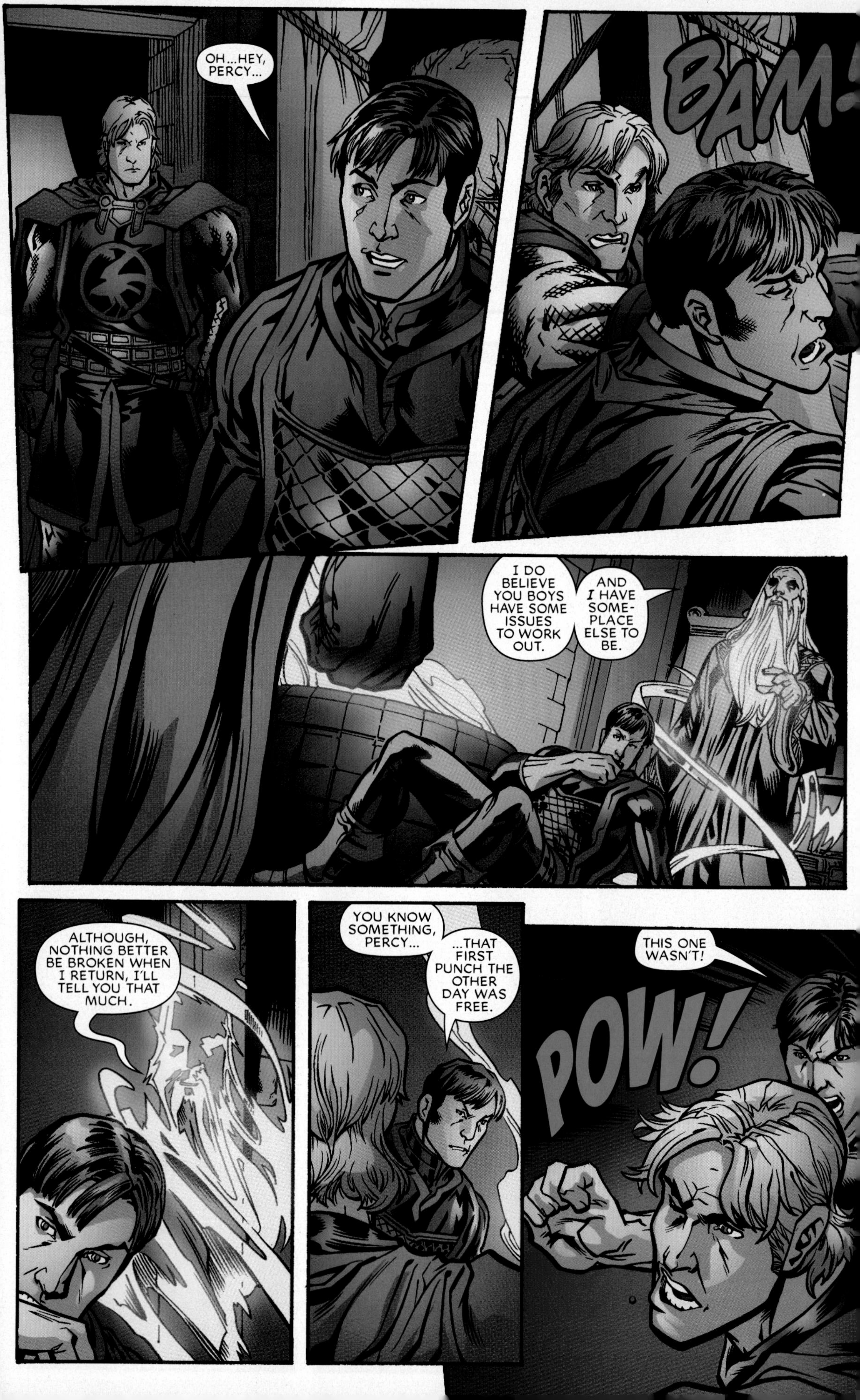
OH...HEY, PERCY...
BAM!
I DO BELIEVE YOU BOYS HAVE SOME ISSUES TO WORK OUT.
AND I HAVE SOME-PLACE ELSE TO BE.
ALTHOUGH, NOTHING BETTER BE BROKEN WHEN I RETURN, I'LL TELL YOU THAT MUCH.
YOU KNOW SOMETHING, PERCY...
...THAT FIRST PUNCH THE OTHER DAY WAS FREE.
THIS ONE WASN'T!
POW!

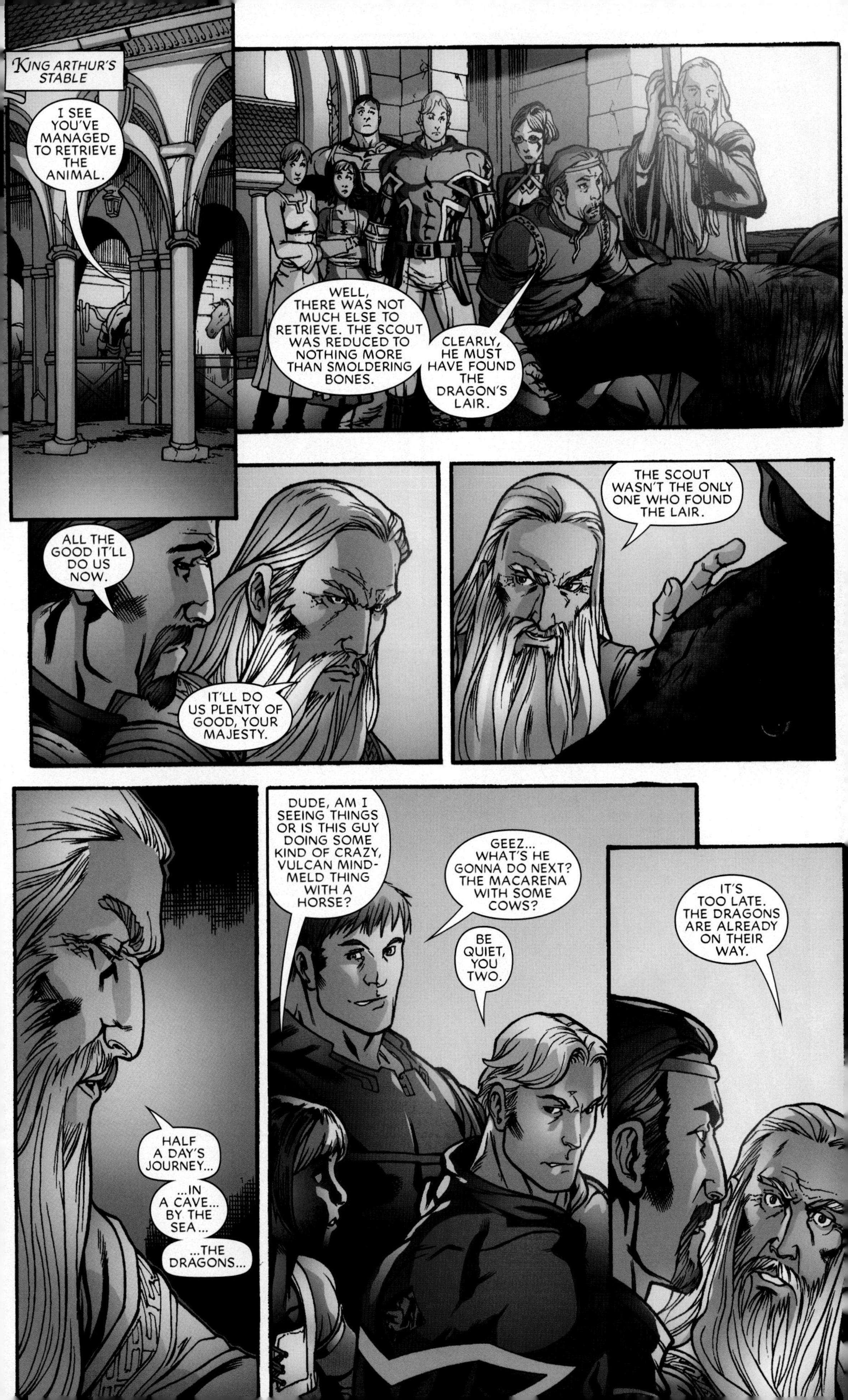
KING ARTHUR'S STABLE
I SEE YOU'VE MANAGED TO RETRIEVE THE ANIMAL.
WELL, THERE WAS NOT MUCH ELSE TO RETRIEVE. THE SCOUT WAS REDUCED TO NOTHING MORE THAN SMOLDERING BONES.
CLEARLY, HE MUST HAVE FOUND THE DRAGON'S LAIR.
ALL THE GOOD IT'LL DO US NOW.
IT'LL DO US PLENTY OF GOOD, YOUR MAJESTY.
THE SCOUT WASN'T THE ONLY ONE WHO FOUND THE LAIR.
HALF A DAY'S JOURNEY...
...IN A CAVE... BY THE SEA...
...THE DRAGONS...
DUDE, AM I SEEING THINGS OR IS THIS GUY DOING SOME KIND OF CRAZY, VULCAN MIND-MELD THING WITH A HORSE?
GEEZ... WHAT'S HE GONNA DO NEXT? THE MACARENA WITH SOME COWS?
BE QUIET, YOU TWO.
IT'S TOO LATE. THE DRAGONS ARE ALREADY ON THEIR WAY.

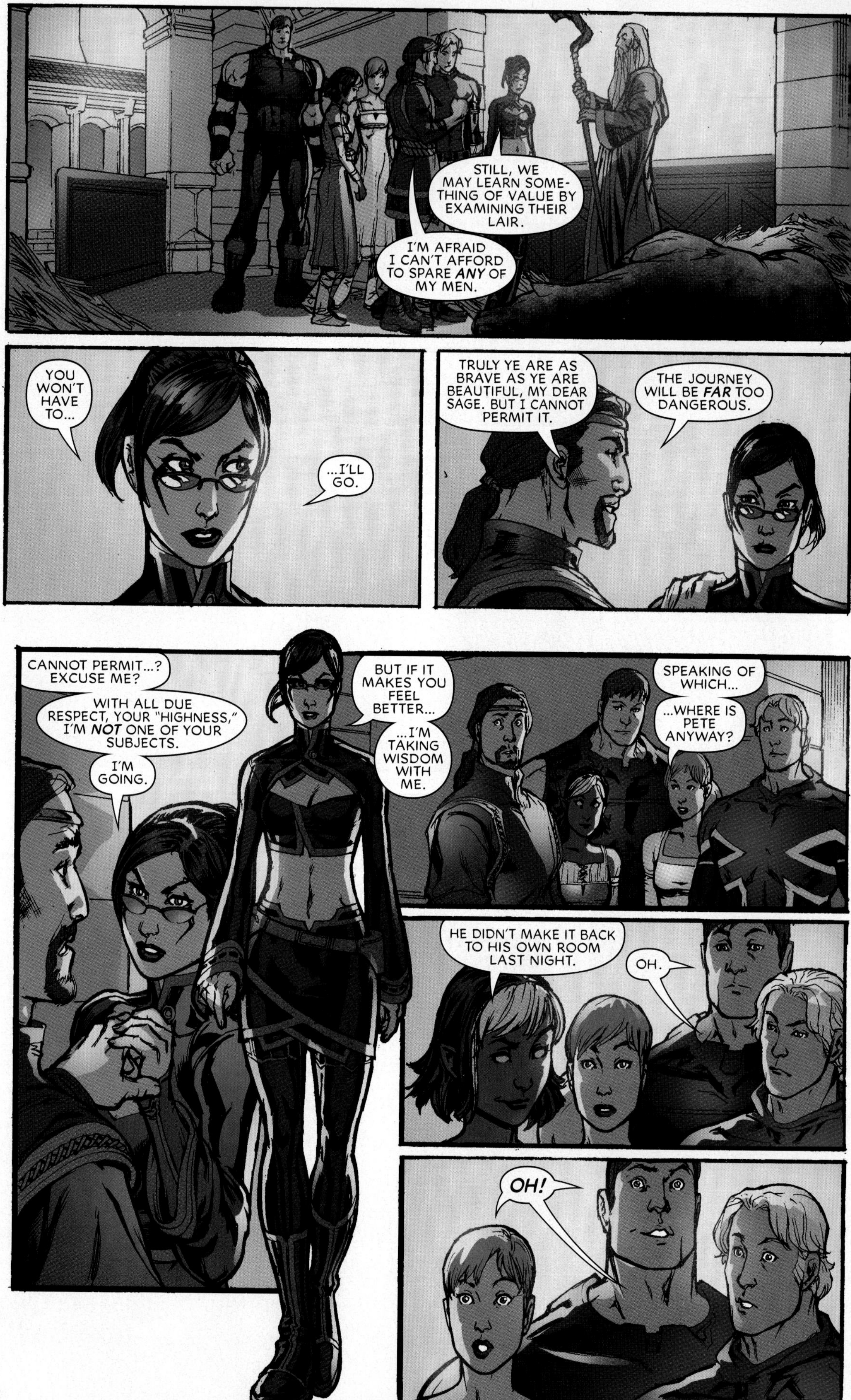
STILL, WE MAY LEARN SOME-THING OF VALUE BY EXAMINING THEIR LAIR.
I'M AFRAID I CAN'T AFFORD TO SPARE ANY OF MY MEN.
YOU WON'T HAVE TO...
...I'LL GO.
TRULY YE ARE AS BRAVE AS YE ARE BEAUTIFUL, MY DEAR SAGE. BUT I CANNOT PERMIT IT.
THE JOURNEY WILL BE FAR TOO DANGEROUS.
CANNOT PERMIT...? EXCUSE ME?
WITH ALL DUE RESPECT, YOUR "HIGHNESS," I'M NOT ONE OF YOUR SUBJECTS.
I'M GOING.
BUT IF IT MAKES YOU FEEL BETTER...
...I'M TAKING WISDOM WITH ME.
SPEAKING OF WHICH...
...WHERE IS PETE ANYWAY?
HE DIDN'T MAKE IT BACK TO HIS OWN ROOM LAST NIGHT.
OH.
OH!

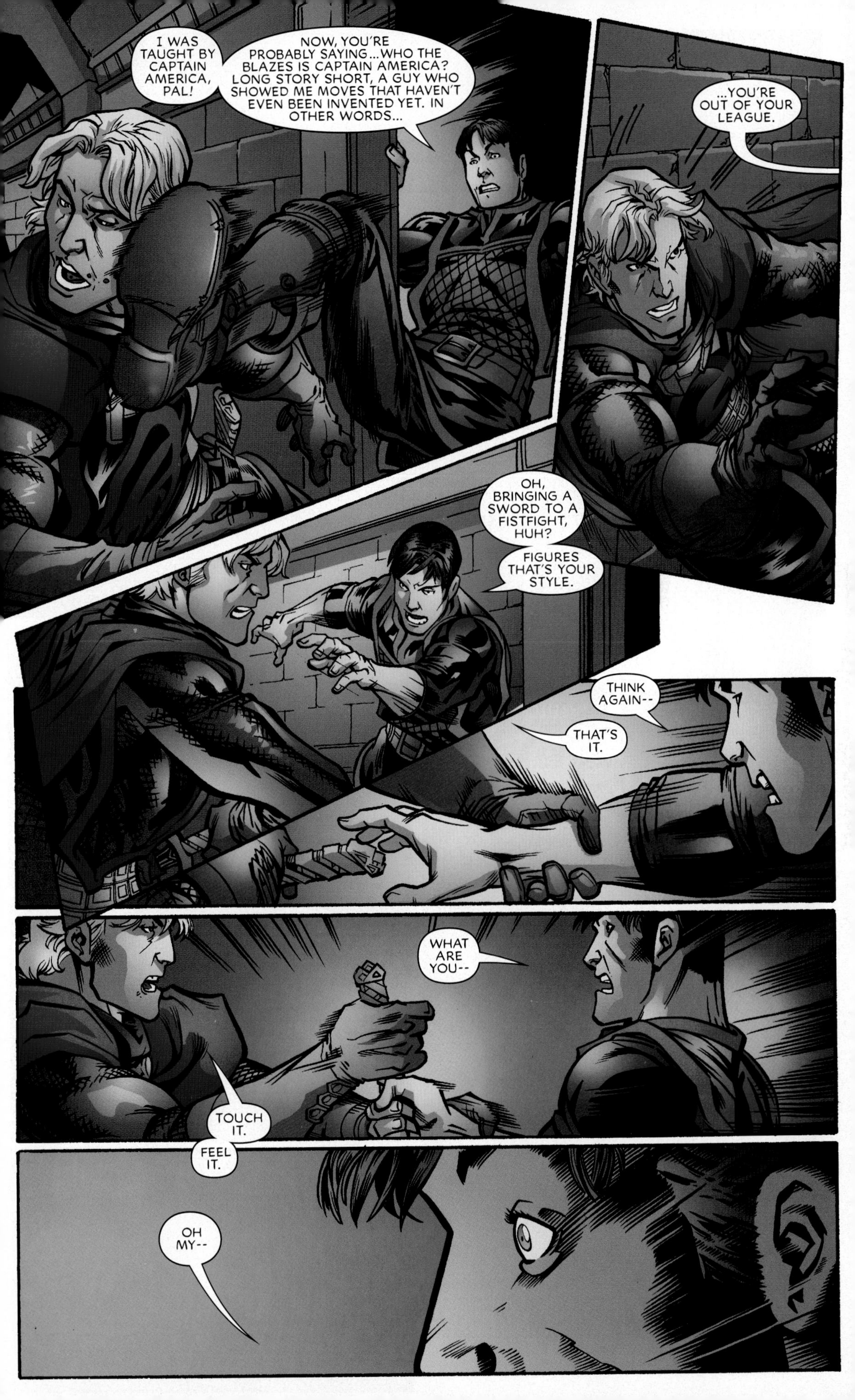
I WAS TAUGHT BY CAPTAIN AMERICA, PAL!
NOW, YOU'RE PROBABLY SAYING...WHO THE BLAZES IS CAPTAIN AMERICA? LONG STORY SHORT, A GUY WHO SHOWED ME MOVES THAT HAVEN'T EVEN BEEN INVENTED YET. IN OTHER WORDS...
...YOU'RE OUT OF YOUR LEAGUE.
OH, BRINGING A SWORD TO A FISTFIGHT, HUH?
FIGURES THAT'S YOUR STYLE.
THINK AGAIN--
THAT'S IT.
WHAT ARE YOU--
TOUCH IT.
FEEL IT.
OH MY--

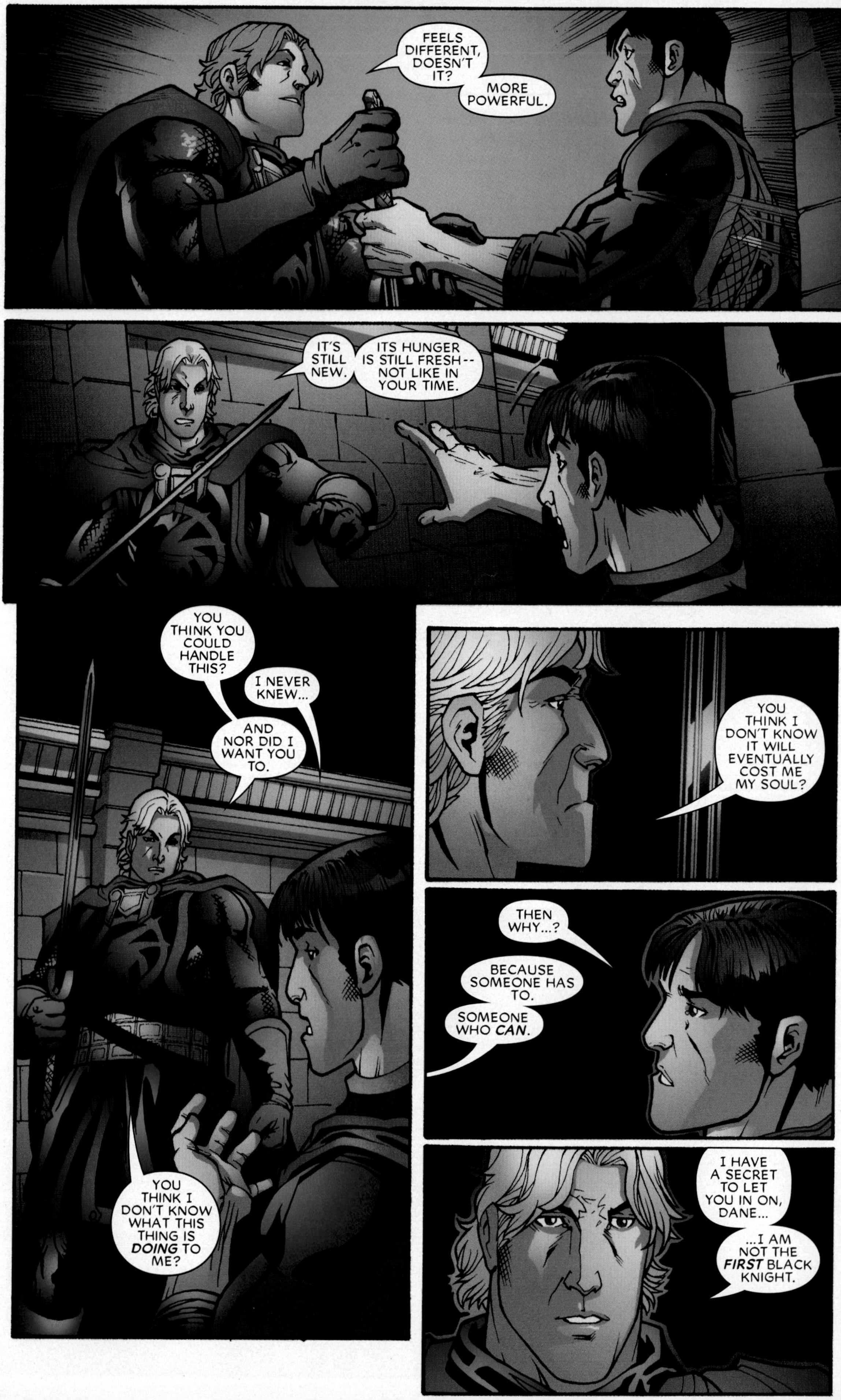
FEELS DIFFERENT, DOESN'T IT?
MORE POWERFUL.
IT'S STILL NEW.
ITS HUNGER IS STILL FRESH-- NOT LIKE IN YOUR TIME.
YOU THINK YOU COULD HANDLE THIS?
I NEVER KNEW...
AND NOR DID I WANT YOU TO.
YOU THINK I DON'T KNOW WHAT THIS THING IS DOING TO ME?
YOU THINK I DON'T KNOW IT WILL EVENTUALLY COST ME MY SOUL?
THEN WHY...?
BECAUSE SOMEONE HAS TO.
SOMEONE WHO CAN.
I HAVE A SECRET TO LET YOU IN ON, DANE...
...I AM NOT THE FIRST BLACK KNIGHT.

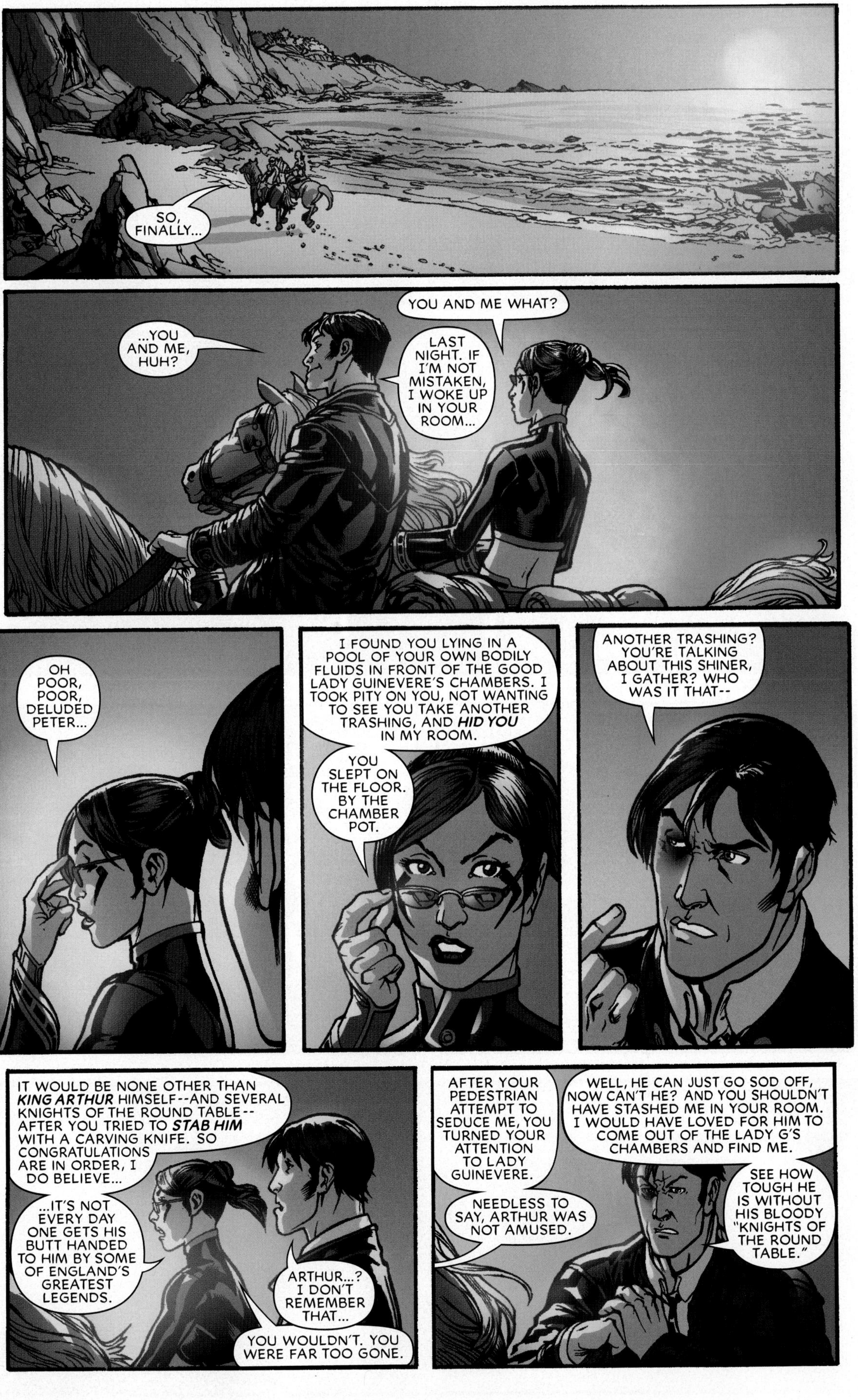
SO, FINALLY...
...YOU AND ME, HUH?
YOU AND ME WHAT?
LAST NIGHT. IF I'M NOT MISTAKEN, I WOKE UP IN YOUR ROOM...
OH POOR, POOR, DELUDED PETER...
I FOUND YOU LYING IN A POOL OF YOUR OWN BODILY FLUIDS IN FRONT OF THE GOOD LADY GUINEVERE'S CHAMBERS. I TOOK PITY ON YOU, NOT WANTING TO SEE YOU TAKE ANOTHER TRASHING, AND HID YOU IN MY ROOM.
YOU SLEPT ON THE FLOOR. BY THE CHAMBER POT.
ANOTHER TRASHING? YOU'RE TALKING ABOUT THIS SHINER, I GATHER? WHO WAS IT THAT--
IT WOULD BE NONE OTHER THAN KING ARTHUR HIMSELF--AND SEVERAL KNIGHTS OF THE ROUND TABLE--AFTER YOU TRIED TO STAB HIM WITH A CARVING KNIFE. SO CONGRATULATIONS ARE IN ORDER, I DO BELIEVE...
...IT'S NOT EVERY DAY ONE GETS HIS BUTT HANDED TO HIM BY SOME OF ENGLAND'S GREATEST LEGENDS.
ARTHUR...? I DON'T REMEMBER THAT...
YOU WOULDN'T. YOU WERE FAR TOO GONE.
AFTER YOUR PEDESTRIAN ATTEMPT TO SEDUCE ME, YOU TURNED YOUR ATTENTION TO LADY GUINEVERE.
NEEDLESS TO SAY, ARTHUR WAS NOT AMUSED.
WELL, HE CAN JUST GO SOD OFF, NOW CAN'T HE? AND YOU SHOULDN'T HAVE STASHED ME IN YOUR ROOM. I WOULD HAVE LOVED FOR HIM TO COME OUT OF THE LADY G'S CHAMBERS AND FIND ME.
SEE HOW TOUGH HE IS WITHOUT HIS BLOODY "KNIGHTS OF THE ROUND TABLE."

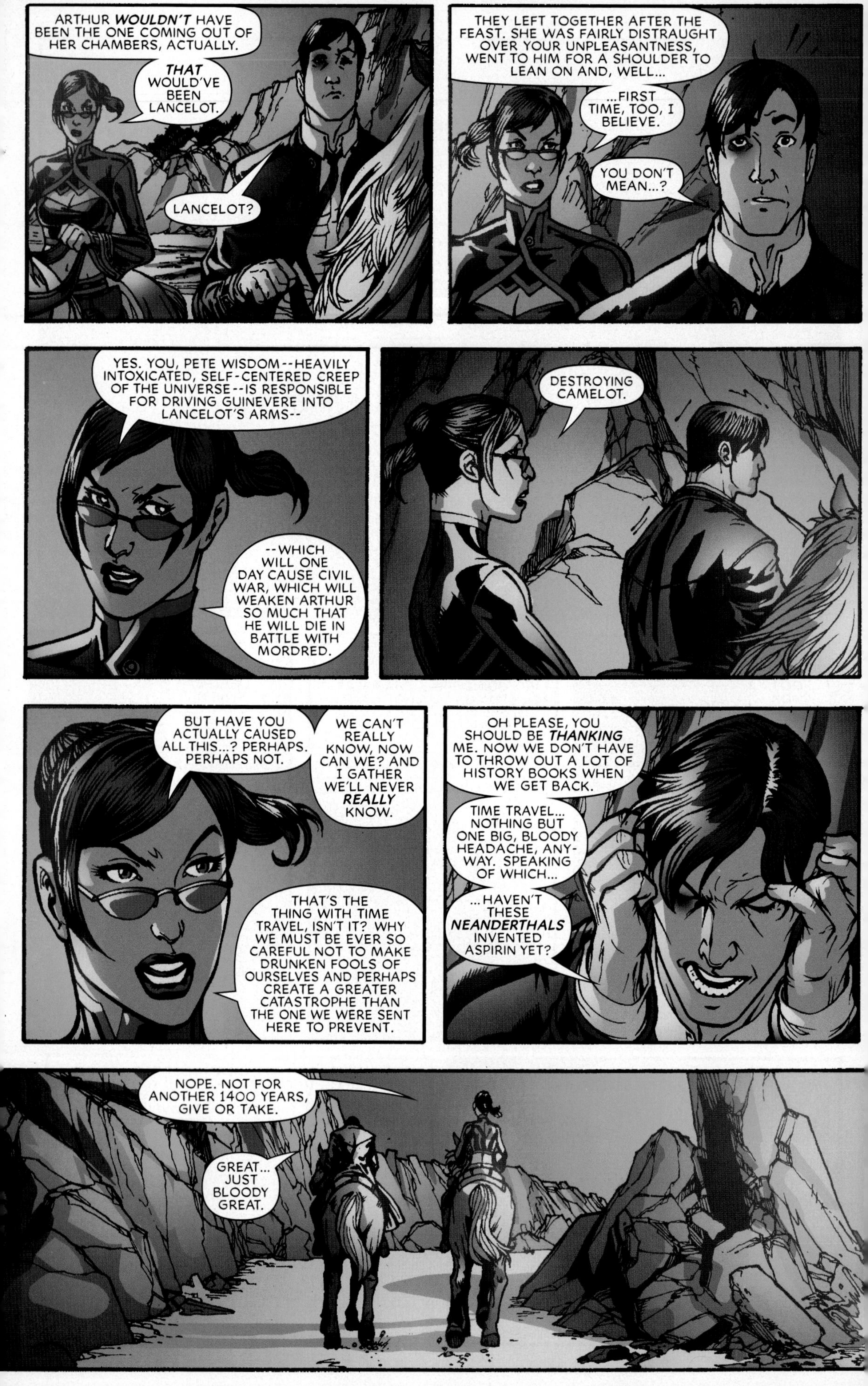
ARTHUR *WOULDN'T* HAVE BEEN THE ONE COMING OUT OF HER CHAMBERS, ACTUALLY.
THAT WOULD'VE BEEN LANCELOT.
LANCELOT?
THEY LEFT TOGETHER AFTER THE FEAST. SHE WAS FAIRLY DISTRAUGHT OVER YOUR UNPLEASANTNESS, WENT TO HIM FOR A SHOULDER TO LEAN ON AND, WELL...
...FIRST TIME, TOO, I BELIEVE.
YOU DON'T MEAN...?
YES. YOU, PETE WISDOM--HEAVILY INTOXICATED, SELF-CENTERED CREEP OF THE UNIVERSE--IS RESPONSIBLE FOR DRIVING GUINEVERE INTO LANCELOT'S ARMS--
--WHICH WILL ONE DAY CAUSE CIVIL WAR, WHICH WILL WEAKEN ARTHUR SO MUCH THAT HE WILL DIE IN BATTLE WITH MORDRED.
DESTROYING CAMELOT.
BUT HAVE YOU ACTUALLY CAUSED ALL THIS...? PERHAPS. PERHAPS NOT.
WE CAN'T REALLY KNOW, NOW CAN WE? AND I GATHER WE'LL NEVER *REALLY* KNOW.
THAT'S THE THING WITH TIME TRAVEL, ISN'T IT? WHY WE MUST BE EVER SO CAREFUL NOT TO MAKE DRUNKEN FOOLS OF OURSELVES AND PERHAPS CREATE A GREATER CATASTROPHE THAN THE ONE WE WERE SENT HERE TO PREVENT.
OH PLEASE, YOU SHOULD BE *THANKING* ME. NOW WE DON'T HAVE TO THROW OUT A LOT OF HISTORY BOOKS WHEN WE GET BACK.
TIME TRAVEL... NOTHING BUT ONE BIG, BLOODY HEADACHE, ANY-WAY. SPEAKING OF WHICH...
...HAVEN'T THESE *NEANDERTHALS* INVENTED ASPIRIN YET?
NOPE. NOT FOR ANOTHER 1400 YEARS, GIVE OR TAKE.
GREAT... JUST BLOODY GREAT.

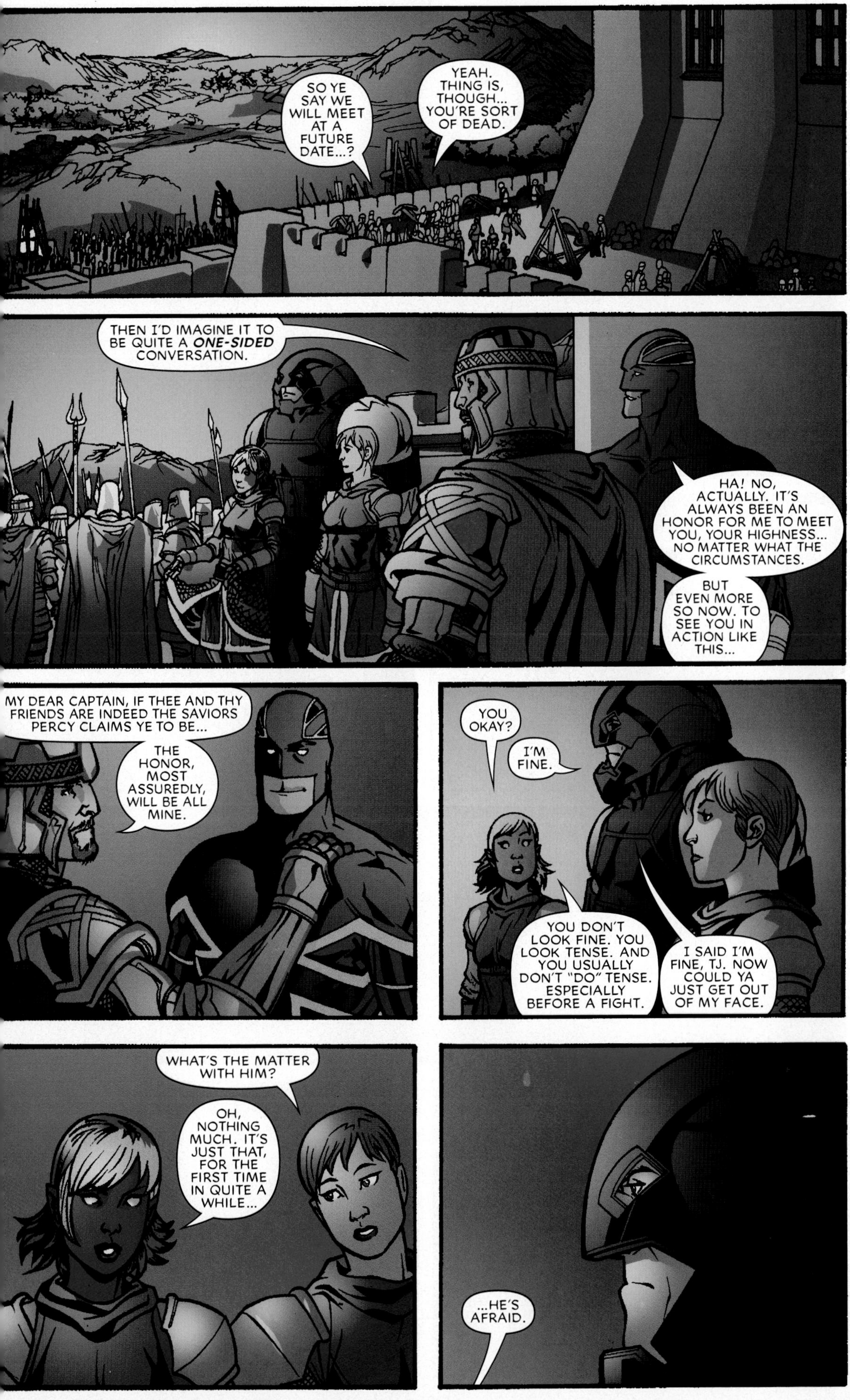
SO YE SAY WE WILL MEET AT A FUTURE DATE...?
YEAH. THING IS, THOUGH... YOU'RE SORT OF DEAD.
THEN I'D IMAGINE IT TO BE QUITE A *ONE-SIDED* CONVERSATION.
HA! NO, ACTUALLY. IT'S ALWAYS BEEN AN HONOR FOR ME TO MEET YOU, YOUR HIGHNESS... NO MATTER WHAT THE CIRCUMSTANCES.
BUT EVEN MORE SO NOW. TO SEE YOU IN ACTION LIKE THIS...
MY DEAR CAPTAIN, IF THEE AND THY FRIENDS ARE INDEED THE SAVIORS PERCY CLAIMS YE TO BE...
THE HONOR, MOST ASSUREDLY, WILL BE ALL MINE.
YOU OKAY?
I'M FINE.
YOU DON'T LOOK FINE. YOU LOOK TENSE. AND YOU USUALLY DON'T "DO" TENSE. ESPECIALLY BEFORE A FIGHT.
I SAID I'M FINE, TJ. NOW COULD YA JUST GET OUT OF MY FACE.
WHAT'S THE MATTER WITH HIM?
OH, NOTHING MUCH. IT'S JUST THAT, FOR THE FIRST TIME IN QUITE A WHILE...
...HE'S AFRAID.

"EIGHT MEN HELD THE BLADE BEFORE I DID."

"EACH ONE WAS AN HONORABLE MAN...EACH ONE WAS A GOOD MAN.

"YET EACH ONE, THE SWORD DROVE MAD.

"AND EACH ONE, EVENTUALLY, HAD TO BE PUT DOWN.

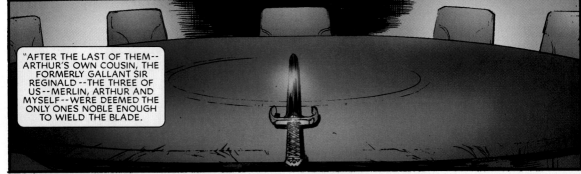

"AFTER THE LAST OF THEM--ARTHUR'S OWN COUSIN, THE FORMERLY GALLANT SIR REGINALD--THE THREE OF US--MERLIN, ARTHUR AND MYSELF--WERE DEEMED THE ONLY ONES NOBLE ENOUGH TO WIELD THE BLADE.

"BUT ARTHUR WAS OUR KING... AND CAMELOT NEEDED HIS STEADY RULE.

"AND MERLIN...WELL, IF MERLIN WERE TO BE CORRUPTED BY THE BLADE, I'M AFRAID NOTHING ON THE FACE OF THE EARTH WOULD BE ABLE TO STOP HIM.

"AND SO, THERE WAS LITTLE CHOICE LEFT..."

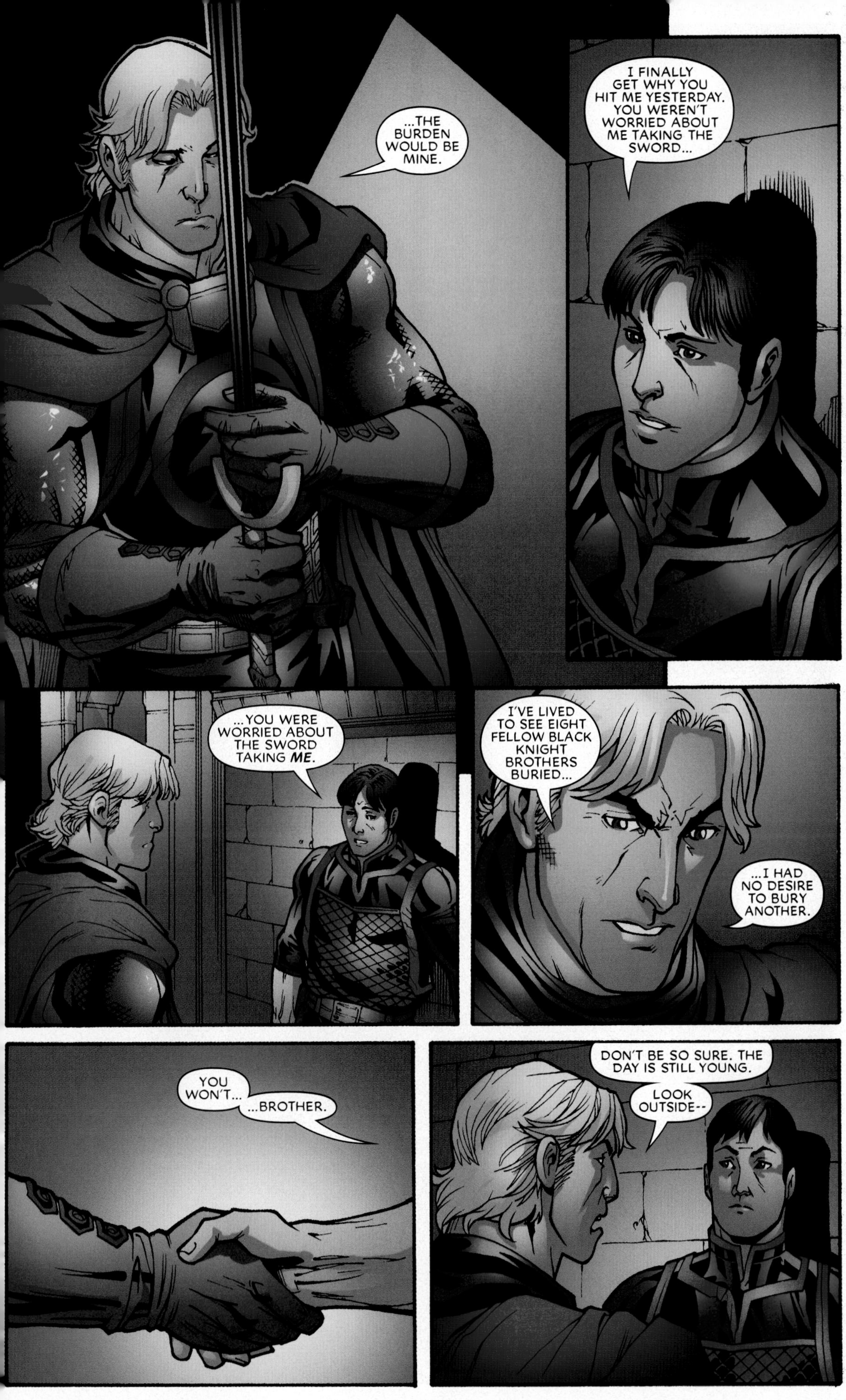
...THE BURDEN WOULD BE MINE.
I FINALLY GET WHY YOU HIT ME YESTERDAY. YOU WEREN'T WORRIED ABOUT ME TAKING THE SWORD...
...YOU WERE WORRIED ABOUT THE SWORD TAKING *ME*.
I'VE LIVED TO SEE EIGHT FELLOW BLACK KNIGHT BROTHERS BURIED...
...I HAD NO DESIRE TO BURY ANOTHER.
YOU WON'T...
...BROTHER.
DON'T BE SO SURE. THE DAY IS STILL YOUNG.
LOOK OUTSIDE--

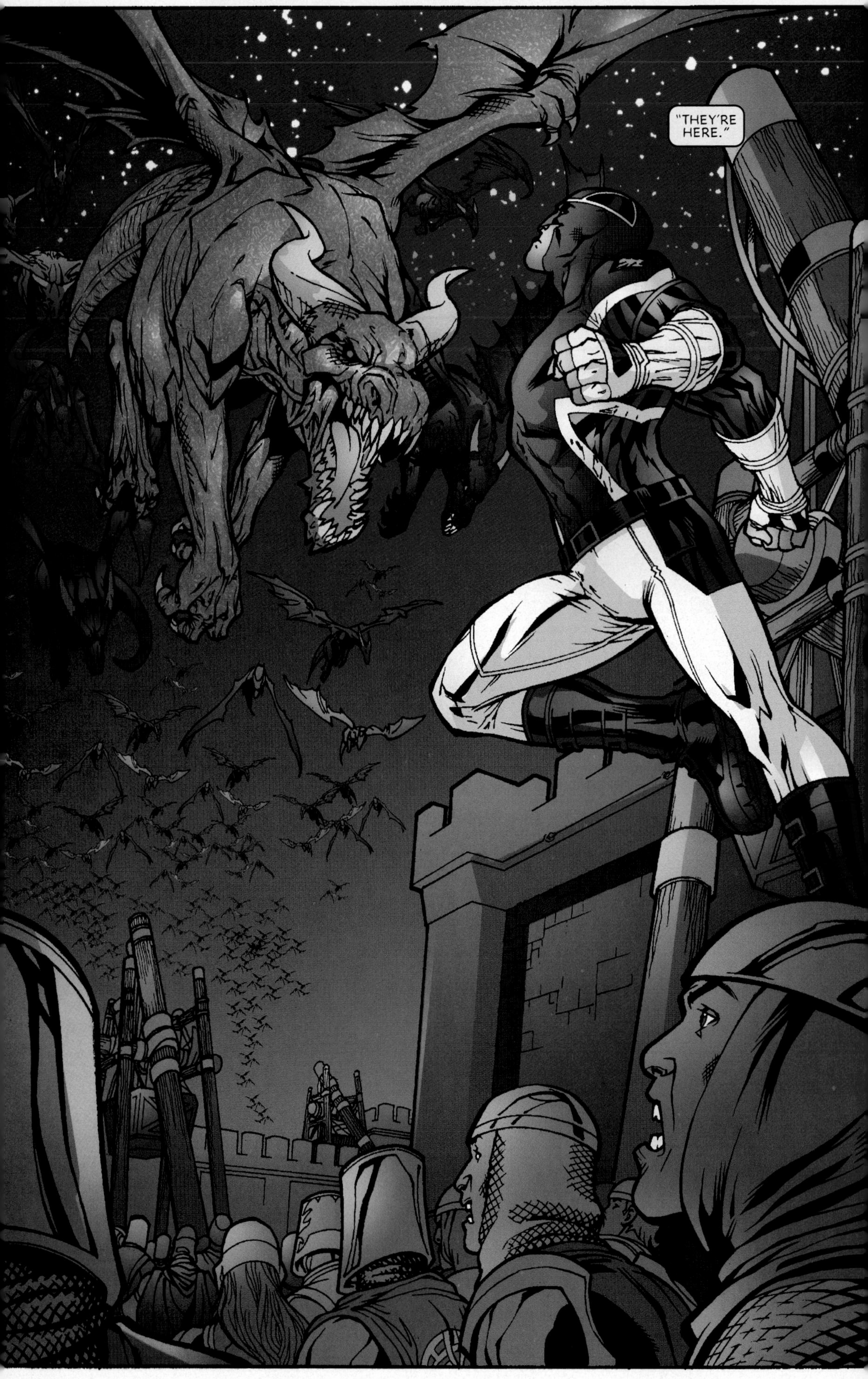
"THEY'RE HERE."

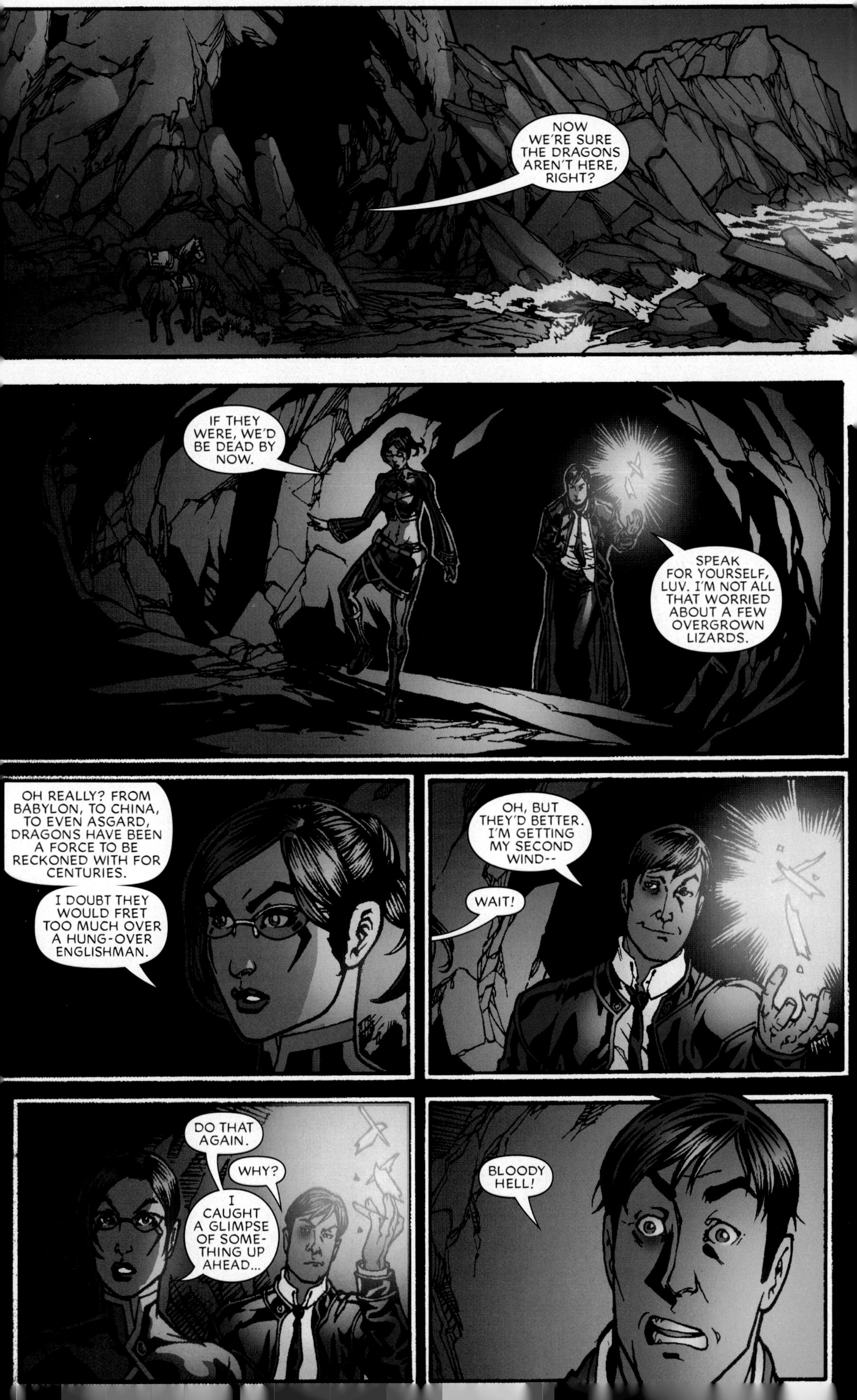
NOW WE'RE SURE THE DRAGONS AREN'T HERE, RIGHT?
IF THEY WERE, WE'D BE DEAD BY NOW.
SPEAK FOR YOURSELF, LUV. I'M NOT ALL THAT WORRIED ABOUT A FEW OVERGROWN LIZARDS.
OH REALLY? FROM BABYLON, TO CHINA, TO EVEN ASGARD, DRAGONS HAVE BEEN A FORCE TO BE RECKONED WITH FOR CENTURIES.
I DOUBT THEY WOULD FRET TOO MUCH OVER A HUNG-OVER ENGLISHMAN.
OH, BUT THEY'D BETTER. I'M GETTING MY SECOND WIND--
WAIT!
DO THAT AGAIN.
WHY?
I CAUGHT A GLIMPSE OF SOME-THING UP AHEAD...
BLOODY HELL!

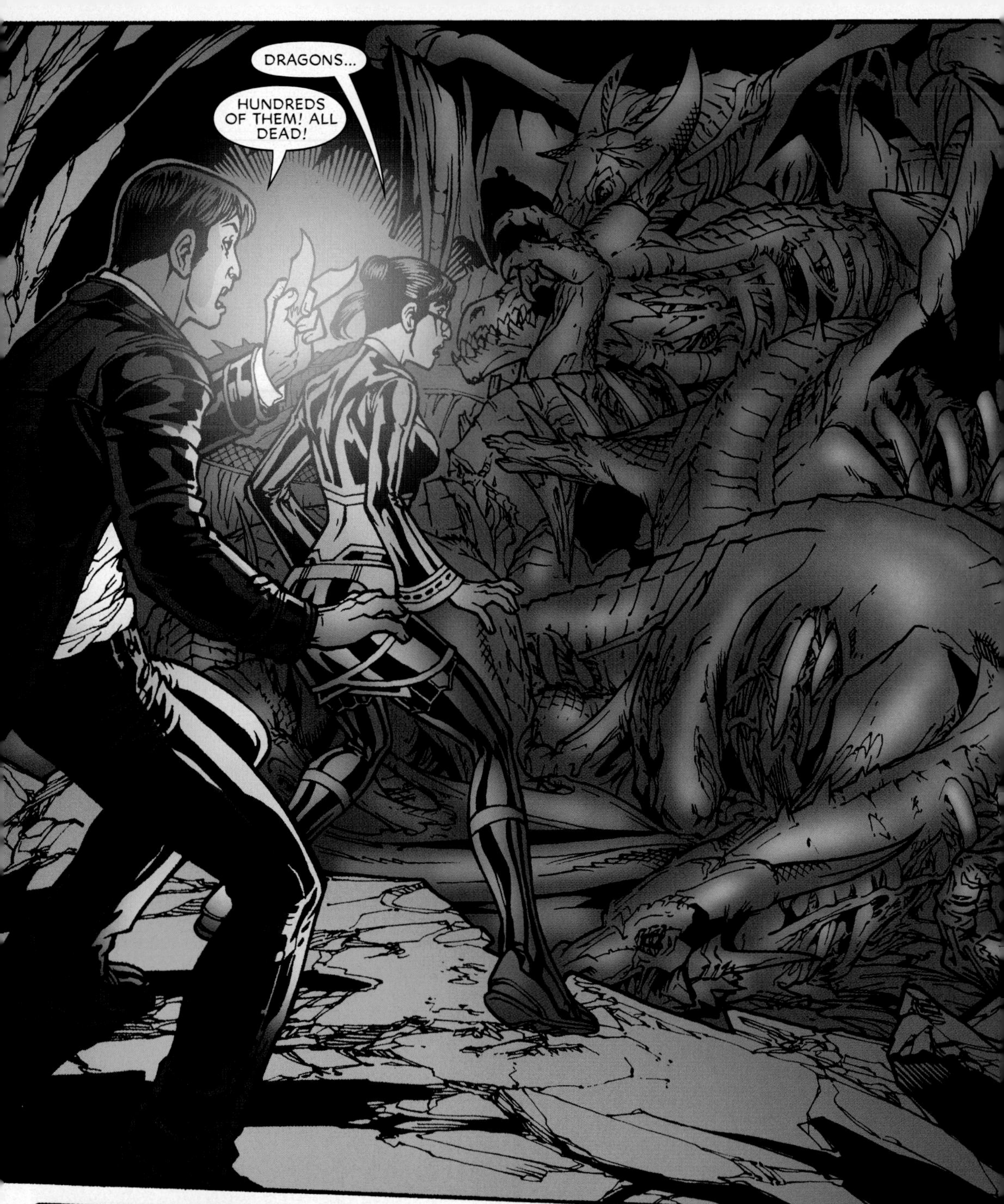
DRAGONS...
HUNDREDS OF THEM! ALL DEAD!

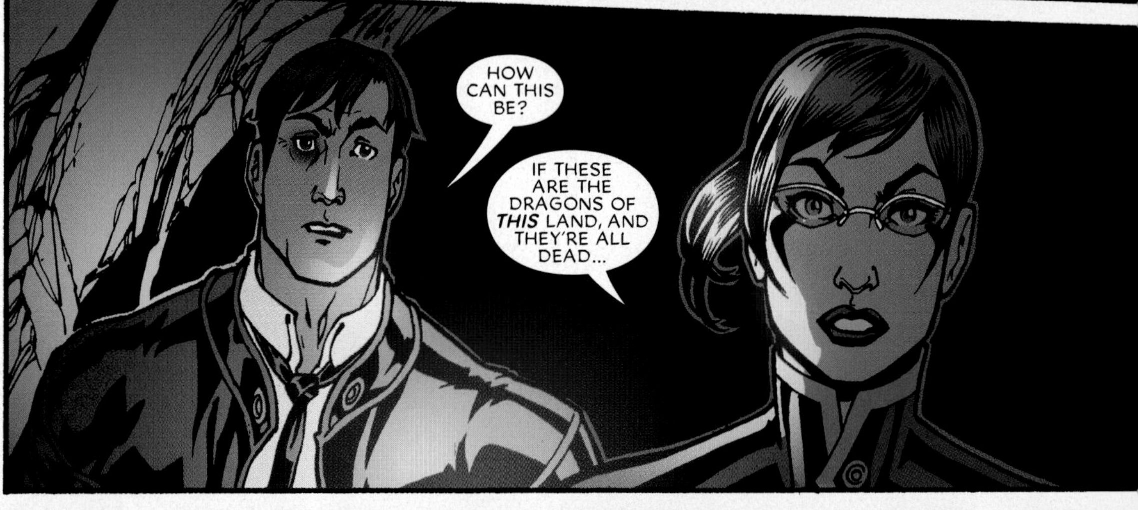
HOW CAN THIS BE?
IF THESE ARE THE DRAGONS OF *THIS* LAND, AND THEY'RE ALL DEAD...

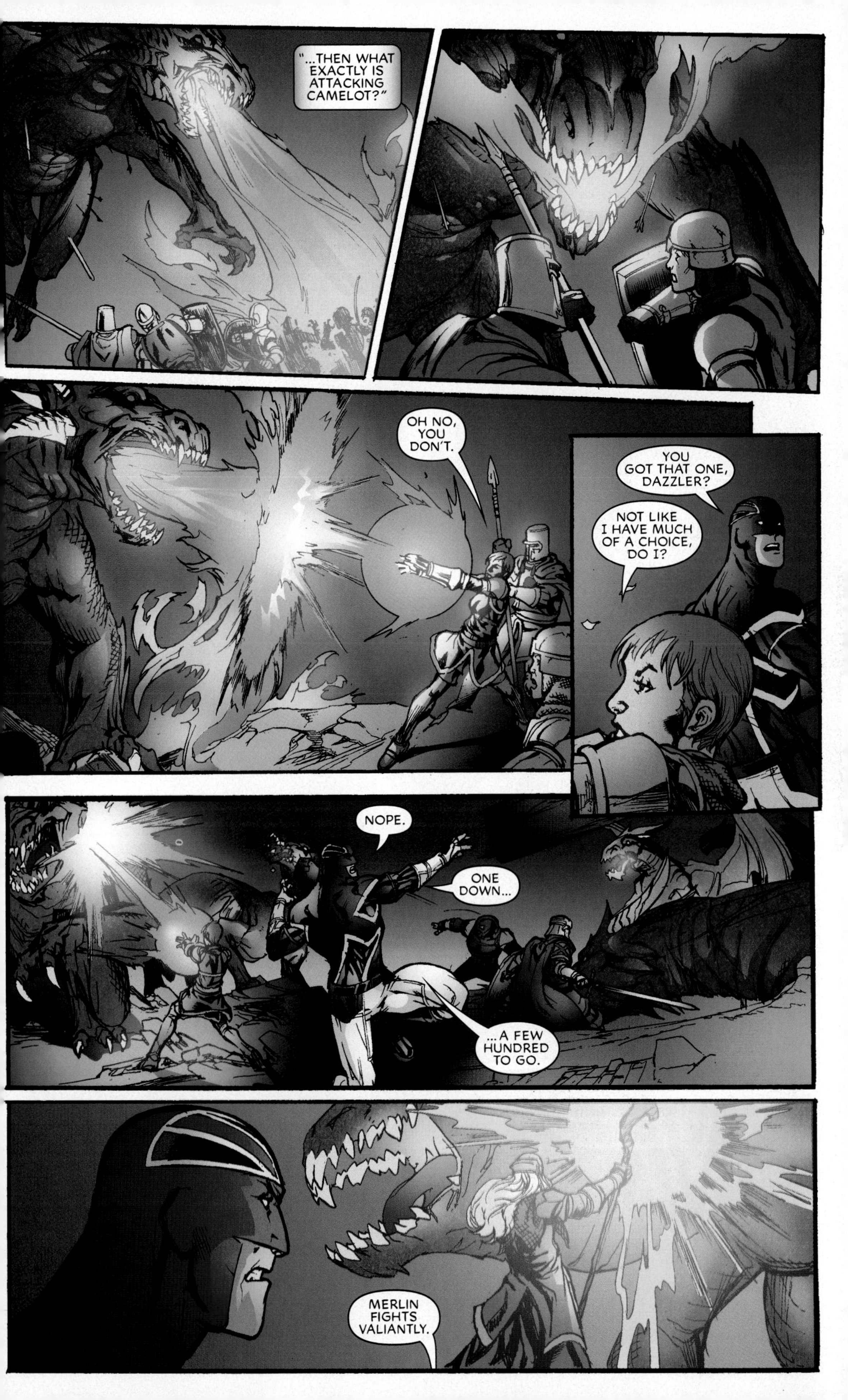
"...THEN WHAT EXACTLY IS ATTACKING CAMELOT?"
OH NO, YOU DON'T.
YOU GOT THAT ONE, DAZZLER?
NOT LIKE I HAVE MUCH OF A CHOICE, DO I?
NOPE.
ONE DOWN...
...A FEW HUNDRED TO GO.
MERLIN FIGHTS VALIANTLY.

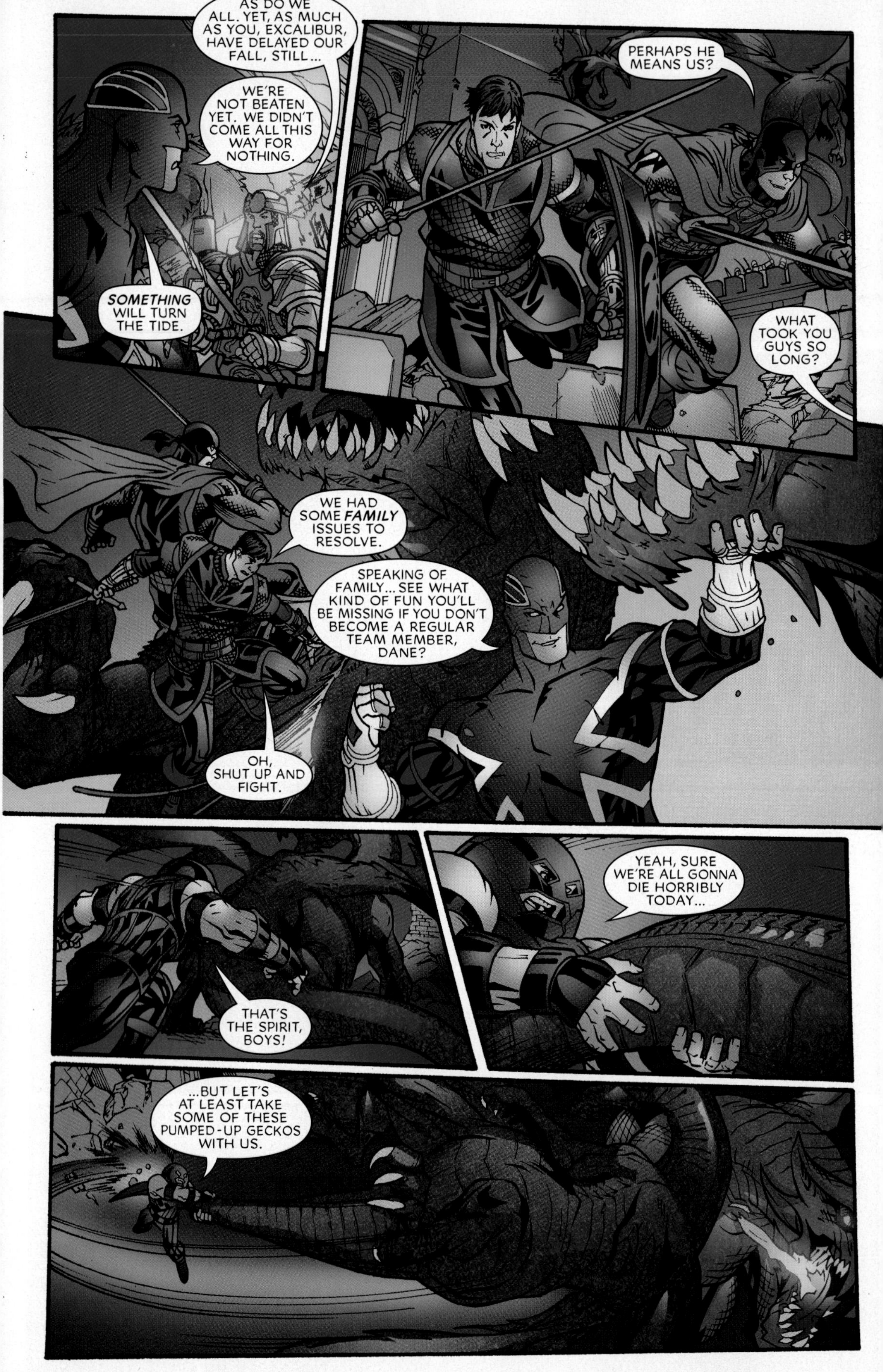
AS DO WE ALL. YET, AS MUCH AS YOU, EXCALIBUR, HAVE DELAYED OUR FALL, STILL...
WE'RE NOT BEATEN YET. WE DIDN'T COME ALL THIS WAY FOR NOTHING.
SOMETHING WILL TURN THE TIDE.
PERHAPS HE MEANS US?
WHAT TOOK YOU GUYS SO LONG?
WE HAD SOME FAMILY ISSUES TO RESOLVE.
SPEAKING OF FAMILY... SEE WHAT KIND OF FUN YOU'LL BE MISSING IF YOU DON'T BECOME A REGULAR TEAM MEMBER, DANE?
OH, SHUT UP AND FIGHT.
THAT'S THE SPIRIT, BOYS!
YEAH, SURE WE'RE ALL GONNA DIE HORRIBLY TODAY...
...BUT LET'S AT LEAST TAKE SOME OF THESE PUMPED-UP GECKOS WITH US.

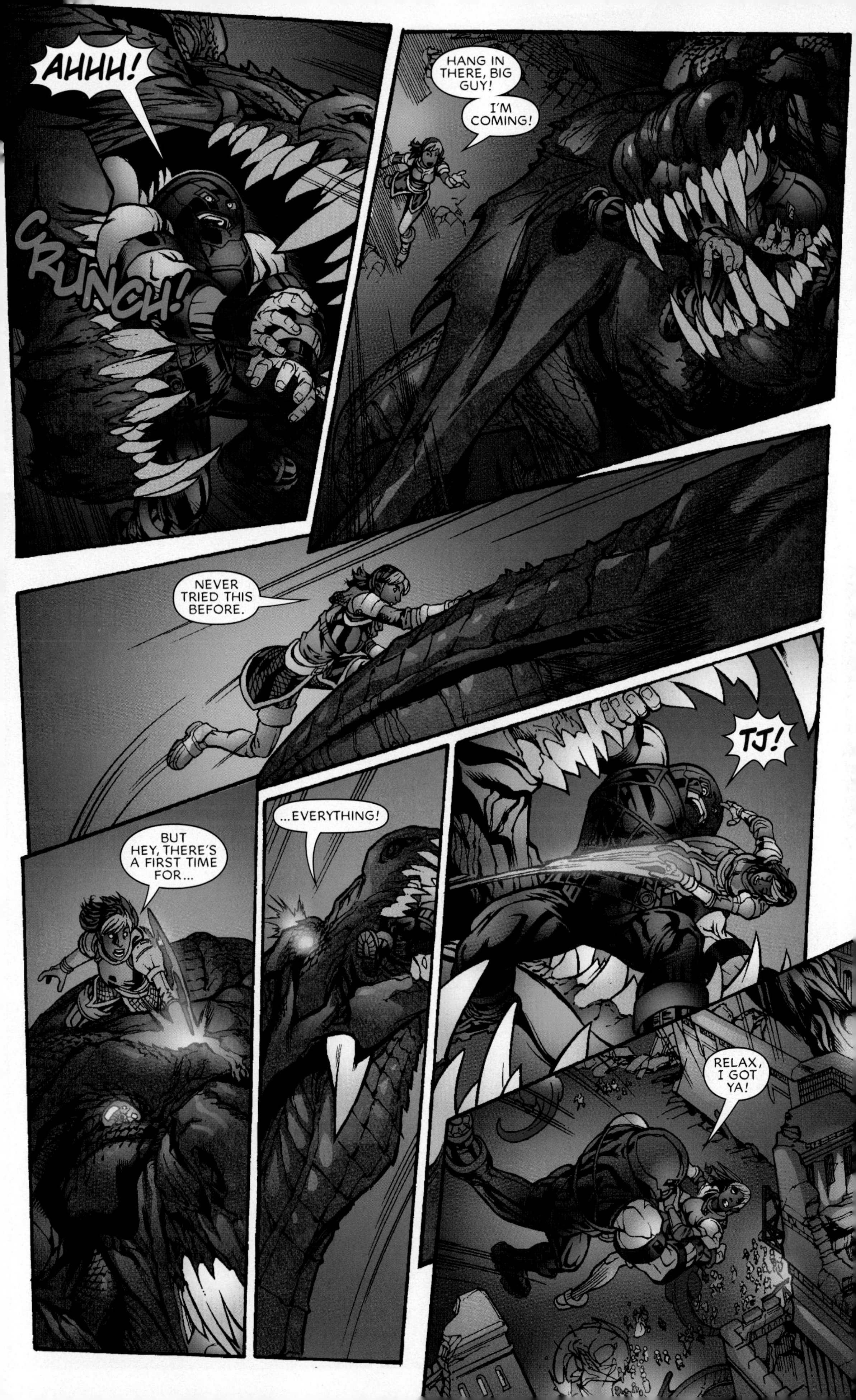
AHHH!
CRUNCH!
HANG IN THERE, BIG GUY!
I'M COMING!
NEVER TRIED THIS BEFORE.
TJ!
BUT HEY, THERE'S A FIRST TIME FOR...
...EVERYTHING!
RELAX, I GOT YA!

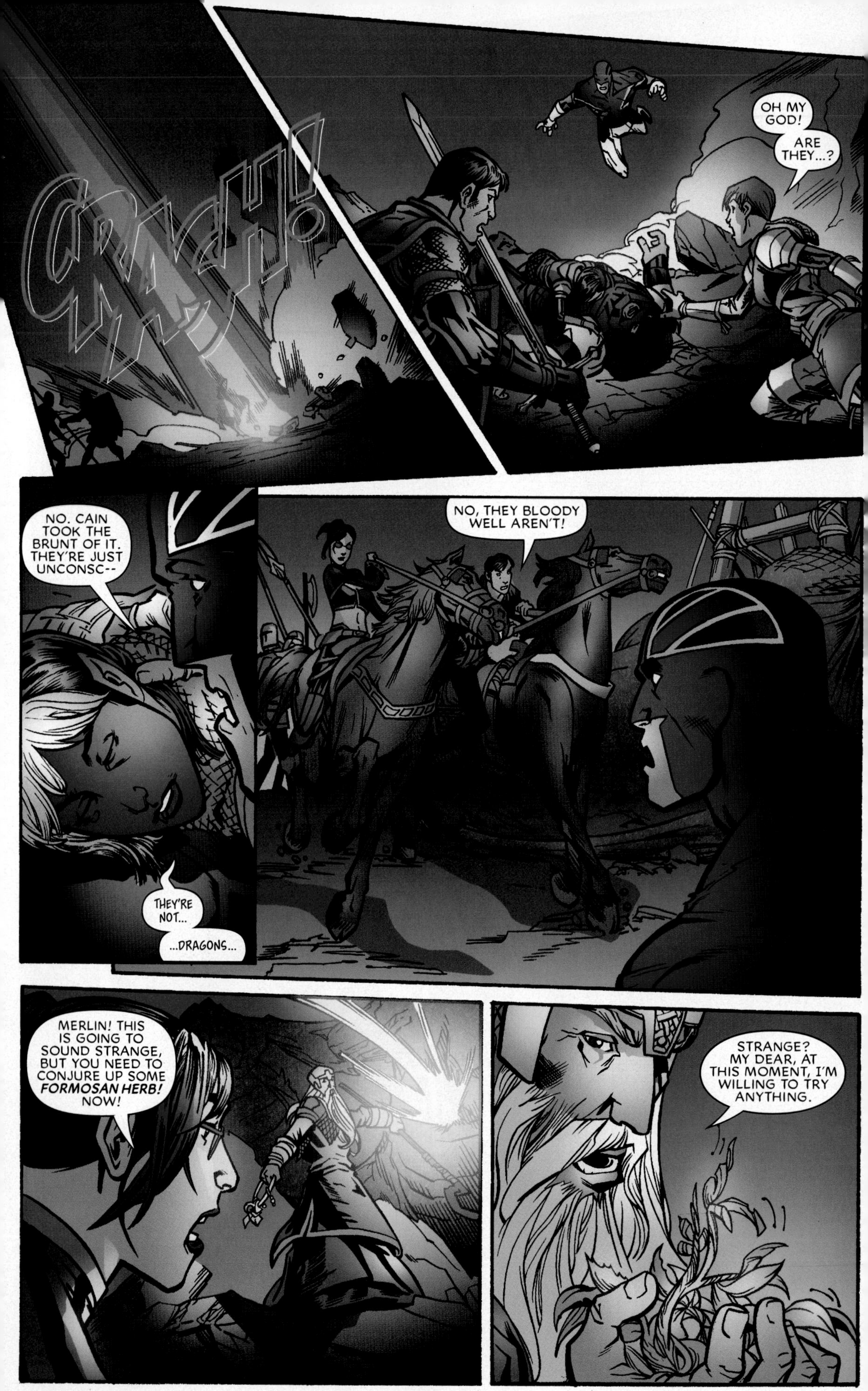
CRAAASH!
OH MY GOD!
ARE THEY...?
NO. CAIN TOOK THE BRUNT OF IT. THEY'RE JUST UNCONSC--
NO, THEY BLOODY WELL AREN'T!
THEY'RE NOT...
...DRAGONS...
MERLIN! THIS IS GOING TO SOUND STRANGE, BUT YOU NEED TO CONJURE UP SOME ***FORMOSAN HERB!*** NOW!
STRANGE? MY DEAR, AT THIS MOMENT, I'M WILLING TO TRY ANYTHING.

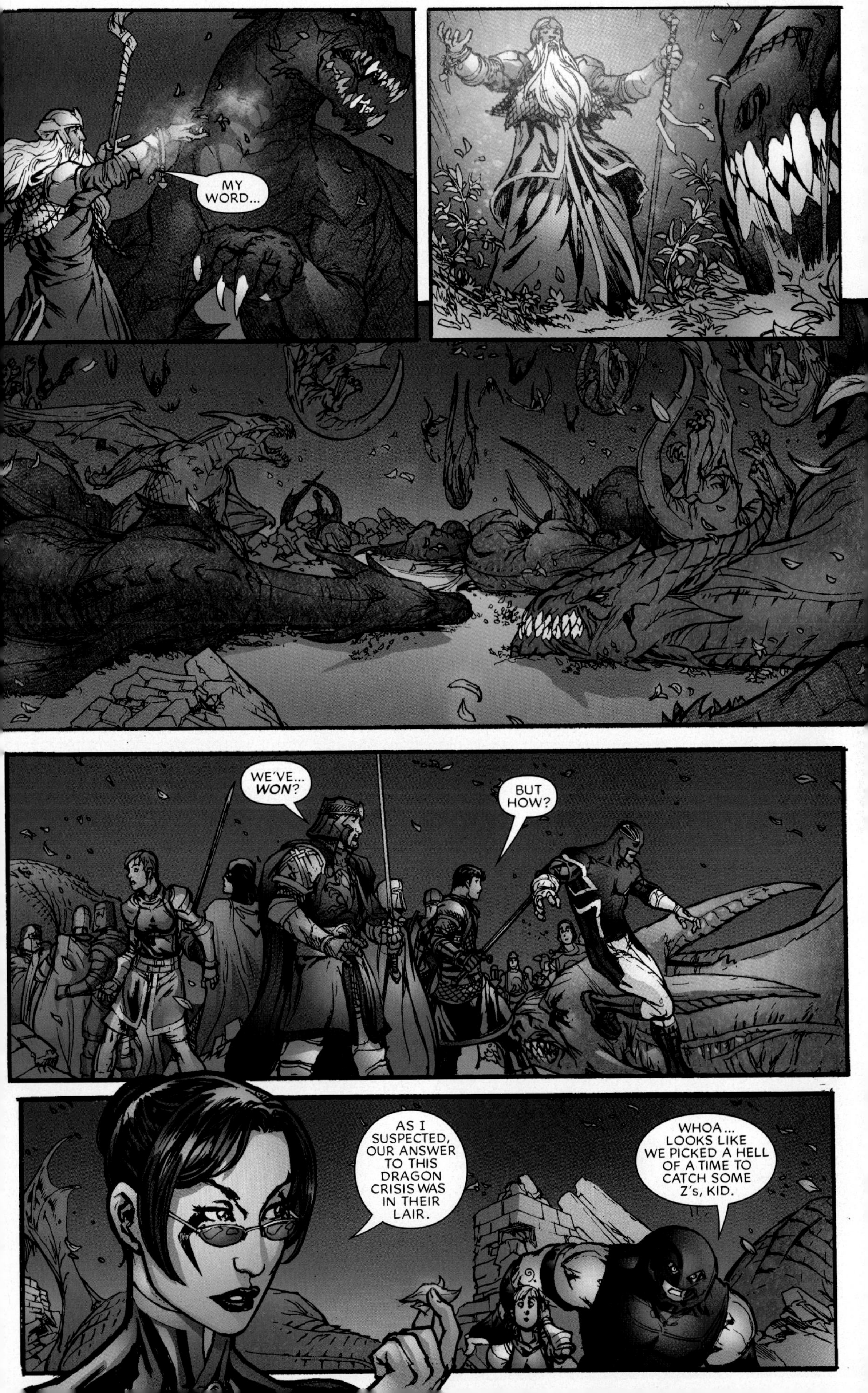
MY WORD...
WE'VE... *WON*?
BUT HOW?
AS I SUSPECTED, OUR ANSWER TO THIS DRAGON CRISIS WAS IN THEIR LAIR.
WHOA... LOOKS LIKE WE PICKED A HELL OF A TIME TO CATCH SOME Z's, KID.

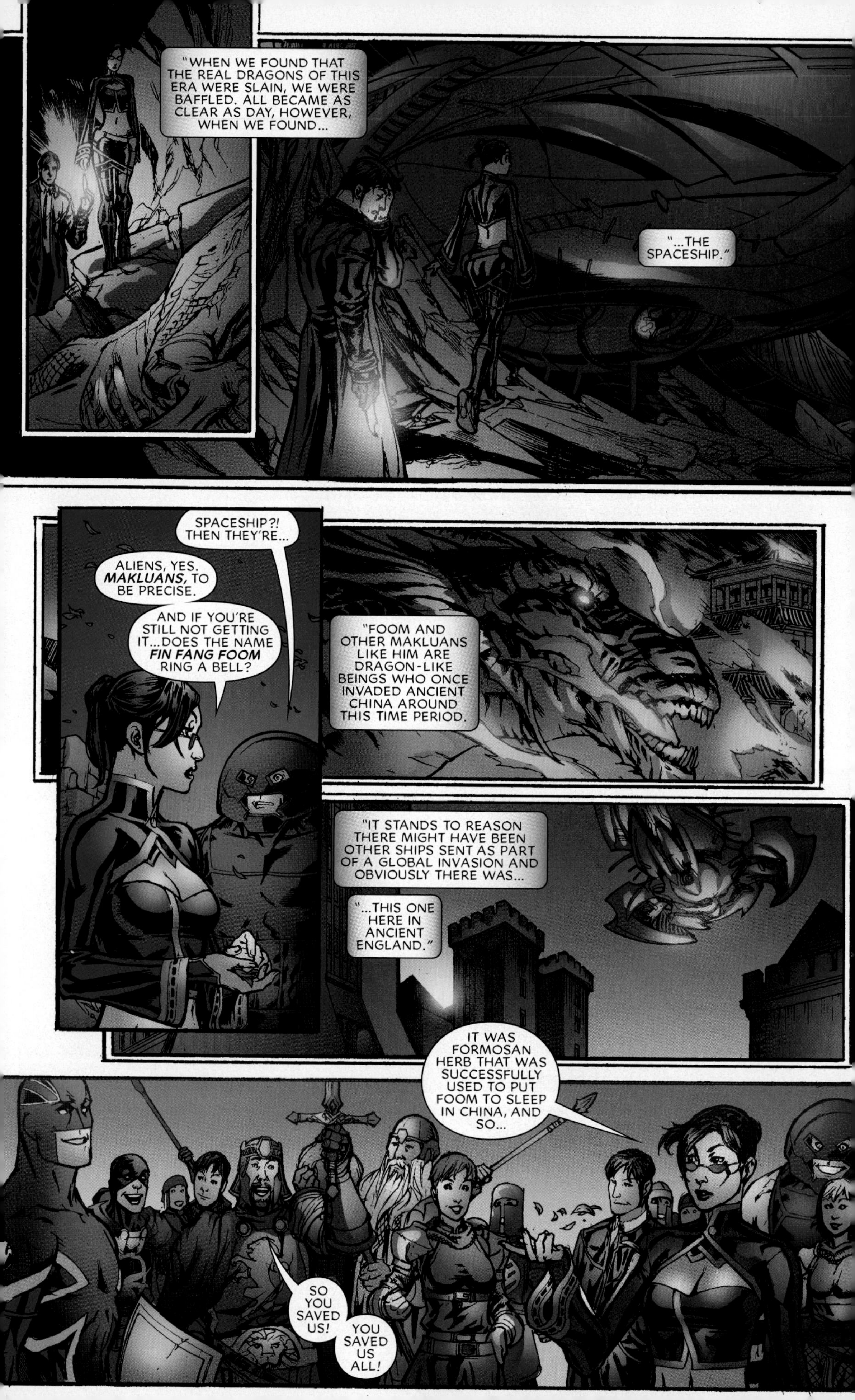
"WHEN WE FOUND THAT THE REAL DRAGONS OF THIS ERA WERE SLAIN, WE WERE BAFFLED. ALL BECAME AS CLEAR AS DAY, HOWEVER, WHEN WE FOUND...
"...THE SPACESHIP."
SPACESHIP?! THEN THEY'RE...
ALIENS, YES. MAKLUANS, TO BE PRECISE.
AND IF YOU'RE STILL NOT GETTING IT...DOES THE NAME FIN FANG FOOM RING A BELL?
"FOOM AND OTHER MAKLUANS LIKE HIM ARE DRAGON-LIKE BEINGS WHO ONCE INVADED ANCIENT CHINA AROUND THIS TIME PERIOD.
"IT STANDS TO REASON THERE MIGHT HAVE BEEN OTHER SHIPS SENT AS PART OF A GLOBAL INVASION AND OBVIOUSLY THERE WAS...
"...THIS ONE HERE IN ANCIENT ENGLAND."
IT WAS FORMOSAN HERB THAT WAS SUCCESSFULLY USED TO PUT FOOM TO SLEEP IN CHINA, AND SO...
SO YOU SAVED US!
YOU SAVED US ALL!

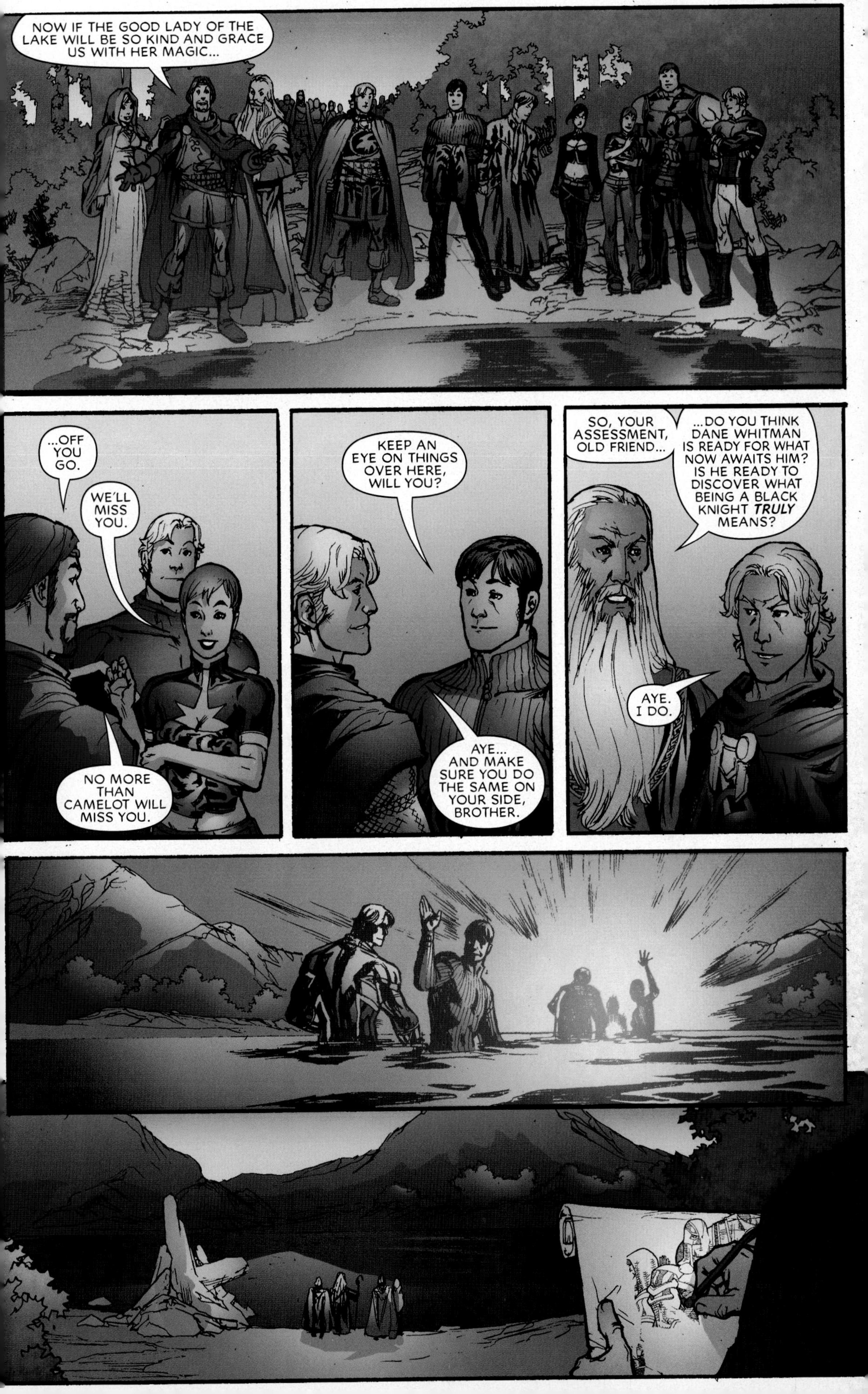
NOW IF THE GOOD LADY OF THE LAKE WILL BE SO KIND AND GRACE US WITH HER MAGIC...
...OFF YOU GO.
WE'LL MISS YOU.
NO MORE THAN CAMELOT WILL MISS YOU.
KEEP AN EYE ON THINGS OVER HERE, WILL YOU?
AYE... AND MAKE SURE YOU DO THE SAME ON YOUR SIDE, BROTHER.
SO, YOUR ASSESSMENT, OLD FRIEND...
...DO YOU THINK DANE WHITMAN IS READY FOR WHAT NOW AWAITS HIM? IS HE READY TO DISCOVER WHAT BEING A BLACK KNIGHT TRULY MEANS?
AYE. I DO.

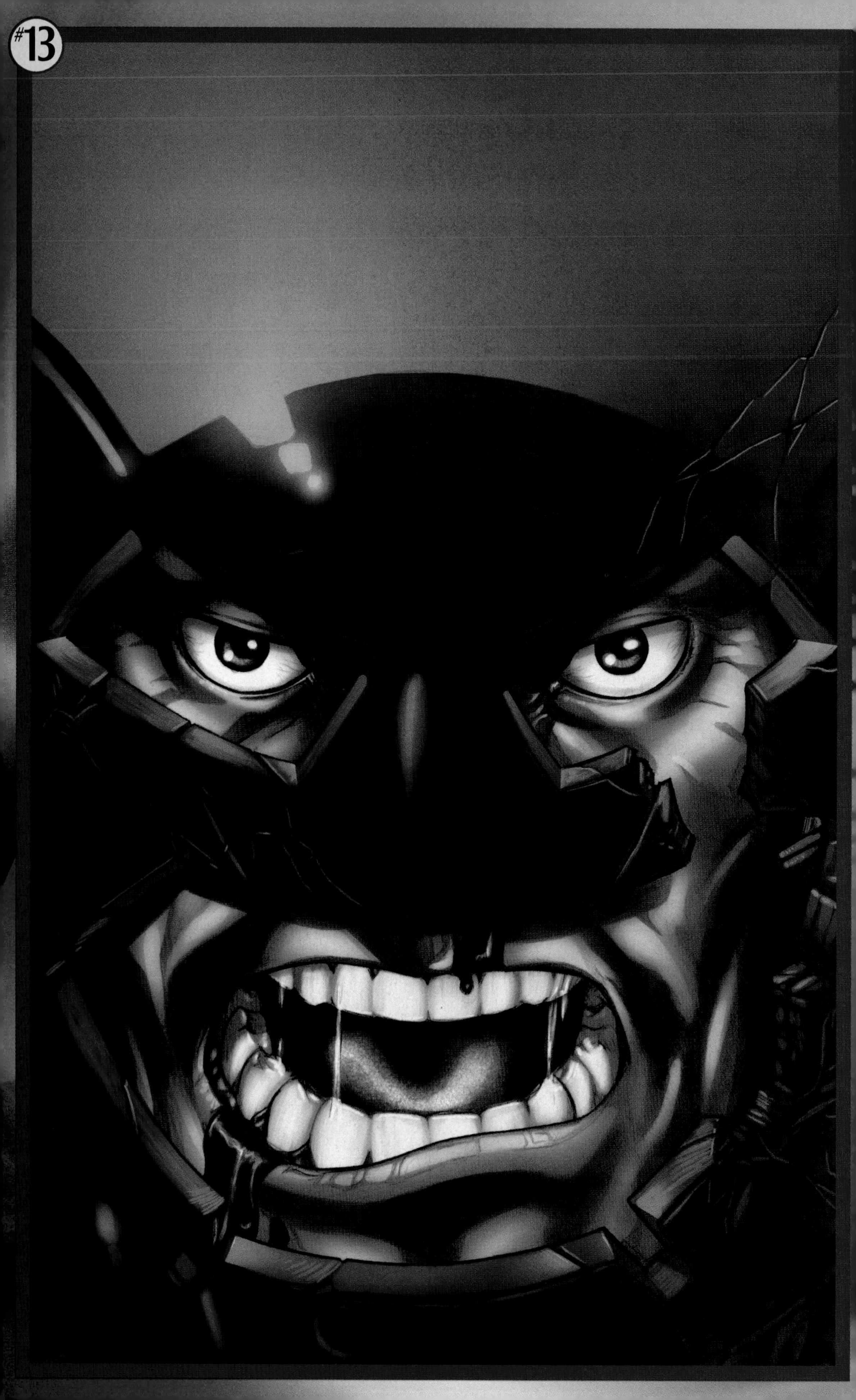
#13

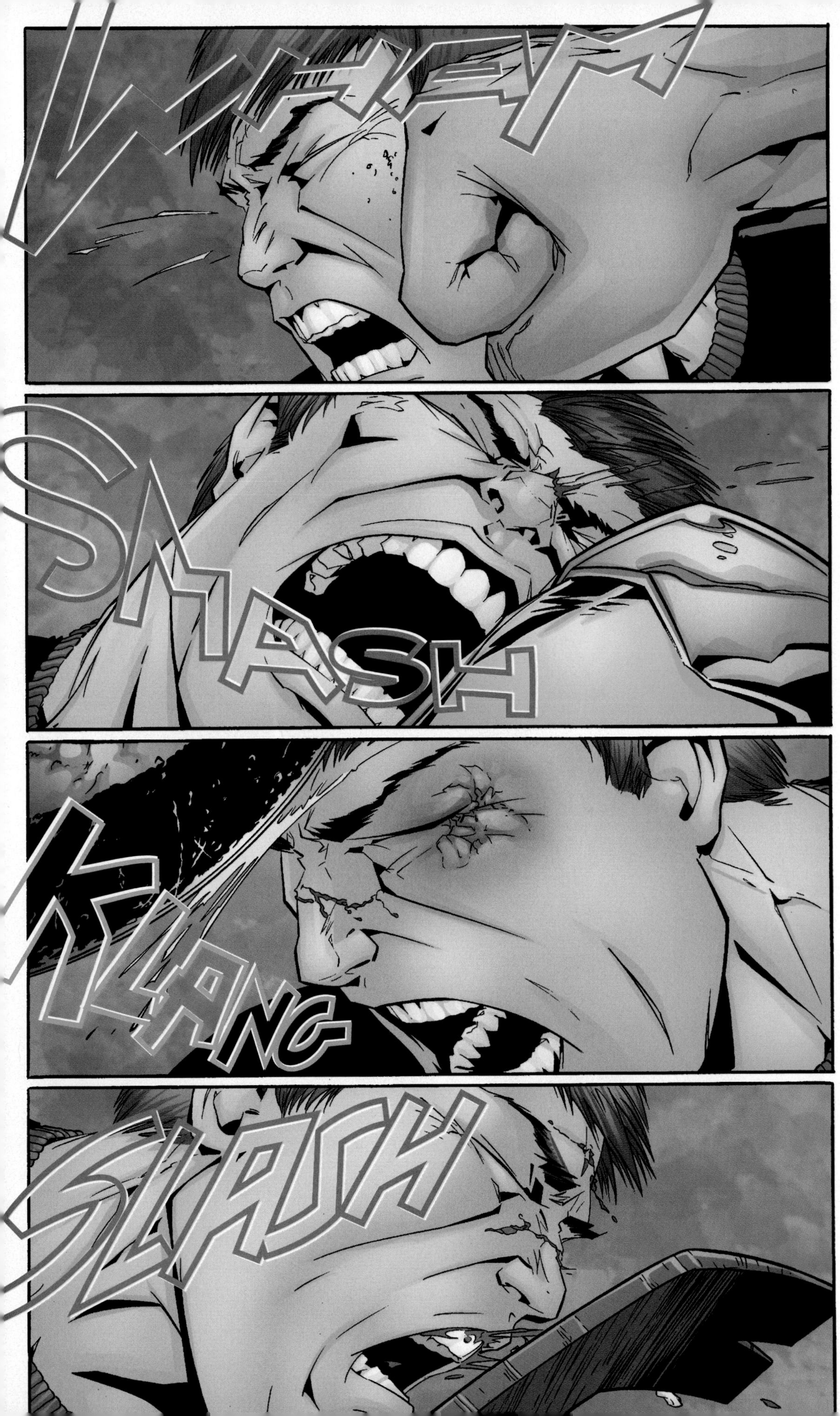
WHAM
SMASH
KLANG
SLASH

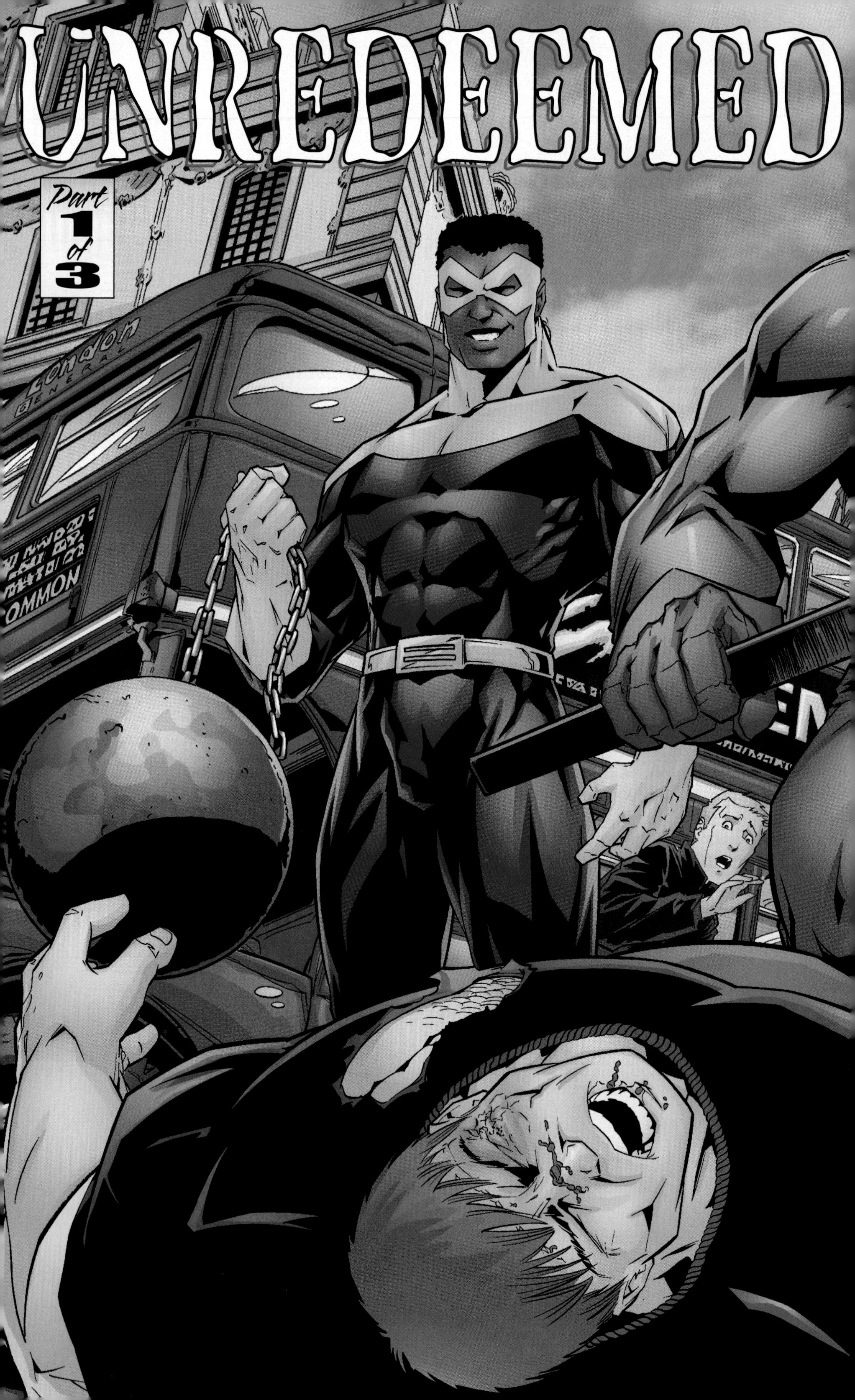
UNREDEEMED
Part 1 of 3
London General
COMMON

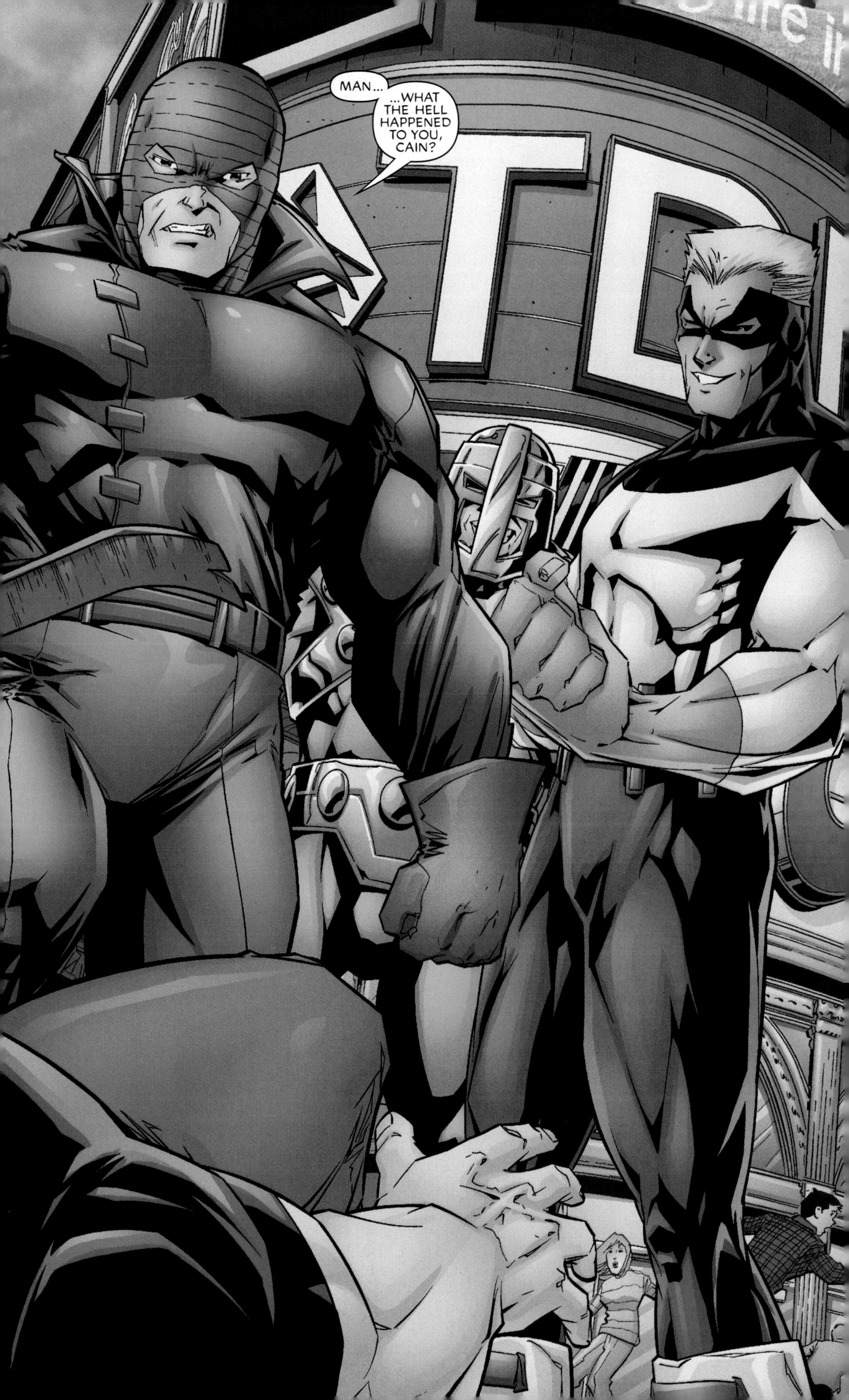
MAN...
...WHAT THE HELL HAPPENED TO YOU, CAIN?

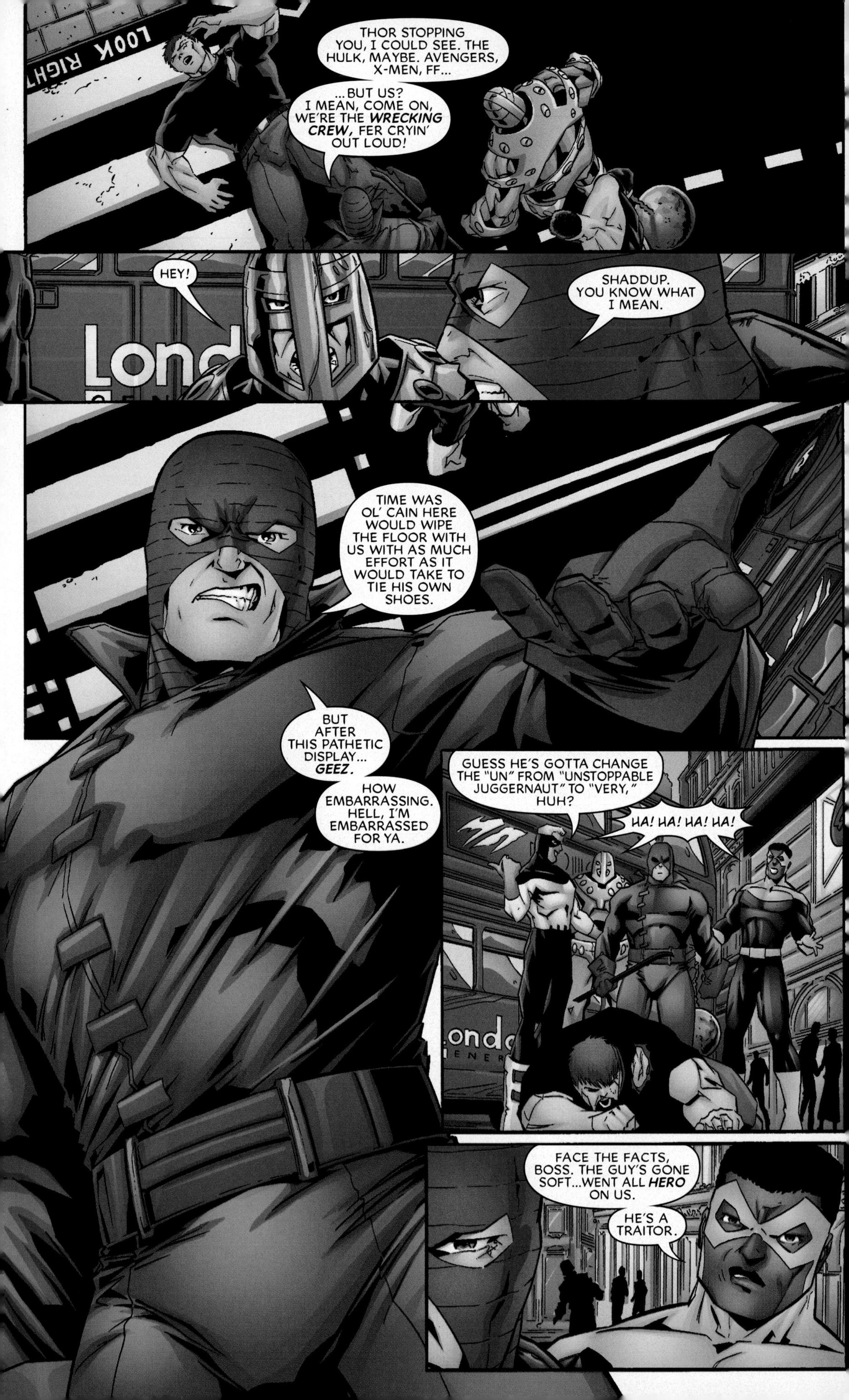
LOOK RIGHT
THOR STOPPING YOU, I COULD SEE. THE HULK, MAYBE. AVENGERS, X-MEN, FF...
...BUT US? I MEAN, COME ON, WE'RE THE **WRECKING CREW,** FER CRYIN' OUT LOUD!
HEY!
SHADDUP. YOU KNOW WHAT I MEAN.
London
TIME WAS OL' CAIN HERE WOULD WIPE THE FLOOR WITH US WITH AS MUCH EFFORT AS IT WOULD TAKE TO TIE HIS OWN SHOES.
BUT AFTER THIS PATHETIC DISPLAY... **GEEZ.**
HOW EMBARRASSING. HELL, I'M EMBARRASSED FOR YA.
GUESS HE'S GOTTA CHANGE THE "UN" FROM "UNSTOPPABLE JUGGERNAUT" TO "VERY," HUH?
HA! HA! HA! HA!
FACE THE FACTS, BOSS. THE GUY'S GONE SOFT...WENT ALL **HERO** ON US.
HE'S A TRAITOR.

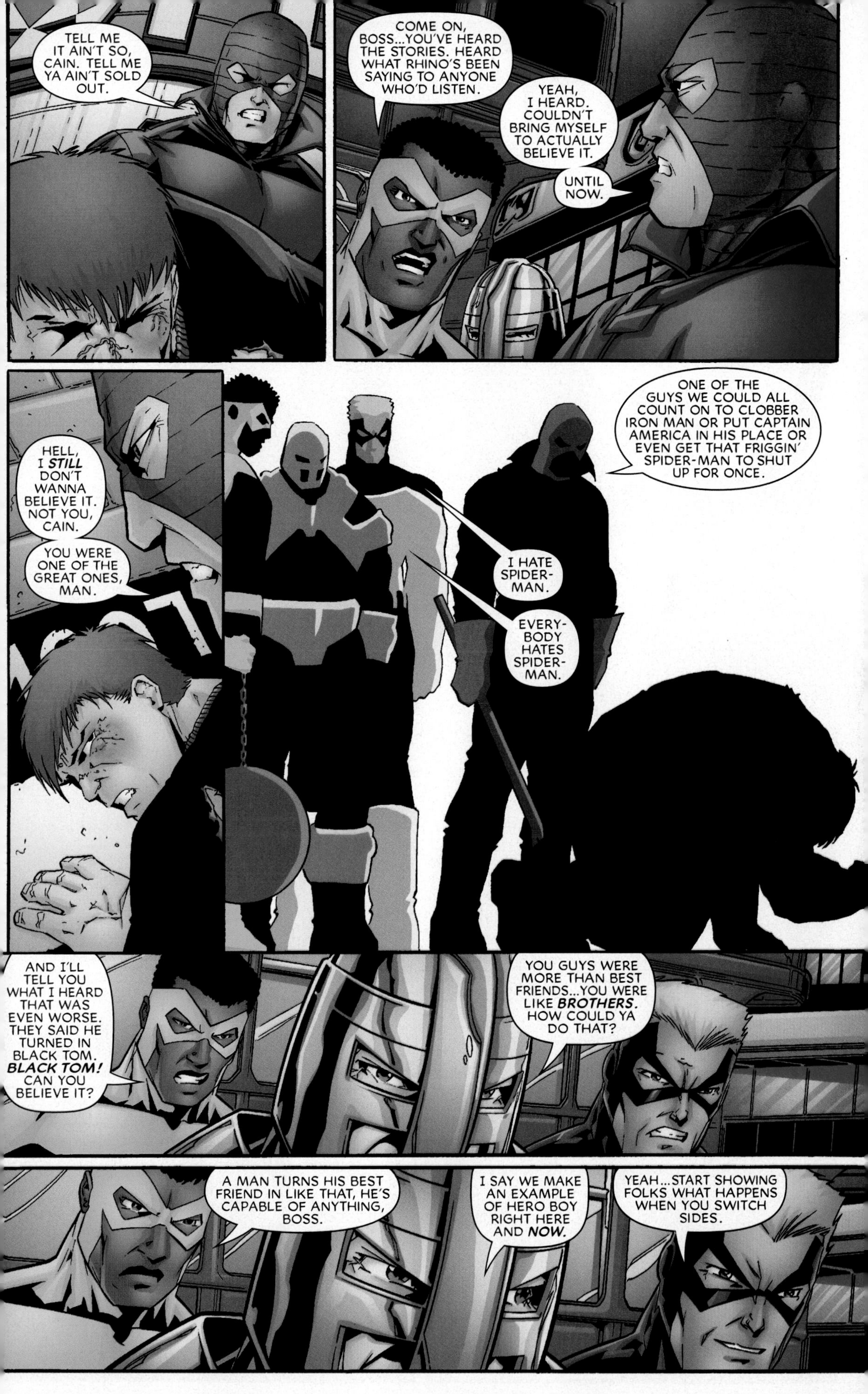
TELL ME IT AIN'T SO, CAIN. TELL ME YA AIN'T SOLD OUT.
COME ON, BOSS...YOU'VE HEARD THE STORIES. HEARD WHAT RHINO'S BEEN SAYING TO ANYONE WHO'D LISTEN.
YEAH, I HEARD. COULDN'T BRING MYSELF TO ACTUALLY BELIEVE IT.
UNTIL NOW.
HELL, I *STILL* DON'T WANNA BELIEVE IT. NOT YOU, CAIN.
YOU WERE ONE OF THE GREAT ONES, MAN.
ONE OF THE GUYS WE COULD ALL COUNT ON TO CLOBBER IRON MAN OR PUT CAPTAIN AMERICA IN HIS PLACE OR EVEN GET THAT FRIGGIN' SPIDER-MAN TO SHUT UP FOR ONCE.
I HATE SPIDER-MAN.
EVERY-BODY HATES SPIDER-MAN.
AND I'LL TELL YOU WHAT I HEARD THAT WAS EVEN WORSE. THEY SAID HE TURNED IN BLACK TOM. ***BLACK TOM!*** CAN YOU BELIEVE IT?
YOU GUYS WERE MORE THAN BEST FRIENDS...YOU WERE LIKE ***BROTHERS***. HOW COULD YA DO THAT?
A MAN TURNS HIS BEST FRIEND IN LIKE THAT, HE'S CAPABLE OF ANYTHING, BOSS.
I SAY WE MAKE AN EXAMPLE OF HERO BOY RIGHT HERE AND ***NOW***.
YEAH...START SHOWING FOLKS WHAT HAPPENS WHEN YOU SWITCH SIDES.

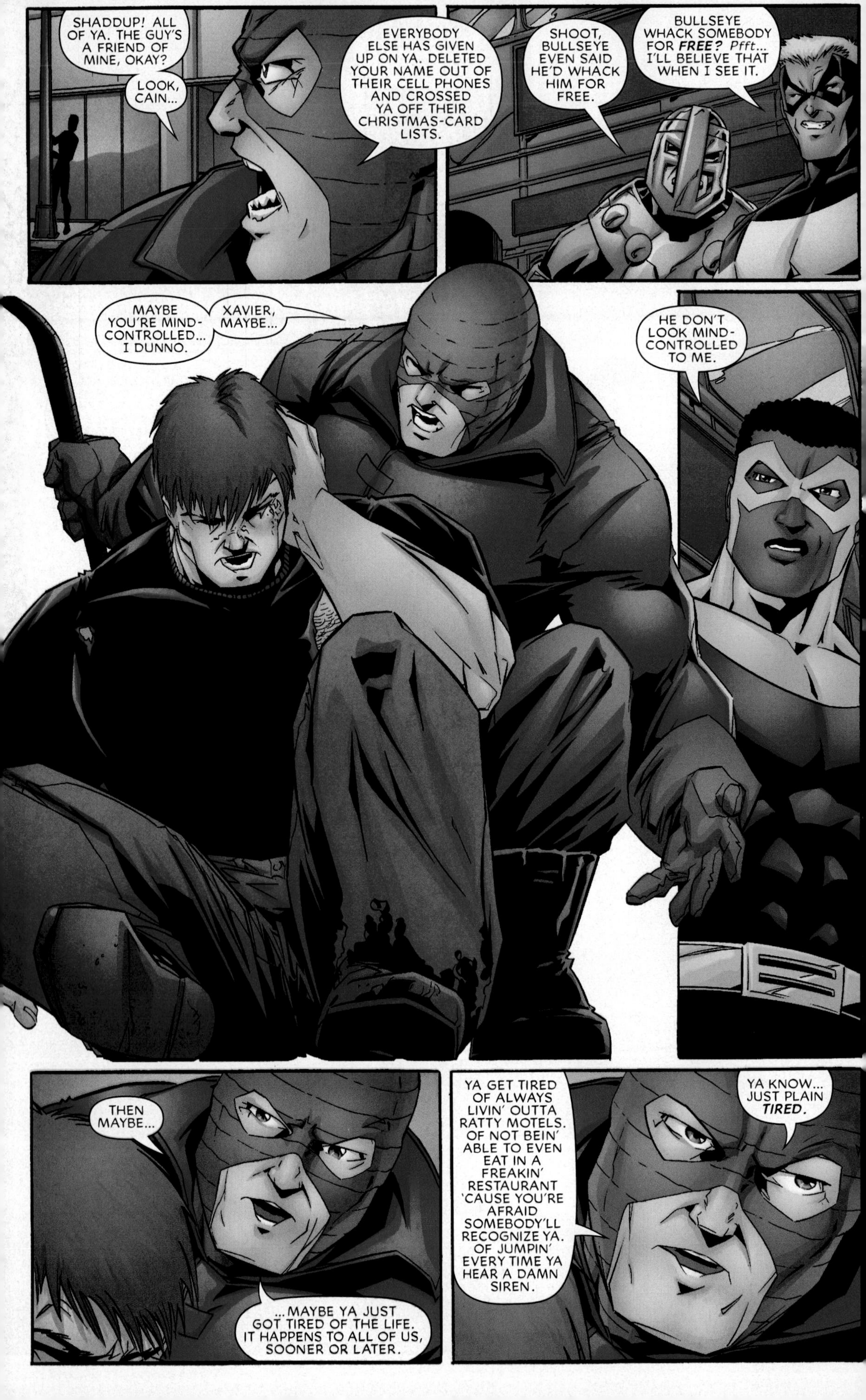
SHADDUP! ALL OF YA. THE GUY'S A FRIEND OF MINE, OKAY?
LOOK, CAIN...
EVERYBODY ELSE HAS GIVEN UP ON YA. DELETED YOUR NAME OUT OF THEIR CELL PHONES AND CROSSED YA OFF THEIR CHRISTMAS-CARD LISTS.
SHOOT, BULLSEYE EVEN SAID HE'D WHACK HIM FOR FREE.
BULLSEYE WHACK SOMEBODY FOR ***FREE?*** *Pfft...* I'LL BELIEVE THAT WHEN I SEE IT.
MAYBE YOU'RE MIND-CONTROLLED... I DUNNO.
XAVIER, MAYBE...
HE DON'T LOOK MIND-CONTROLLED TO ME.
THEN MAYBE...
...MAYBE YA JUST GOT TIRED OF THE LIFE. IT HAPPENS TO ALL OF US, SOONER OR LATER.
YA GET TIRED OF ALWAYS LIVIN' OUTTA RATTY MOTELS. OF NOT BEIN' ABLE TO EVEN EAT IN A FREAKIN' RESTAURANT 'CAUSE YOU'RE AFRAID SOMEBODY'LL RECOGNIZE YA. OF JUMPIN' EVERY TIME YA HEAR A DAMN SIREN.
YA KNOW... JUST PLAIN ***TIRED.***

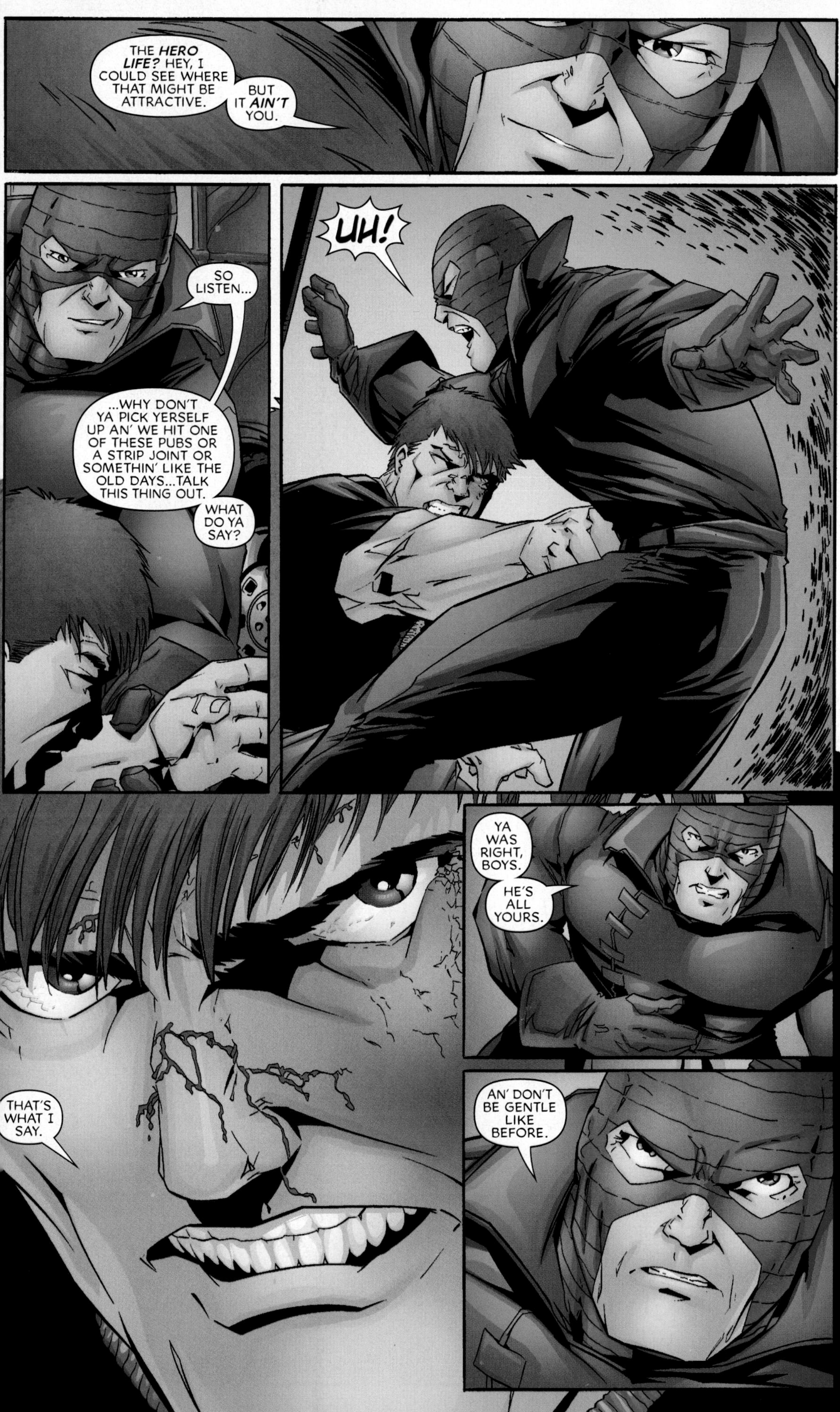
THE HERO LIFE? HEY, I COULD SEE WHERE THAT MIGHT BE ATTRACTIVE.
BUT IT AIN'T YOU.
SO LISTEN...
...WHY DON'T YA PICK YERSELF UP AN' WE HIT ONE OF THESE PUBS OR A STRIP JOINT OR SOMETHIN' LIKE THE OLD DAYS...TALK THIS THING OUT.
WHAT DO YA SAY?
UH!
THAT'S WHAT I SAY.
YA WAS RIGHT, BOYS.
HE'S ALL YOURS.
AN' DON'T BE GENTLE LIKE BEFORE.

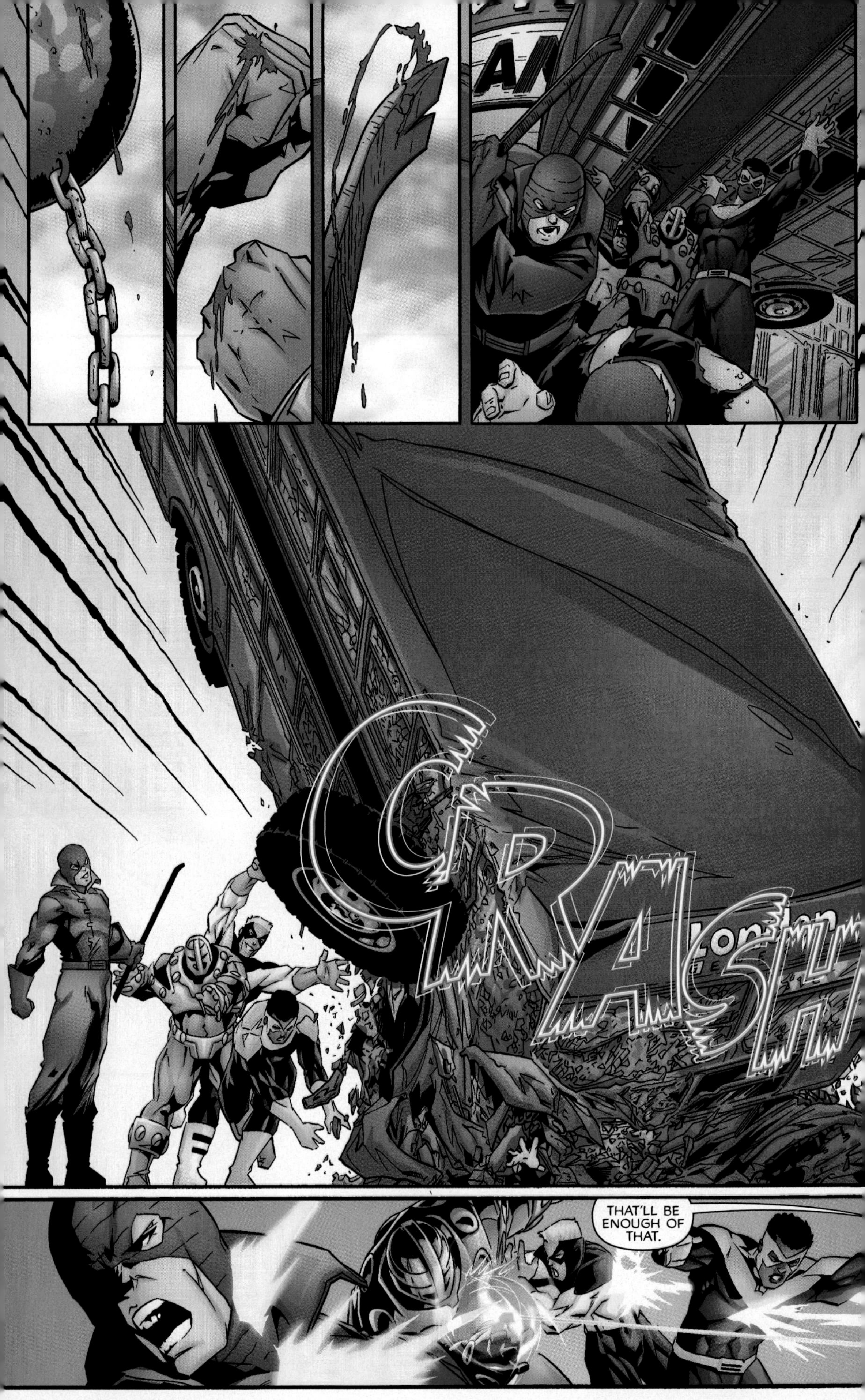
CRASH
THAT'LL BE ENOUGH OF THAT.

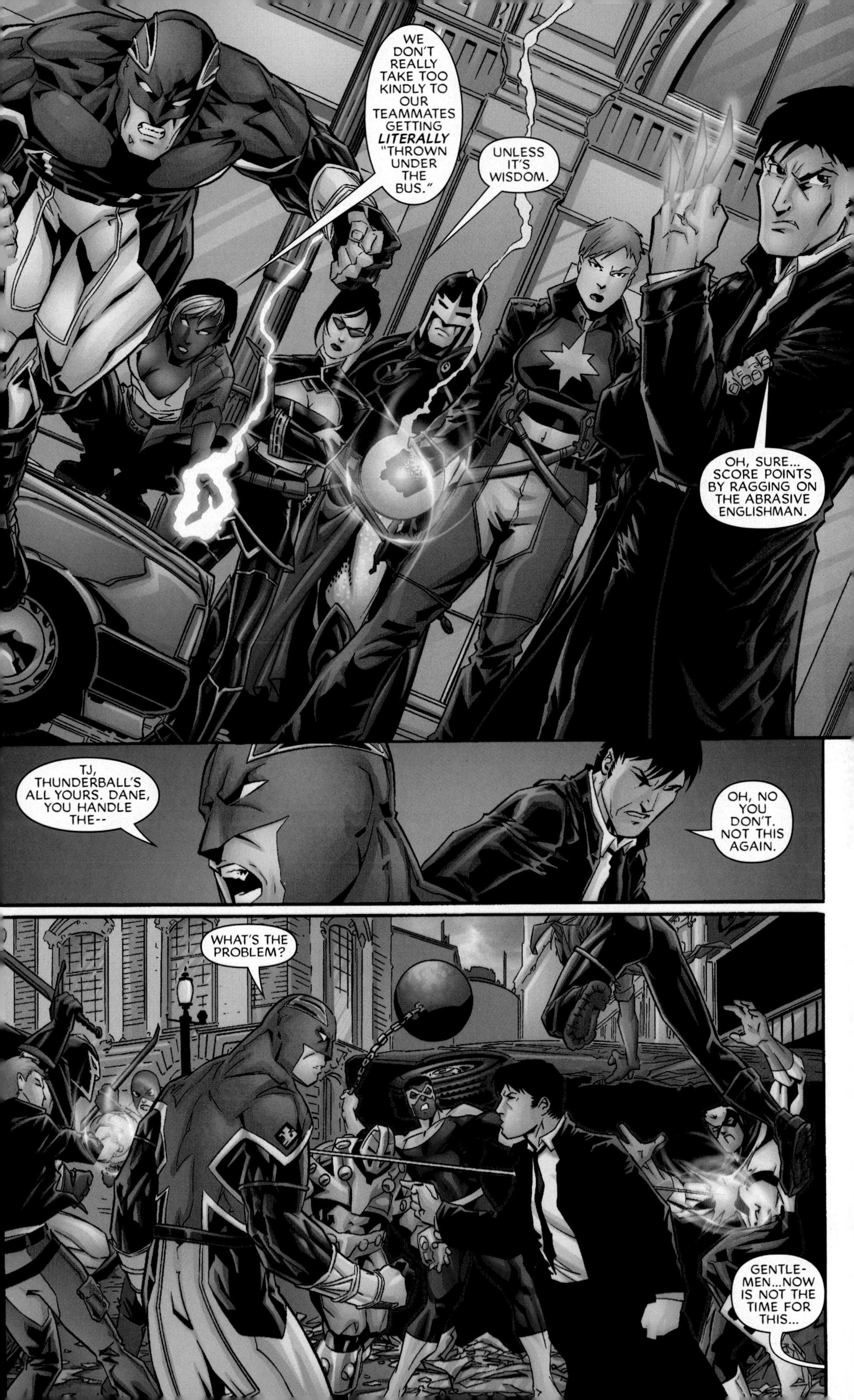
WE DON'T REALLY TAKE TOO KINDLY TO OUR TEAMMATES GETTING *LITERALLY* "THROWN UNDER THE BUS."
UNLESS IT'S WISDOM.
OH, SURE... SCORE POINTS BY RAGGING ON THE ABRASIVE ENGLISHMAN.
TJ, THUNDERBALL'S ALL YOURS. DANE, YOU HANDLE THE--
OH, NO YOU DON'T. NOT THIS AGAIN.
WHAT'S THE PROBLEM?
GENTLE-MEN...NOW IS NOT THE TIME FOR THIS...

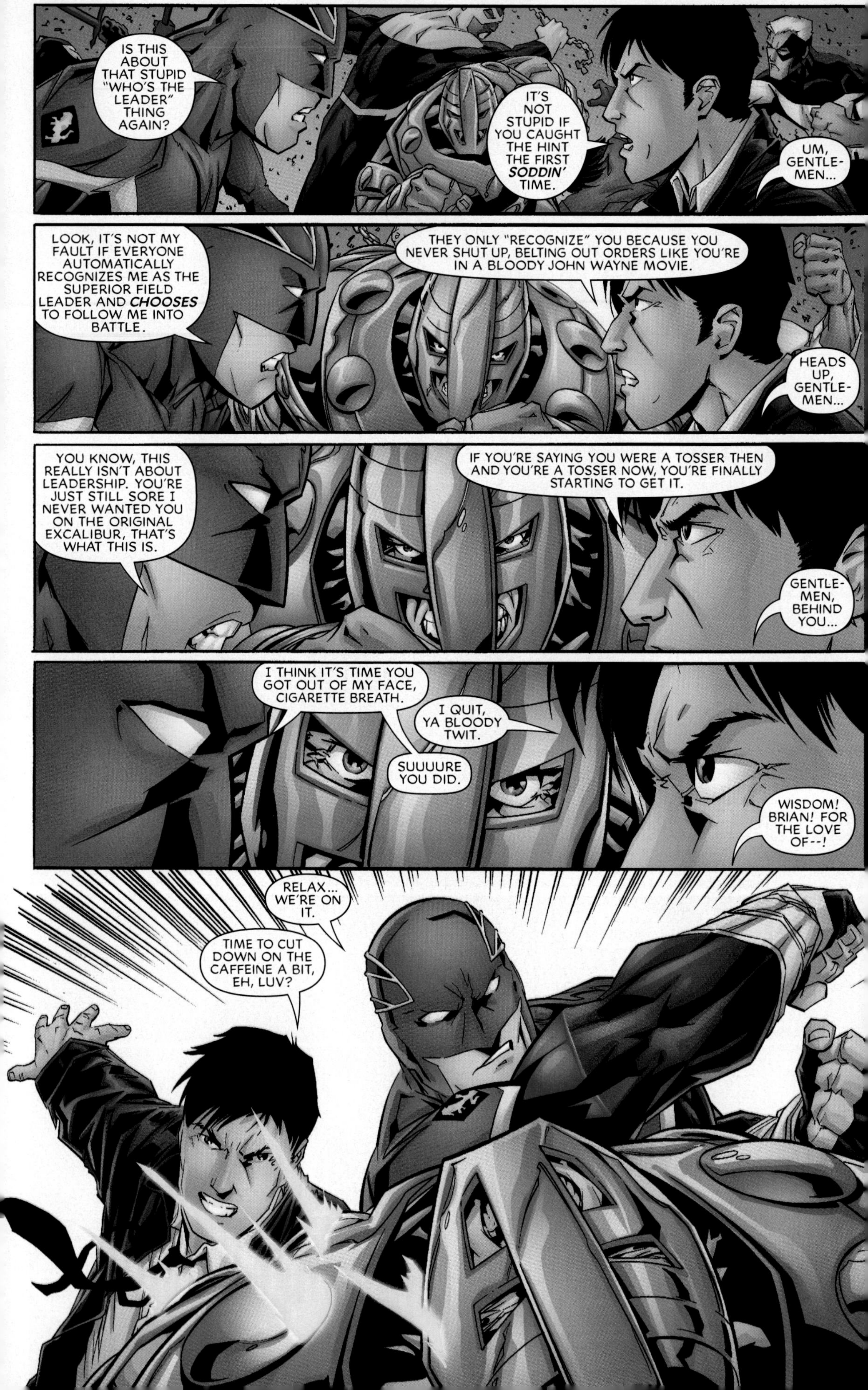
IS THIS ABOUT THAT STUPID "WHO'S THE LEADER" THING AGAIN?
IT'S NOT STUPID IF YOU CAUGHT THE HINT THE FIRST *SODDIN'* TIME.
UM, GENTLE-MEN...
LOOK, IT'S NOT MY FAULT IF EVERYONE AUTOMATICALLY RECOGNIZES ME AS THE SUPERIOR FIELD LEADER AND *CHOOSES* TO FOLLOW ME INTO BATTLE.
THEY ONLY "RECOGNIZE" YOU BECAUSE YOU NEVER SHUT UP, BELTING OUT ORDERS LIKE YOU'RE IN A BLOODY JOHN WAYNE MOVIE.
HEADS UP, GENTLE-MEN...
YOU KNOW, THIS REALLY ISN'T ABOUT LEADERSHIP. YOU'RE JUST STILL SORE I NEVER WANTED YOU ON THE ORIGINAL EXCALIBUR, THAT'S WHAT THIS IS.
IF YOU'RE SAYING YOU WERE A TOSSER THEN AND YOU'RE A TOSSER NOW, YOU'RE FINALLY STARTING TO GET IT.
GENTLE-MEN, BEHIND YOU...
I THINK IT'S TIME YOU GOT OUT OF MY FACE, CIGARETTE BREATH.
I QUIT, YA BLOODY TWIT.
SUUUURE YOU DID.
WISDOM! BRIAN! FOR THE LOVE OF--!
RELAX... WE'RE ON IT.
TIME TO CUT DOWN ON THE CAFFEINE A BIT, EH, LUV?

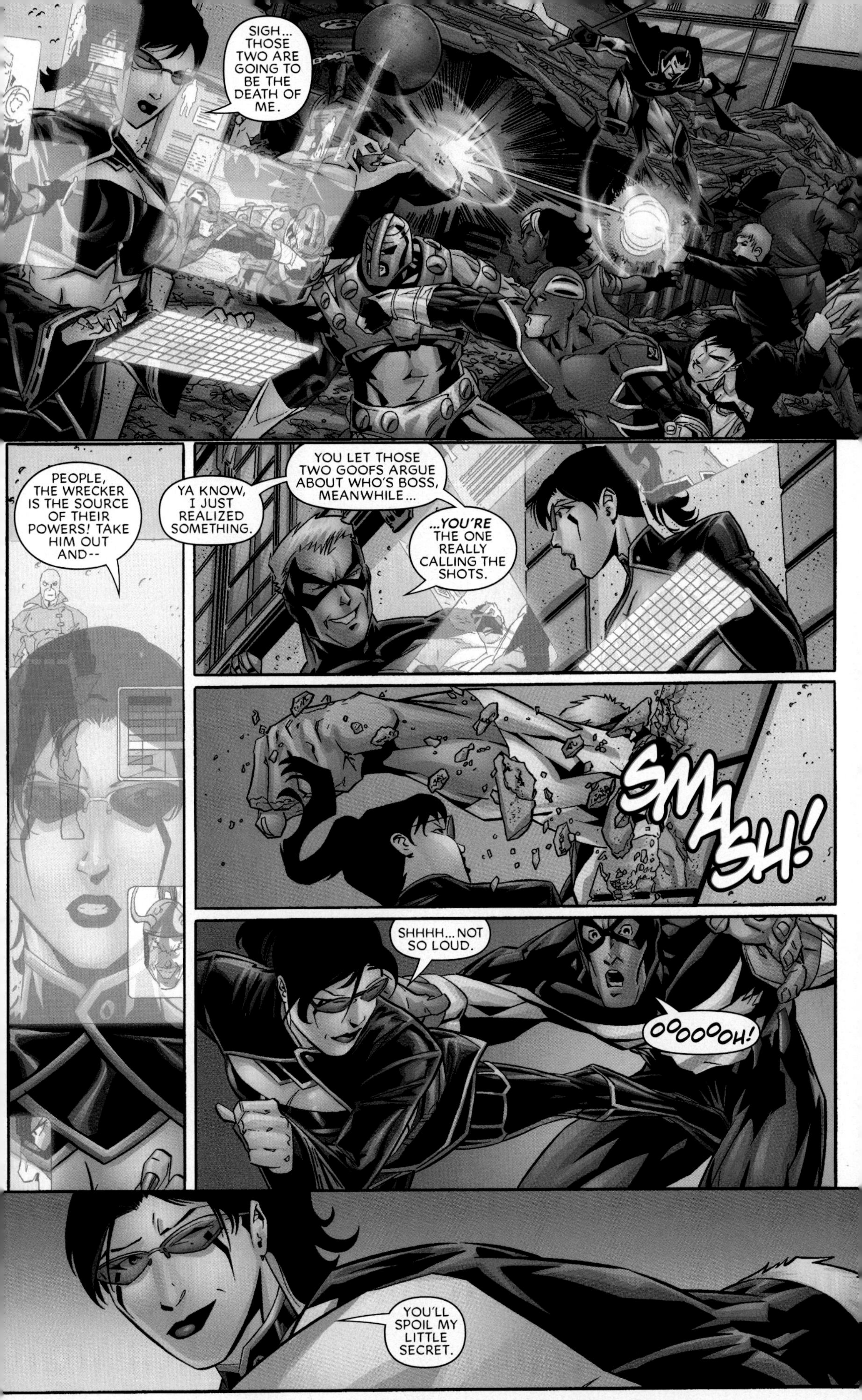
SIGH... THOSE TWO ARE GOING TO BE THE DEATH OF ME.
PEOPLE, THE WRECKER IS THE SOURCE OF THEIR POWERS! TAKE HIM OUT AND--
YA KNOW, I JUST REALIZED SOMETHING.
YOU LET THOSE TWO GOOFS ARGUE ABOUT WHO'S BOSS, MEANWHILE...
...YOU'RE THE ONE REALLY CALLING THE SHOTS.
SMASH!
SHHHH... NOT SO LOUD.
OOOOOOH!
YOU'LL SPOIL MY LITTLE SECRET.

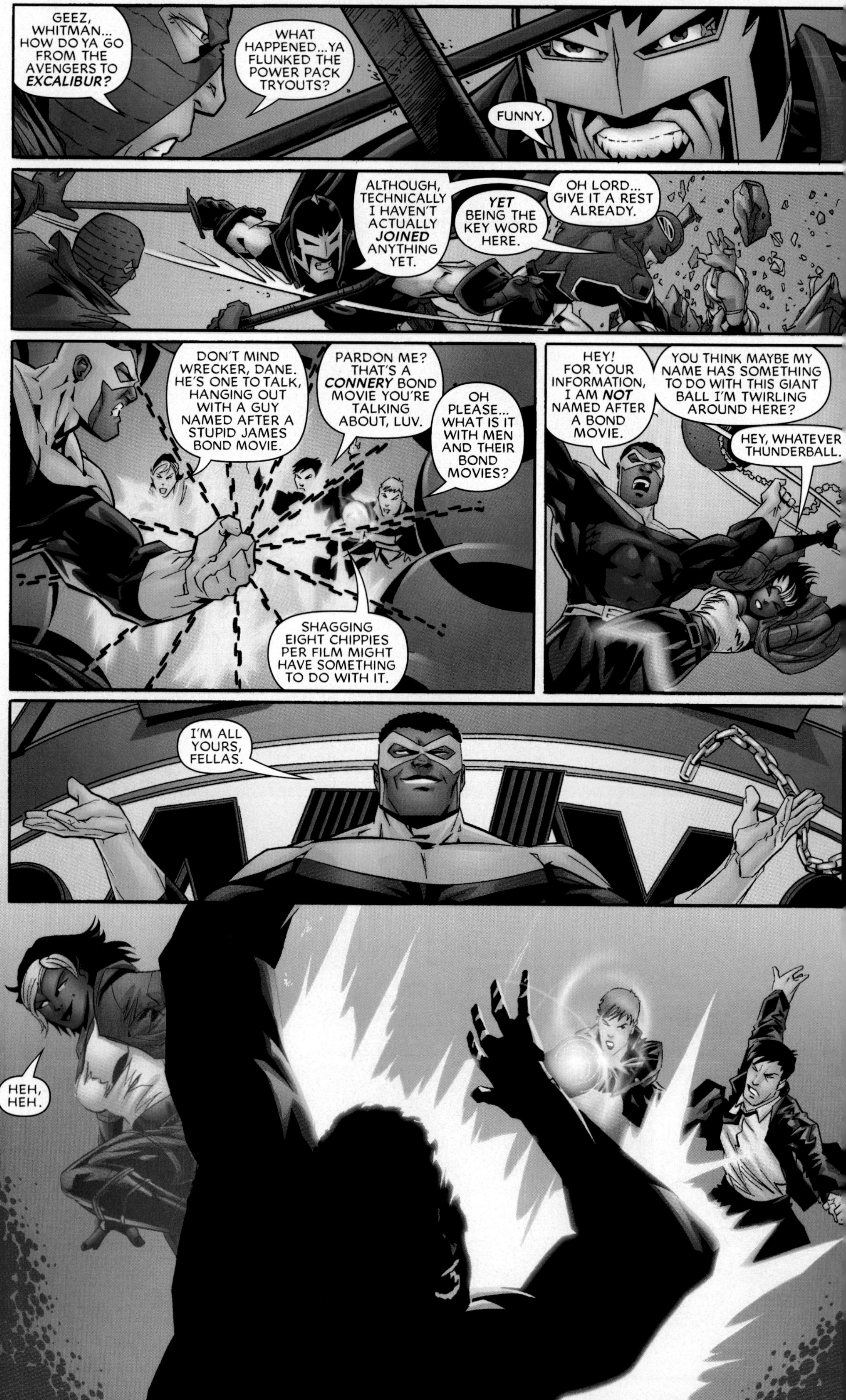
GEEZ, WHITMAN... HOW DO YA GO FROM THE AVENGERS TO *EXCALIBUR?*
WHAT HAPPENED...YA FLUNKED THE POWER PACK TRYOUTS?
FUNNY.
ALTHOUGH, TECHNICALLY I HAVEN'T ACTUALLY *JOINED* ANYTHING YET.
YET BEING THE KEY WORD HERE.
OH LORD... GIVE IT A REST ALREADY.
DON'T MIND WRECKER, DANE. HE'S ONE TO TALK, HANGING OUT WITH A GUY NAMED AFTER A STUPID JAMES BOND MOVIE.
PARDON ME? THAT'S A *CONNERY* BOND MOVIE YOU'RE TALKING ABOUT, LUV.
OH PLEASE... WHAT IS IT WITH MEN AND THEIR BOND MOVIES?
SHAGGING EIGHT CHIPPIES PER FILM MIGHT HAVE SOMETHING TO DO WITH IT.
HEY! FOR YOUR INFORMATION, I AM *NOT* NAMED AFTER A BOND MOVIE.
YOU THINK MAYBE MY NAME HAS SOMETHING TO DO WITH THIS GIANT BALL I'M TWIRLING AROUND HERE?
HEY, WHATEVER THUNDERBALL.
I'M ALL YOURS, FELLAS.
HEH, HEH.

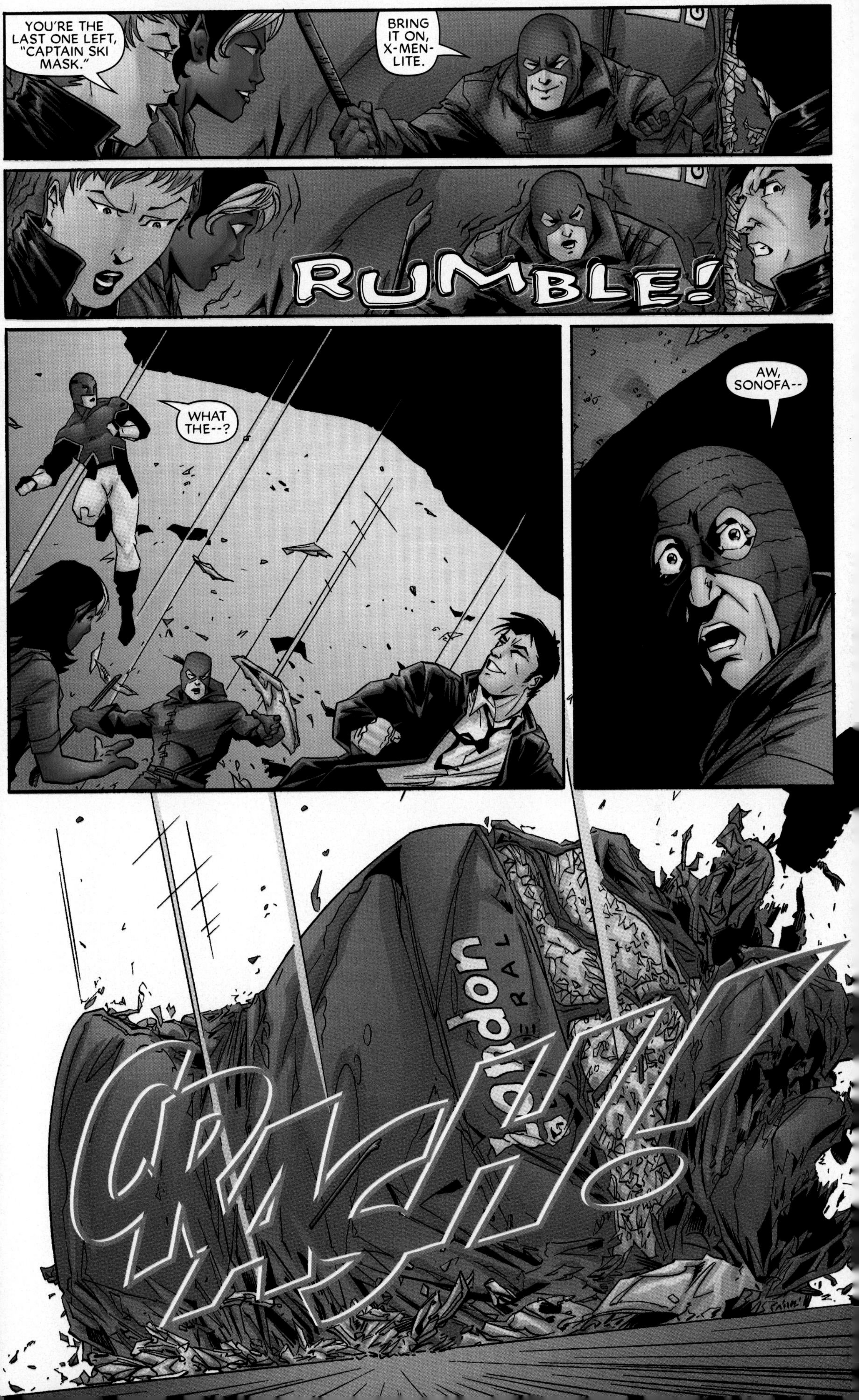

YOU'RE THE LAST ONE LEFT, "CAPTAIN SKI MASK."
BRING IT ON, X-MEN-LITE.
RUMBLE!
WHAT THE--?
AW, SONOFA--
CRASH!

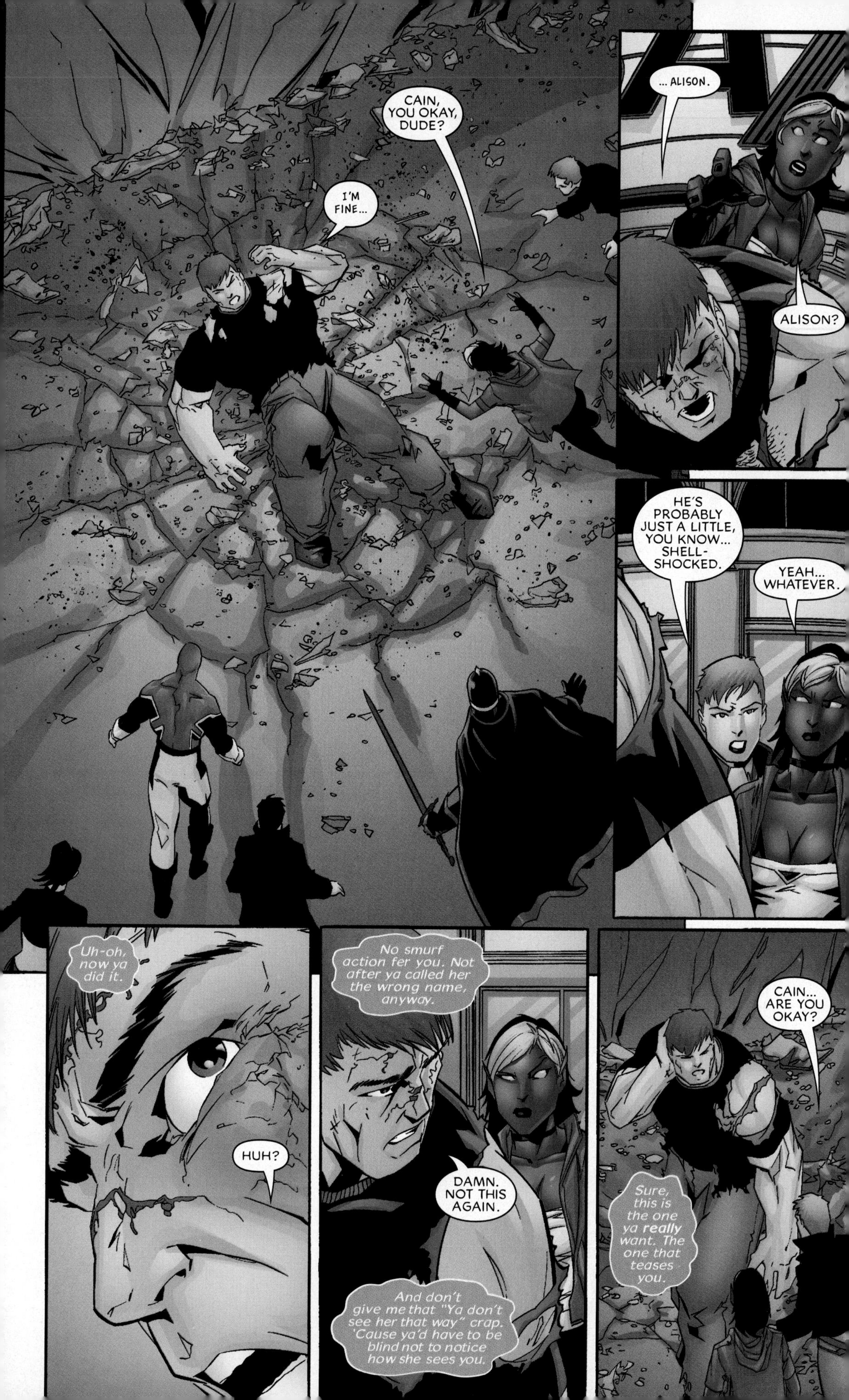
CAIN, YOU OKAY, DUDE?
I'M FINE...
... ALISON.
ALISON?
HE'S PROBABLY JUST A LITTLE, YOU KNOW... SHELL-SHOCKED.
YEAH... WHATEVER.
Uh-oh, now ya did it.
HUH?
No smurf action fer you. Not after ya called her the wrong name, anyway.
DAMN. NOT THIS AGAIN.
And don't give me that "Ya don't see her that way" crap. 'Cause ya'd have to be blind not to notice how she sees you.
CAIN... ARE YOU OKAY?
Sure, this is the one ya **really** want. The one that teases you.

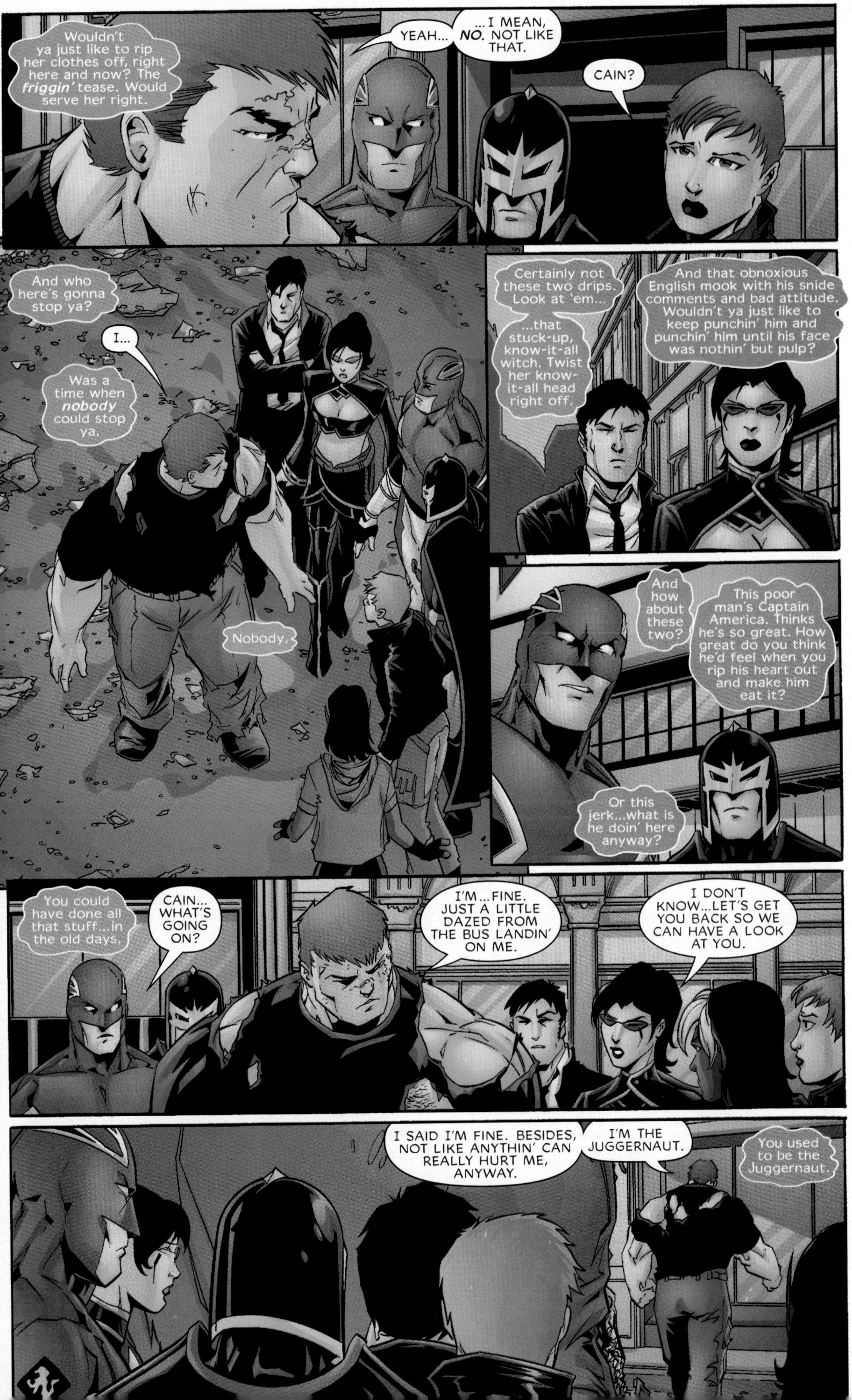
Wouldn't ya just like to rip her clothes off, right here and now? The *friggin'* tease. Would serve her right.
YEAH...
...I MEAN, **NO.** NOT LIKE THAT.
CAIN?
And who here's gonna stop ya?
I...
Was a time when *nobody* could stop ya.
Nobody.
Certainly not these two drips. Look at 'em...
...that stuck-up, know-it-all witch. Twist her know-it-all head right off.
And that obnoxious English mook with his snide comments and bad attitude. Wouldn't ya just like to keep punchin' him and punchin' him until his face was nothin' but pulp?
And how about these two?
This poor man's Captain America. Thinks he's so great. How great do you think he'd feel when you rip his heart out and make him eat it?
Or this jerk...what is he doin' here anyway?
You could have done all that stuff...in the old days.
CAIN... WHAT'S GOING ON?
I'M...FINE. JUST A LITTLE DAZED FROM THE BUS LANDIN' ON ME.
I DON'T KNOW...LET'S GET YOU BACK SO WE CAN HAVE A LOOK AT YOU.
I SAID I'M FINE. BESIDES, NOT LIKE ANYTHIN' CAN REALLY HURT ME, ANYWAY.
I'M THE JUGGERNAUT.
You used to be the Juggernaut.

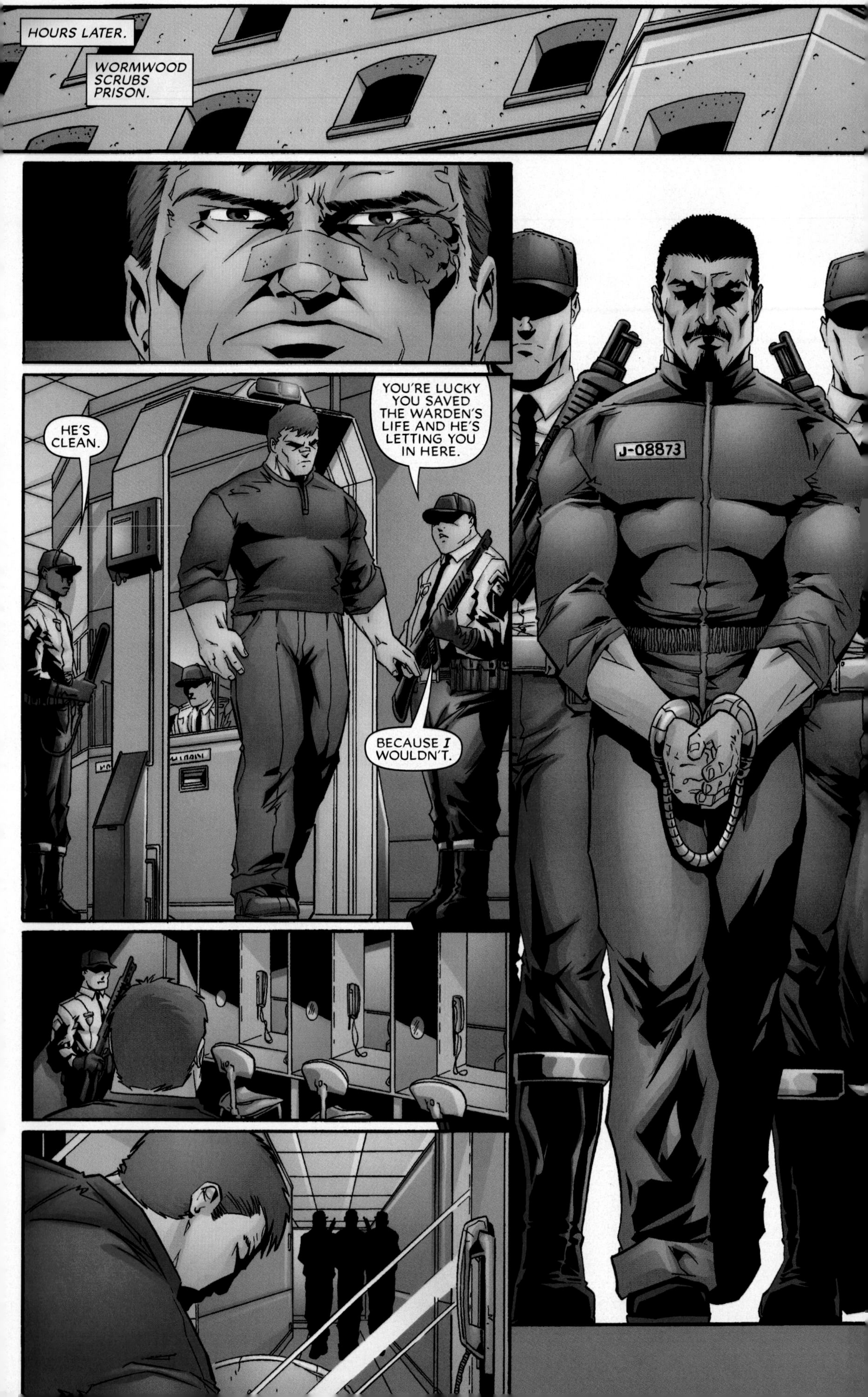
HOURS LATER.
WORMWOOD SCRUBS PRISON.
HE'S CLEAN.
YOU'RE LUCKY YOU SAVED THE WARDEN'S LIFE AND HE'S LETTING YOU IN HERE.
BECAUSE *I* WOULDN'T.
J-08873

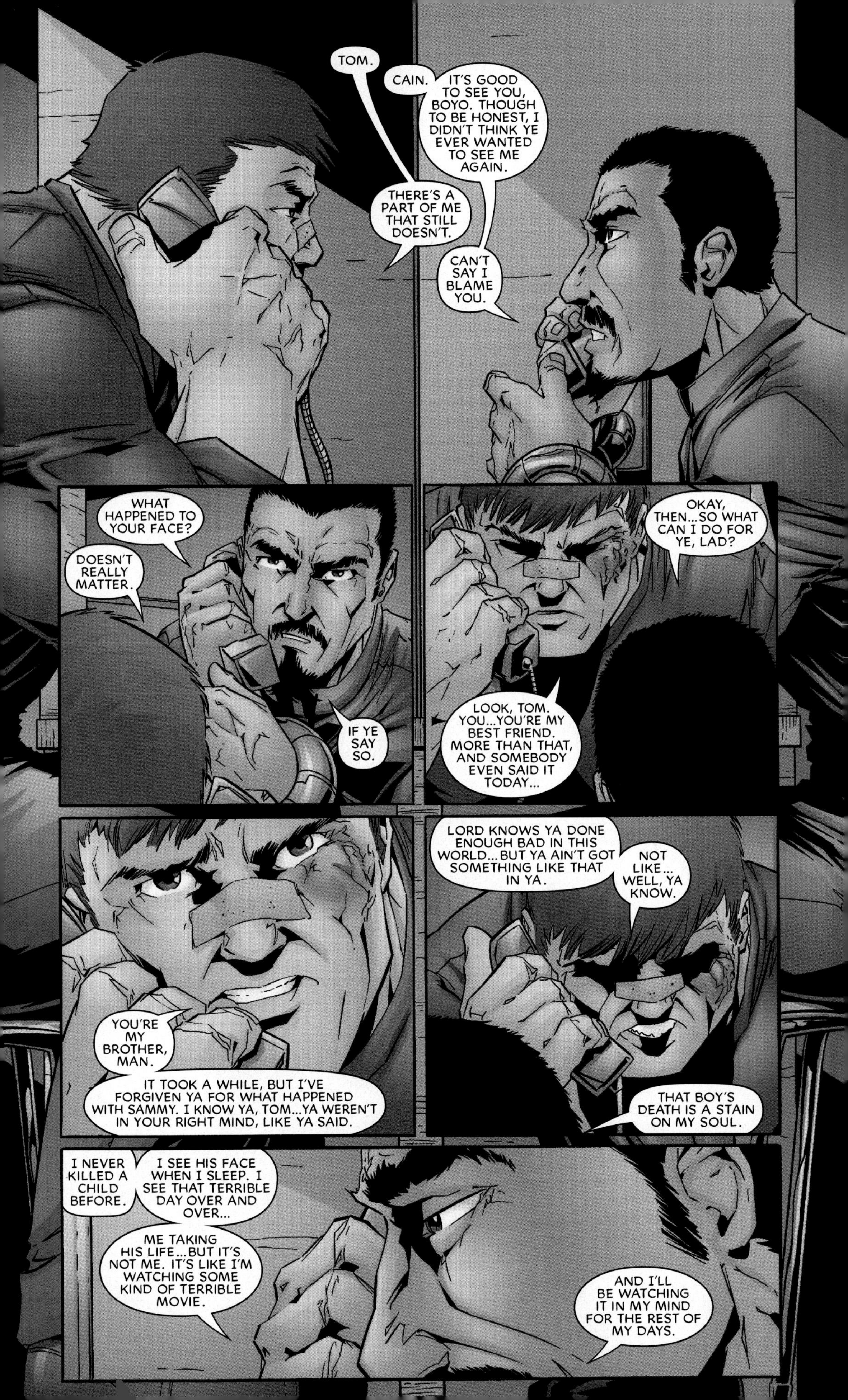
TOM.
CAIN.
IT'S GOOD TO SEE YOU, BOYO. THOUGH TO BE HONEST, I DIDN'T THINK YE EVER WANTED TO SEE ME AGAIN.
THERE'S A PART OF ME THAT STILL DOESN'T.
CAN'T SAY I BLAME YOU.
WHAT HAPPENED TO YOUR FACE?
DOESN'T REALLY MATTER.
IF YE SAY SO.
OKAY, THEN...SO WHAT CAN I DO FOR YE, LAD?
LOOK, TOM. YOU...YOU'RE MY BEST FRIEND. MORE THAN THAT, AND SOMEBODY EVEN SAID IT TODAY...
YOU'RE MY BROTHER, MAN.
IT TOOK A WHILE, BUT I'VE FORGIVEN YA FOR WHAT HAPPENED WITH SAMMY. I KNOW YA, TOM...YA WEREN'T IN YOUR RIGHT MIND, LIKE YA SAID.
LORD KNOWS YA DONE ENOUGH BAD IN THIS WORLD... BUT YA AIN'T GOT SOMETHING LIKE THAT IN YA.
NOT LIKE... WELL, YA KNOW.
THAT BOY'S DEATH IS A STAIN ON MY SOUL.
I NEVER KILLED A CHILD BEFORE.
I SEE HIS FACE WHEN I SLEEP. I SEE THAT TERRIBLE DAY OVER AND OVER...
ME TAKING HIS LIFE...BUT IT'S NOT ME. IT'S LIKE I'M WATCHING SOME KIND OF TERRIBLE MOVIE.
AND I'LL BE WATCHING IT IN MY MIND FOR THE REST OF MY DAYS.

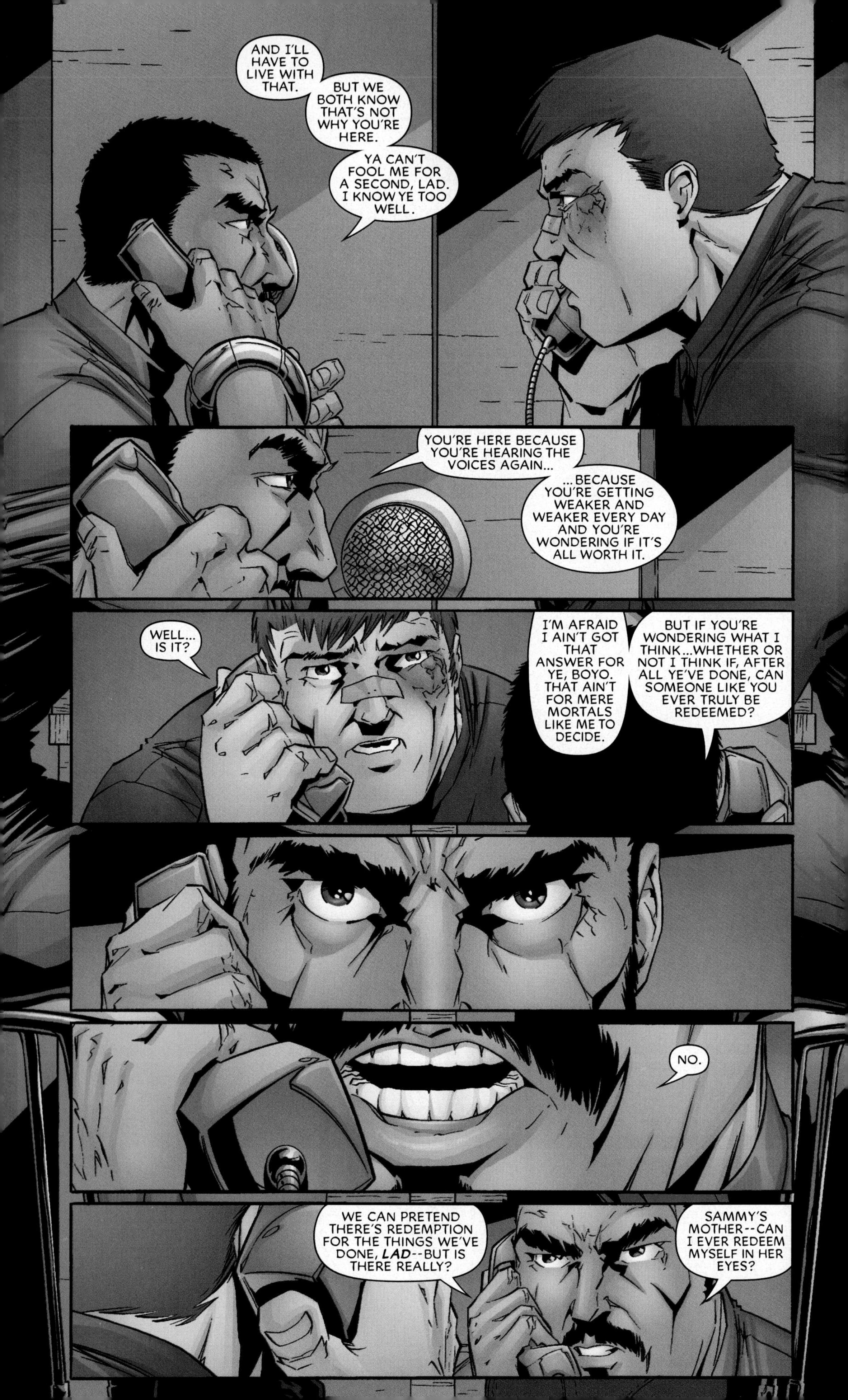
AND I'LL HAVE TO LIVE WITH THAT.
BUT WE BOTH KNOW THAT'S NOT WHY YOU'RE HERE.
YA CAN'T FOOL ME FOR A SECOND, LAD. I KNOW YE TOO WELL.
YOU'RE HERE BECAUSE YOU'RE HEARING THE VOICES AGAIN...
...BECAUSE YOU'RE GETTING WEAKER AND WEAKER EVERY DAY AND YOU'RE WONDERING IF IT'S ALL WORTH IT.
WELL... IS IT?
I'M AFRAID I AIN'T GOT THAT ANSWER FOR YE, BOYO. THAT AIN'T FOR MERE MORTALS LIKE ME TO DECIDE.
BUT IF YOU'RE WONDERING WHAT I THINK...WHETHER OR NOT I THINK IF, AFTER ALL YE'VE DONE, CAN SOMEONE LIKE YOU EVER TRULY BE REDEEMED?
NO.
WE CAN PRETEND THERE'S REDEMPTION FOR THE THINGS WE'VE DONE, *LAD*--BUT IS THERE REALLY?
SAMMY'S MOTHER--CAN I EVER REDEEM MYSELF IN HER EYES?

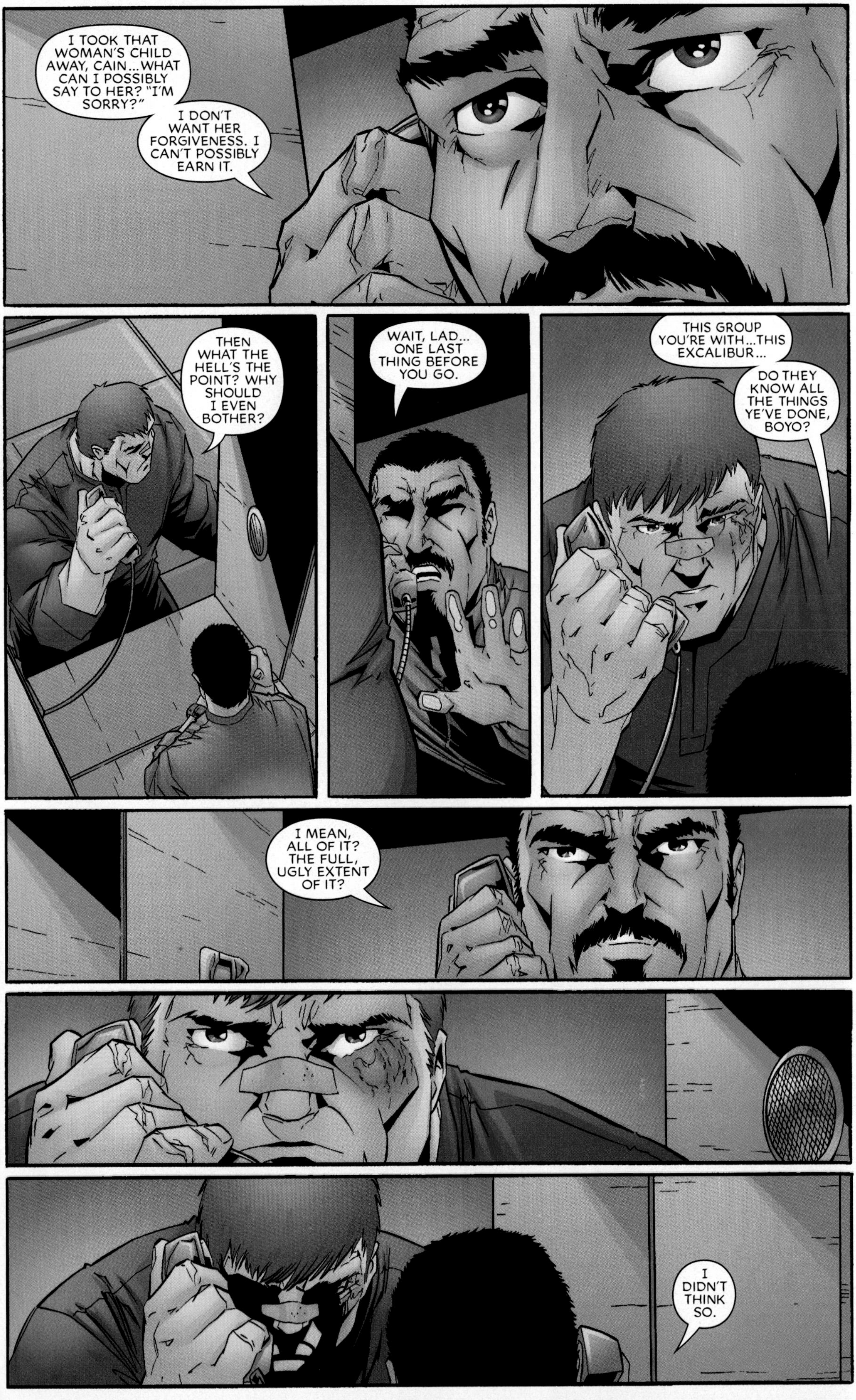

I TOOK THAT WOMAN'S CHILD AWAY, CAIN...WHAT CAN I POSSIBLY SAY TO HER? "I'M SORRY?"
I DON'T WANT HER FORGIVENESS. I CAN'T POSSIBLY EARN IT.
THEN WHAT THE HELL'S THE POINT? WHY SHOULD I EVEN BOTHER?
WAIT, LAD... ONE LAST THING BEFORE YOU GO.
THIS GROUP YOU'RE WITH...THIS EXCALIBUR...
DO THEY KNOW ALL THE THINGS YE'VE DONE, BOYO?
I MEAN, ALL OF IT? THE FULL, UGLY EXTENT OF IT?
I DIDN'T THINK SO.

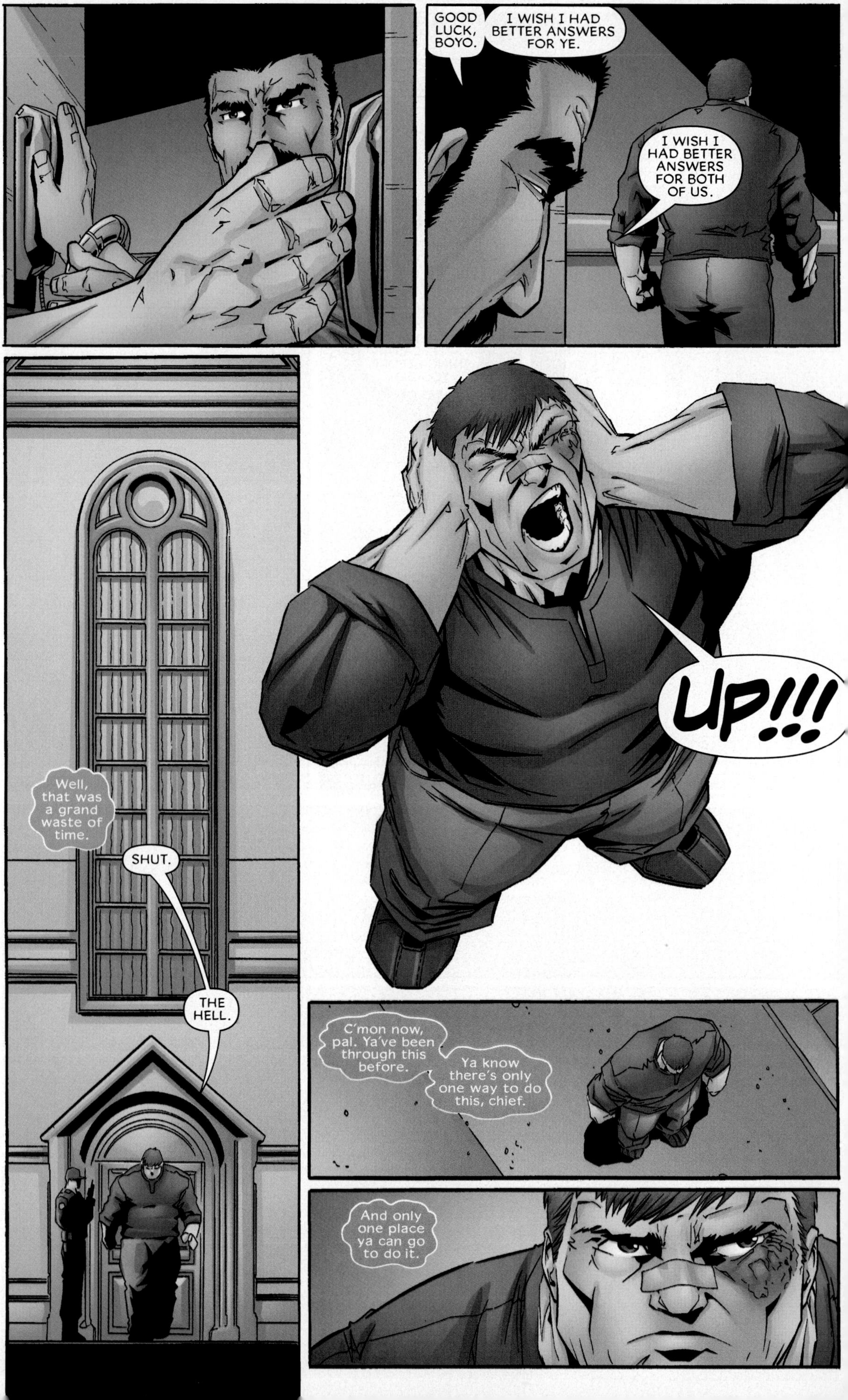
GOOD LUCK, BOYO.
I WISH I HAD BETTER ANSWERS FOR YE.
I WISH I HAD BETTER ANSWERS FOR BOTH OF US.
Well, that was a grand waste of time.
SHUT.
THE HELL.
UP!!!
C'mon now, pal. Ya've been through this before.
Ya know there's only one way to do this, chief.
And only one place ya can go to do it.

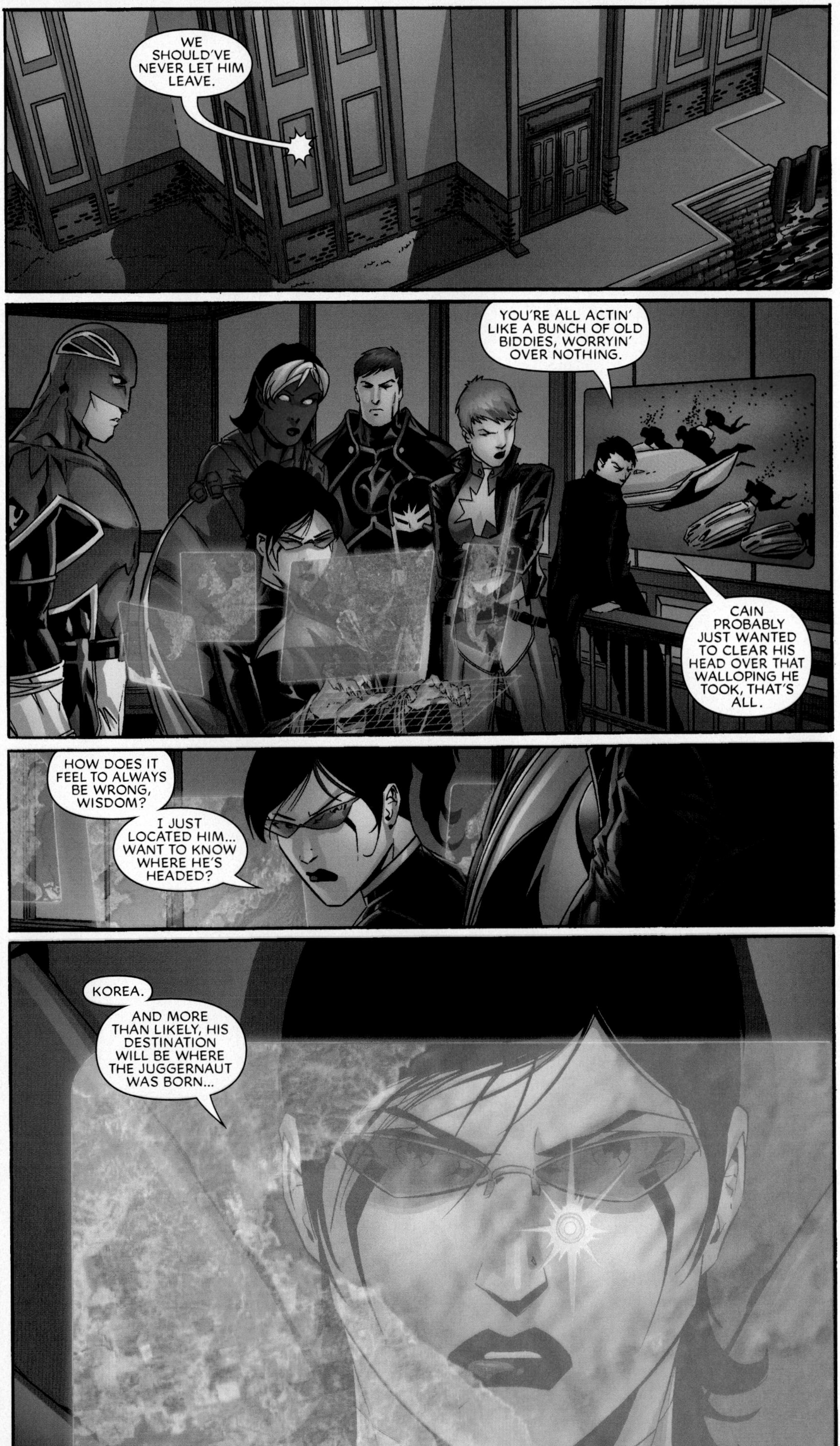
WE SHOULD'VE NEVER LET HIM LEAVE.
YOU'RE ALL ACTIN' LIKE A BUNCH OF OLD BIDDIES, WORRYIN' OVER NOTHING.
CAIN PROBABLY JUST WANTED TO CLEAR HIS HEAD OVER THAT WALLOPING HE TOOK, THAT'S ALL.
HOW DOES IT FEEL TO ALWAYS BE WRONG, WISDOM?
I JUST LOCATED HIM... WANT TO KNOW WHERE HE'S HEADED?
KOREA.
AND MORE THAN LIKELY, HIS DESTINATION WILL BE WHERE THE JUGGERNAUT WAS BORN...

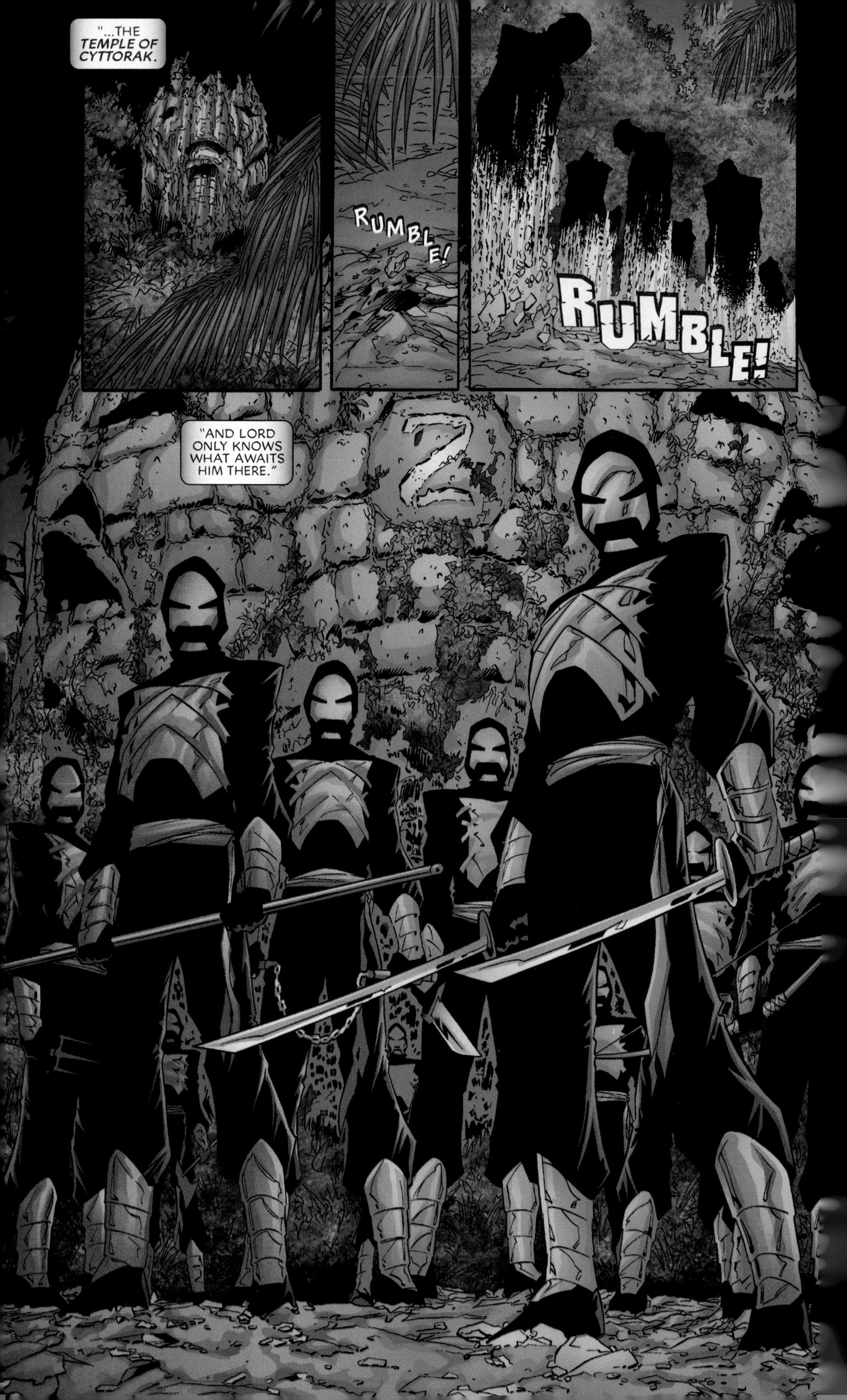
"...THE TEMPLE OF CYTTORAK.
RUMBLE!
RUMBLE!
"AND LORD ONLY KNOWS WHAT AWAITS HIM THERE."

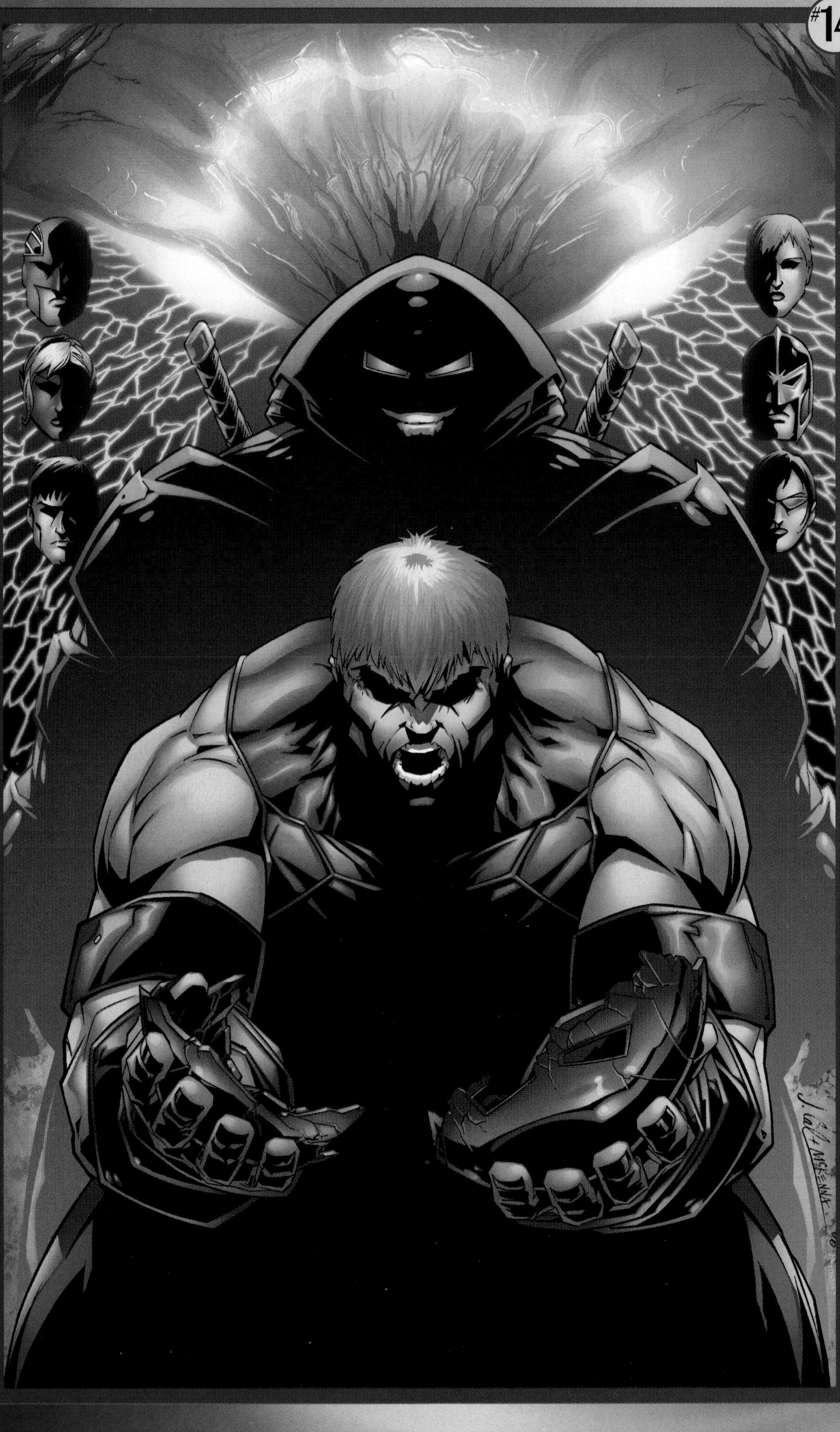
#14

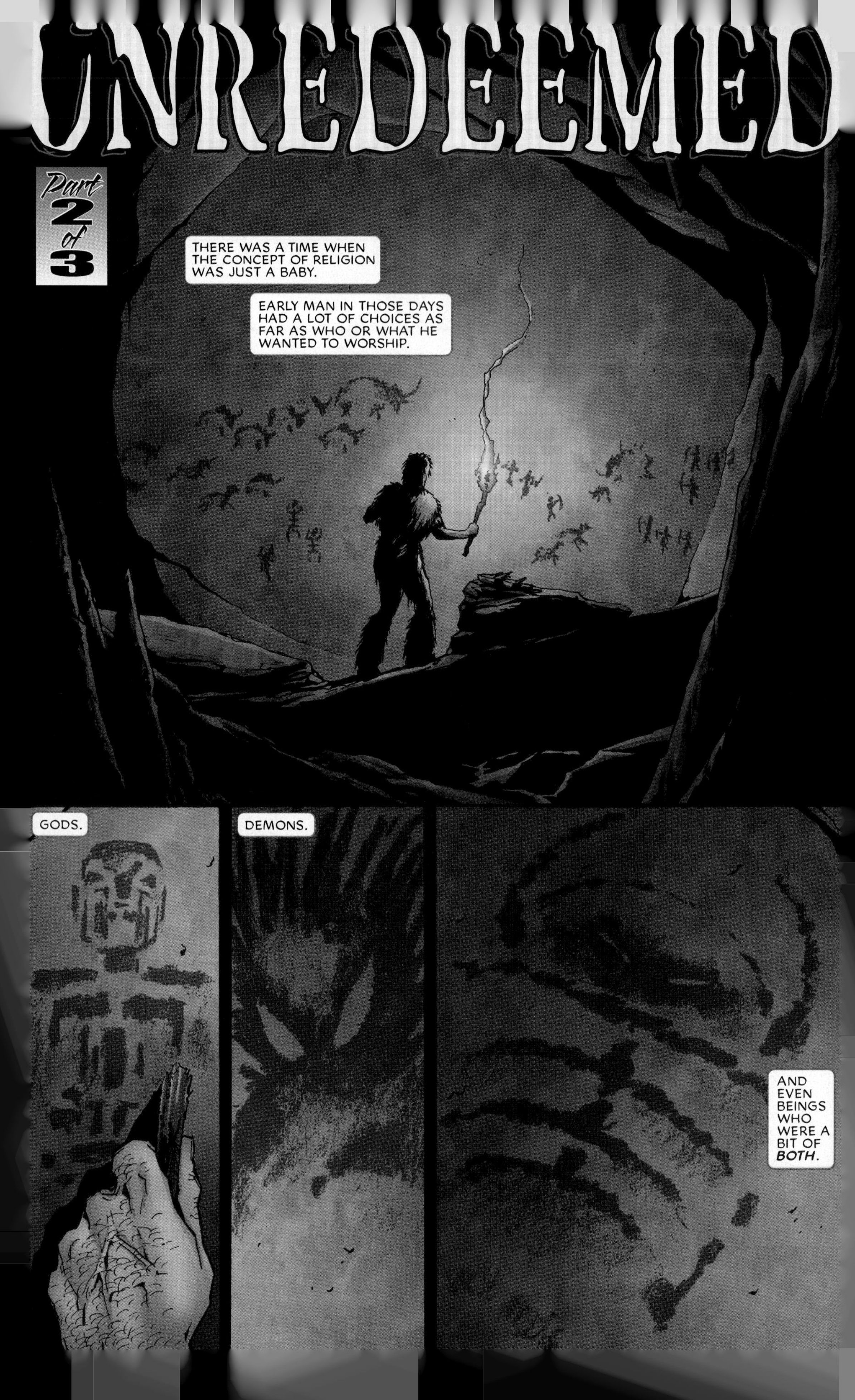
UNREDEEMED
Part 2 of 3
THERE WAS A TIME WHEN THE CONCEPT OF RELIGION WAS JUST A BABY.
EARLY MAN IN THOSE DAYS HAD A LOT OF CHOICES AS FAR AS WHO OR WHAT HE WANTED TO WORSHIP.
GODS.
DEMONS.
AND EVEN BEINGS WHO WERE A BIT OF *BOTH*.

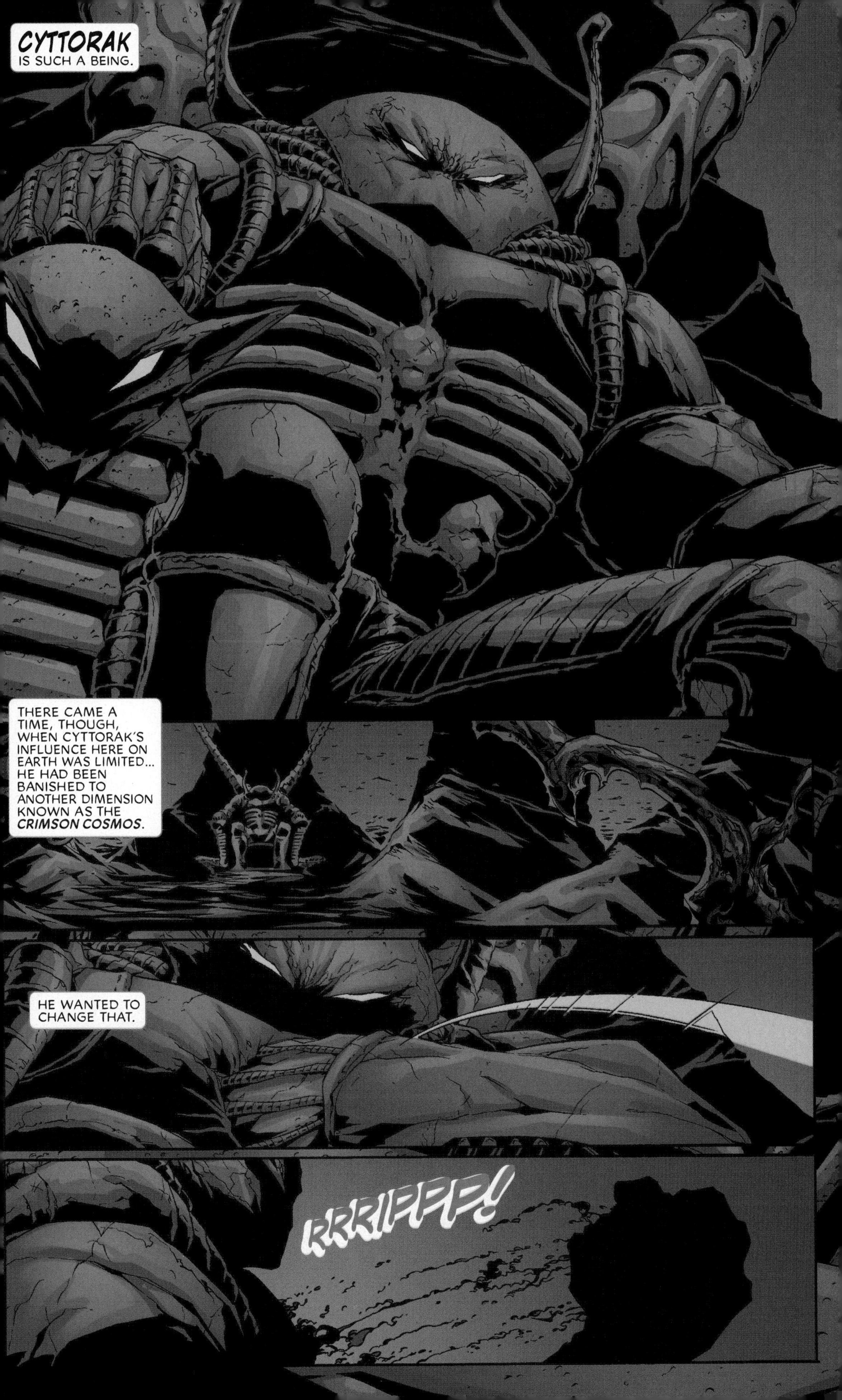
CYTTORAK IS SUCH A BEING.
THERE CAME A TIME, THOUGH, WHEN CYTTORAK'S INFLUENCE HERE ON EARTH WAS LIMITED... HE HAD BEEN BANISHED TO ANOTHER DIMENSION KNOWN AS THE CRIMSON COSMOS.
HE WANTED TO CHANGE THAT.
RRRIPPP!

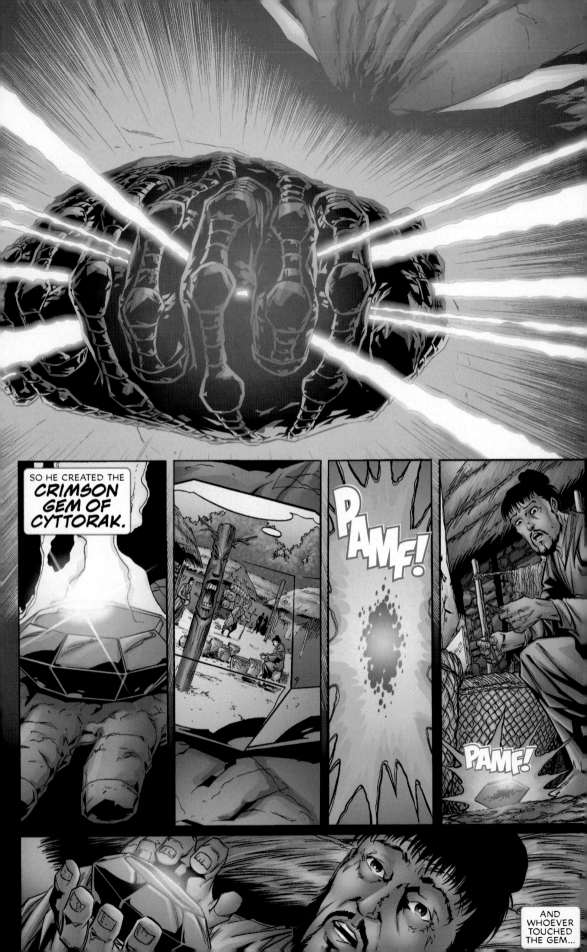

SO HE CREATED THE **CRIMSON GEM OF CYTTORAK.**

PAMF!

PAMF!

AND WHOEVER TOUCHED THE GEM...

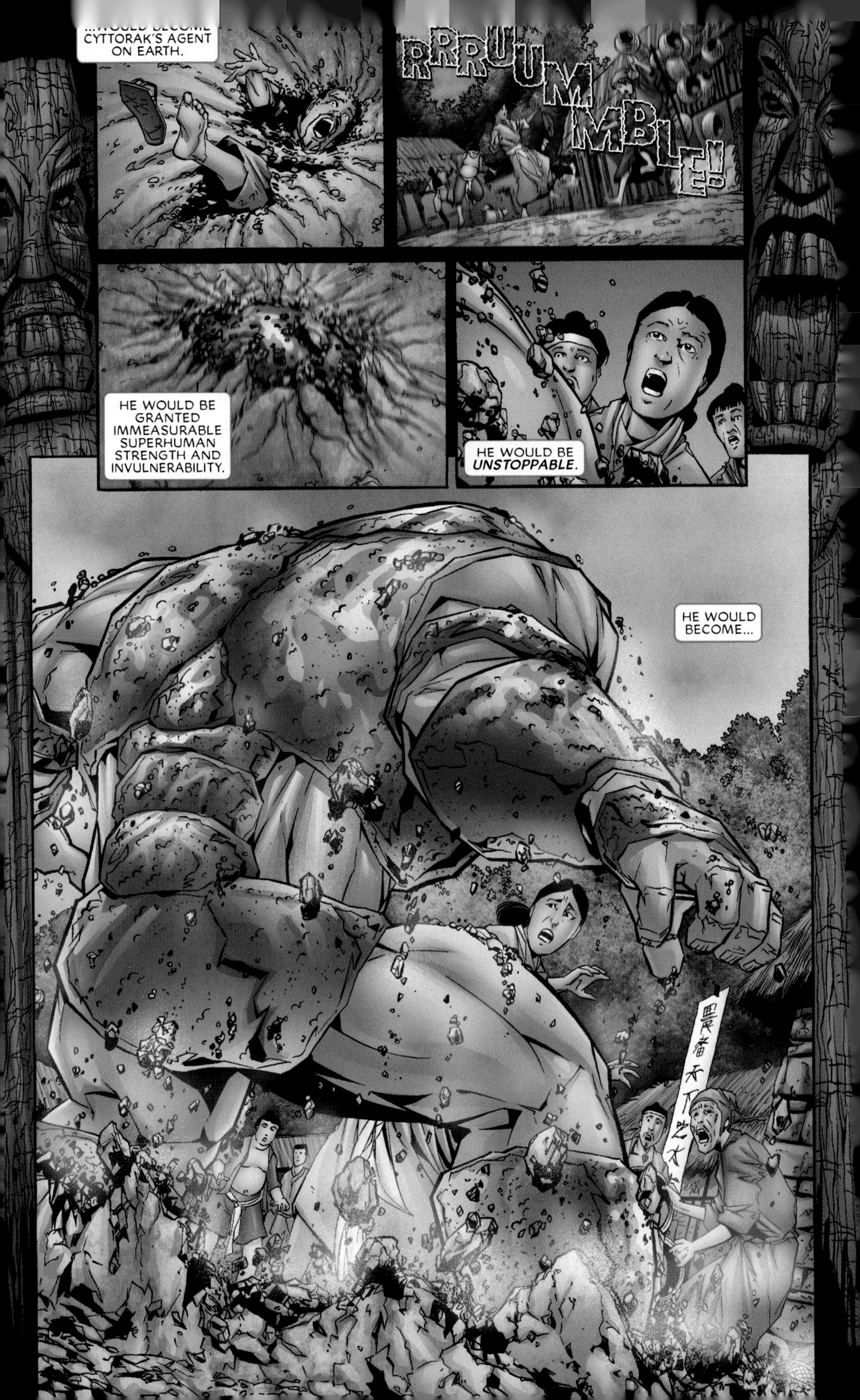
...WOULD BECOME CYTTORAK'S AGENT ON EARTH.
RRRUUMMBLE!
HE WOULD BE GRANTED IMMEASURABLE SUPERHUMAN STRENGTH AND INVULNERABILITY.
HE WOULD BE *UNSTOPPABLE*.
HE WOULD BECOME...

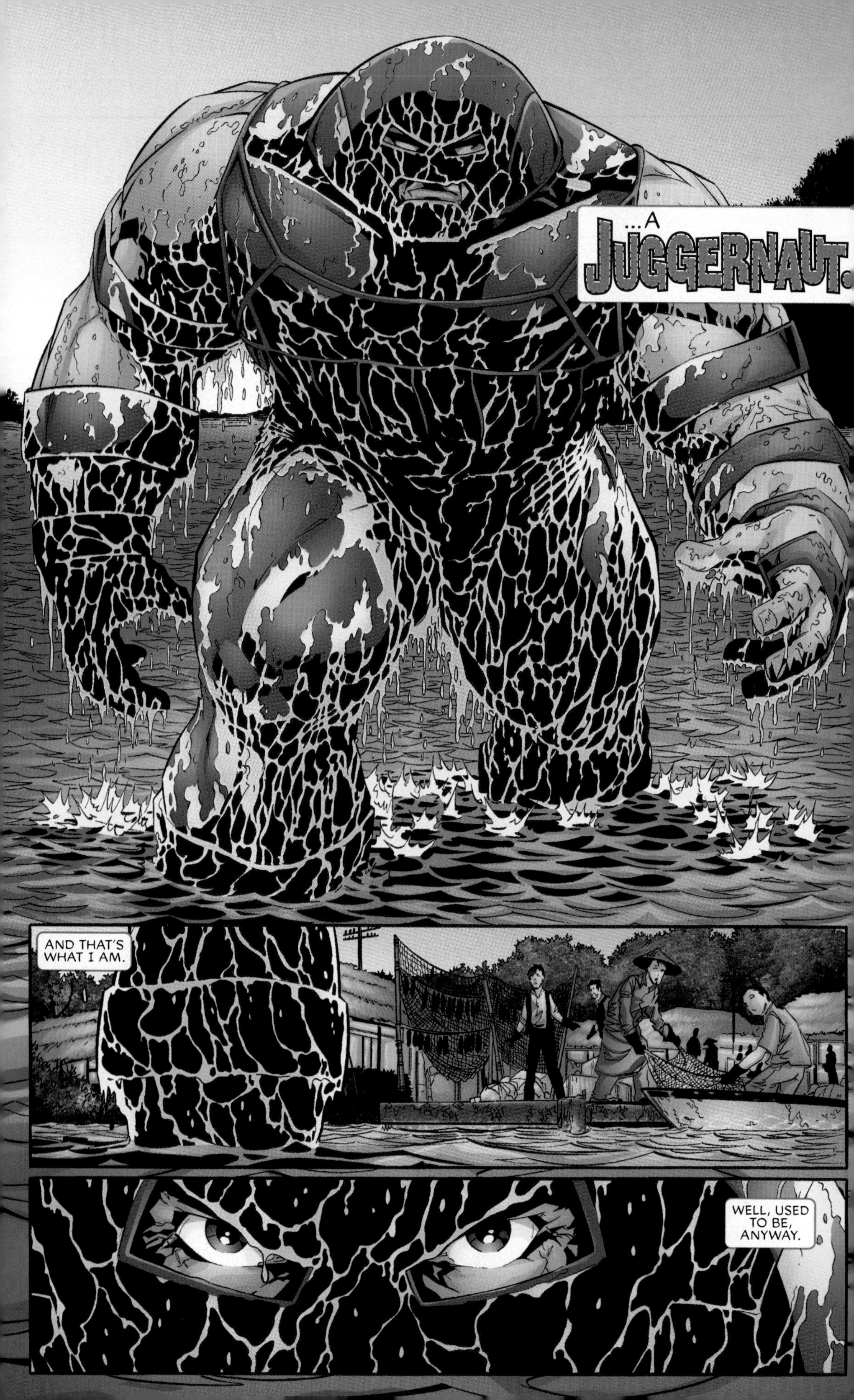
...A JUGGERNAUT.
AND THAT'S WHAT I AM.
WELL, USED TO BE, ANYWAY.

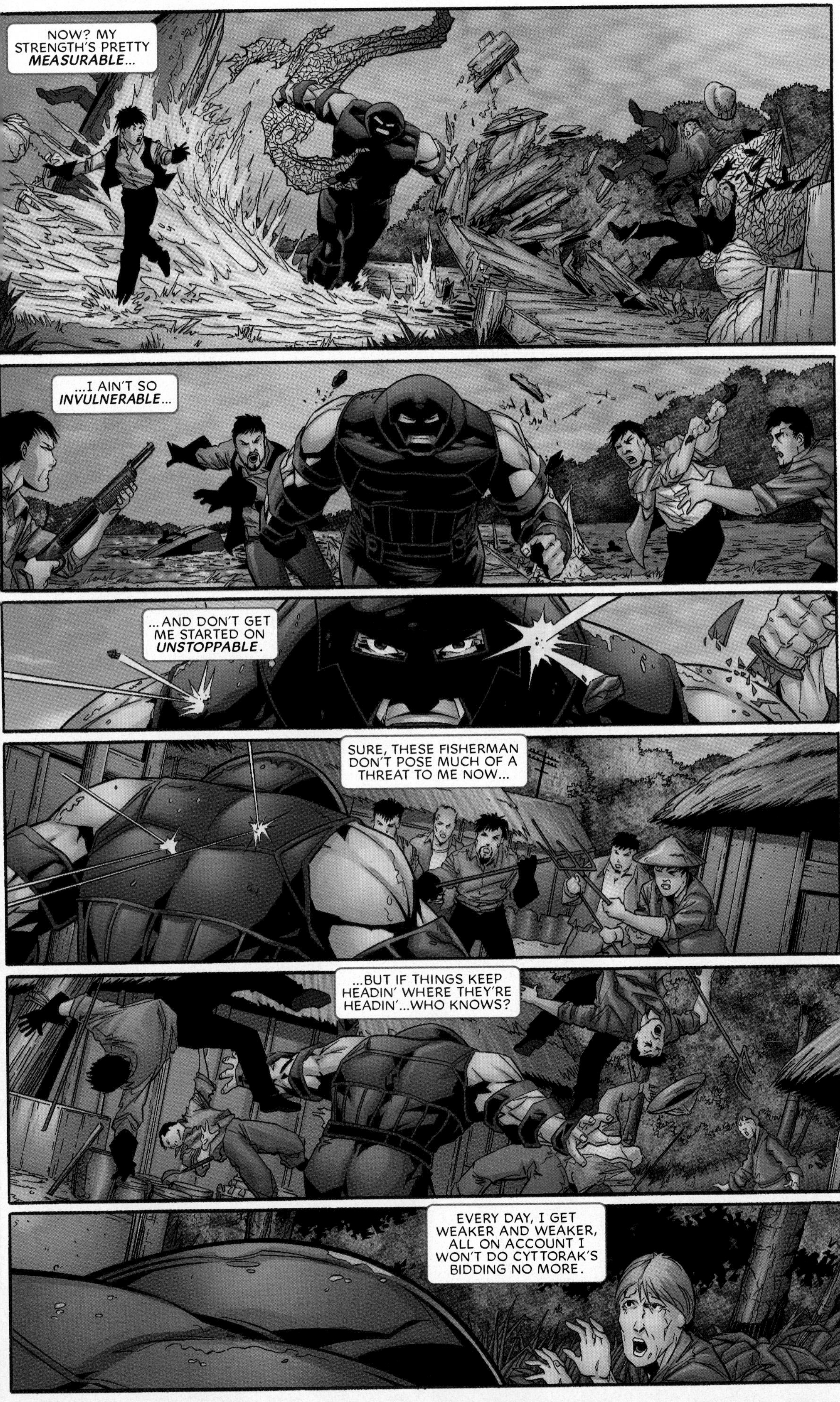
NOW? MY STRENGTH'S PRETTY MEASURABLE...
...I AIN'T SO INVULNERABLE...
...AND DON'T GET ME STARTED ON UNSTOPPABLE.
SURE, THESE FISHERMAN DON'T POSE MUCH OF A THREAT TO ME NOW...
...BUT IF THINGS KEEP HEADIN' WHERE THEY'RE HEADIN'...WHO KNOWS?
EVERY DAY, I GET WEAKER AND WEAKER, ALL ON ACCOUNT I WON'T DO CYTTORAK'S BIDDING NO MORE.

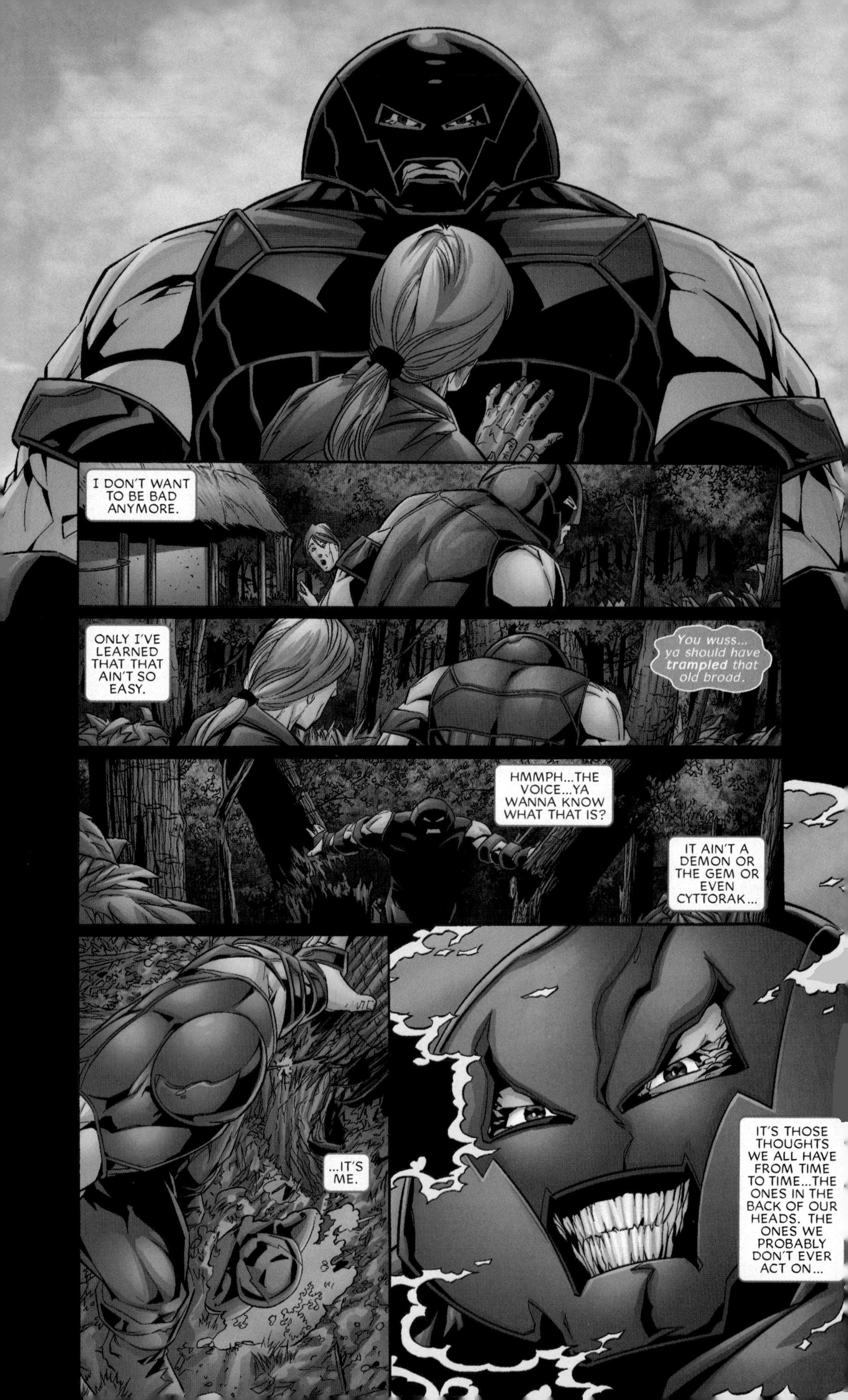
I DON'T WANT TO BE BAD ANYMORE.
ONLY I'VE LEARNED THAT THAT AIN'T SO EASY.
You wuss... ya should have **trampled** that old broad.
HMMPH...THE VOICE...YA WANNA KNOW WHAT THAT IS?
IT AIN'T A DEMON OR THE GEM OR EVEN CYTTORAK...
...IT'S ME.
IT'S THOSE THOUGHTS WE ALL HAVE FROM TIME TO TIME...THE ONES IN THE BACK OF OUR HEADS. THE ONES WE PROBABLY DON'T EVER ACT ON...

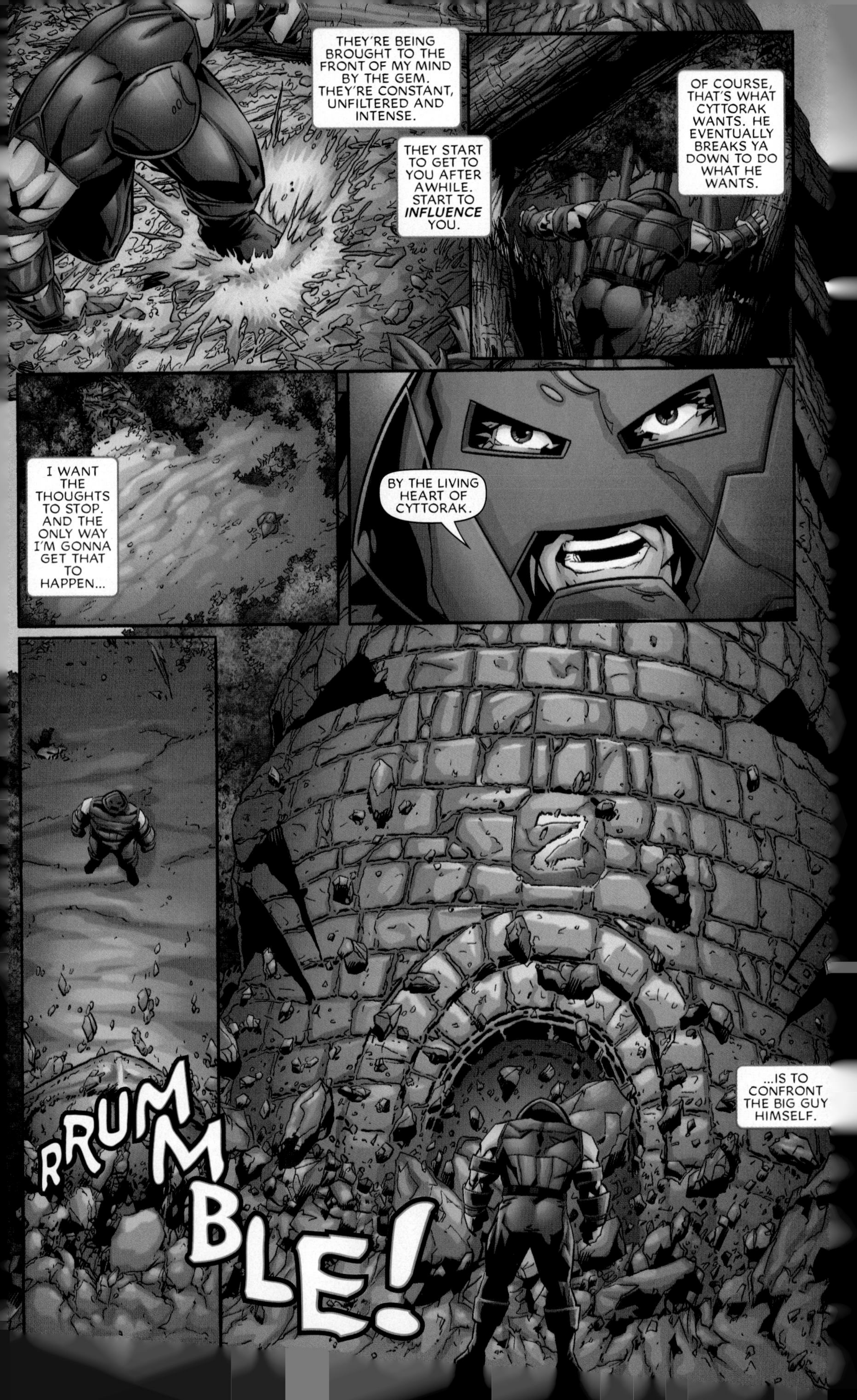
THEY'RE BEING BROUGHT TO THE FRONT OF MY MIND BY THE GEM. THEY'RE CONSTANT, UNFILTERED AND INTENSE.
THEY START TO GET TO YOU AFTER AWHILE. START TO *INFLUENCE* YOU.
OF COURSE, THAT'S WHAT CYTTORAK WANTS. HE EVENTUALLY BREAKS YA DOWN TO DO WHAT HE WANTS.
I WANT THE THOUGHTS TO STOP. AND THE ONLY WAY I'M GONNA GET THAT TO HAPPEN...
BY THE LIVING HEART OF CYTTORAK.
...IS TO CONFRONT THE BIG GUY HIMSELF.
RRUMMBLE!

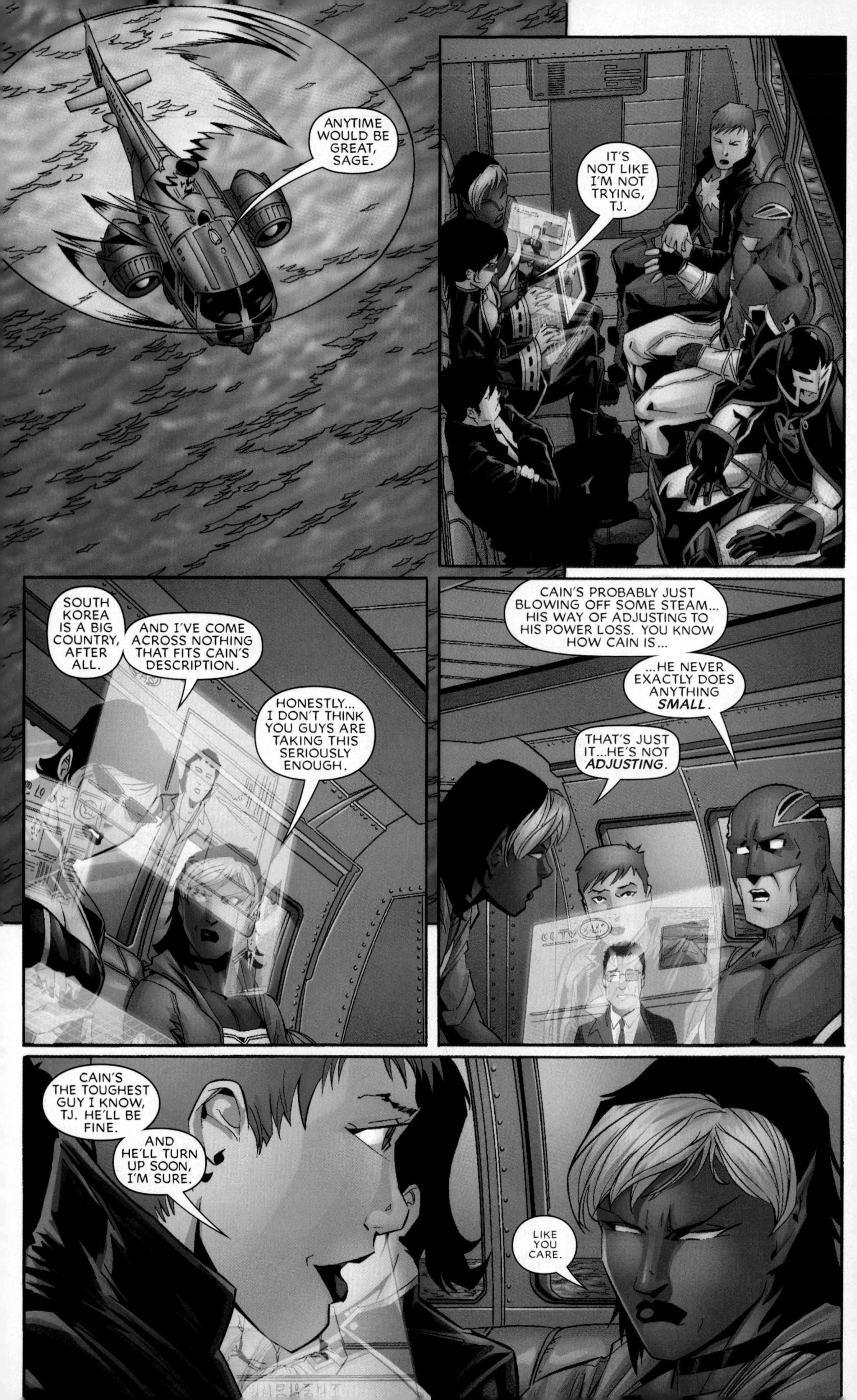
ANYTIME WOULD BE GREAT, SAGE.
IT'S NOT LIKE I'M NOT TRYING, TJ.
SOUTH KOREA IS A BIG COUNTRY, AFTER ALL.
AND I'VE COME ACROSS NOTHING THAT FITS CAIN'S DESCRIPTION.
HONESTLY... I DON'T THINK YOU GUYS ARE TAKING THIS SERIOUSLY ENOUGH.
CAIN'S PROBABLY JUST BLOWING OFF SOME STEAM... HIS WAY OF ADJUSTING TO HIS POWER LOSS. YOU KNOW HOW CAIN IS...
...HE NEVER EXACTLY DOES ANYTHING ***SMALL***.
THAT'S JUST IT...HE'S NOT ***ADJUSTING***.
CAIN'S THE TOUGHEST GUY I KNOW, TJ. HE'LL BE FINE.
AND HE'LL TURN UP SOON, I'M SURE.
LIKE YOU CARE.

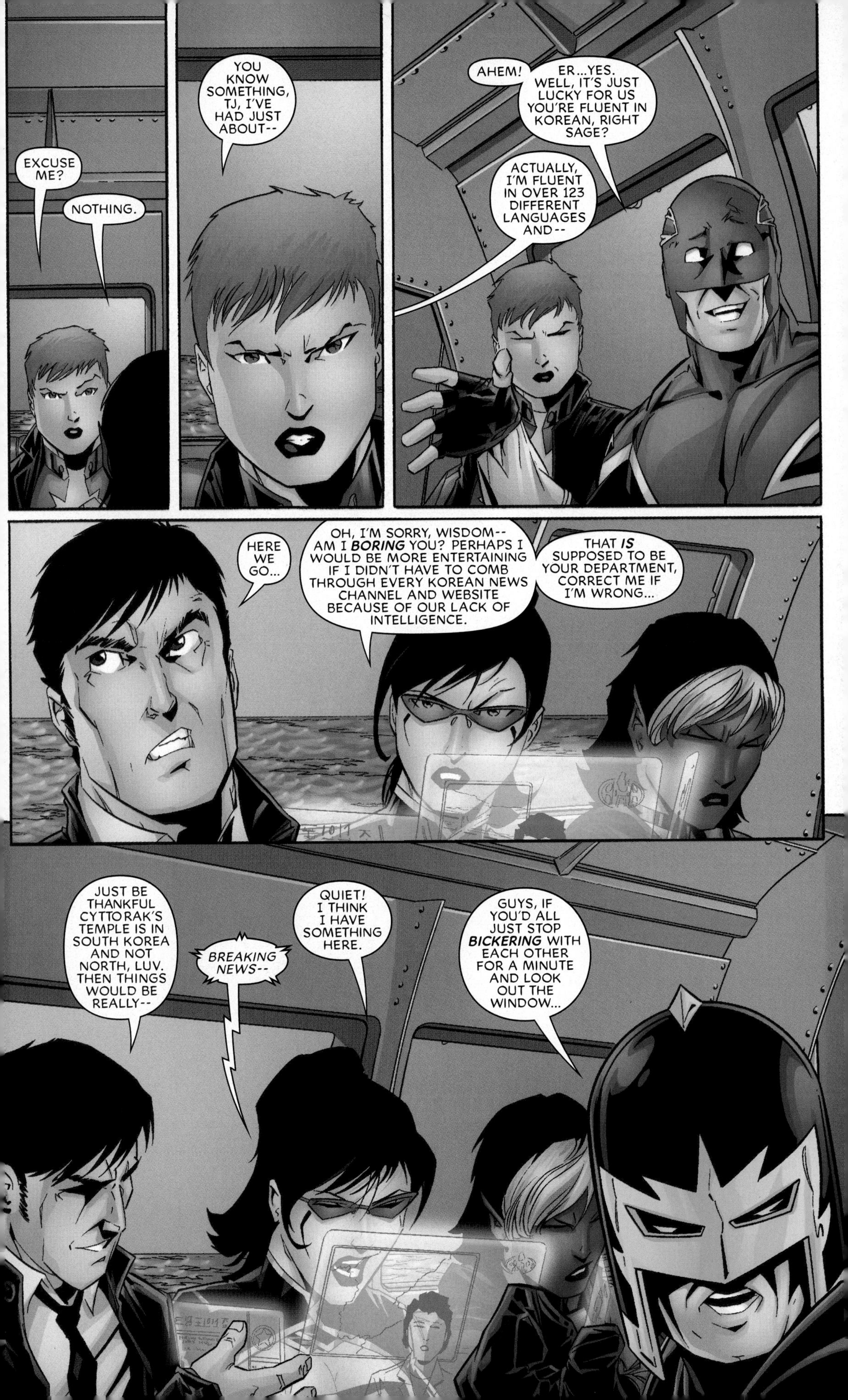
EXCUSE ME?
NOTHING.
YOU KNOW SOMETHING, TJ, I'VE HAD JUST ABOUT--
AHEM!
ER...YES. WELL, IT'S JUST LUCKY FOR US YOU'RE FLUENT IN KOREAN, RIGHT SAGE?
ACTUALLY, I'M FLUENT IN OVER 123 DIFFERENT LANGUAGES AND--
HERE WE GO...
OH, I'M SORRY, WISDOM-- AM I *BORING* YOU? PERHAPS I WOULD BE MORE ENTERTAINING IF I DIDN'T HAVE TO COMB THROUGH EVERY KOREAN NEWS CHANNEL AND WEBSITE BECAUSE OF OUR LACK OF INTELLIGENCE.
THAT *IS* SUPPOSED TO BE YOUR DEPARTMENT, CORRECT ME IF I'M WRONG...
JUST BE THANKFUL CYTTORAK'S TEMPLE IS IN SOUTH KOREA AND NOT NORTH, LUV. THEN THINGS WOULD BE REALLY--
BREAKING NEWS--
QUIET! I THINK I HAVE SOMETHING HERE.
GUYS, IF YOU'D ALL JUST STOP *BICKERING* WITH EACH OTHER FOR A MINUTE AND LOOK OUT THE WINDOW...

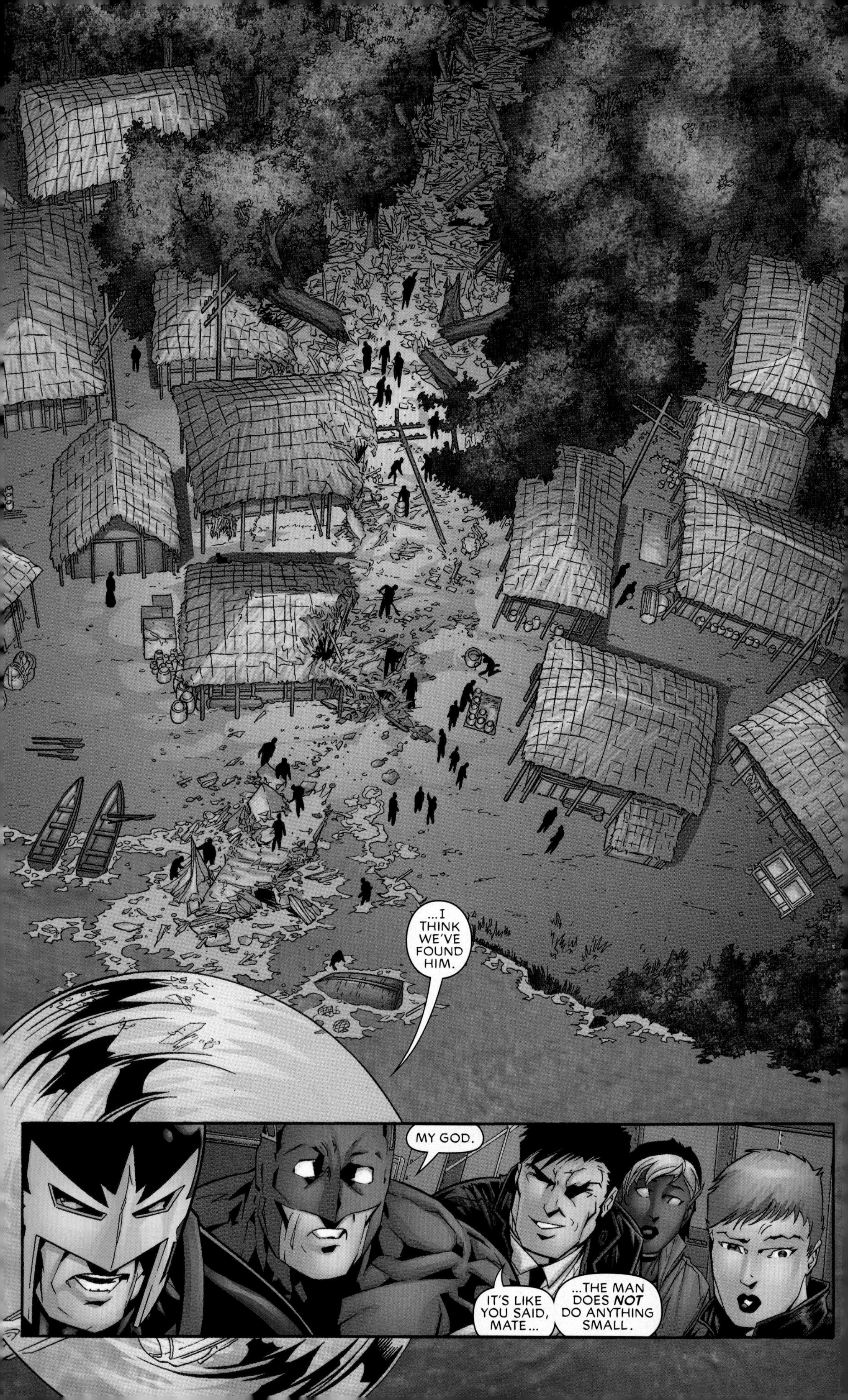
...I THINK WE'VE FOUND HIM.
MY GOD.
IT'S LIKE YOU SAID, MATE...
...THE MAN DOES *NOT* DO ANYTHING SMALL.

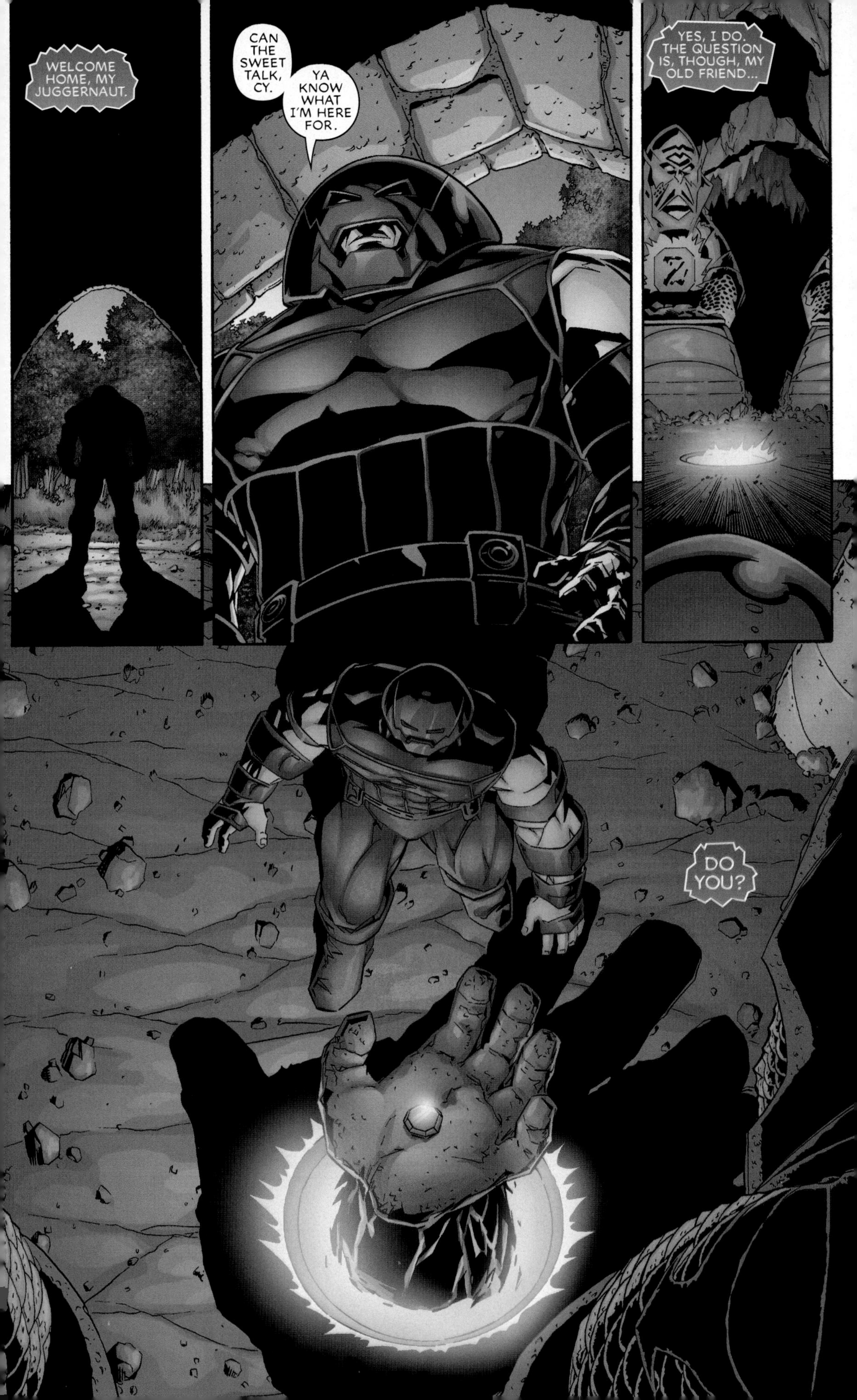
WELCOME HOME, MY JUGGERNAUT.
CAN THE SWEET TALK, CY.
YA KNOW WHAT I'M HERE FOR.
YES, I DO. THE QUESTION IS, THOUGH, MY OLD FRIEND...
DO YOU?

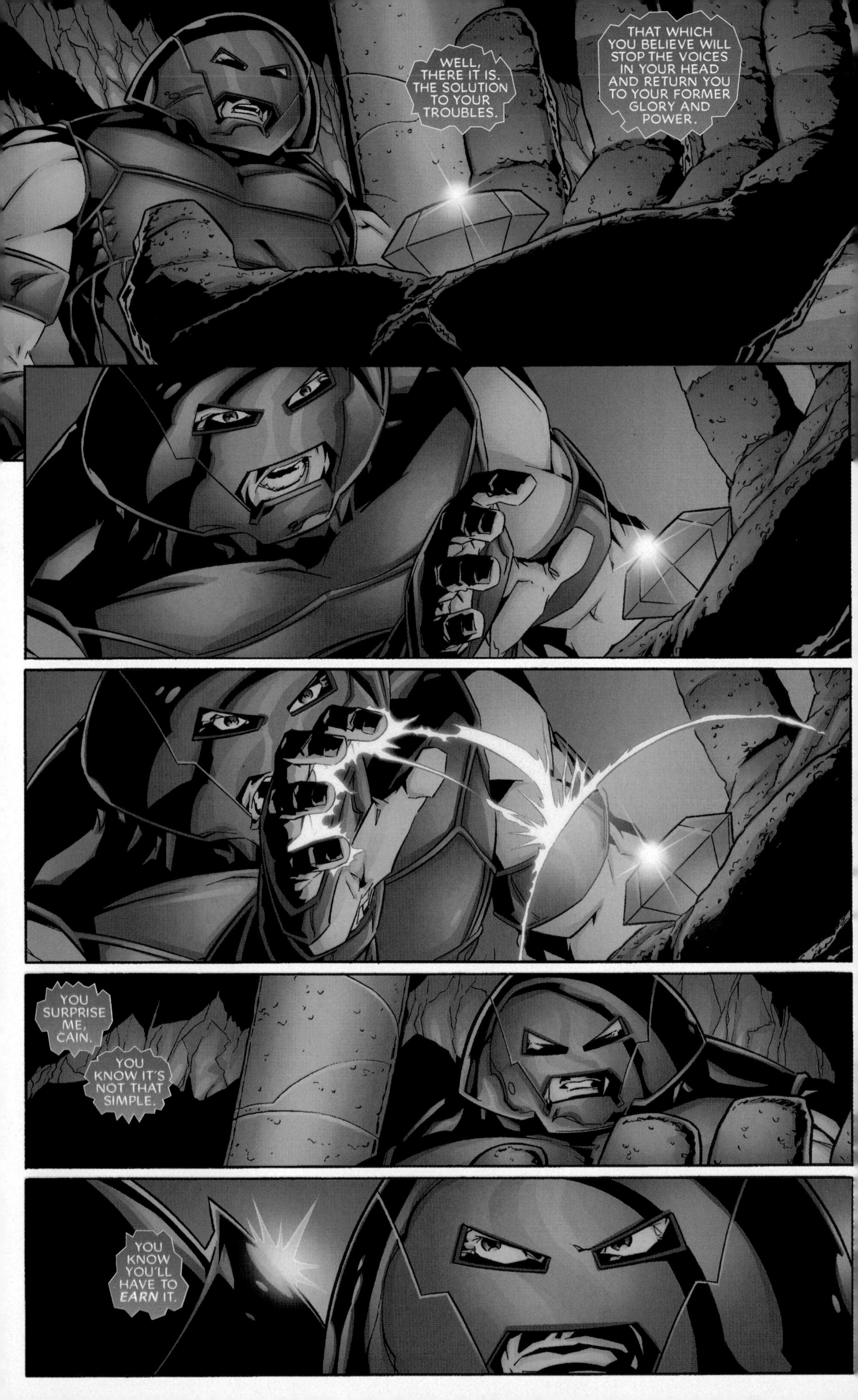
WELL, THERE IT IS. THE SOLUTION TO YOUR TROUBLES.
THAT WHICH YOU BELIEVE WILL STOP THE VOICES IN YOUR HEAD AND RETURN YOU TO YOUR FORMER GLORY AND POWER.
YOU SURPRISE ME, CAIN.
YOU KNOW IT'S NOT THAT SIMPLE.
YOU KNOW YOU'LL HAVE TO *EARN* IT.

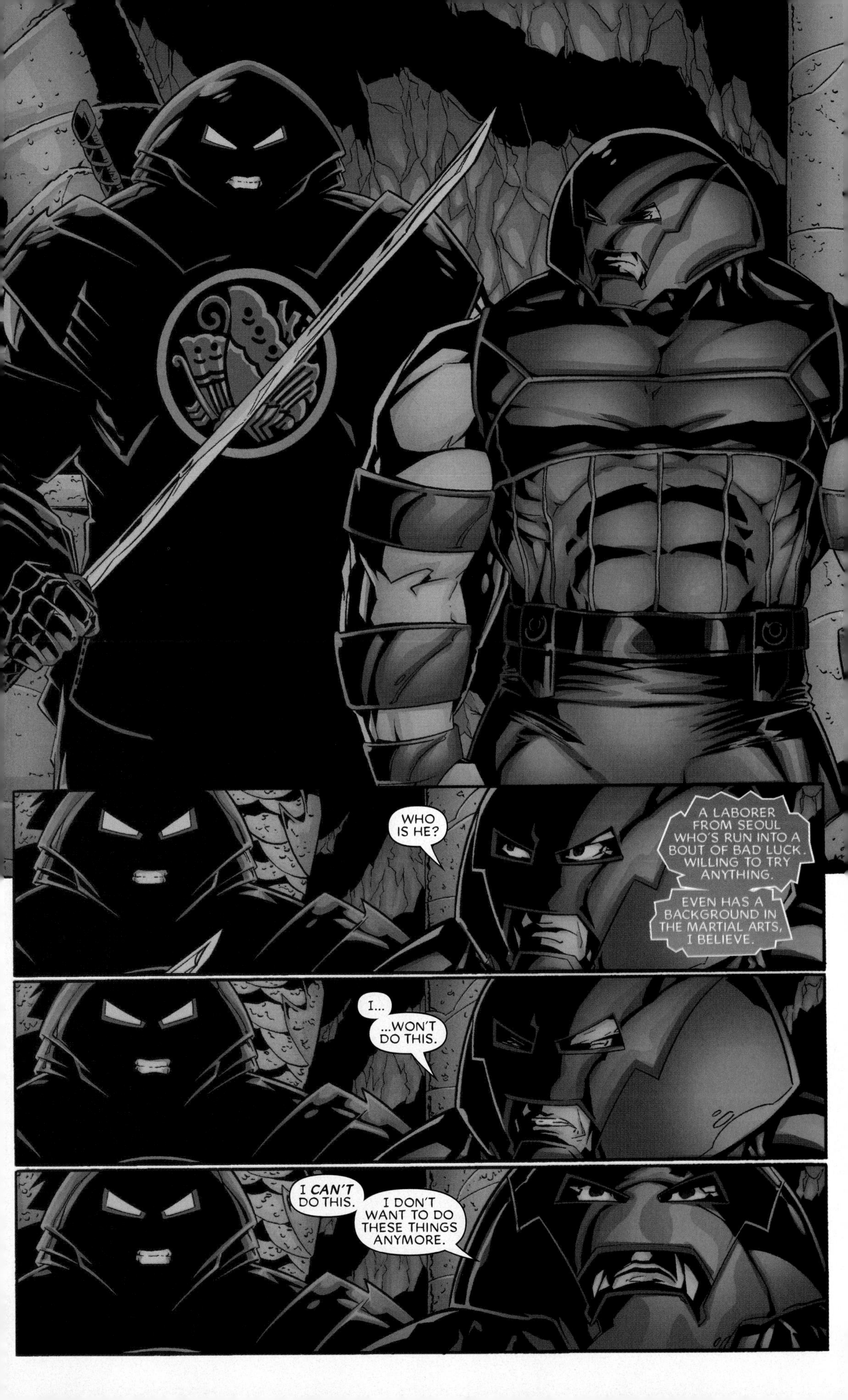
WHO IS HE?
A LABORER FROM SEOUL WHO'S RUN INTO A BOUT OF BAD LUCK. WILLING TO TRY ANYTHING.
EVEN HAS A BACKGROUND IN THE MARTIAL ARTS, I BELIEVE.
I...
...WON'T DO THIS.
I *CAN'T* DO THIS.
I DON'T WANT TO DO THESE THINGS ANYMORE.

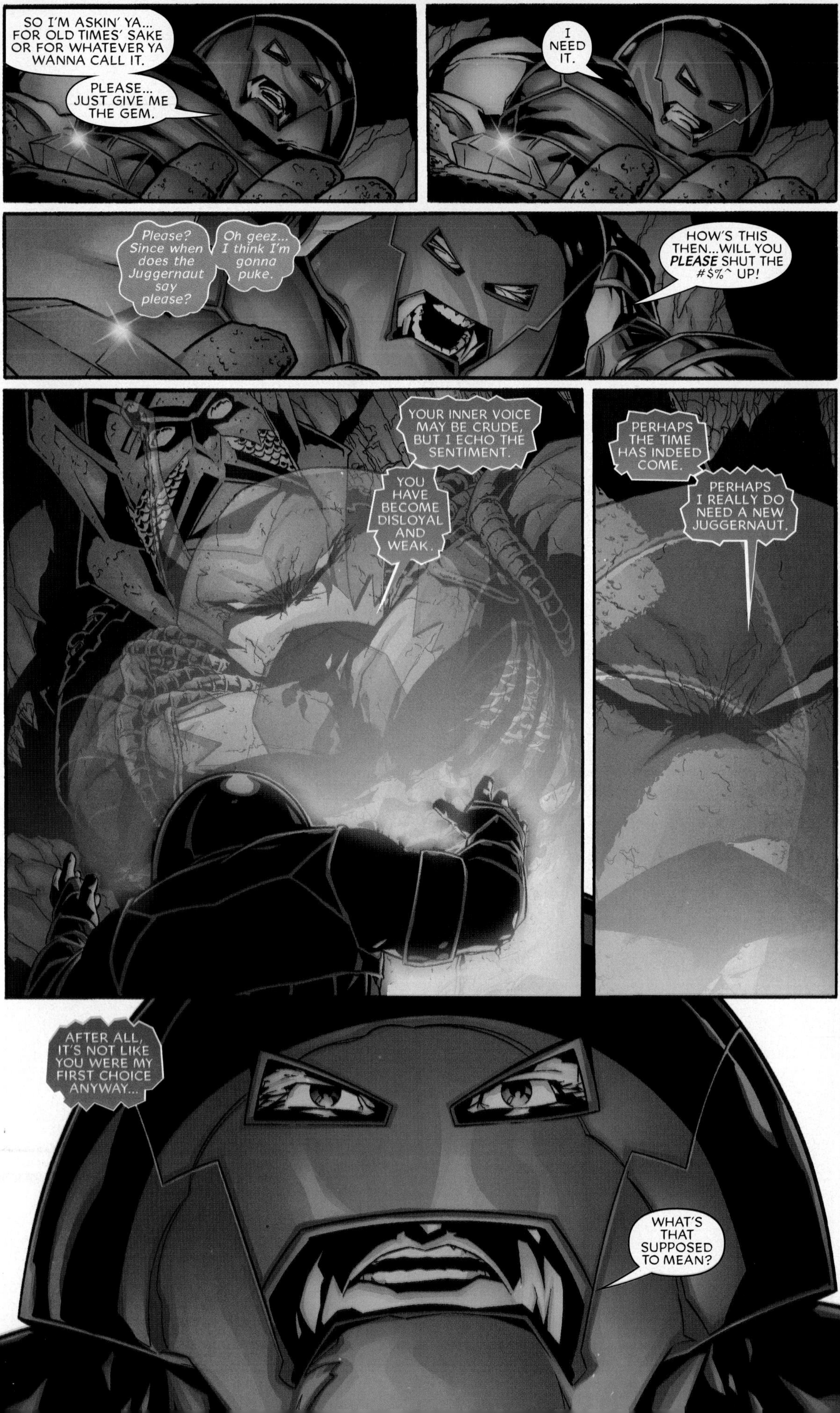
SO I'M ASKIN' YA... FOR OLD TIMES' SAKE OR FOR WHATEVER YA WANNA CALL IT.
PLEASE... JUST GIVE ME THE GEM.
I NEED IT.
Please? Since when does the Juggernaut say please?
Oh geez... I think I'm gonna puke.
HOW'S THIS THEN...WILL YOU **PLEASE** SHUT THE #$%^ UP!
YOUR INNER VOICE MAY BE CRUDE, BUT I ECHO THE SENTIMENT.
YOU HAVE BECOME DISLOYAL AND WEAK.
PERHAPS THE TIME HAS INDEED COME.
PERHAPS I REALLY DO NEED A NEW JUGGERNAUT.
AFTER ALL, IT'S NOT LIKE YOU WERE MY FIRST CHOICE ANYWAY...
WHAT'S THAT SUPPOSED TO MEAN?

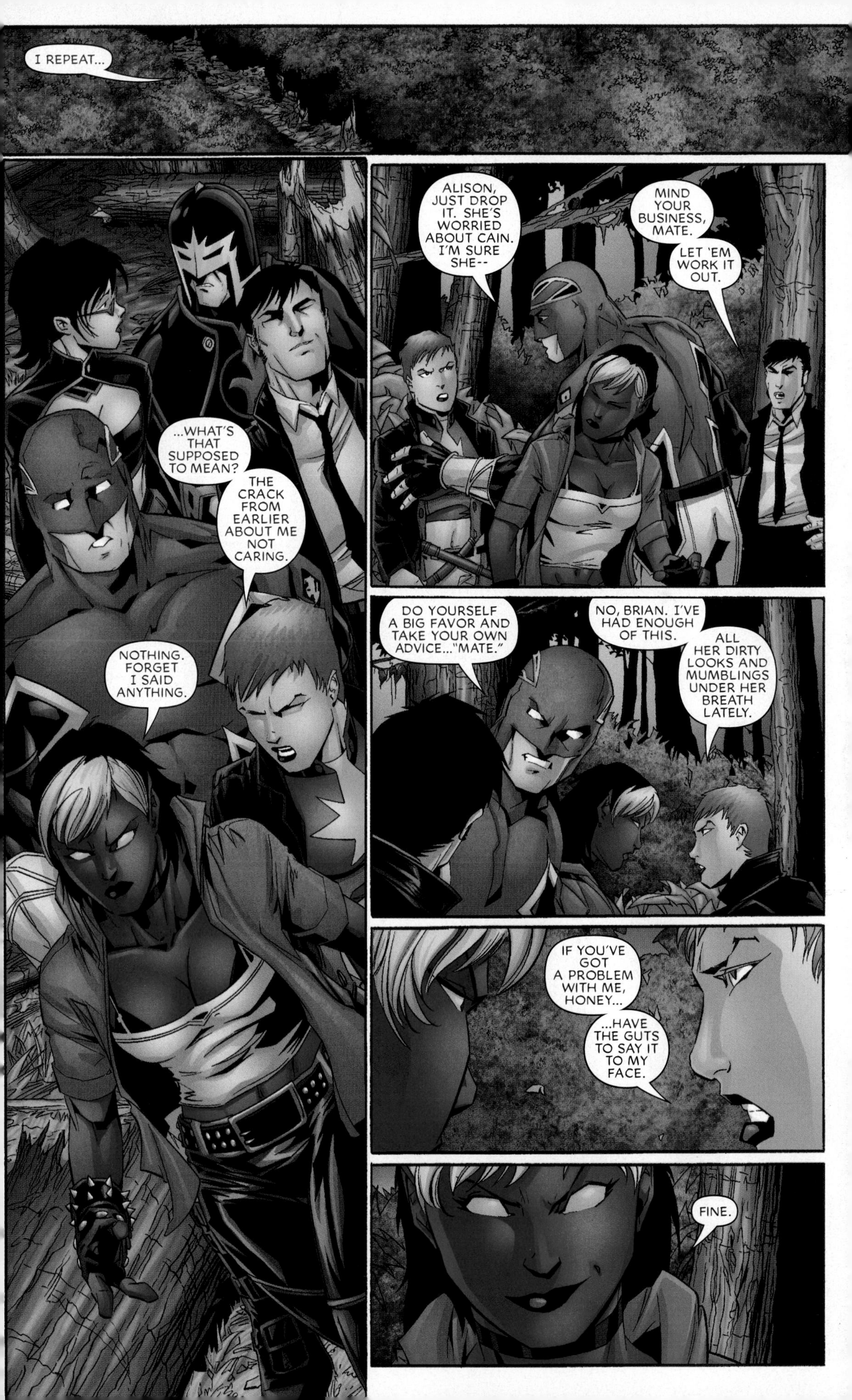
I REPEAT...
...WHAT'S THAT SUPPOSED TO MEAN?
THE CRACK FROM EARLIER ABOUT ME NOT CARING.
NOTHING. FORGET I SAID ANYTHING.
ALISON, JUST DROP IT. SHE'S WORRIED ABOUT CAIN. I'M SURE SHE--
MIND YOUR BUSINESS, MATE.
LET 'EM WORK IT OUT.
DO YOURSELF A BIG FAVOR AND TAKE YOUR OWN ADVICE..."MATE."
NO, BRIAN. I'VE HAD ENOUGH OF THIS.
ALL HER DIRTY LOOKS AND MUMBLINGS UNDER HER BREATH LATELY.
IF YOU'VE GOT A PROBLEM WITH ME, HONEY...
...HAVE THE GUTS TO SAY IT TO MY FACE.
FINE.

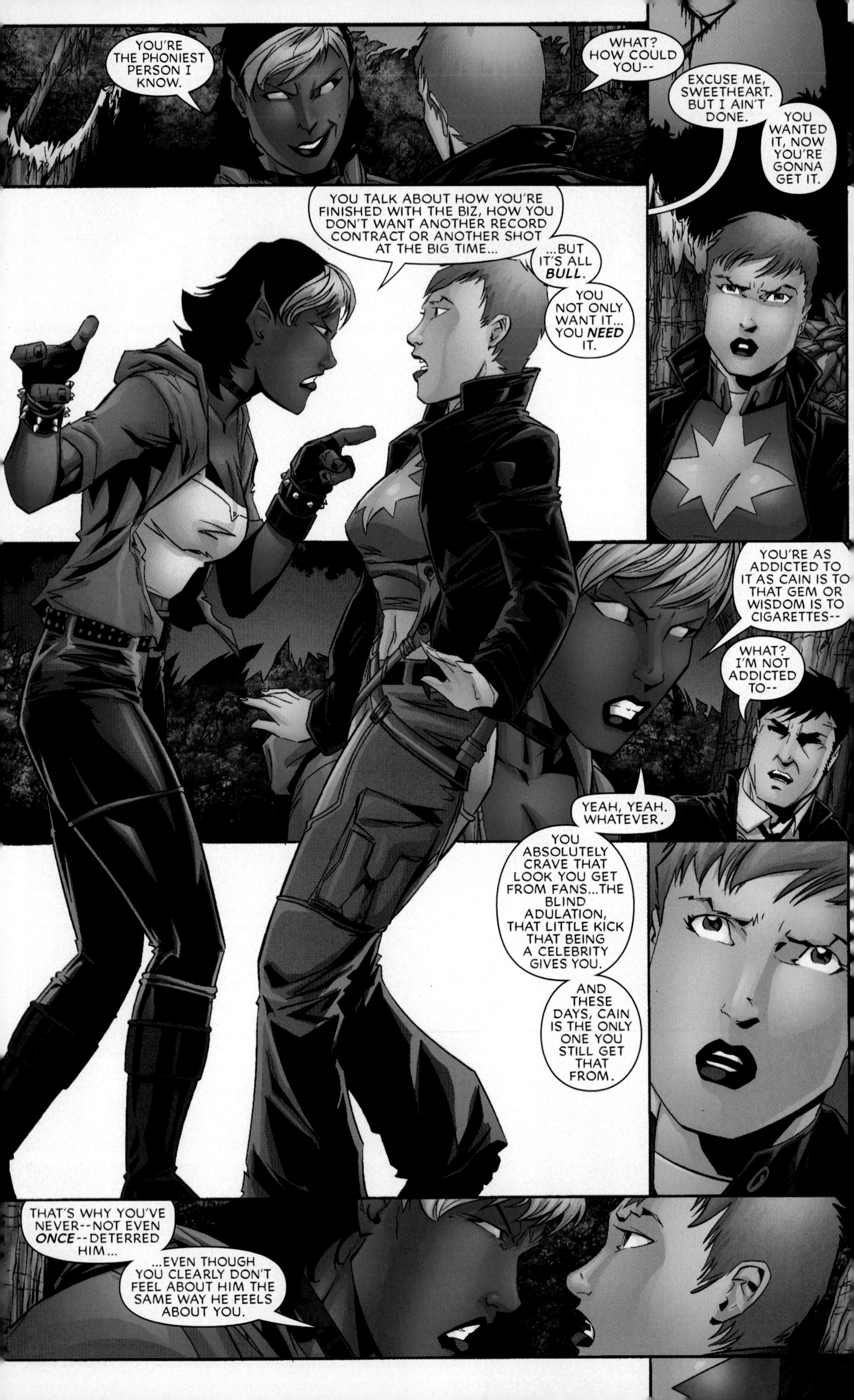
YOU'RE THE PHONIEST PERSON I KNOW.
WHAT? HOW COULD YOU--
EXCUSE ME, SWEETHEART. BUT I AIN'T DONE.
YOU WANTED IT, NOW YOU'RE GONNA GET IT.
YOU TALK ABOUT HOW YOU'RE FINISHED WITH THE BIZ, HOW YOU DON'T WANT ANOTHER RECORD CONTRACT OR ANOTHER SHOT AT THE BIG TIME...
...BUT IT'S ALL *BULL*.
YOU NOT ONLY WANT IT... YOU *NEED* IT.
YOU'RE AS ADDICTED TO IT AS CAIN IS TO THAT GEM OR WISDOM IS TO CIGARETTES--
WHAT? I'M NOT ADDICTED TO--
YEAH, YEAH. WHATEVER.
YOU ABSOLUTELY CRAVE THAT LOOK YOU GET FROM FANS...THE BLIND ADULATION, THAT LITTLE KICK THAT BEING A CELEBRITY GIVES YOU.
AND THESE DAYS, CAIN IS THE ONLY ONE YOU STILL GET THAT FROM.
THAT'S WHY YOU'VE NEVER--NOT EVEN *ONCE*--DETERRED HIM...
...EVEN THOUGH YOU CLEARLY DON'T FEEL ABOUT HIM THE SAME WAY HE FEELS ABOUT YOU.

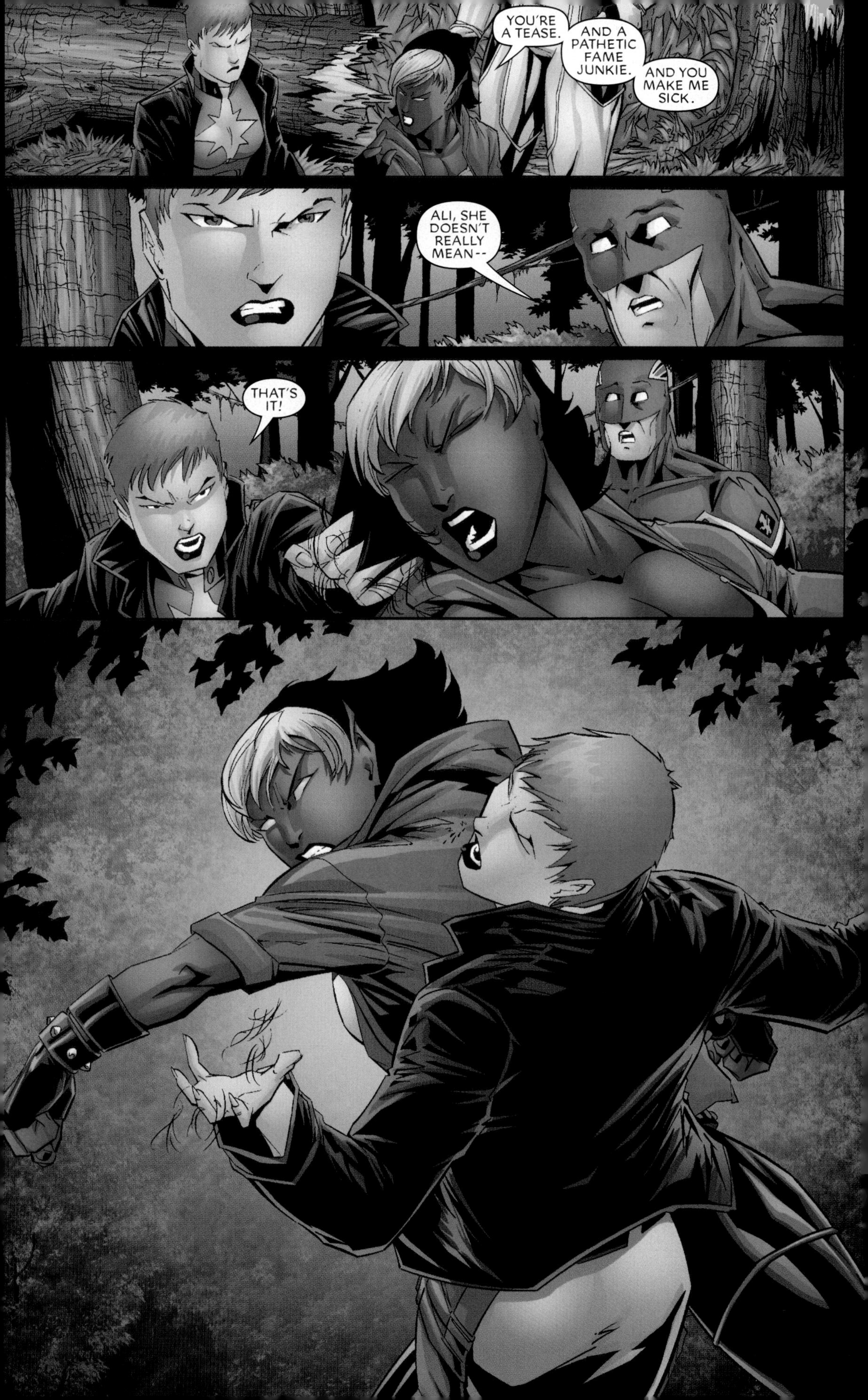
YOU'RE A TEASE.
AND A PATHETIC FAME JUNKIE.
AND YOU MAKE ME SICK.
ALI, SHE DOESN'T REALLY MEAN--
THAT'S IT!

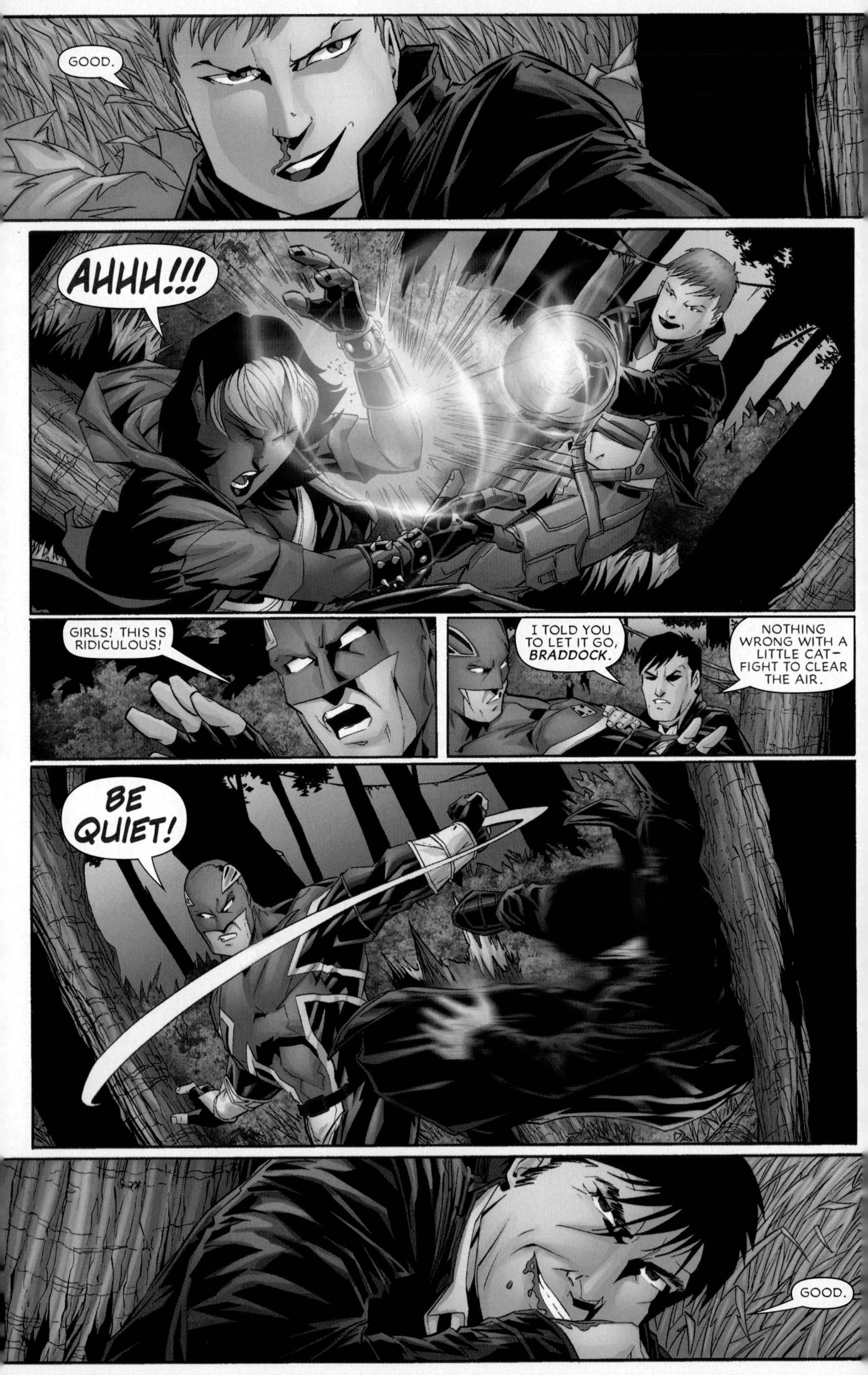
GOOD.
AHHH!!!
GIRLS! THIS IS RIDICULOUS!
I TOLD YOU TO LET IT GO, BRADDOCK.
NOTHING WRONG WITH A LITTLE CAT-FIGHT TO CLEAR THE AIR.
BE QUIET!
GOOD.

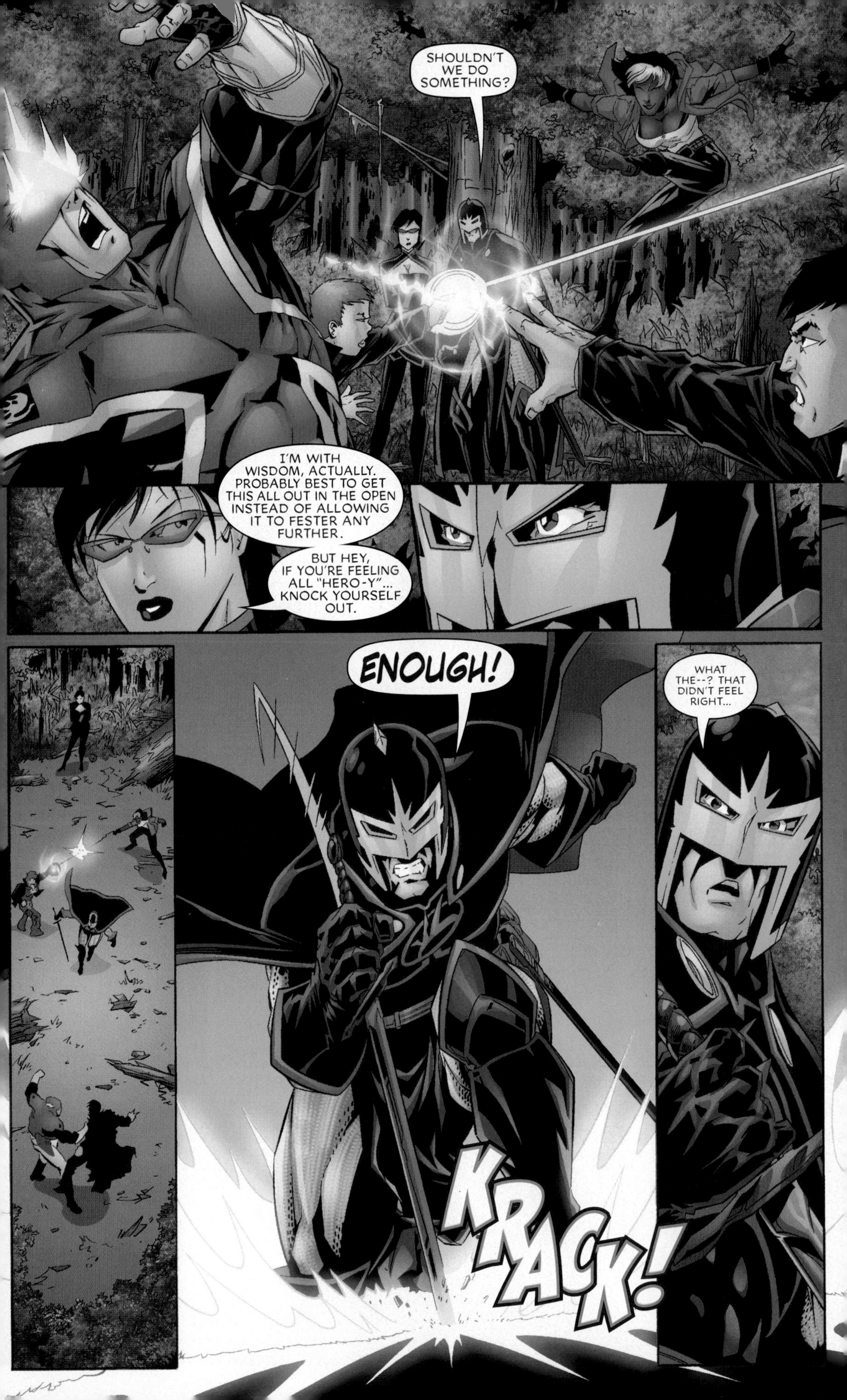
SHOULDN'T WE DO SOMETHING?
I'M WITH WISDOM, ACTUALLY. PROBABLY BEST TO GET THIS ALL OUT IN THE OPEN INSTEAD OF ALLOWING IT TO FESTER ANY FURTHER.
BUT HEY, IF YOU'RE FEELING ALL "HERO-Y"... KNOCK YOURSELF OUT.
ENOUGH!
WHAT THE--? THAT DIDN'T FEEL RIGHT...
KRACK!

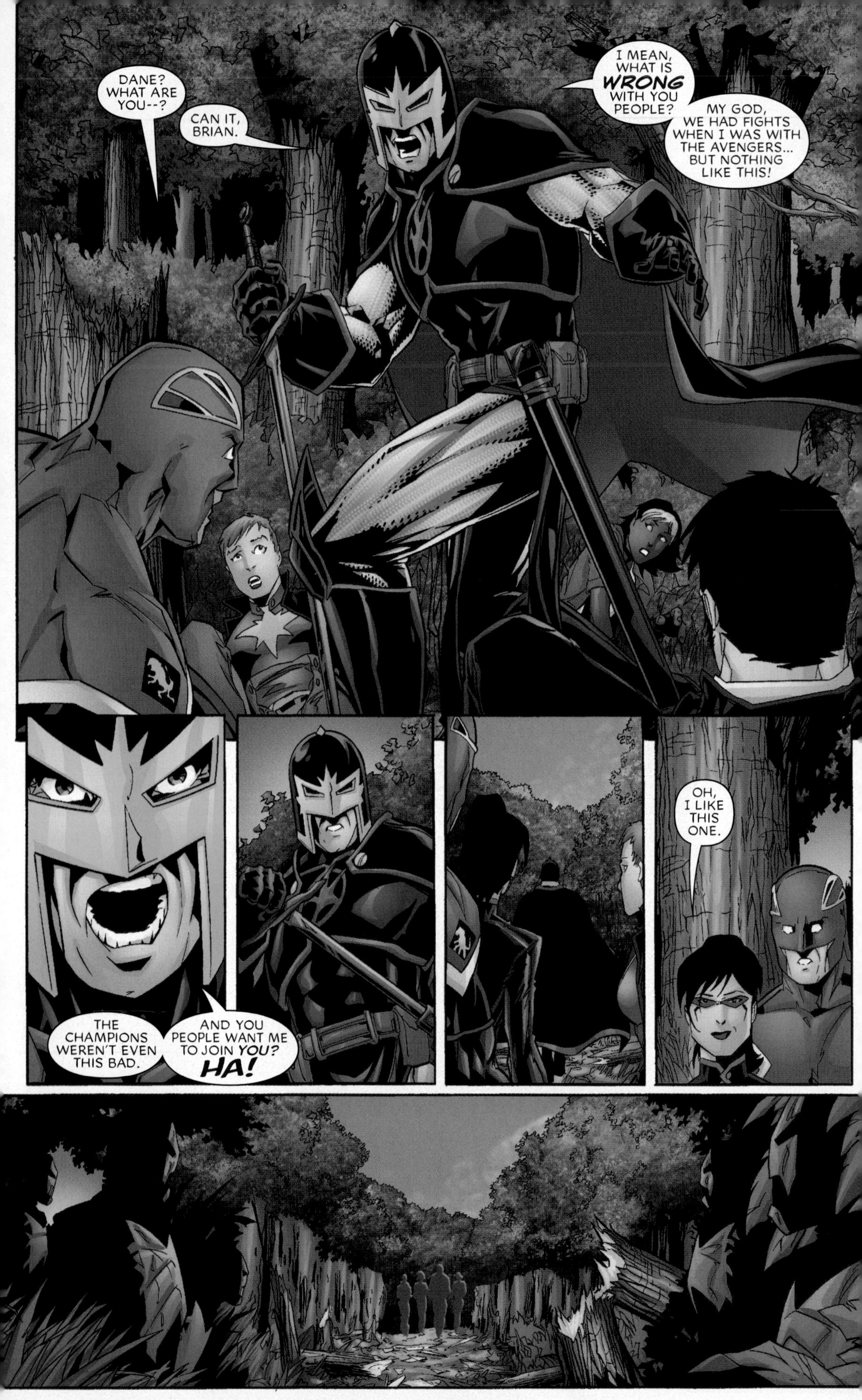
DANE? WHAT ARE YOU--?
CAN IT, BRIAN.
I MEAN, WHAT IS WRONG WITH YOU PEOPLE?
MY GOD, WE HAD FIGHTS WHEN I WAS WITH THE AVENGERS... BUT NOTHING LIKE THIS!
THE CHAMPIONS WEREN'T EVEN THIS BAD.
AND YOU PEOPLE WANT ME TO JOIN YOU? HA!
OH, I LIKE THIS ONE.

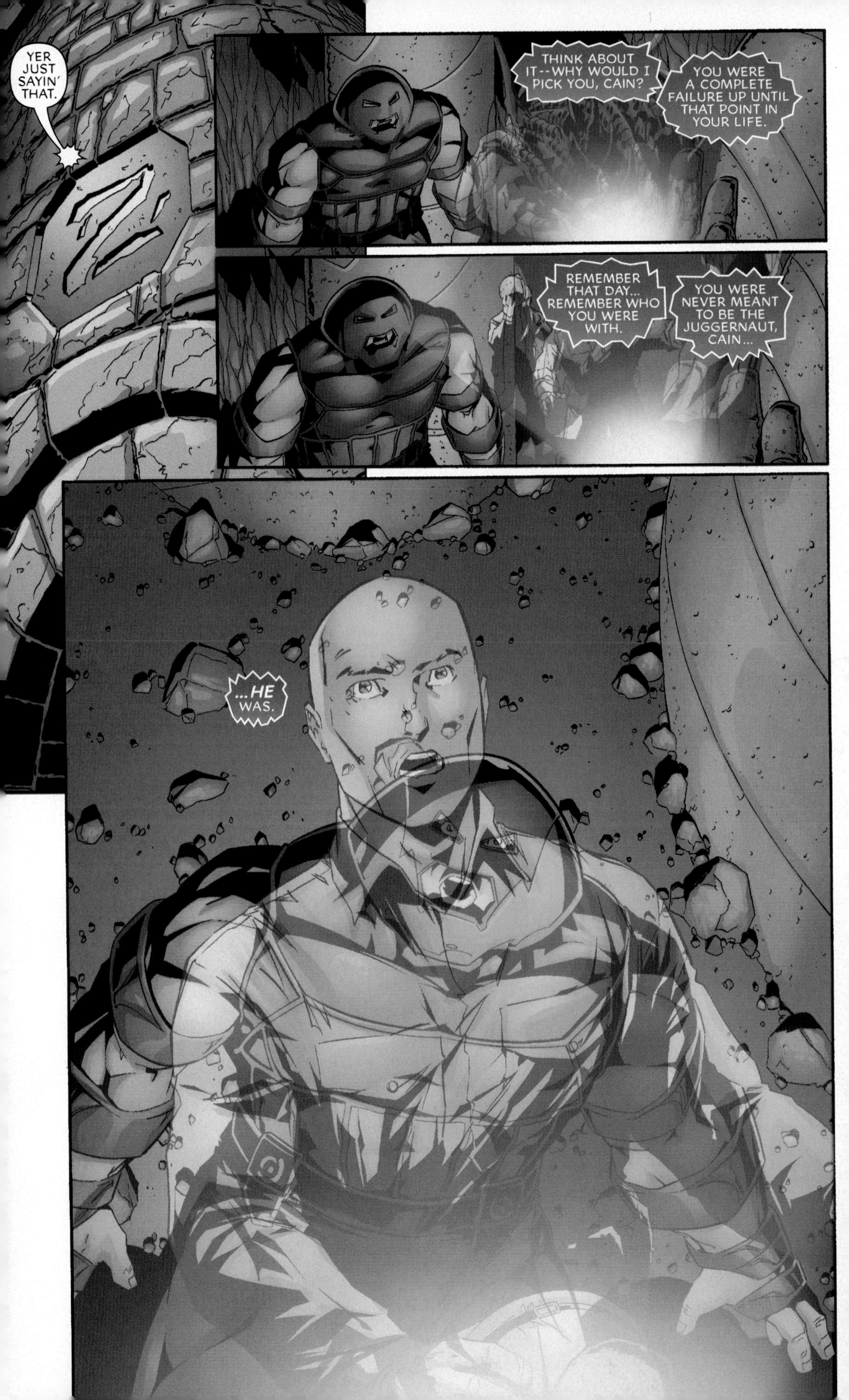
YER JUST SAYIN' THAT.
THINK ABOUT IT--WHY WOULD I PICK YOU, CAIN?
YOU WERE A COMPLETE FAILURE UP UNTIL THAT POINT IN YOUR LIFE.
REMEMBER THAT DAY... REMEMBER WHO YOU WERE WITH.
YOU WERE NEVER MEANT TO BE THE JUGGERNAUT, CAIN...
...HE WAS.

#15

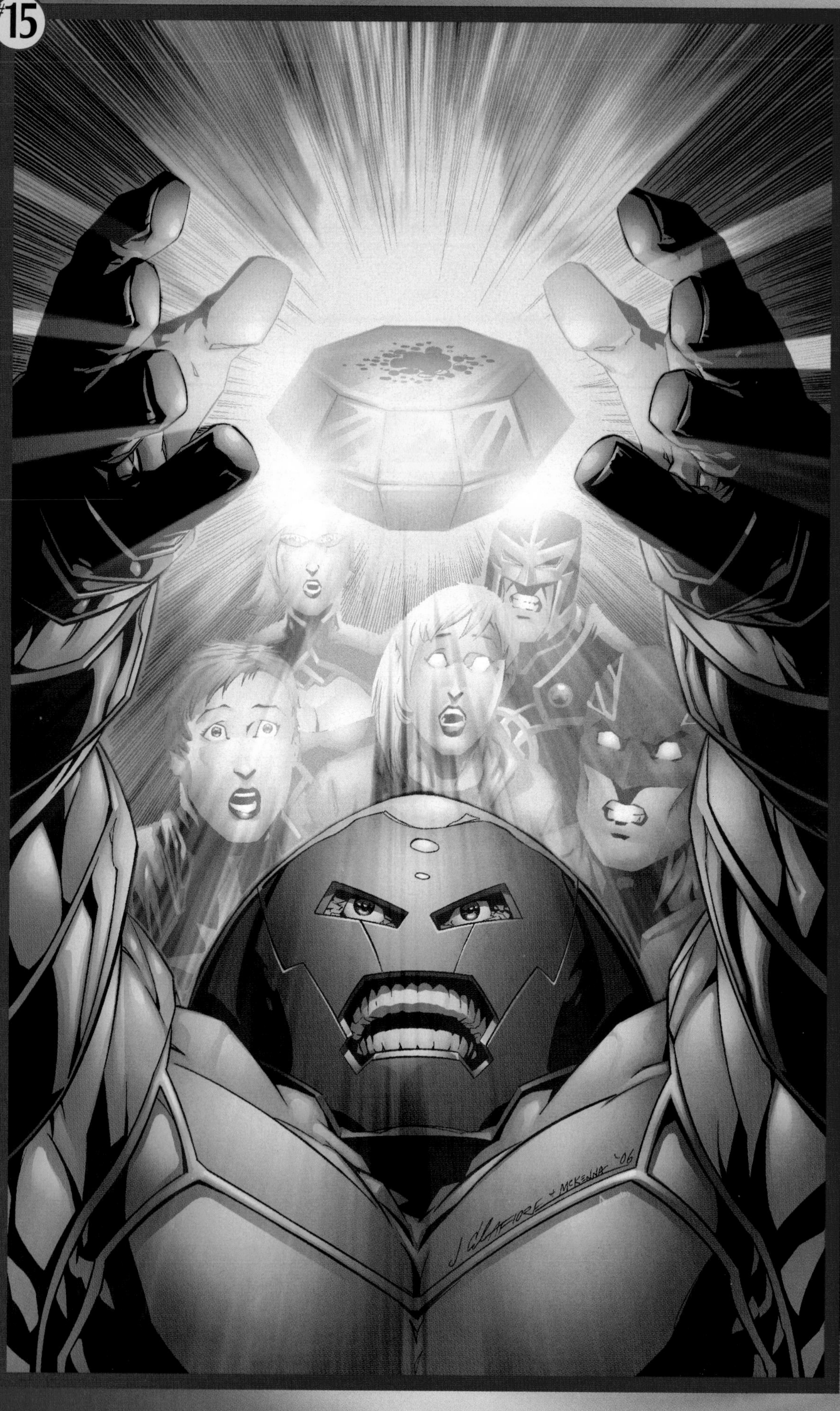
J CALAFIORE + McKENNA '06

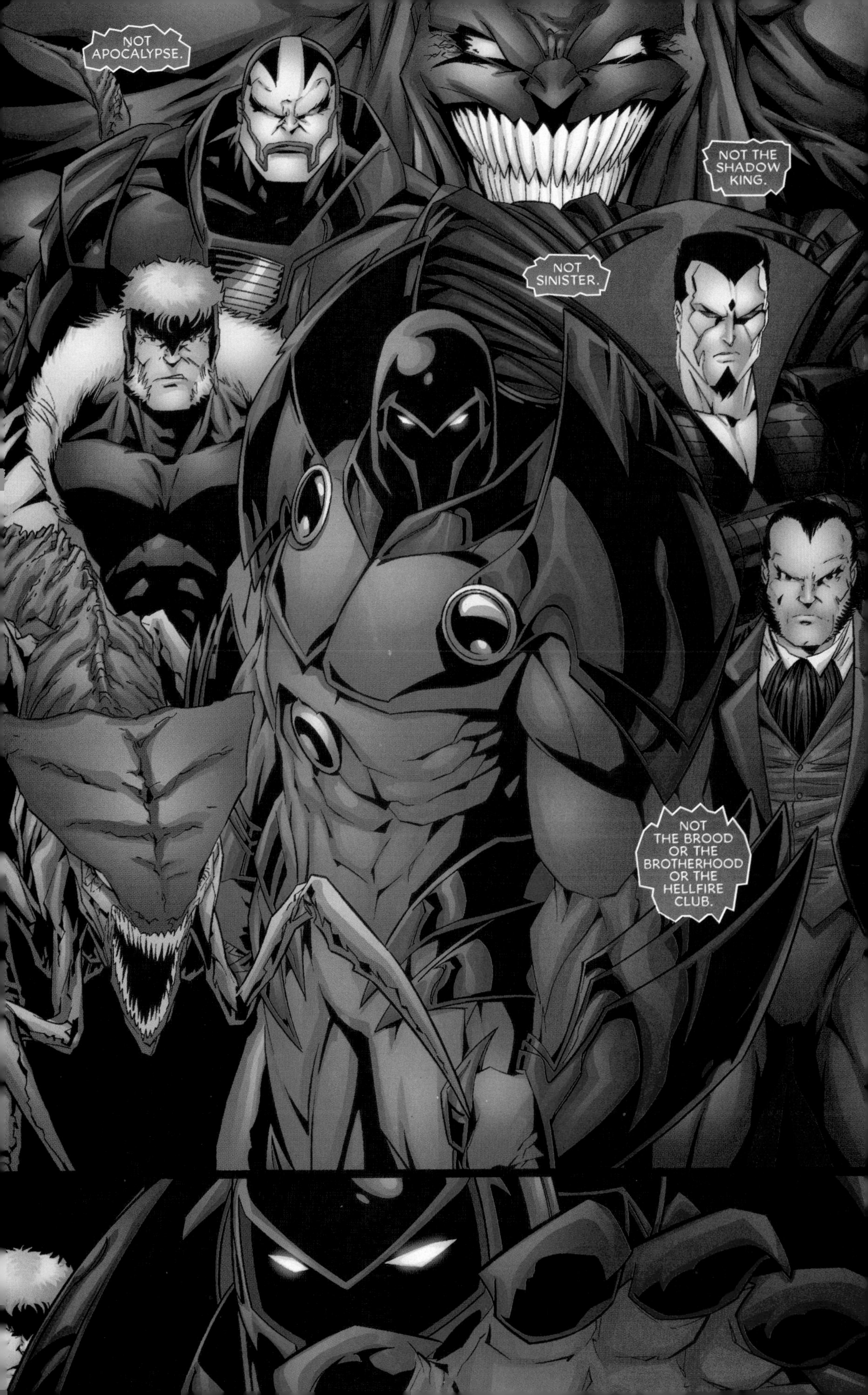
NOT APOCALYPSE.
NOT THE SHADOW KING.
NOT SINISTER.
NOT THE BROOD OR THE BROTHERHOOD OR THE HELLFIRE CLUB.

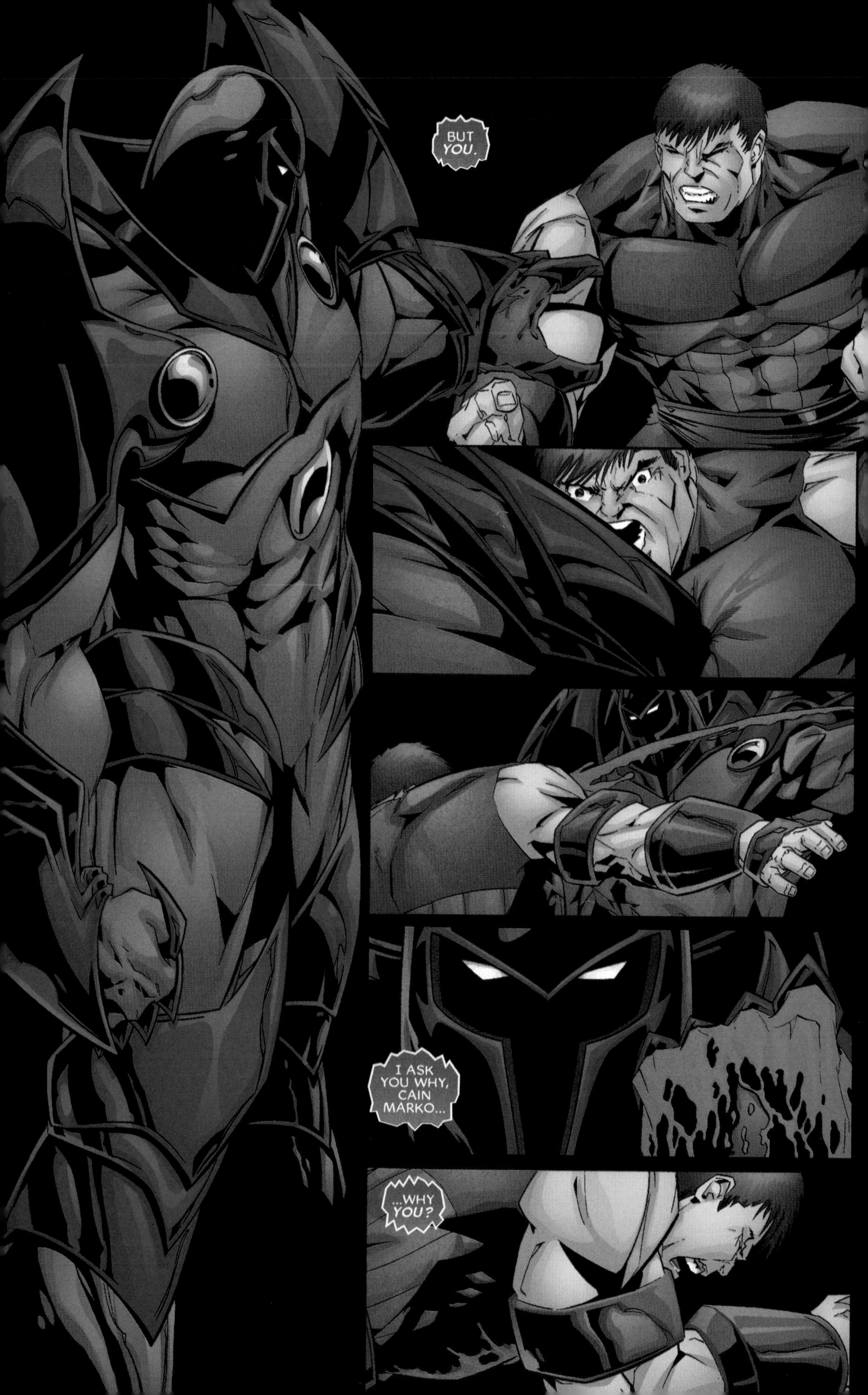
BUT YOU.
I ASK YOU WHY, CAIN MARKO...
...WHY YOU?

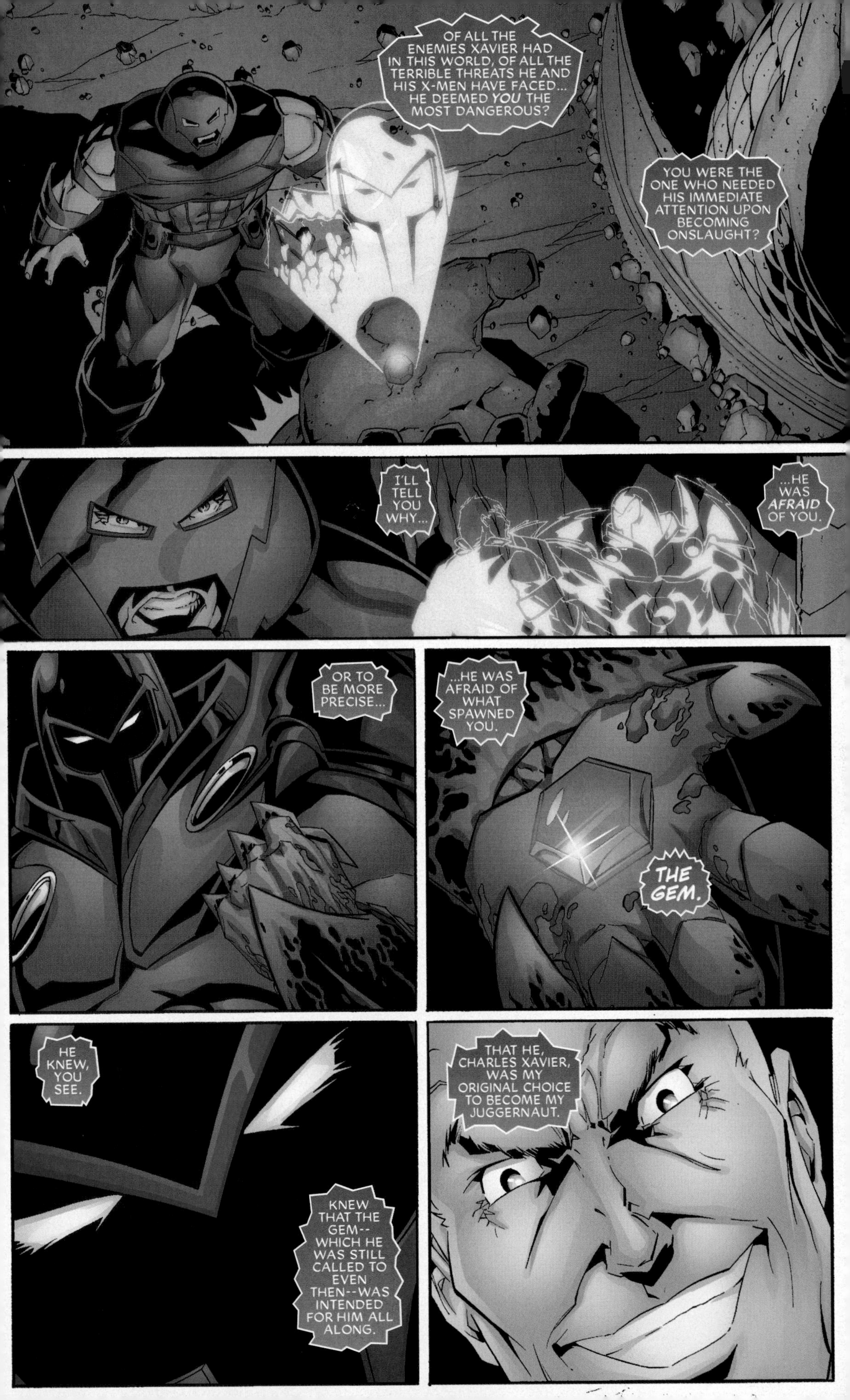
OF ALL THE ENEMIES XAVIER HAD IN THIS WORLD, OF ALL THE TERRIBLE THREATS HE AND HIS X-MEN HAVE FACED... HE DEEMED YOU THE MOST DANGEROUS?
YOU WERE THE ONE WHO NEEDED HIS IMMEDIATE ATTENTION UPON BECOMING ONSLAUGHT?
I'LL TELL YOU WHY...
...HE WAS AFRAID OF YOU.
OR TO BE MORE PRECISE...
...HE WAS AFRAID OF WHAT SPAWNED YOU.
THE GEM.
HE KNEW, YOU SEE.
KNEW THAT THE GEM-- WHICH HE WAS STILL CALLED TO EVEN THEN--WAS INTENDED FOR HIM ALL ALONG.
THAT HE, CHARLES XAVIER, WAS MY ORIGINAL CHOICE TO BECOME MY JUGGERNAUT.

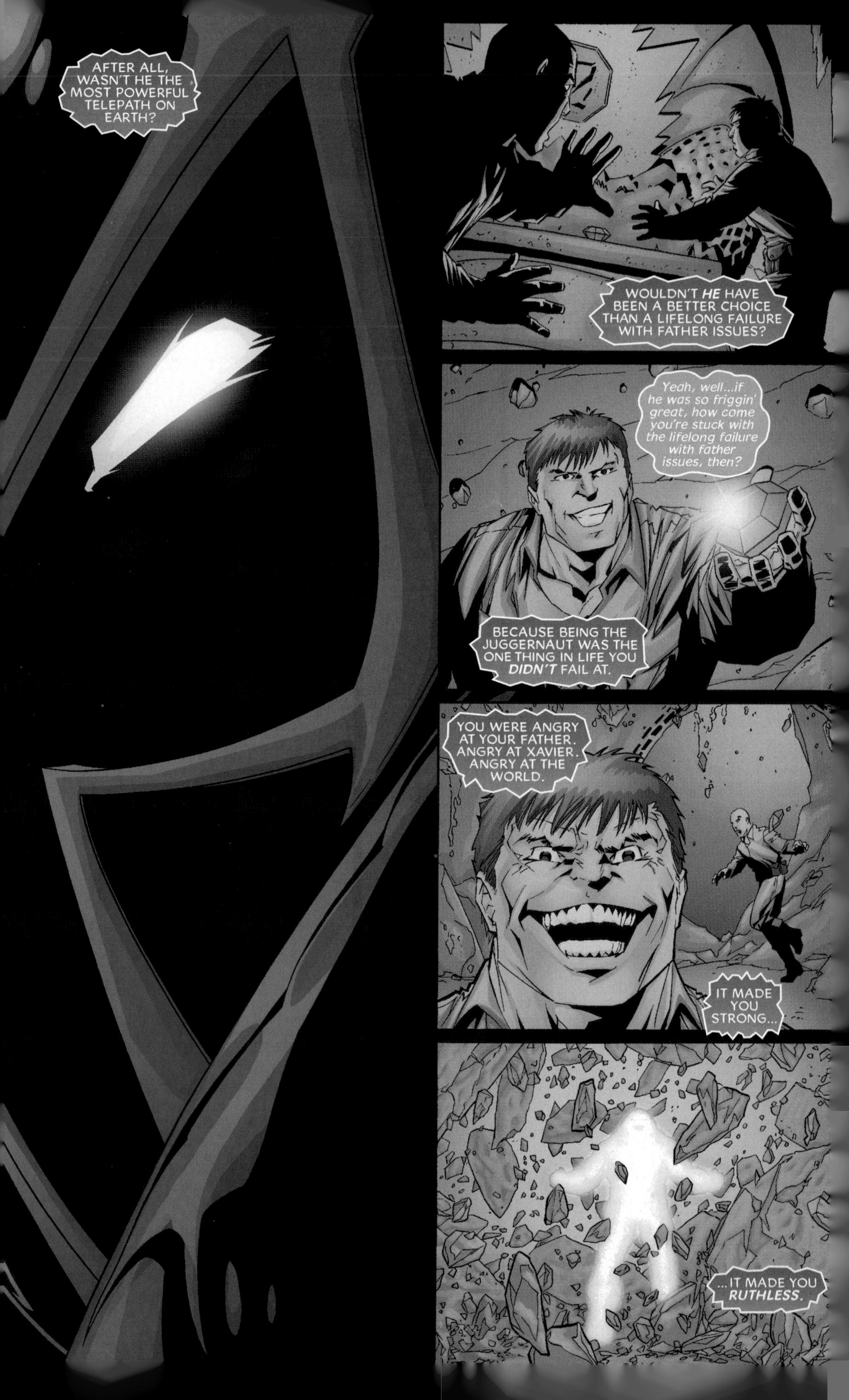
AFTER ALL, WASN'T HE THE MOST POWERFUL TELEPATH ON EARTH?
WOULDN'T *HE* HAVE BEEN A BETTER CHOICE THAN A LIFELONG FAILURE WITH FATHER ISSUES?
Yeah, well...if he was so friggin' great, how come you're stuck with the lifelong failure with father issues, then?
BECAUSE BEING THE JUGGERNAUT WAS THE ONE THING IN LIFE YOU *DIDN'T* FAIL AT.
YOU WERE ANGRY AT YOUR FATHER. ANGRY AT XAVIER. ANGRY AT THE WORLD.
IT MADE YOU STRONG...
...IT MADE YOU *RUTHLESS.*

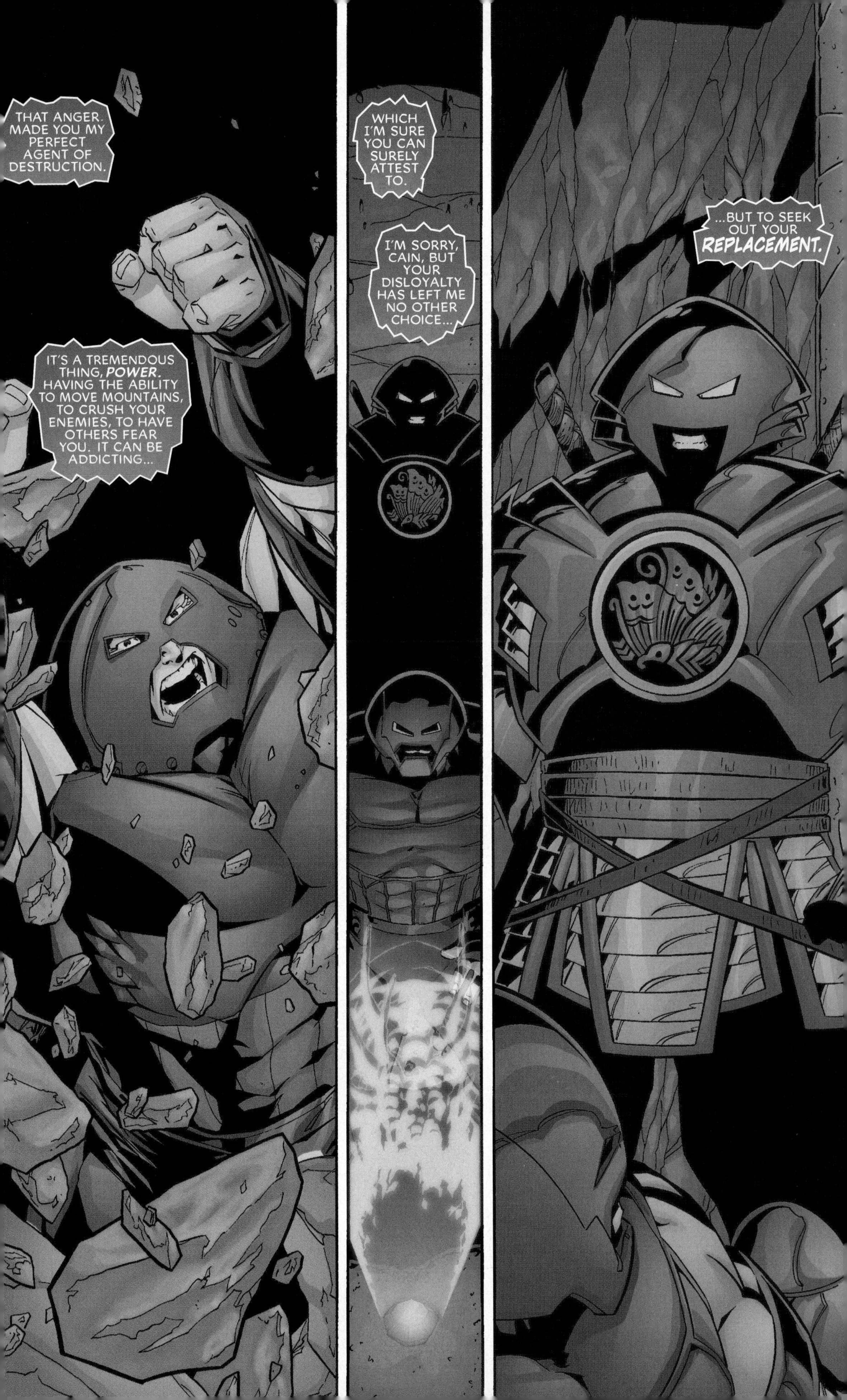
THAT ANGER. MADE YOU MY PERFECT AGENT OF DESTRUCTION.
IT'S A TREMENDOUS THING, POWER. HAVING THE ABILITY TO MOVE MOUNTAINS, TO CRUSH YOUR ENEMIES, TO HAVE OTHERS FEAR YOU. IT CAN BE ADDICTING...
WHICH I'M SURE YOU CAN SURELY ATTEST TO.
I'M SORRY, CAIN, BUT YOUR DISLOYALTY HAS LEFT ME NO OTHER CHOICE...
...BUT TO SEEK OUT YOUR REPLACEMENT.

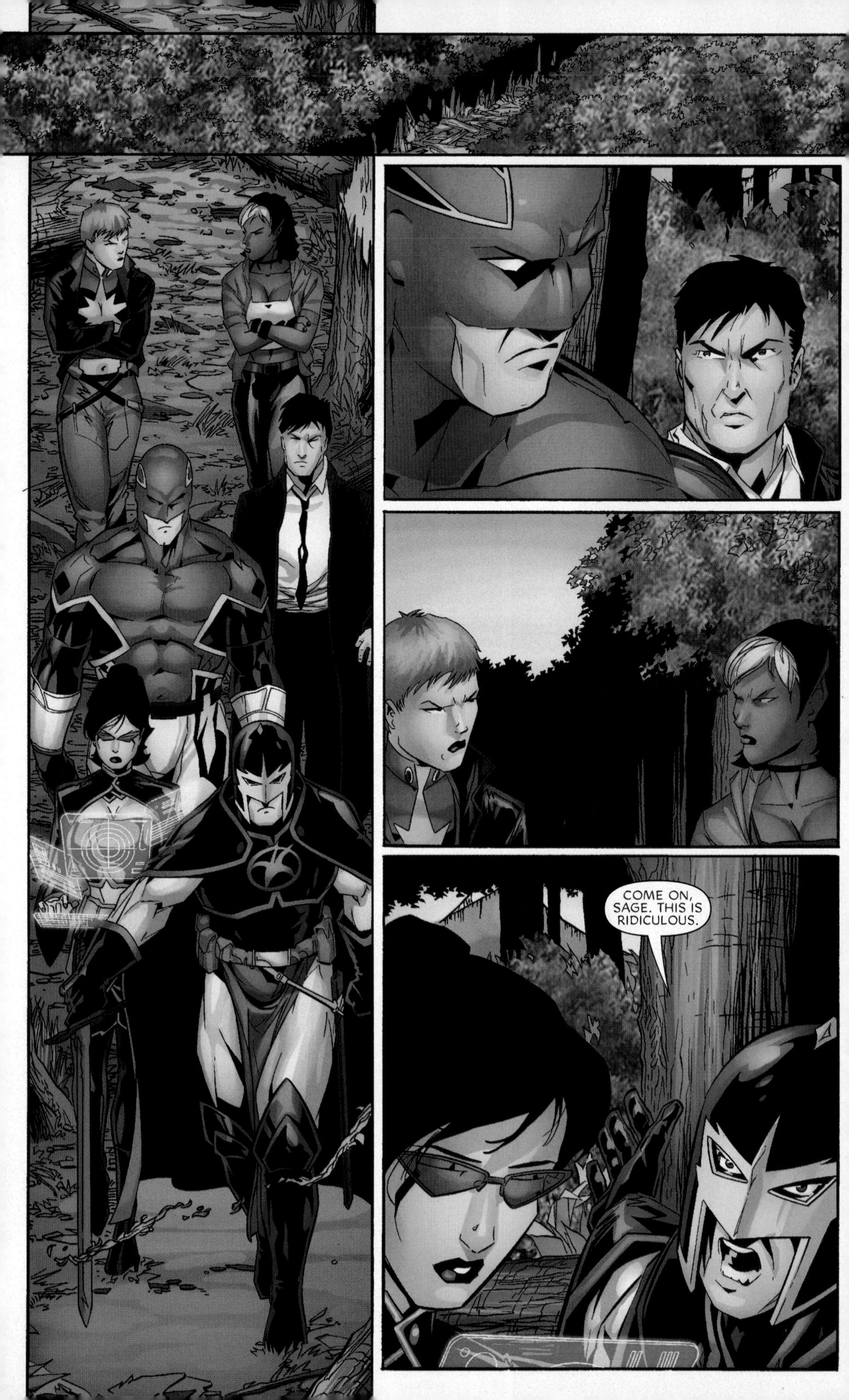
COME ON, SAGE. THIS IS RIDICULOUS.

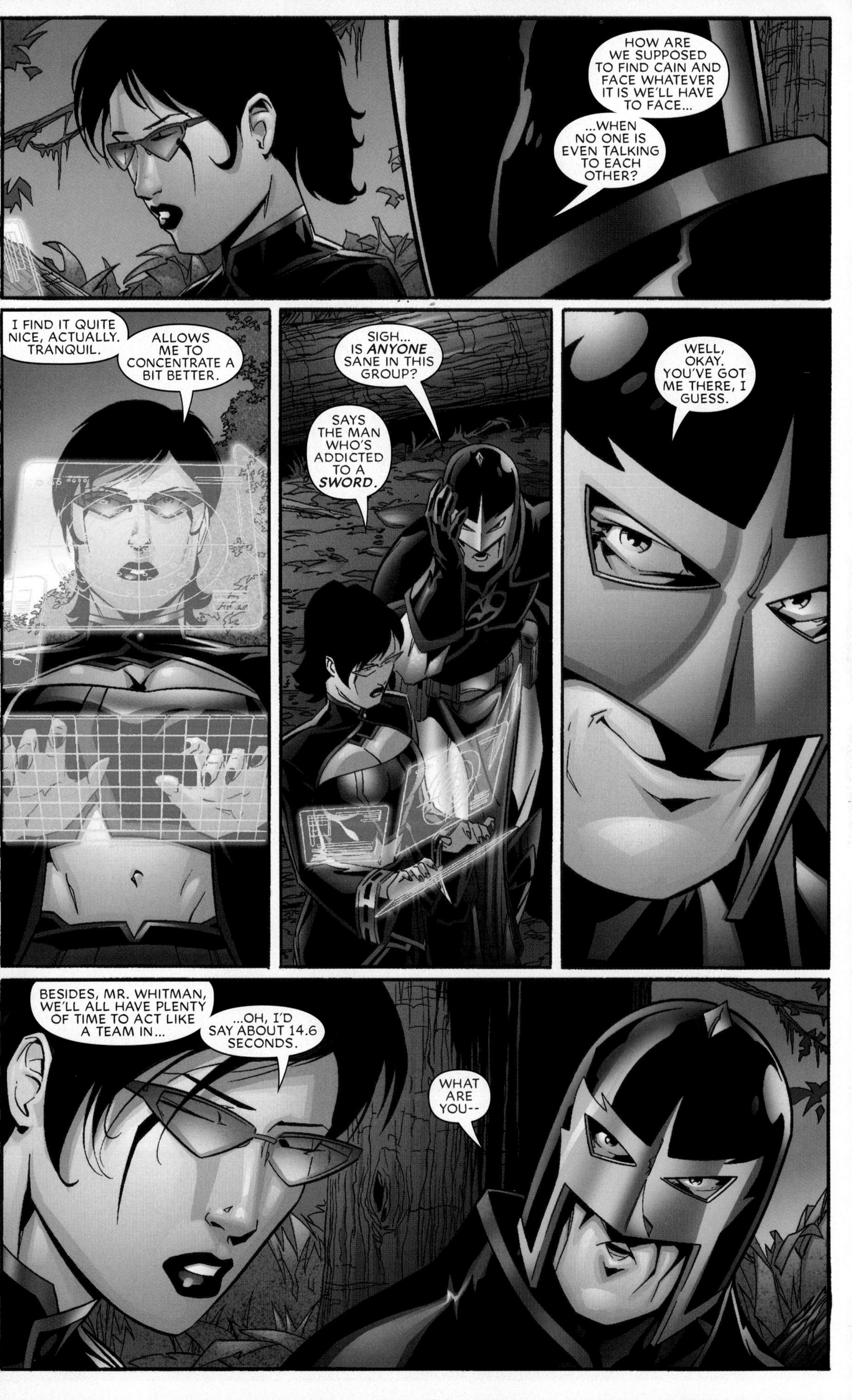
HOW ARE WE SUPPOSED TO FIND CAIN AND FACE WHATEVER IT IS WE'LL HAVE TO FACE...
...WHEN NO ONE IS EVEN TALKING TO EACH OTHER?
I FIND IT QUITE NICE, ACTUALLY. TRANQUIL.
ALLOWS ME TO CONCENTRATE A BIT BETTER.
SIGH... IS *ANYONE* SANE IN THIS GROUP?
SAYS THE MAN WHO'S ADDICTED TO A ***SWORD***.
WELL, OKAY. YOU'VE GOT ME THERE, I GUESS.
BESIDES, MR. WHITMAN, WE'LL ALL HAVE PLENTY OF TIME TO ACT LIKE A TEAM IN...
...OH, I'D SAY ABOUT 14.6 SECONDS.
WHAT ARE YOU--

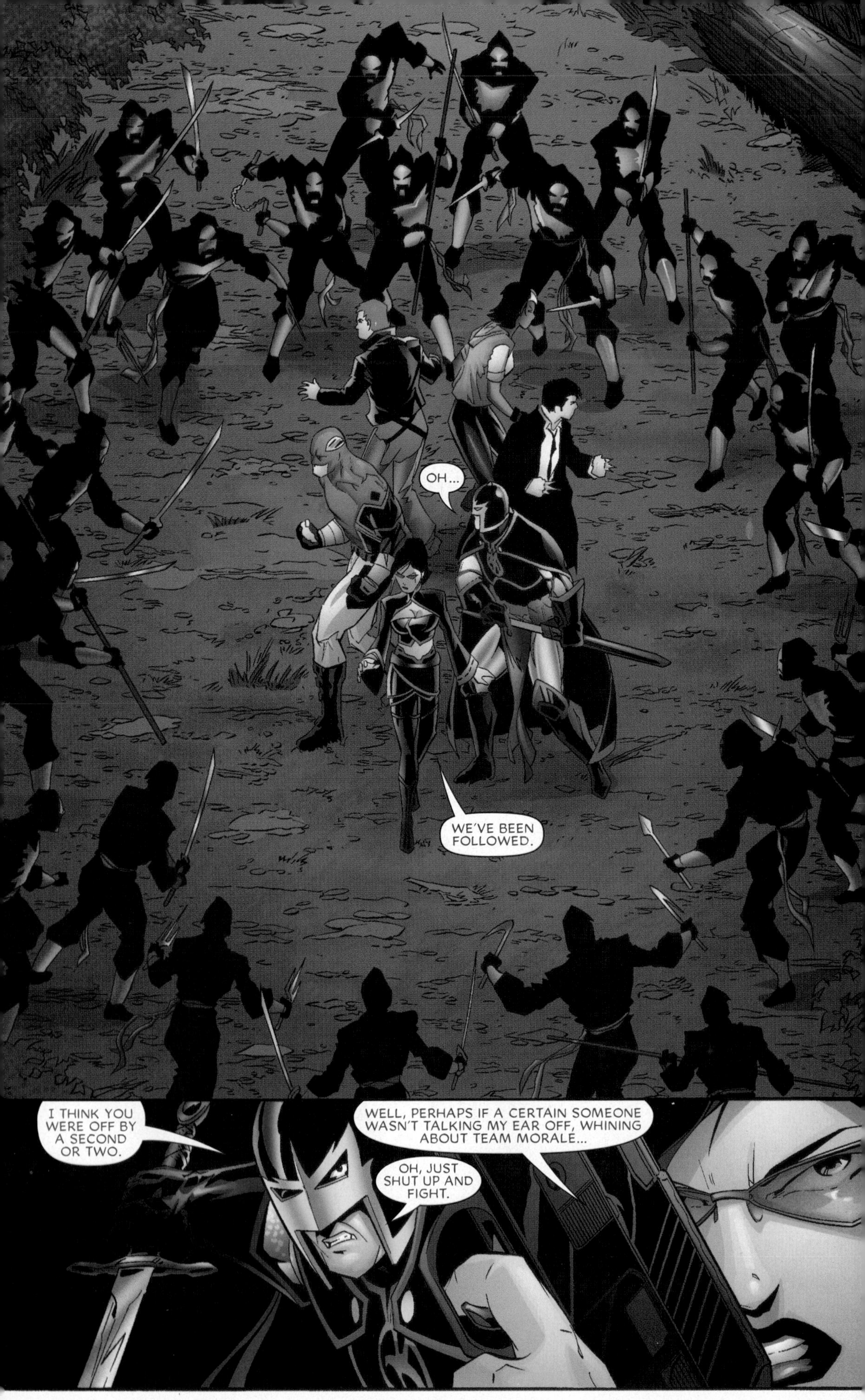
OH...
WE'VE BEEN FOLLOWED.
I THINK YOU WERE OFF BY A SECOND OR TWO.
WELL, PERHAPS IF A CERTAIN SOMEONE WASN'T TALKING MY EAR OFF, WHINING ABOUT TEAM MORALE...
OH, JUST SHUT UP AND FIGHT.

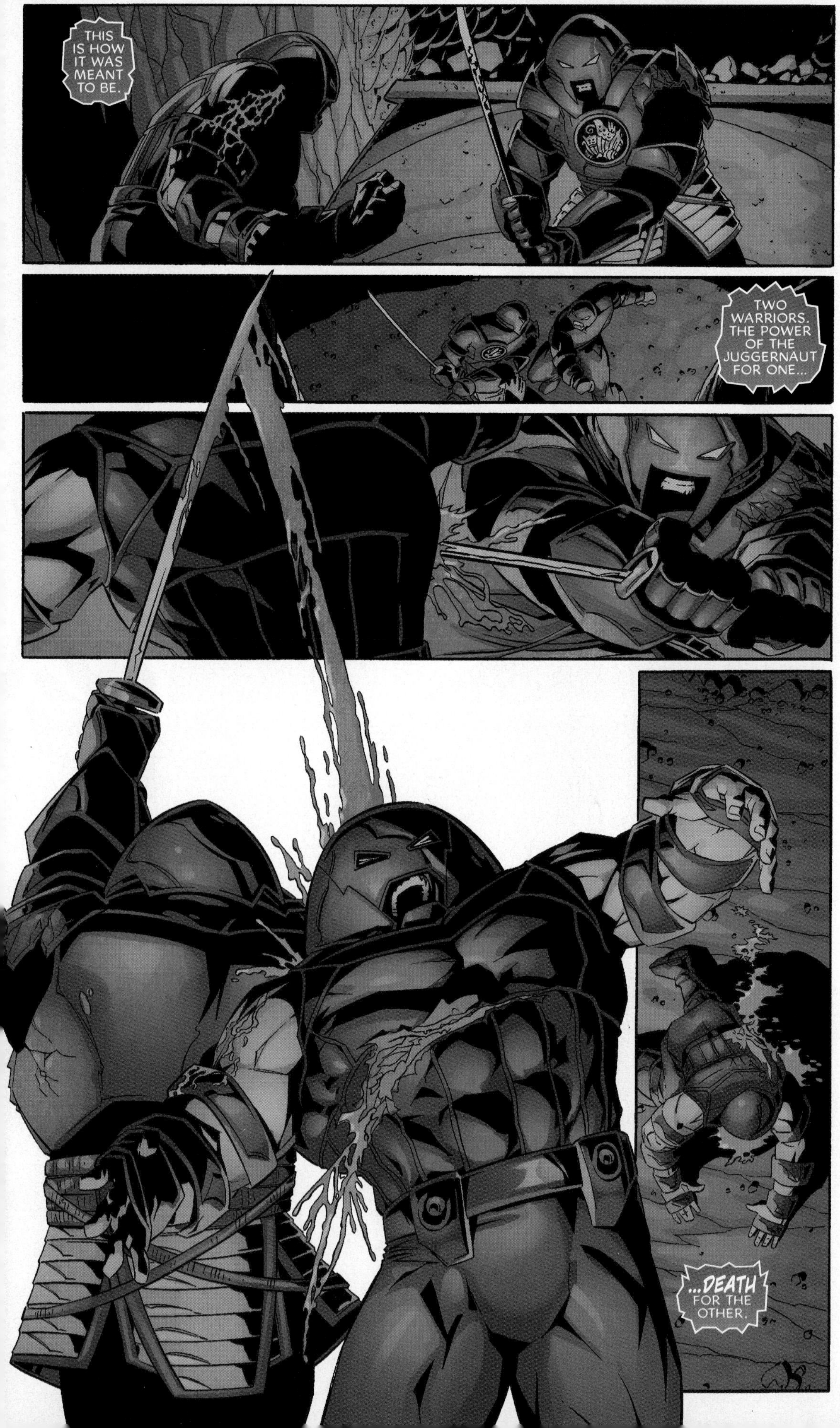
THIS IS HOW IT WAS MEANT TO BE.
TWO WARRIORS. THE POWER OF THE JUGGERNAUT FOR ONE...
...DEATH FOR THE OTHER.

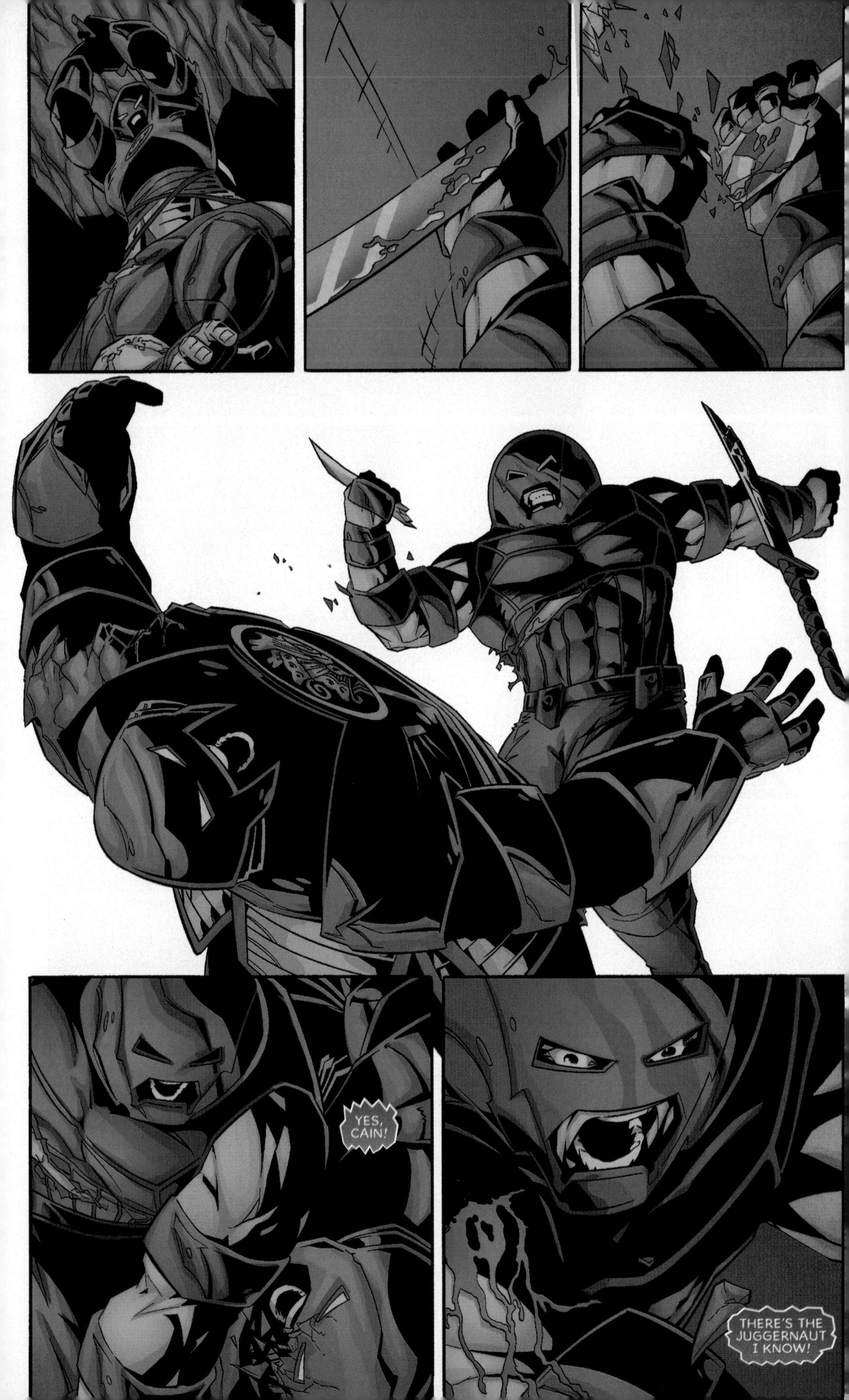
YES, CAIN!
THERE'S THE JUGGERNAUT I KNOW!

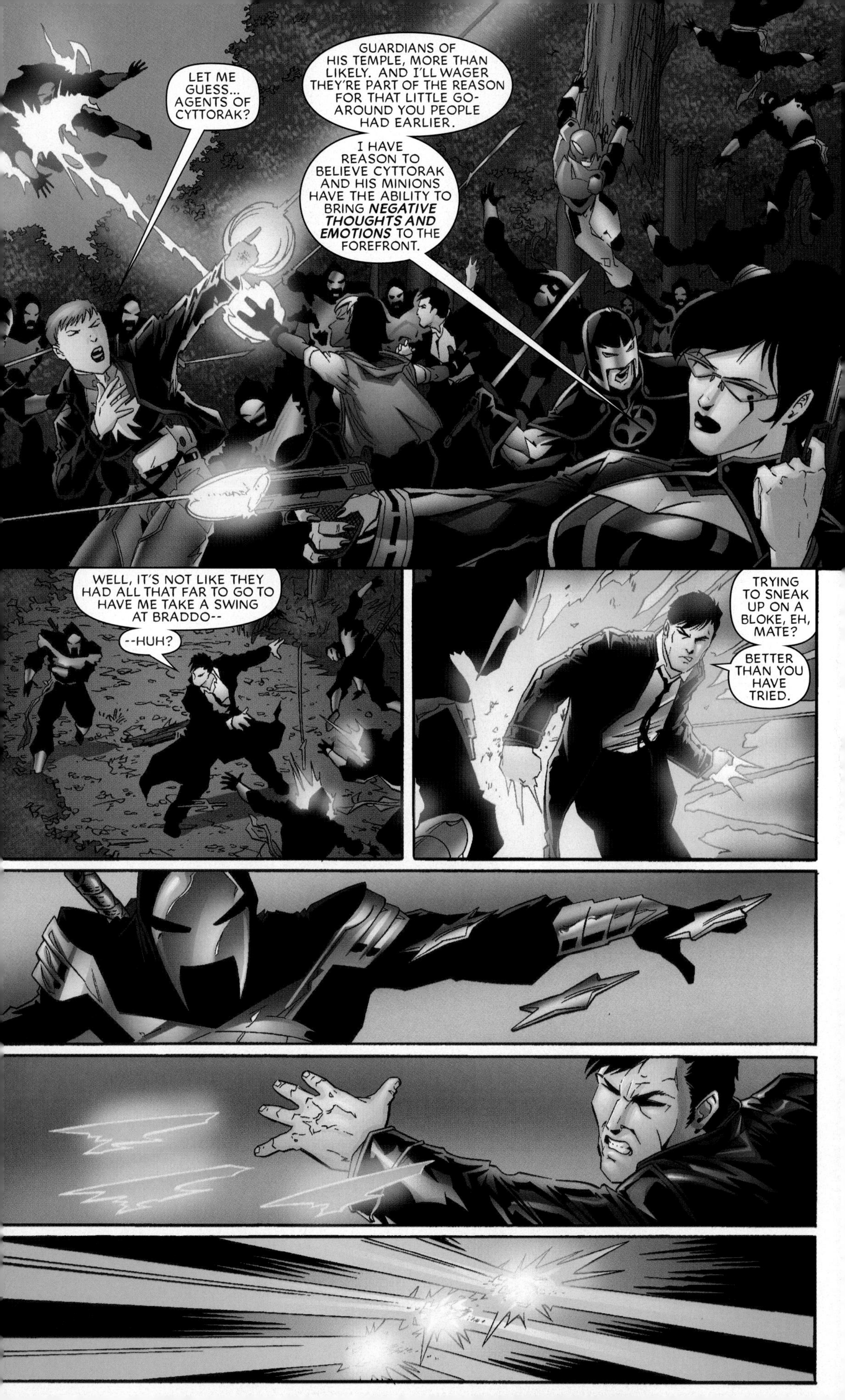
LET ME GUESS... AGENTS OF CYTTORAK?
GUARDIANS OF HIS TEMPLE, MORE THAN LIKELY. AND I'LL WAGER THEY'RE PART OF THE REASON FOR THAT LITTLE GO-AROUND YOU PEOPLE HAD EARLIER.
I HAVE REASON TO BELIEVE CYTTORAK AND HIS MINIONS HAVE THE ABILITY TO BRING **NEGATIVE THOUGHTS AND EMOTIONS** TO THE FOREFRONT.
WELL, IT'S NOT LIKE THEY HAD ALL THAT FAR TO GO TO HAVE ME TAKE A SWING AT BRADDO--
--HUH?
TRYING TO SNEAK UP ON A BLOKE, EH, MATE?
BETTER THAN YOU HAVE TRIED.

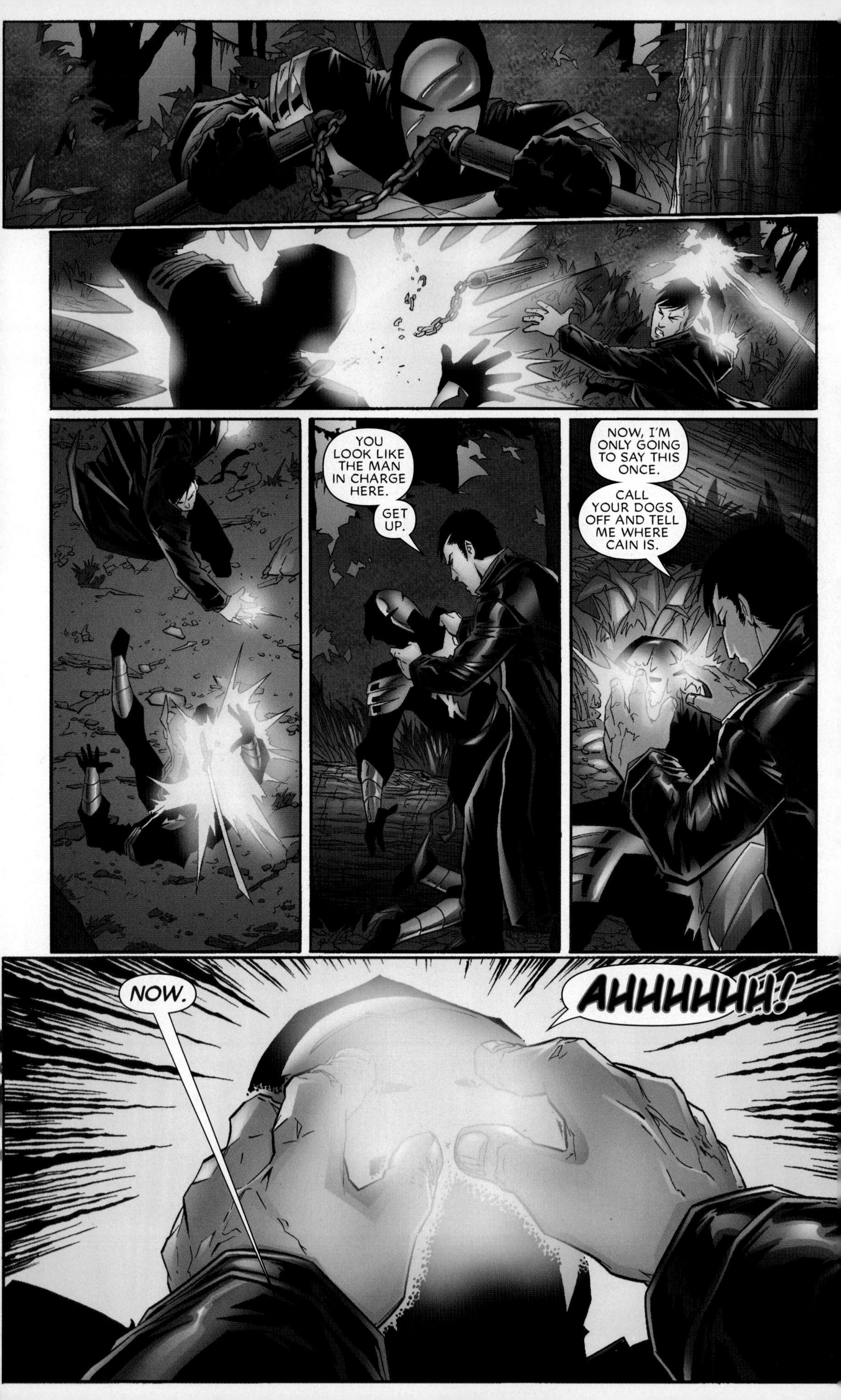
YOU LOOK LIKE THE MAN IN CHARGE HERE.
GET UP.
NOW, I'M ONLY GOING TO SAY THIS ONCE.
CALL YOUR DOGS OFF AND TELL ME WHERE CAIN IS.
NOW.
AHHHHHH!

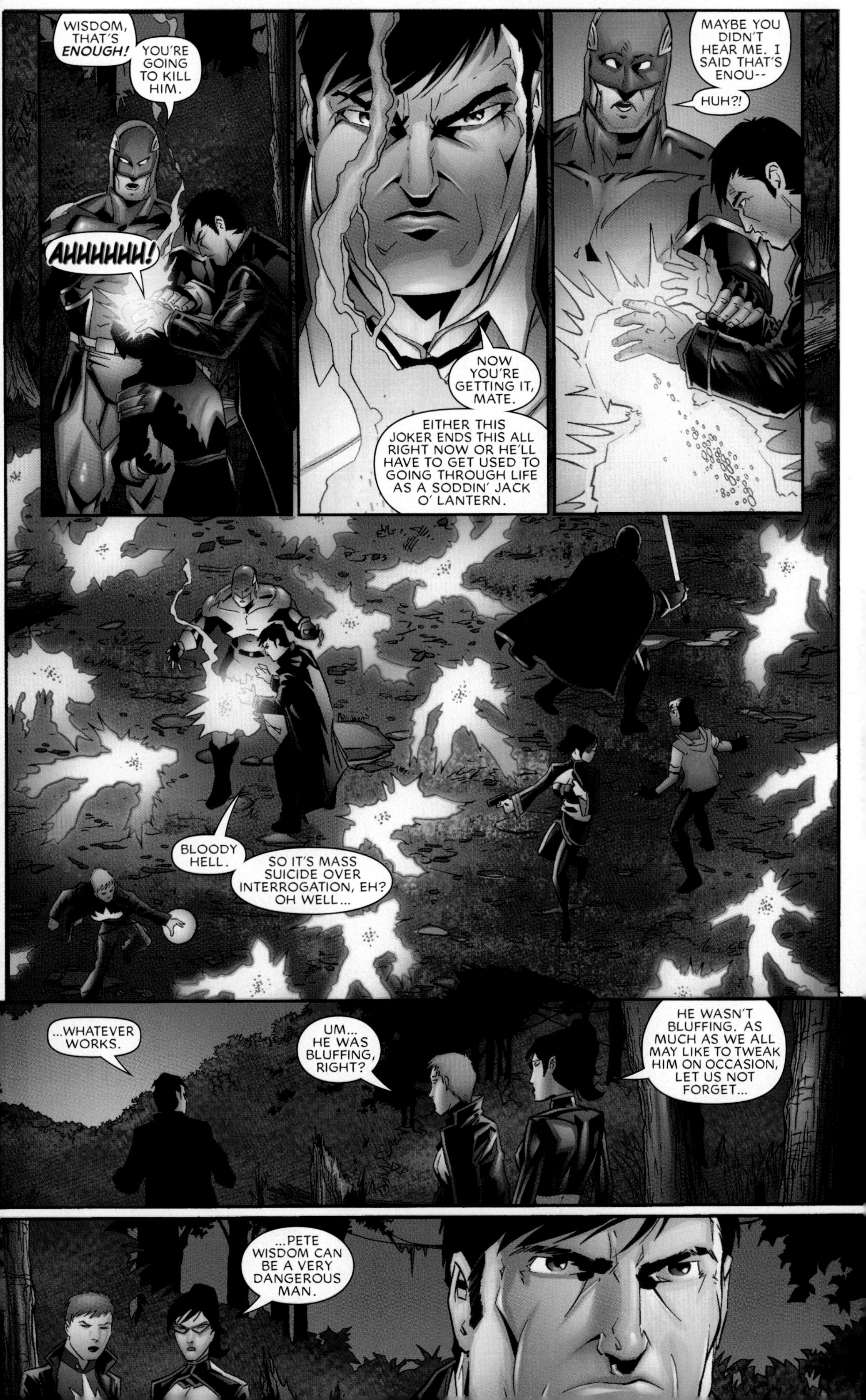
WISDOM, THAT'S *ENOUGH!*
YOU'RE GOING TO KILL HIM.
AHHHHHH!
NOW YOU'RE GETTING IT, MATE.
EITHER THIS JOKER ENDS THIS ALL RIGHT NOW OR HE'LL HAVE TO GET USED TO GOING THROUGH LIFE AS A SODDIN' JACK O' LANTERN.
MAYBE YOU DIDN'T HEAR ME. I SAID THAT'S ENOU--
HUH?!
BLOODY HELL.
SO IT'S MASS SUICIDE OVER INTERROGATION, EH? OH WELL...
...WHATEVER WORKS.
UM... HE WAS BLUFFING, RIGHT?
HE WASN'T BLUFFING. AS MUCH AS WE ALL MAY LIKE TO TWEAK HIM ON OCCASION, LET US NOT FORGET...
...PETE WISDOM CAN BE A VERY DANGEROUS MAN.

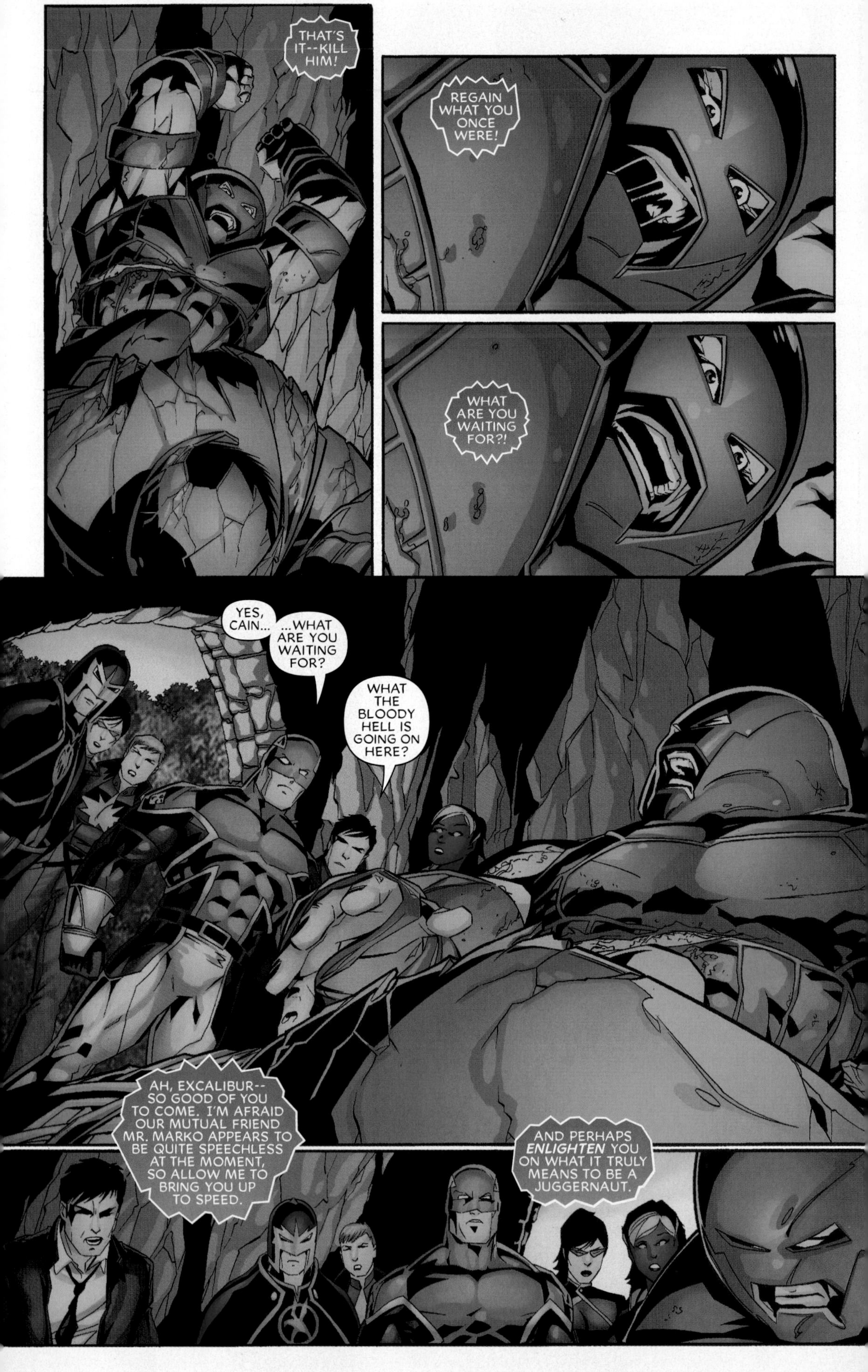
THAT'S IT--KILL HIM!
REGAIN WHAT YOU ONCE WERE!
WHAT ARE YOU WAITING FOR?!
YES, CAIN...
...WHAT ARE YOU WAITING FOR?
WHAT THE BLOODY HELL IS GOING ON HERE?
AH, EXCALIBUR--SO GOOD OF YOU TO COME. I'M AFRAID OUR MUTUAL FRIEND MR. MARKO APPEARS TO BE QUITE SPEECHLESS AT THE MOMENT, SO ALLOW ME TO BRING YOU UP TO SPEED.
AND PERHAPS *ENLIGHTEN* YOU ON WHAT IT TRULY MEANS TO BE A JUGGERNAUT.

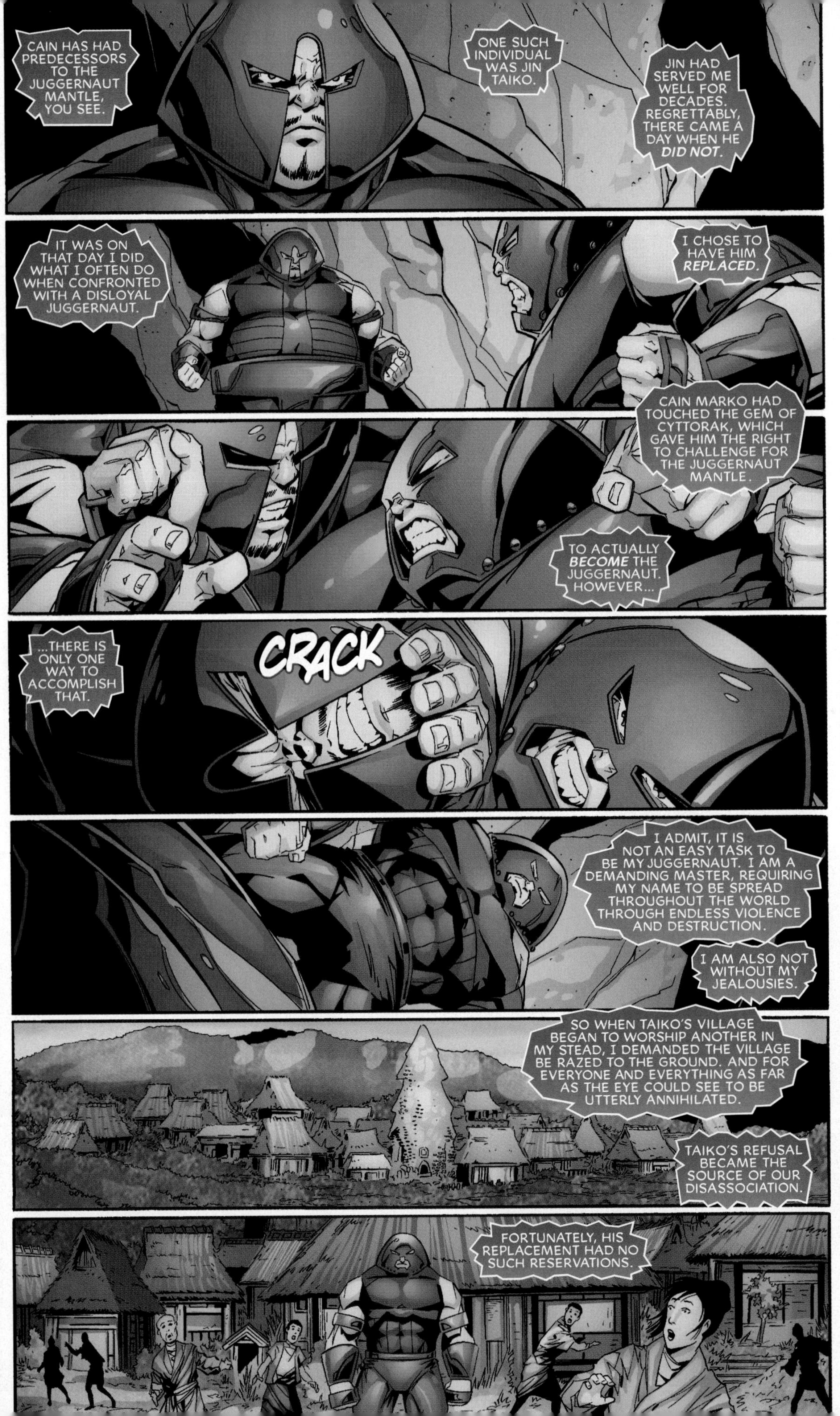
CAIN HAS HAD PREDECESSORS TO THE JUGGERNAUT MANTLE, YOU SEE.
ONE SUCH INDIVIDUAL WAS JIN TAIKO.
JIN HAD SERVED ME WELL FOR DECADES. REGRETTABLY, THERE CAME A DAY WHEN HE *DID NOT*.
IT WAS ON THAT DAY I DID WHAT I OFTEN DO WHEN CONFRONTED WITH A DISLOYAL JUGGERNAUT.
I CHOSE TO HAVE HIM *REPLACED*.
CAIN MARKO HAD TOUCHED THE GEM OF CYTTORAK, WHICH GAVE HIM THE RIGHT TO CHALLENGE FOR THE JUGGERNAUT MANTLE.
TO ACTUALLY *BECOME* THE JUGGERNAUT. HOWEVER...
...THERE IS ONLY ONE WAY TO ACCOMPLISH THAT.
CRACK
I ADMIT, IT IS NOT AN EASY TASK TO BE MY JUGGERNAUT. I AM A DEMANDING MASTER, REQUIRING MY NAME TO BE SPREAD THROUGHOUT THE WORLD THROUGH ENDLESS VIOLENCE AND DESTRUCTION.
I AM ALSO NOT WITHOUT MY JEALOUSIES.
SO WHEN TAIKO'S VILLAGE BEGAN TO WORSHIP ANOTHER IN MY STEAD, I DEMANDED THE VILLAGE BE RAZED TO THE GROUND. AND FOR EVERYONE AND EVERYTHING AS FAR AS THE EYE COULD SEE TO BE UTTERLY ANNIHILATED.
TAIKO'S REFUSAL BECAME THE SOURCE OF OUR DISASSOCIATION.
FORTUNATELY, HIS REPLACEMENT HAD NO SUCH RESERVATIONS.

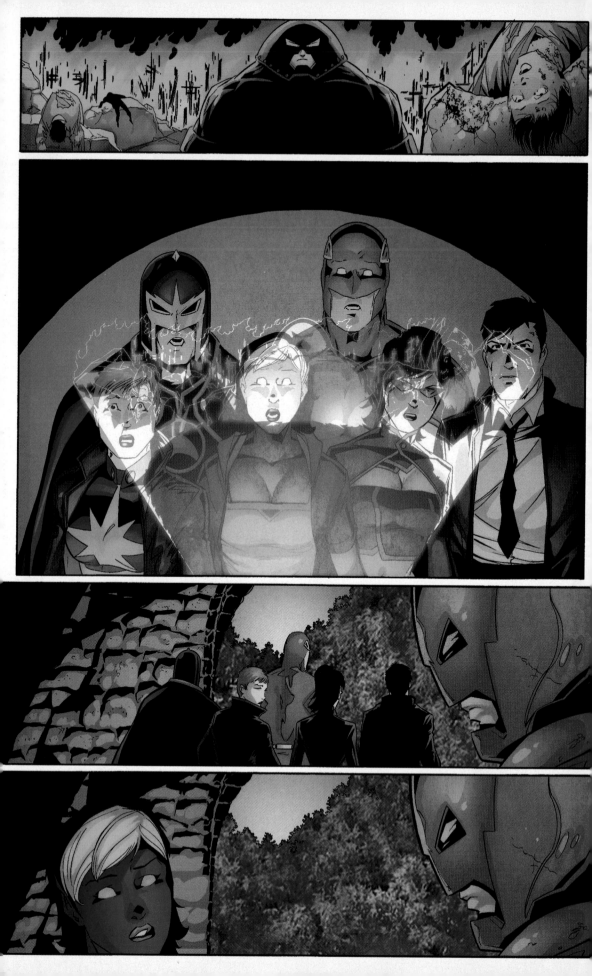

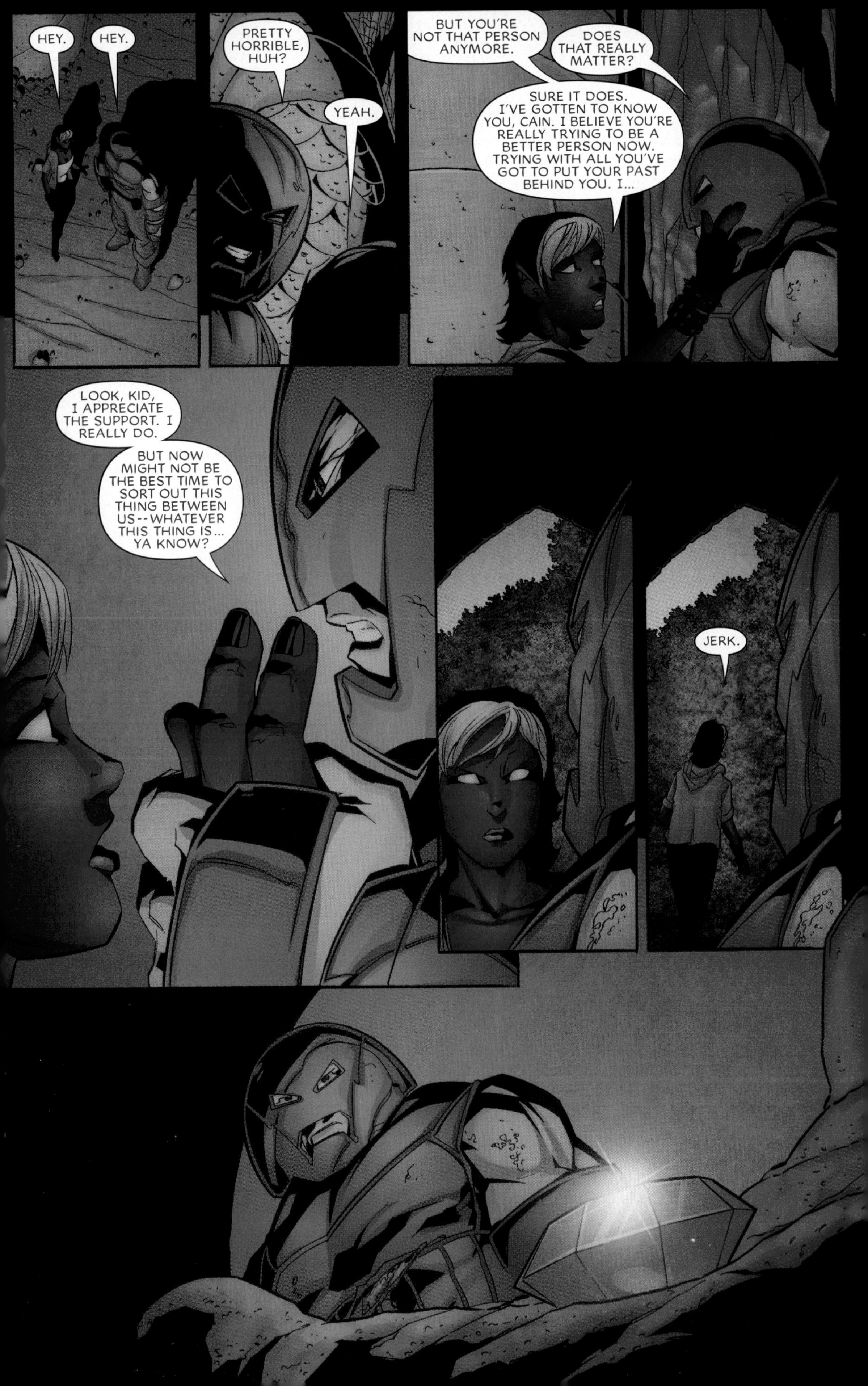
HEY.
HEY.
PRETTY HORRIBLE, HUH?
YEAH.
BUT YOU'RE NOT THAT PERSON ANYMORE.
DOES THAT REALLY MATTER?
SURE IT DOES. I'VE GOTTEN TO KNOW YOU, CAIN. I BELIEVE YOU'RE REALLY TRYING TO BE A BETTER PERSON NOW. TRYING WITH ALL YOU'VE GOT TO PUT YOUR PAST BEHIND YOU. I...
LOOK, KID, I APPRECIATE THE SUPPORT. I REALLY DO.
BUT NOW MIGHT NOT BE THE BEST TIME TO SORT OUT THIS THING BETWEEN US--WHATEVER THIS THING IS... YA KNOW?
JERK.

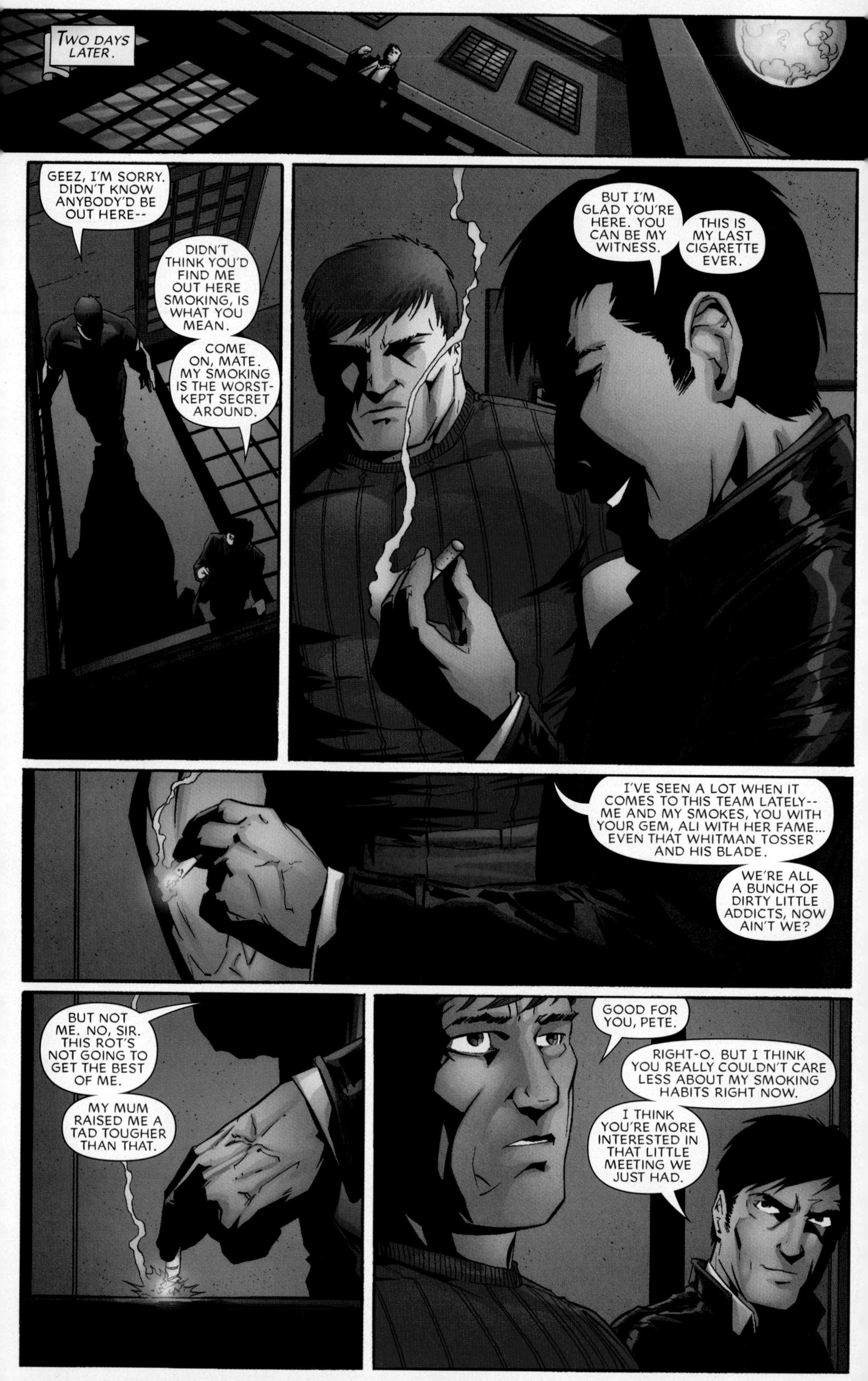
TWO DAYS LATER.
GEEZ, I'M SORRY. DIDN'T KNOW ANYBODY'D BE OUT HERE--
DIDN'T THINK YOU'D FIND ME OUT HERE SMOKING, IS WHAT YOU MEAN.
COME ON, MATE. MY SMOKING IS THE WORST-KEPT SECRET AROUND.
BUT I'M GLAD YOU'RE HERE. YOU CAN BE MY WITNESS.
THIS IS MY LAST CIGARETTE EVER.
I'VE SEEN A LOT WHEN IT COMES TO THIS TEAM LATELY-- ME AND MY SMOKES, YOU WITH YOUR GEM, ALI WITH HER FAME... EVEN THAT WHITMAN TOSSER AND HIS BLADE.
WE'RE ALL A BUNCH OF DIRTY LITTLE ADDICTS, NOW AIN'T WE?
BUT NOT ME. NO, SIR. THIS ROT'S NOT GOING TO GET THE BEST OF ME.
MY MUM RAISED ME A TAD TOUGHER THAN THAT.
GOOD FOR YOU, PETE.
RIGHT-O. BUT I THINK YOU REALLY COULDN'T CARE LESS ABOUT MY SMOKING HABITS RIGHT NOW.
I THINK YOU'RE MORE INTERESTED IN THAT LITTLE MEETING WE JUST HAD.

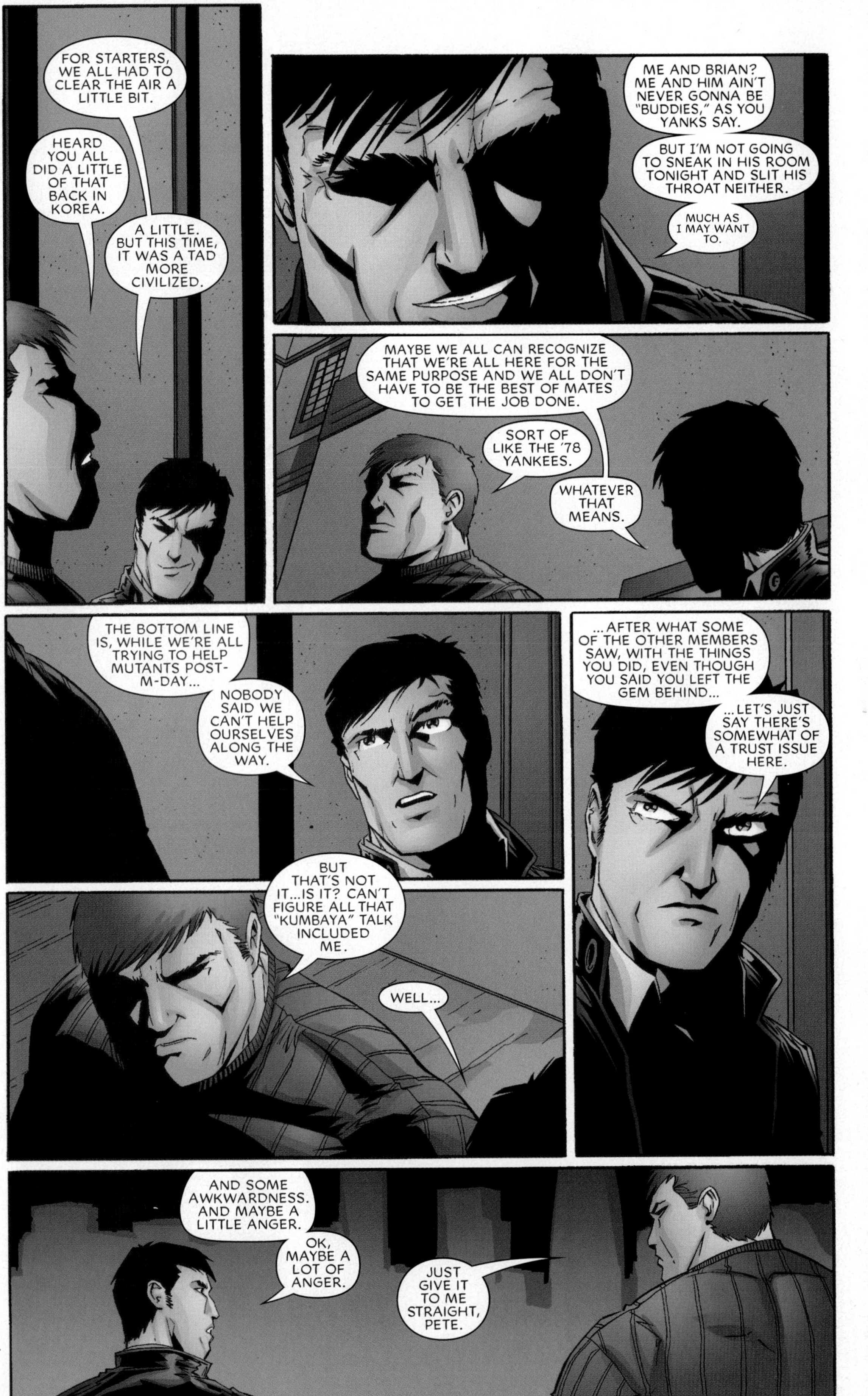

FOR STARTERS, WE ALL HAD TO CLEAR THE AIR A LITTLE BIT.
HEARD YOU ALL DID A LITTLE OF THAT BACK IN KOREA.
A LITTLE. BUT THIS TIME, IT WAS A TAD MORE CIVILIZED.
ME AND BRIAN? ME AND HIM AIN'T NEVER GONNA BE "BUDDIES," AS YOU YANKS SAY.
BUT I'M NOT GOING TO SNEAK IN HIS ROOM TONIGHT AND SLIT HIS THROAT NEITHER.
MUCH AS I MAY WANT TO.
MAYBE WE ALL CAN RECOGNIZE THAT WE'RE ALL HERE FOR THE SAME PURPOSE AND WE ALL DON'T HAVE TO BE THE BEST OF MATES TO GET THE JOB DONE.
SORT OF LIKE THE '78 YANKEES.
WHATEVER THAT MEANS.
THE BOTTOM LINE IS, WHILE WE'RE ALL TRYING TO HELP MUTANTS POST-M-DAY...
NOBODY SAID WE CAN'T HELP OURSELVES ALONG THE WAY.
...AFTER WHAT SOME OF THE OTHER MEMBERS SAW, WITH THE THINGS YOU DID, EVEN THOUGH YOU SAID YOU LEFT THE GEM BEHIND...
...LET'S JUST SAY THERE'S SOMEWHAT OF A TRUST ISSUE HERE.
BUT THAT'S NOT IT...IS IT? CAN'T FIGURE ALL THAT "KUMBAYA" TALK INCLUDED ME.
WELL...
AND SOME AWKWARDNESS. AND MAYBE A LITTLE ANGER.
OK, MAYBE A LOT OF ANGER.
JUST GIVE IT TO ME STRAIGHT, PETE.

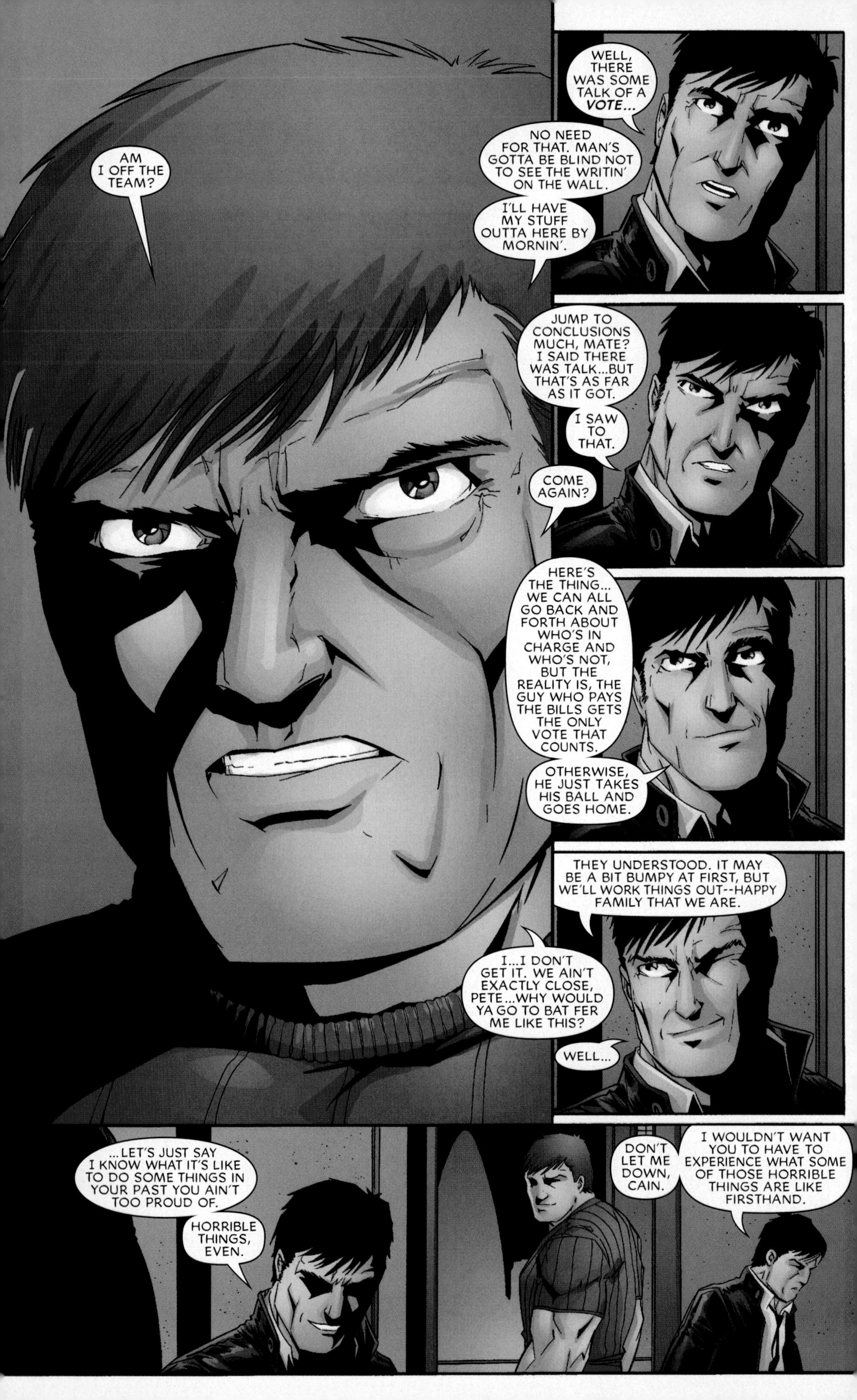
AM I OFF THE TEAM?
WELL, THERE WAS SOME TALK OF A *VOTE...*
NO NEED FOR THAT. MAN'S GOTTA BE BLIND NOT TO SEE THE WRITIN' ON THE WALL.
I'LL HAVE MY STUFF OUTTA HERE BY MORNIN'.
JUMP TO CONCLUSIONS MUCH, MATE? I SAID THERE WAS TALK...BUT THAT'S AS FAR AS IT GOT.
I SAW TO THAT.
COME AGAIN?
HERE'S THE THING... WE CAN ALL GO BACK AND FORTH ABOUT WHO'S IN CHARGE AND WHO'S NOT, BUT THE REALITY IS, THE GUY WHO PAYS THE BILLS GETS THE ONLY VOTE THAT COUNTS.
OTHERWISE, HE JUST TAKES HIS BALL AND GOES HOME.
THEY UNDERSTOOD. IT MAY BE A BIT BUMPY AT FIRST, BUT WE'LL WORK THINGS OUT--HAPPY FAMILY THAT WE ARE.
I...I DON'T GET IT. WE AIN'T EXACTLY CLOSE, PETE...WHY WOULD YA GO TO BAT FER ME LIKE THIS?
WELL...
...LET'S JUST SAY I KNOW WHAT IT'S LIKE TO DO SOME THINGS IN YOUR PAST YOU AIN'T TOO PROUD OF.
HORRIBLE THINGS, EVEN.
DON'T LET ME DOWN, CAIN.
I WOULDN'T WANT YOU TO HAVE TO EXPERIENCE WHAT SOME OF THOSE HORRIBLE THINGS ARE LIKE FIRSTHAND.

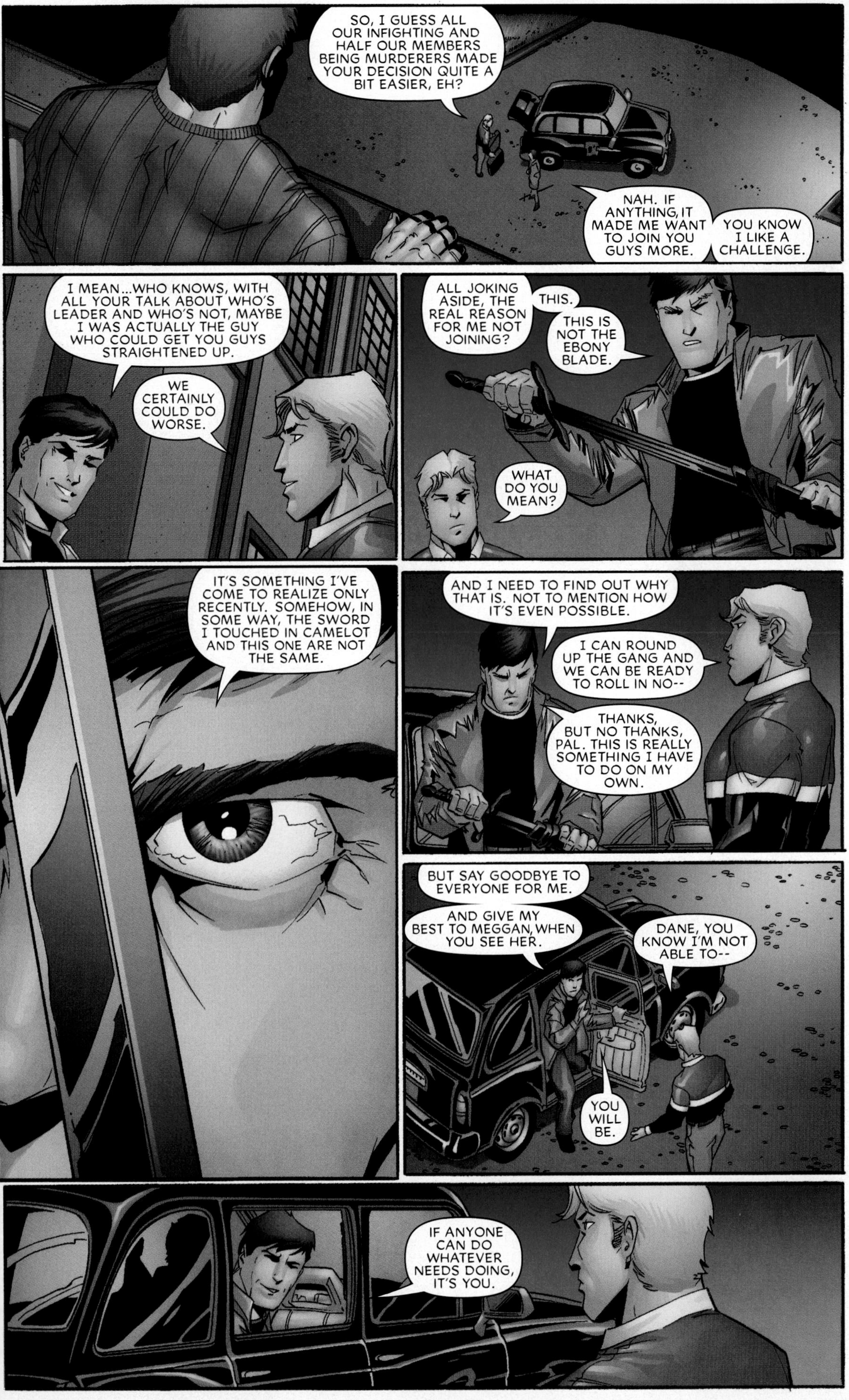
SO, I GUESS ALL OUR INFIGHTING AND HALF OUR MEMBERS BEING MURDERERS MADE YOUR DECISION QUITE A BIT EASIER, EH?
NAH. IF ANYTHING, IT MADE ME WANT TO JOIN YOU GUYS MORE.
YOU KNOW I LIKE A CHALLENGE.
I MEAN...WHO KNOWS, WITH ALL YOUR TALK ABOUT WHO'S LEADER AND WHO'S NOT, MAYBE I WAS ACTUALLY THE GUY WHO COULD GET YOU GUYS STRAIGHTENED UP.
WE CERTAINLY COULD DO WORSE.
ALL JOKING ASIDE, THE REAL REASON FOR ME NOT JOINING?
THIS.
THIS IS NOT THE EBONY BLADE.
WHAT DO YOU MEAN?
IT'S SOMETHING I'VE COME TO REALIZE ONLY RECENTLY. SOMEHOW, IN SOME WAY, THE SWORD I TOUCHED IN CAMELOT AND THIS ONE ARE NOT THE SAME.
AND I NEED TO FIND OUT WHY THAT IS. NOT TO MENTION HOW IT'S EVEN POSSIBLE.
I CAN ROUND UP THE GANG AND WE CAN BE READY TO ROLL IN NO--
THANKS, BUT NO THANKS, PAL. THIS IS REALLY SOMETHING I HAVE TO DO ON MY OWN.
BUT SAY GOODBYE TO EVERYONE FOR ME.
AND GIVE MY BEST TO MEGGAN, WHEN YOU SEE HER.
DANE, YOU KNOW I'M NOT ABLE TO--
YOU WILL BE.
IF ANYONE CAN DO WHATEVER NEEDS DOING, IT'S YOU.

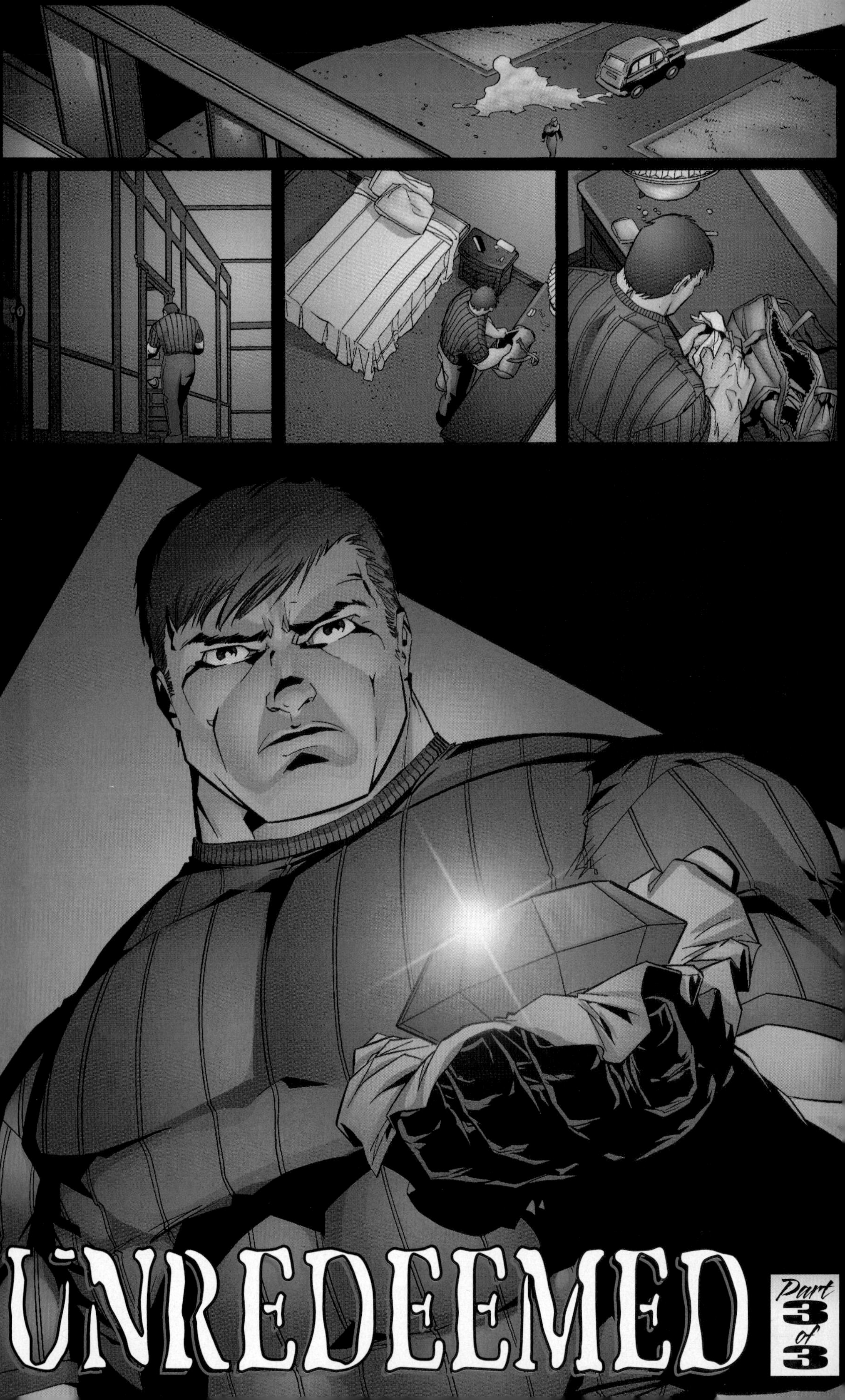
UNREDEEMED
Part 3 of 3

HISTORY: Pete Wisdom's parents divorced by the time he entered his 20s, perhaps earlier. His father Harold had been a Detective Sergeant in New Scotland Yard, specializing in profiling serial killers, but by his retirement he had apparently gone slightly insane, believing in various bizarre occult-related conspiracy theories. Pete's mother informed her son over the phone that she had never loved Harold, and never wanted Pete, prompting a huge argument; Pete never told his father his mother's comments, though she wasted no time in telling Harold of the horrible things Pete said to her. Pete was due to visit her a week later, but decided not to bother; unaware her son wasn't coming, she stood waiting for him by the front window. That day a spree killer decided to walk round her quiet village and shoot anyone he saw. Pete blamed himself for causing his mother's death; so did Harold, leaving a permanent gulf between them.

Both Pete and his elder sister Romany entered the intelligence community. Romany maintained a cover as an eccentric occult specialist while rising to run her own above-top secret organization, while 20-something Pete joined the Secret Intelligence Service, MI-6. He became involved with contract killer Sari St. Hubbins; they promised their work would never come between them, but when Sari planned assassinating Queen Elizabeth II, Pete turned her in. "It needed doing." Those three words became Pete's mantra. Between his dysfunctional family life and working in a duplicitous profession, Pete put up emotional barriers, hiding behind a cynical front, but underneath he remained a good man, and would risk his life without hesitation when the right thing needed doing.

Pete transferred to Black Air, a Ministry of Defense unit charged with recovering unusual artifacts for weapons research. Pete was one of their killers, though he tried to stick to slaying other killers, people "in the lifestyle." For a time Pete was partnered with Ed Culley, one of his few friends in Black Air. Pete was sent in alone to Cold Grey, a fortress in British Antarctica taken over by terrorists armed with unusual technology; under orders, Pete slew everyone, but was haunted by memories of spilled entrails steaming in the snow. One of Pete's old MI-6 friends, Archie Fogg, a research scientist, killed himself testing a new device to duplicate people's neural patterns into a computer, surviving as a computerized brain; he designed an android body for himself, but before it was completed, Black Air installed him in the Faraway, an experimental satellite with a sub-space engine. Pete promised Archie he would ensure he got his new body when he returned. Pete built a network of friends in other agencies, including Pitman at MI-5; MI-6's Doyle, whose life Pete saved when Doyle's appendix burst; and Jardine, head of Criminal Intelligence, after he saved Jardine's photojournalist daughter Amanda from gunmen. Alongside other Black Air operatives, including his then-superior officer, the voltcasting Scratch, Wisdom monitored a supposedly magical Scottish cairn. Unaware of their presence, members of fellow UK intelligence agency WHO approached the cairn during war games with the X-Men. Not wanting any interference with their mission, Black Air (including Wisdom) slaughtered the WHO agents, then fought the X-Men, but the bloodletting released N'Garai demons from the cairn; the Black Air agents worked with the X-Men to drive them back and destroy the cairn. Scratch and Wisdom, the only Black Air survivors, then escaped. Pete subsequently posed as a WHO agent, to enlist aid from Sean Cassidy (the X-Man Banshee) to take down Justin Hammer's European Sentinel-like hounds operation. As his doubts grew about the people he worked with, Pete's relationships with other Black Air operatives became strained; learning Scratch had slaughtered everyone in a remote Norfolk School while retrieving an alien artifact which had come down near there, Pete punctured Scratch's lung and tore half his face off before other agents stopped him. Increasingly disillusioned, things worsened when Black Air took over from WHO (Weird Happenings Organization) as British Intelligence's paranormality specialists.

Things came to a head after Pete killed everyone at a terrorist training camp in Ronsaphan, Thailand. Vowing his killing days were over, he agreed to one final Black Air mission. His superior Michele Scicluna assigned him

REAL NAME: Peter Paul Wisdom
ALIASES: Winston, Mr. W
IDENTITY: No dual identity
OCCUPATION: Government agent
CITIZENSHIP: U.K.
PLACE OF BIRTH: London, England, U.K.
KNOWN RELATIVES: Harold Wisdom (father), unidentified mother (deceased), Romany Wisdom (sister), Tink (wife), Oberon (father-in-law)
GROUP AFFILIATION: MI-13, Excalibur; formerly X-Force, Black Air, MI-6, possibly the Factory
EDUCATION: Unrevealed
FIRST APPEARANCE: Excalibur #86 (1995)

to accompany mutant super-team Excalibur to Genosha to locate British-manufactured anti-mutant ammunition. Excalibur disliked the acerbic, chain-smoking spy, especially Shadowcat (Kitty Pryde), ten years Pete's junior. Instantly annoyed by his demeanor, she hid her attraction to him beneath verbal jabs at his faults, which Pete reciprocated. After Genosha, Pete returned with Excalibur to their base on Muir Island, Scotland; receiving a message from Culley begging for help, Pete requested to borrow Excalibur's plane to get to London. Kitty offered to pilot it, wanting to keep an eye on Pete. Finding Culley dead of an unidentified contagion, they followed the trail back to RAF Utterleigh, codenamed Dream Nails, where Black Air were developing a stress-activated flesh-eating virus, Blood Eagle, extracted from alien bacteria taken from the Uncreated. With Kitty's help, Pete destroyed both base and virus, resigning from Black Air. Having seen through Pete's façade, Kitty gave in to her attraction; Pete reciprocated, though terrified of being hurt again.

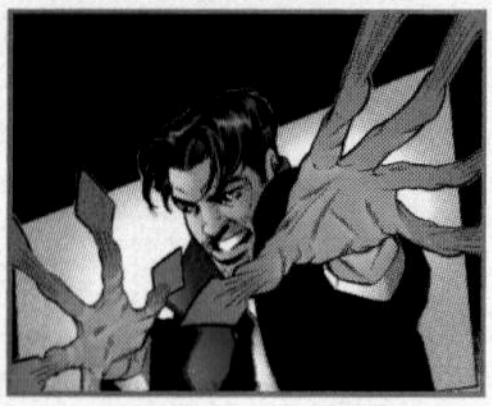

Kitty suggested Pete join Excalibur, and only a couple of days later they informed their teammates of their relationship; while the Excalibur women found the revelation romantic, Captain Britain and Nightcrawler were less certain, but accepted Kitty's choice after they warned Pete of dire consequences should he ever hurt Kitty. Later that night Kitty's superhumanly strong ex-boyfriend, Piotr Rasputin (Colossus), arrived at Muir Island in time to see them kissing; already somewhat irrational, Piotr brutally assaulted Pete. Severely injured and hanging on to life by a thread, Pete used the last of his strength to down Piotr when he thought he was threatening Kitty. Pete narrowly survived, and was confined to a wheelchair for three weeks; recognizing Piotr had been unstable at the time of the assault, Colossus was allowed to join Excalibur while they monitored his mental state. Kitty's pet alien dragon, Lockheed, also disapproved of Wisdom and began stealing the spy's suits and cigarettes.

After learning Black Air were helping the London Hellfire Club seize control of the U.K., Pete's insider knowledge proved vital in thwarting them; with Lockheed's assistance, Pete also settled accounts with Scratch at the same time. When Jardine asked for Pete's help in finding Amanda, who had gone undercover trying to find a mutant serial killer, Kitty got to meet Harold and Romany as Pete turned to them for their respective expertise. Shortly afterwards, Captain Britain cajoled Pete into admitting to Kitty that he loved her; however, remnants of Black Air plotted assassinating Excalibur. They sent Sari St. Hubbins after Pete, but he overpowered her and sent her back with a warning that if any of Excalibur went down, Pete would ensure Black Air went next.

Kitty was unexpectedly called away to work for S.H.I.E.L.D. temporarily, leaving Pete mid-argument. In her absence Pete wondered if he was any good for her or Excalibur; she had helped him reclaim his soul, but in return he felt all he had done was endanger them. Kitty returned from S.H.I.E.L.D. hiding guilt over nearly cheating on Pete; sensing she was shutting him out, Pete tried to talk to her about their relationship, but was interrupted when Nightmare attacked. Nightmare tried to play on Pete's fear that he was making Kitty grow up too fast and that she would one day hate him for it, but the dream lord found Pete unaffected, as he was already living that terror and it couldn't get any worse. With Nightmare driven off, Kitty admitted her indiscretion to Pete but assured him nothing had happened; heartbroken, and certain he was bad for her, Pete broke up with Kitty and left Excalibur.

Pete began working with other disillusioned intelligence operatives and techno-anarchists such as Abel, Baker and Charlie, trying to make up for the things they did during their service, cleaning up some of the dirtier spy secrets around the globe. Learning the Faraway had crashed back to Earth near Genosha, Pete enlisted X-Force's assistance stealing Archie's brain before Genosha's ruler Magneto learned what he had in his possession. They succeeded, and Pete successfully transferred Archie's mind to an android form. Discovering his sister Romany's agency was plotting to modify humanity to make them more compatible with an alien World Engine, Pete approached the nominal head of British paranormal intelligence, Alistaire Stuart, making him aware of her plans and enlisting his aid. X-Force, having kept in touch following the Genoshan escapade, asked Pete if he could train them to be a more proactive force; after six months teaching them new uses for their powers, he took them to Russia to destroy Meatspore Stormtroopers, then to San Francisco to disable a Cold War bioreactor which was transforming the citizenry into murderous mutates. While X-Force were dealing with the bioreactor, Pete was confronted at gunpoint by its creator, Dr. Niles Roman; when X-Force returned to base, they found Pete's corpse, seemingly shot dead; however Pete had survived and faked his death. Spurred by Wisdom's seeming demise and guided by files he had compiled over the years regarding crimes against mutantkind, X-Force eventually faced Romany and her Worldengine, which they destroyed.

Possibly at Alistaire's behest, Pete returned to British intelligence, now working for MI-13, the department of the British National Intelligence Directorate Responsible for Enhanced Human Affairs. In the wake of M-Day depowering most of the world's mutants, causing widespread instability in the superhuman community, and threats to national security such as Earth-6141's Shadow Mob, Pete decided Britain needed back both Excalibur and Captain Britain. With some minor manipulating he achieved both goals, in time to confront Black Air when they resurfaced. As well as his public Excalibur missions, Pete has recently led a covert MI-13 combat squad to Otherworld to stop a faerie invasion, a mission which ended with Pete's arranged marriage to the faerie king's daughter.

NOTE: *Romany claimed that Prior to working at Black Air, Pete was with the Factory, a covert unit whose remit was to extract data from genetic anomalies such as mutants, until the work became too much; unable to resign, his employers tortured him until he suffered a breakdown. Romany nursed him back to health, and once he recovered he launched a single-minded crusade to atone for his sins; however, she was trying to dissuade his X-Force protégés from continuing the investigations that ultimately exposed her World Engine when she said this, it seems unlikely Black Air would recruit someone who had already suffered a breakdown over immoral working methods, and Pete's actions while working for Black Air do not fit with someone on an atonement crusade, so it seems probable Romany was lying when she discussed this aspect of Pete's past.*

HEIGHT: 5'9" **WEIGHT:** 158 lbs.
EYES: Blue **HAIR:** Black

ABILITIES/ACCESSORIES: Pete can generate "hot knives," plates of plasma force hot as the heart of the sun. He can fire these likes bullets, hold them on his finger tips like claws, generate burning shields to destroy incoming missiles, or deploy them beneath him as he falls to create thermal updrafts to slow his descent to safe speeds. While he usually produces these from his fingers, he can generate them from any part of his hands.

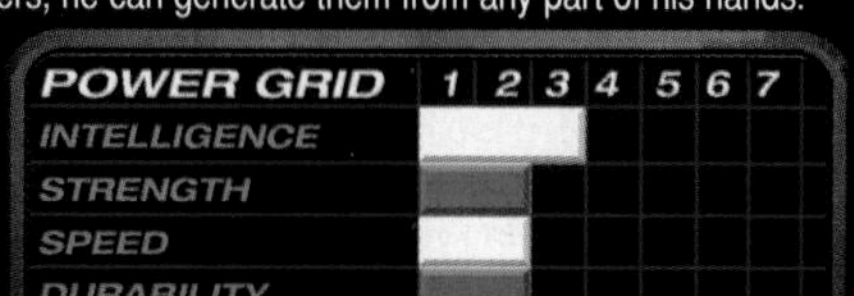
POWER GRID
1 2 3 4 5 6 7
INTELLIGENCE
STRENGTH
SPEED
DURABILITY
ENERGY PROJECTION
FIGHTING SKILLS